The Emergence of the Eastern Powers, 1756–1775

Throughout the nineteenth century, international relations in Europe were dominated by the five great powers – Britain, France, Russia, Austria and Prussia – who collectively determined the continent's political destiny. The creation of this system has been located traditionally in the long struggle with Revolutionary and Napoleonic France, and specifically in the peace settlement at Vienna of 1814–15 which ended a generation of intensive warfare. By contrast, this study demonstrates that its origins lie half a century earlier.

During the third quarter of the eighteenth century, the European states system was transformed by the military rise of Russia and Prussia in the Seven Years War of 1756–63. Simultaneously the actual term 'great power' and the concept of the five leading states together dominating Europe became established both among theorists and practical statesmen. Until the middle of the eighteenth century western European issues had dominated international relations, and France had been the pre-eminent power. This now ceased to be the case. Eastern Europe became pre-eminent. During the 1770s Poland was partitioned for the first time by her three powerful neighbours, while Russia and Austria also seized territory from the Ottoman empire. Europe's centre of gravity moved sharply eastwards, and by the later 1770s Russia was emerging as the leading continental power.

This study, based upon manuscript and printed sources from six countries, provides the first comprehensive study of these critical events.

H.M. SCOTT is Professor of International History, University of St Andrews

CAMBRIDGE STUDIES IN EARLY MODERN HISTORY

Edited by Professor Sir John Elliott, University of Oxford
Professor Olwen Hufton, University of Oxford
Professor H.G. Koenigsberger, University of London
Professor H.M. Scott, University of St Andrews

The idea of an 'early modern' period of European history from the fifteenth to the late eighteenth century is now widely accepted among historians. The purpose of Cambridge Studies in Early Modern History is to publish monographs and studies which illuminate the character of the period as a whole, and in particular focus attention on a dominant theme within it, the interplay of continuity and change as they are presented by the continuity of medieval ideas, political and social organisation, and by the impact of new ideas, new methods, and new demands on the traditional structure.

For a list of titles published in the series, please see end of the book

The Emergence of the Eastern Powers, 1756–1775

H.M. SCOTT

CAMBRIDGE
UNIVERSITY PRESS

PUBLISHED BY THE PRESS SYNDICATE OF THE UNIVERSITY OF CAMBRIDGE
The Pitt Building, Trumpington Street, Cambridge, United Kingdom

CAMBRIDGE UNIVERSITY PRESS
The Edinburgh Building, Cambridge CB2 2RU, UK
40 West 20th Street, New York, NY 10011-4211, USA
10 Stamford Road, Oakleigh, VIC 3166, Australia
Ruiz de Alarcón 13, 28014 Madrid, Spain
Dock House, The Waterfront, Cape Town 8001, South Africa

http://www.cambridge.org

First published 2001

Printed in the United Kingdom at the University Press, Cambridge

Typeface Monotype Ehrhardt 10/12pt   *System* QuarkXPress™ [SE]

A catalogue record for this book is available from the British Library

Library of Congress Cataloguing in Publication data
Scott, H. M. (Hamish M.), 1946–
The emergence of the eastern powers, 1756–1775 / H. M. Scott.
p.   cm. – (Cambridge studies in early modern history)
Includes bibliographical references and index.
ISBN 0 521 79269 X
1. Europe, Eastern – Politics and government – 18th century.   I. Title.   II. Series.
DJK47.S38   2001
947′.0009′033–dc21   2001025199

ISBN 0 521 79269 X hardback

To Isabel de Madariaga

Contents

Maps and genealogical table

Acknowledgements

In the research and writing of the book, I have incurred numerous obligations which it is a pleasure to be able to acknowledge here. The staff of the archives and libraries in which I have worked have been unfailingly helpful, while in St Andrews Mrs Margaret Grundy and her Inter-Library Loans colleagues have secured many important and often rare items. Research in continental archives was made possible by generous grants from the British Academy, the Carnegie Trust for the Universities of Scotland, the Royal Society of Edinburgh (through its Caledonian Research Awards scheme) and the University of St Andrews: I am grateful to them all. The final typescript was completed during the early part of my tenure of a Leverhulme Fellowship awarded for a different project, and I express my gratitude to the Trust.

The support of individuals has been even more important. Mrs Marian Dawson graciously provided a base for research trips to Cambridge, enabling much crucial work to be accomplished by a preoccupied son-in-law, while nearer home Jane Dawson has helped in numerous ways. Successive versions of the text have been speedily and uncomplainingly typed by Nancy Bailey, who has also been a shrewd critic of presentation. In my own institution, Michael Bentley and, over a more extended period, Bruce Lenman have done most to maintain morale and to defend scholarly values during a difficult period for our University and Department. My editorial colleagues Sir John Elliott, Helli Koenigsberger and Olwen Hufton have all offered friendly encouragement. Helli first suggested to me that this study should appear in 'Cambridge Studies in Early Modern History'; my real pleasure that it should finally do so is inevitably much reduced by the Press' decision not to continue with a Series which has defined the subject and area of early modern history throughout my own professional lifetime. At Cambridge University Press Bill Davies has been the best of editors, wise, patient and always supportive, while Linda Randall copy-edited the manuscript with remarkable speed and care. Twenty years ago J.T. Lukowski generously gave me a copy of his important monograph on the Radom confederacy; this, along with his subsequent publications have compensated for my ignorance of Poland-Lithuania and its languages; while more recently Virginia Aksan has performed a similar service for the Ottoman empire. P.G.M. Dickson provided significant advice concerning public finance. Robert Oresko's friendship and his encouragement to think about the enduring role of courts within diplomacy have been important.

Acknowledgements

One advantage of the growing revival of interest in international history is the number of fellow specialists on whom authors can try out their ideas in advance of publication. The text has been read by T.C.W. Blanning, H.G. Koenigsberger, Derek McKay, M.J. Rodríguez-Salgado and Paul W. Schroeder, whose comments and suggestions have been invaluable in the process of revision. Mia Rodríguez-Salgado's detailed and rigorous critique was particularly helpful. Though dealing with her penetrating criticisms took me far longer than I hoped or intended, it also confirmed my admiration for her as Britain's foremost early modern international historian. Paul Schroeder's invitation to speak at a conference forced me to reconsider quite fundamentally the role of France in the pages which follow, and I am grateful to him for the stimulus this provided. It goes without saying that any errors or misunderstandings which remain are all my own work.

I owe most to two senior scholars. Derek Beales has been the shrewdest and also the friendliest of critics for as long as I have been researching in the area explored by this book. His willingness to discuss, with the incisiveness which is his trademark, problems of evidence and interpretation has been crucial, while his own magisterial study of Joseph II has provided a secure foundation for its Austrian dimension. My debt to Isabel de Madariaga, the *doyenne* of eighteenth-century Russian historians, is even greater. Her own publications mapped out the terrain traversed in this study and have been frequently drawn upon. This is only a small part of my obligations to her, which now extend over thirty years. When I began doctoral research I was sent off to read her seminal study of Sir James Harris' mission to Russia, in order to see what could be achieved in a diplomatic history PhD, though this advice was properly accompanied with the caution that I would never produce anything as important or impressive! I was then despatched to consult her about my own thesis, to my enduring benefit. Her advice, encouragement and friendship have been very important to me throughout my career, and deserve a far better return than this book can ever be.

Dates and place names

Unless otherwise indicated, all dates in this study are given in the New Style. During the second half of the eighteenth century, the Russian calendar was still eleven days behind that in use throughout the rest of Europe, and all such dates are indicated by OS.

The wide geographical focus of this study, together with the frequent later changes of political geography, creates an obvious problem over personal and proper names. The solution adopted is pragmatic rather than linguistically correct. Where an established English form exists it has been used: thus 'Vienna' rather than 'Wien'. In a similar way I have written 'Prussia' rather than 'Brandenburg-Prussia' and 'Poland' instead of the more correct 'Poland-Lithuania', and also utilised 'Austria' as a synonym for the 'Habsburg Monarchy', exactly as it was used at the time. 'Empire' where it stands alone and is capitalised designates the 'Holy Roman Empire'. Otherwise the most familiar version has been utilised, with the present-day equivalent sometimes given in brackets on the first occasion it is mentioned.

Abbreviations

AAE	Archives du Ministère des Affaires Etrangères (Paris)
ABB	*Acta Borussica: Denkmäler der Preussischen Staatsverwaltung im 18. Jahrhundert – Die Behördenorganisation und die allgemeine Staatsverwaltung Preussens im 18. Jahrhundert*, ed. G. Schmoller *et al.* (16 vols., Berlin, 1894–1982)
Add. MSS	Additional Manuscripts
AKV	*Arkiv kniazia Vorontsova*, ed. P. Bartenev (40 vols., Moscow, 1870–95)
AÖG	*Archiv für Österreichische Geschichte*
Arneth, *GMT*	Alfred Ritter von Arneth, *Geschichte Maria Theresias* (10 vols., Vienna, 1863–79)
Beales, *Joseph II*	Derek Beales, *Joseph II*, vol. 1: *In the Shadow of Maria Theresa, 1741–1780* (Cambridge, 1987)
Beer, *Erste Theilung Polens*	Adolf Beer, *Die Erste Theilung Polens* (3 vols., Vienna, 1873)
Bernstorff Corr.	*Correspondance Ministérielle du Comte J.H.E. Bernstorff 1751–1770*, ed. P. Vedel (2 vols., Copenhagen, 1882)
Bernstorffsche Papiere	*Bernstorffsche Papiere*, ed. Aage Friis (3 vols., Copenhagen, 1904–13)
Bielfeld, *Institutions politiques*	J.F. von Bielfeld, *Institutions politiques* (2 vols., The Hague, 1760)
BL	British Library, London
CP	Correspondance Politique
Danske Tractater	*Danske Tractater, 1751–1800* (Copenhagen, 1882)
Dickson, *Finance*	P.G.M. Dickson, *Finance and Government under Maria Theresia 1740–1780* (2 vols., Oxford, 1987)
Die politischen Testamente, ed. Dietrich	*Die politischen Testamente der Hohenzollern*, ed. R. Dietrich (Cologne and Vienna, 1986)
Doniol, *Participation de la France*	Henri Doniol, *Histoire de la participation de la France à l'établissement des Etats-Unis d'Amérique* (5 vols., Paris, 1886–92)

xiv

List of abbreviations

FBPG	*Forschungen zur brandenburgischen und preussischen Geschichte*
GStAPK	Geheimes Staatsarchiv Preussischer Kulturbesitz, Berlin-Dahlem
Hammer, *Histoire de l'empire Ottoman*	J. de Hammer (Joseph von Hammer-Purgstall), *Histoire de l'empire Ottoman, depuis son origine jusqu'à nos jours* (18 vols., Paris, 1835–41)
HHStA	Haus-, Hof- und Staatsarchiv, Vienna
JGO	*Jahrbücher für Geschichte Osteuropas*
KuF	*Briefe der Kaiserin Maria Theresia an ihre Kinder und Freunde*, ed Alfred Ritter von Arneth (4 vols., Vienna, 1881)
Madariaga, *Russia*	Isabel de Madariaga, *Russia in the Age of Catherine the Great* (London, 1981)
MA–JII	*Correspondance secrète du comte de Mercy-Argenteau avec l'Empereur Joseph II et le Prince de Kaunitz*, ed. Alfred Ritter von Arneth and Jules Flammermont (2 vols., Paris, 1889–91)
Mémoires de Choiseul, ed. Calmettes	*Mémoires du duc de Choiseul 1719–85*, ed. F. Calmettes (Paris, 1904)
MD	Mémoires et Documents
Martens, *Recueil des traités*	F. von Martens, *Recueil des traités et conventions conclus par la Russie avec les puissances étrangères* (15 vols., St Petersburg, 1874–1909)
MT–JII	*Maria Theresia und Joseph II: ihre Correspondenz*, ed. Alfred Ritter von Arneth (3 vols., Vienna, 1867–8)
MT–MA	*Marie Antoinette: correspondance secrète entre Marie-Thérèse et le comte de Mercy-Argenteau*, ed. Alfred Ritter von Arneth (3 vols., 2nd edn, Paris, 1874–5)
NF	Neue Folge
NLS	National Library of Scotland, Edinburgh
Œuvres	*Œuvres de Frédéric le Grand*, ed. J.D.E. Preuss (30 vols., Berlin, 1846–56)
Pol. Corr.	*Politische Correspondenz Friedrichs des Grossen*, ed. J.G. Droysen *et al.* (46 vols., Berlin, 1879–1939)
PRO	Public Record Office, London
Recueil	*Recueil des instructions données aux ambassadeurs et ministres de France, depuis les traités de Westphalie jusqu'à la Révolution Française* (32 vols. to date, Paris, 1884–)
Repertorium	*Repertorium der diplomatischen Vertreter aller Länder*, ed. L. Bittner, L. Gross and L. Santifaller (3 vols., Berlin, Zürich and Graz, 1936–65)

List of abbreviations

Roberts, *British Diplomacy* Michael Roberts, *British diplomacy and Swedish politics 1758–1773* (London, 1980)

Schieder, *Friedrich* Theodor Schieder, *Friedrich der Grosse: ein Königtum der Widersprüche* (Frankfurt-am-Main, 1983)

Ségur, *Politique de tous les cabinets* L.P. de Ségur, *Politique de tous les cabinets de l'Europe pendant les règnes de Louis XV et de Louis XVI* (3 vols., Paris, 1802)

SHAT Service Historique de l'Armée de Terre, Vincennes

Soloviev, *History of Russia* Sergei M. Soloviev, *History of Russia from the Earliest Times* (multi-volume English translation, Gulf Breeze, FL, 1981–)

SIRIO *Sbornik imperatorskogo russkogo istoricheskogo obshchestva* (148 vols., St Petersburg, 1867–1916)

SP State Papers (Foreign) series

The eighteenth-century European states system and its transformations

On 17 March 1778 the House of Commons began to consider the treaties between France and Britain's rebellious North American colonists. These had been signed early in February, and their formal communication to London signalled open French intervention in the War of American Independence. In the course of this debate Charles Jenkinson offered an incisive if pessimistic analysis of the predicament facing Britain. Her diplomatic isolation and accompanying political decline, he declared, were due to a wider and quite fundamental transformation:

> The great military powers in the interior parts of Europe, who have amassed together their great treasures, and have modelled their subjects into great armies, will in the next and succeeding period of time, become the predominant powers. France and Great Britain, which have been the first and second-rate powers of the European world, will perhaps for the future be but of the third and fourth rate.[1]

Though acute, Jenkinson's analysis was too sanguine. During the 1770s Russia, Prussia and Austria, 'the great military powers in the interior parts of Europe', were already becoming the leading continental states: what he termed the 'predominant powers'. Their political rise during the third quarter of the eighteenth century is the subject of this book.

The emergence of the eastern powers was a turning point in the evolution of the modern European states system. During the century after the Peace of Westphalia (1648) international relations had been shaped primarily by attempts to contain the French monarchy, the one true great power of that era. The efforts had been led by the Dutch Republic (until its strength waned after 1713) and, increasingly, by the British state, and supported by Austria. In the generation after the Peace of Utrecht Britain and Austria were more equal in strength to France, until her notable recovery under Cardinal Fleury's leadership during the 1730s. Memories of recent wars, however, ensured that the Anglo-Dutch alliance with Austria continued in its efforts to restrain French might, which was still feared. These three countries had usually been allies between the 1680s and the 1740s. Lesser states had attached themselves to one side or the other in this struggle. Until the second half of the eighteenth

---

[1] *The Parliamentary History of England from the Earliest Period to the Year 1803* (36 vols., London, 1806–20), XIX. col. 948. Jenkinson, subsequently the first Lord Liverpool, was at this point an Under-Secretary of State.

century this international system extended only over western and central Europe, reflecting the crucial importance of French dominance to its operations.[2] Large regions in northern, eastern and south-eastern Europe were on its fringes. Sweden had been incorporated during its transient career as a leading state in the seventeenth century. After 1700 Russia's increasing power and her dominant role in Poland gave her enhanced importance, though she only became a full member after the Seven Years War. The international system overlapped with the network of resident diplomacy which linked Europe's leading capitals, but it was not identical to it. This distinction was most apparent in the case of the Ottoman empire. The threat which it presented to its European neighbours had been crucial for international relations during the sixteenth and seventeenth centuries. Its retreat, after the severe defeats suffered at the hands of Austria during the wars of 1683–1718, was to be no less important during the eighteenth century and especially the period covered by this study. Yet it only began to become part of the diplomatic network during the 1790s, and its entry was at first hesitant and incomplete.

In its essentials this international system survived down to the Seven Years War of 1756–63. This was the first western and central European conflict for almost a century which was not primarily about the power of France but that of the upstart Hohenzollern monarchy. It witnessed the emergence of two new leading states, Prussia and Russia. By the 1770s their status had increased, and the so-called 'Pentarchy' of Russia, Prussia, Austria, Britain and France had come into existence. With the addition of the newly unified Italy from the 1860s, these states would collectively dominate European diplomacy down to the First World War. The nineteenth-century international system had important foundations during the eighteenth century as well as in the struggle against Revolutionary and Napoleonic France.[3] Though the emergence of the eastern powers was quite central for the development of modern international relations and has been noted by previous scholars, it has not hitherto been the subject of a separate monograph.[4] This neglect has been encouraged by the established tendency for scholars to produce studies of national foreign policies or bilateral diplomatic relations, which has the effect of obscuring broader changes within the states system. This book by contrast is explicitly conceived within the international history tradition. It rests upon the conviction that the trajectory of an individual state can only be fully understood in the

---

[2] See Derek McKay and H.M. Scott, *The Rise of the Great Powers 1648–1815* (London, 1983), chs. 1–6, for this view of its evolution.

[3] Our understanding of the international order at this period has been transformed by the remarkable and distinguished study by Paul W. Schroeder, *The Transformation of European Politics 1763–1848* (Oxford, 1994).

[4] See in particular Heinz Duchhardt, *Balance of Power und Pentarchie: Internationale Beziehungen 1700–1785* (Paderborn, 1997), esp. chs. 1, 2:i, 6 and 7: this is now the best introduction to the eighteenth-century international system; Johannes Kunisch, 'Der Aufstieg neuer Großmächte im 18. Jahrhundert und die Aufteilung der Machtsphären Ostmitteleuropa', in Grete Klingenstein and Franz A.J. Szabo, eds., *Staatskanzler Wenzel Anton von Kaunitz-Rietberg 1711–1794* (Graz, 1996), pp. 70–89.

context of other national foreign policies and the wider evolution of the European system. Though its principal focus is the eastern powers, their emergence is linked to changes in the position and priorities of France and even Britain. It aims to be a study of the entire international system at a decisive point in its evolution.

The rise of Prussia and Russia was brought about by their military victories and territorial gains, in which Austria also shared. Their annexations were accomplished at the expense of the once great and still extensive, but now vulnerable, states of the eastern half of the continent, Poland and the Ottoman empire. These developments, together with France's decline and Britain's insular policies and domestic and colonial preoccupations, conferred diplomatic leadership in Europe upon 'the great military powers', and they were to retain this throughout the next generation. During the 1770s the eastern monarchies, led by Russia, became the continent's most dynamic states. They partitioned Poland in 1772, annexing almost 30 per cent of her territory and 35 per cent of her population. Two years later Russia ended a highly successful war with the Ottoman empire (1768–74) by a dictated peace at Kuchuk-Kainardji, securing sweeping gains to the north of the Black Sea. In the following year Austria plundered the province of Bukovina from the defeated Ottoman empire. These were the most dramatic territorial changes of the entire century and were only to be eclipsed in the 1790s, when Poland was partitioned out of existence and Revolutionary France expanded dramatically by means of successful military imperialism. Eighteenth-century Europe had seen relatively few major changes in political geography, and none on the scale of the 1770s. The Baltic map had been redrawn after the Great Northern War (1700–21), with the emerging state of Russia securing the lion's share of the Swedish empire, which was split up, while in the 1740s Prussia had seized the wealthy province of Silesia from the Austrian Habsburgs. These changes, however, were eclipsed by the scale and importance of the territorial gains made by the three eastern powers in 1772–5. Russia's annexations were particularly striking and suggested that, for the present at least, she was the continent's most expansionist and powerful state.

Throughout the 1770s and beyond, the eastern powers were to grow in confidence and to exhibit increasing initiative and independence. Their emergence was the crucial development in eighteenth-century European diplomacy. It was still incomplete in 1775, and it did not begin overnight in 1756. These dates, however, are the most satisfactory chronological limits for this study. Before the Seven Years War, Prussia and, in a different way, Russia were marginal to the operation of Europe's states system.[5] By the 1770s they had been fully incorporated and the Pentarchy had come into existence. The eastern powers had secured political parity with the states further west. The Russo-Ottoman War of 1768–74 was the first such struggle for a century not to be concluded through western diplomatic intervention, which was proffered but rejected. Throughout the fighting after 1768 the Empress

---

[5] See below, pp. 14–28.

3

Catherine II (1762–96) had successfully eluded all attempts at outside mediation and had retained freedom of action, which enabled her to translate Russia's impressive military victories into striking territorial and political gains. During the Anglo-Bourbon War of 1778–83, the eastern powers, and especially Russia and Austria, themselves sought to mediate in a struggle involving the western states. This was a complete reversal of the pattern hitherto, that of diplomatic intervention by the dominant western states in the conflicts of eastern and southern Europe, and it epitomised the transformation which had taken place.

The political and territorial changes were viewed with alarm and resentment both in Britain and France, where Jenkinson's lament was a familiar theme. The English man of letters Horace Walpole described the Polish partition as 'the most impudent association of robbers that ever existed', while the Scottish philosopher David Hume lamented that 'the two most civilised nations, the English and the French, should be on the decline; and the barbarians, the Goths and Vandals of Germany and Russia, should be rising in power and influence'.[6] Official circles in London in some measure shared this concern. It was not that British ministers were greatly exercised by Poland's fate. That country was remote, Catholic and long viewed as a French client.[7] The extent of British indifference to Russian expansion at the expense of the Ottoman empire can be gauged from the fact that, when news of Kuchuk-Kainardji arrived, the cabinet was not even summoned back from its summer holidays to discuss the treaty's implications.[8] The dramatic territorial changes in themselves did not alarm ministers, long accustomed to view eastern Europe as distant and involving no significant British interests, and preoccupied with internal and colonial problems, particularly in North America. Yet the political realignment which accompanied and facilitated their territorial annexations caused concern. The novel unity of the eastern powers appeared to threaten London's own diplomacy, which aimed to manipulate continental rivalries to secure allies against France.

The impact on the other side of the English Channel was greater and also more immediate. Indeed, traditional Anglo–French rivalry ensured that British observers viewed the events of the 1770s primarily as a defeat for Versailles. Walpole crowed at 'the affronts offered to France, where this partition treaty was not even notified. How that formidable monarchy is fallen, debased.'[9] The French crown had long

---

[6] *The Last Journals of Horace Walpole during the Reign of George III, from 1771 to 1783*, ed. A.F. Steuart (2 vols., London, 1910), I. 159; D.B. Horn, *British Public Opinion and the First Partition of Poland* (Edinburgh, 1945), pp. 18–19.

[7] This latter judgement was certainly exaggerated and probably mistaken. Though France remained influential, Poland had been a Russian puppet since the first decade of the eighteenth century. British observers, however, always viewed European issues through the lens of Anglo-French rivalry and thereby exaggerated Versailles' influence.

[8] H.M. Scott, *British Foreign Policy in the Age of the American Revolution* (Oxford, 1990), pp. 178–80, 195.

[9] To Sir Horace Mann, 1 July 1772, *Horace Walpole's Correspondence*, ed. W.S. Lewis (48 vols., New Haven, CT, 1937–83), XXIII. 419–20.

been the protector and friend of both Poland and the Ottoman empire. These two countries, together with Sweden, comprised the famous *barrière de l'est*, by which French diplomacy had sought to contain first its established Austrian Habsburg rival and then the rising power of Russia. The fact that these two states had been allies during the generation after 1726 strengthened Versailles' efforts to shut the Russian empire out of Europe: any further move westwards could only strengthen France's enemy Austria and menace her own clients, above all Sweden.[10] Versailles had supporters in Poland and traditionally exercised significant influence at Constantinople, but during the 1770s it could do nothing to prevent the first partition, and was even prepared to sacrifice the Ottoman empire to the wider interests of French policy.

France was a continental state and could not simply withdraw from European diplomacy, as her island rival at times appeared to do. In 1772–3 concern at the Polish partition, and at the unprecedented co-operation between the three eastern powers which made it possible, led to an attempted *rapprochement* with Britain, in order to restore the western states' political leadership of Europe. This secret initiative failed, principally because the British government was unwilling and, perhaps, unable to face the repercussions of such a dramatic step as an alliance with the national enemy. With hindsight it is clear that the initiative by France's foreign minister, the duc d'Aiguillon, was never likely to succeed. The Franco-British negotiations were significant primarily because they revealed the common predicament of the two western powers by the early 1770s.[11]

Each had been marginalised by the eastern Leviathans and now exerted little influence on the continent. This was fully apparent to the comte de Vergennes, who became France's foreign minister in July 1774. Vergennes was a career diplomat who had served both in Constantinople (1756–68) and in Stockholm (1771–4).[12] In each post he had been forced to confront Russia's new power at first hand, and he also recognised the wider international transformation of which her rise was part. His own background as a member of Louis XV's private diplomatic network, known as the *secret du roi*, with its anti-Russian purpose, was here important, as were the traditions of the *barrière de l'est*: French opposition to Russia was one of the few constants of the eighteenth-century international system. A major aim of Vergennes' policy came to be that of curbing and, if possible, reversing the political and territorial gains made by the eastern monarchies. Louis XVI's foreign minister was concerned at their new power and alarmed at its implications. Austria had been France's ally since 1756, but her growing intimacy with Russia and Prussia threatened – if it did not actually destroy – this alliance and thus weakened France's position in Europe. Vergennes also disliked the destruction both of the balance of power and of

---

[10] See the Instructions for the Marquis de la Chétardie, 1 July 1739, and for the Marquis de l'Hôpital, 28 Dec. 1756, both in *Recueil des Instructions données aux ambassadeurs et ministres de France, depuis les traités de Westphalie jusqu'à la Révolution Française* (32 vols. to date, Paris, 1884–): *Russie*, ed. A. Rambaud, I. 341, 344–5; II. 32–3.   [11] See below, ch. 8, for a fuller account.

[12] There is an informative biography by Orville T. Murphy, *Charles Gravier, Comte de Vergennes: French Diplomacy in the Age of Revolution 1719–1787* (Albany, NY, 1982).

what would later be known as the 'Public Law of Europe', that matrix of established conventions and dynastic and legal rights which regulated the international conduct of nation states. This had been the consequence of the Polish partition, the product of 'brigandage politique', which he believed had established power, not right, as the main determinant of diplomacy.[13] This view was shared by the Earl of Suffolk, Britain's Northern Secretary, who declared that the partition had established the 'Law of the Strongest'.[14]

These and similar comments by western observers were, at one level, inspired by a recognition of their own diminished importance. Both Britain and, in a different way, France were casualties of the eastern powers' emergence. The diplomatic leadership which they had enjoyed and exploited since the decades around 1700 was first challenged during the Seven Years War and then undermined after 1763. The transformation was no less apparent to Russia, Prussia and Austria, whose leaders appreciated their own enhanced role. It was recognised with particular clarity by Prussia's Frederick the Great, who in February 1772 – as the partition of Poland took shape – penned a brief and lucid analysis of the end of Anglo-French political hegemony. On hearing of the attempted *rapprochement* between the two western powers, he wrote: 'France and England can only console each other over the loss of their influence which had hitherto been dominant within the wider European states system. They retain only the memory of this dominance, and now lack any influence at all.'[15] There was, characteristically, both exaggeration and malice in the King's explanation: it was, he said, 'a natural consequence of their weakness'. His fundamental analysis, however, was well founded. In the previous year Frederick had actually claimed that Europe's only great powers were now Russia and Prussia, and perhaps Austria.[16] The Emperor Joseph II, during a conversation with the Prussian minister in Vienna extolling the merits of a Triple Alliance, threw out the remarkable notion that the eastern half of the continent should become closed to the western states. The partitioning powers should draw a line from the Adriatic to the Baltic, declare it to be their unique sphere of influence, and permit no outside interference within that zone.[17] The Prussian King's brother, Prince Henry, went even further, claiming that they would henceforth determine Europe's entire political destiny, if only they could create an enduring Triple Alliance.[18] By the early 1770s the eastern powers gave the law to the continent: as Russia's foreign minister, Nikita Panin,

---

[13] See, e.g., his 'Mémoire' of Dec. 1774, given to the new King Louis XVI: this is printed in Ségur, *Politique de tous les cabinets*, I. 158–70: the quotation is at p. 159.

[14] Quoted by Beales, *Joseph II*, p. 299.

[15] To Sandoz Rollin (Prussian agent in Paris), 7 Feb. 1772, *Pol. Corr.*, xxxi. 737. Sandoz Rollin had reported on the growing Anglo-French *rapprochement* on 26 Jan. 1772: *Pol. Corr.*, xxxi. 737.

[16] To Solms (minister in St Petersburg), 20 Feb. 1771, *SIRIO*, xxxvii. 393–6.

[17] Edelsheim to Frederick II, 8 Sept. 1772, GStAPK Rep. 96.47.K. Prussia's King ignored this hint: *Pol. Corr.*, xxxii. 490–1.

[18] Soloviev, *History of Russia*, xlviii. 21–2; *Pol. Corr.*, xxxii. 16–17. Frederick, it should be said, was considerably more realistic, recognising that a struggle between Prussia and Austria for influence in St Petersburg would be inevitable: see below, ch. 8.

explicitly noted in February 1772, as the initial treaty partitioning Poland was being signed, a view which was echoed by Maria Theresa six years later.[19] These changes expanded the international system eastwards, incorporating areas on Europe's periphery which had hitherto lain beyond its operations. Russia's full entry during Catherine II's reign was the most immediate symptom of this expansion.[20] The emergence of the eastern powers, however, involved rather more than a geographical extension of the international system, with a corresponding increase in the number of leading states from three to five. It was also central to a far more fundamental transformation: the establishment of a European great power system which would endure until the twentieth century.[21] The archaeology of words and terms is a notoriously difficult and elusive subject, and one where precision is impossible. It appears, however, that the third quarter of the eighteenth century was the period at which the term and, more important, the modern concept of 'great power' definitively entered the political lexicon.[22] This was linked to a simultaneous

---

[19] *SIRIO*, XXXVII. 643; cf. Soloviev, *History of Russia*, XLVIII. 25, for a similar view in summer 1772. For Maria Theresa, see her letter to Mercy-Argenteau, 30 June 1778, *MT-MA*, III. 326.

[20] See below, ch. 5.

[21] Though he did not explore the origins of the term, Leopold von Ranke's seminal essay on 'The Great Powers' remains fundamental to the development of the concept. It was first published in the *Historische Politische Zeitschrift*, vol. 2, for 1833, and can be found in English translation, in T.H. von Laue, *Leopold Ranke: The Formative Years* (Princeton, NJ, 1950), pp. 181–218. On the formative impact of nineteenth-century historiography and Ranke in particular on approaches to the study of early modern international relations, there are some suggestive remarks in Ulrich Muhlack, 'Das europäische Staatensystem in der deutschen Geschichtsschreibung des 19. Jahrhunderts', *Annali dell' Istituto Storico Germanico in Trento* 16 (1990), pp. 43–90. On the wider development there are some interesting reflections in F.H. Hinsley, *Power and the Pursuit of Peace: Theory and Practice in the History of Relations between States* (Cambridge, 1963), chs. 8–9, and in Arno Strohmeyer, *Theorie der Interaktion: das europäische Gleichgewicht der Kräfte in der frühen Neuzeit* (Vienna, Cologne and Weimar, 1994), esp. ch. 6.

[22] Numberous instances of the use of the term 'great power' or 'great powers' can be given. See, for example: J.H.G. von Justi, *Die Chimäre des Gleichgewichts von Europa* (Altona, 1758), p. 86; Bielfeld, *Institutions politiques*, II. 20, 23, 39; Rohan Butler, *Choiseul*, vol. I: *Father and Son, 1719–1754* (Oxford, 1980), 333 (de Bussy (French envoy in London) reporting a conversation with Carteret in 1742); Adolf Beer, 'Denkschriften des Fürsten Wenzel Kaunitz-Rittberg', *AÖG* 48 (1872), pp. 1–162, at p. 61 (Kaunitz in 1755); L. Jay Oliva, *Misalliance: A Study of French Policy in Russia during the Seven Years War* (New York, 1964), 143 (Choiseul in 1759); BL Egerton 1862, fo. 105 (Sir Joseph Yorke (British minister at The Hague) in 1761); AAE CP (Autriche) 304, fo. 131 (Châtelet (French ambassador in Vienna) in 1766); *Pol. Corr.*, XXV. 137 (Sir Andrew Mitchell (British minister in Berlin) in 1766); *Die politischen Testamente*, ed. Dietrich, pp. 622, 646 (Frederick the Great in 1768; in its predecessor, completed in 1752, the King employed the phrase 'grandes puissances' but the concept seems less well developed: *Die politischen Testamente*, ed. Dietrich, p. 334); *SIRIO*, CXXXV. 237 (Panin in 1774). On the general meaning of 'Macht' and 'puissance' at this period, see the entry by Karl-Georg Faber in Otto Brunner, Werner Conze and Reinhart Koselleck, eds., *Geschichtliche Grundbegriffe: Historisches Lexikon zur politisch-sozialen Sprache in Deutschland* (8 vols., Stuttgart, 1972–97), III. 882–8. At the close of the seventeenth century, the word 'Großmacht' had been the German translation of the Latin 'summum imperium': Brunner *et al.*, eds., *Geschichtliche Grundbegriffe*, p. 930 n. 748. This meaning was to be enduring. During the Seven Years War the *Encyclopédie* noted that 'puissance' was a synonym for authority (*pouvoir*) as well as an assessment of strength within the international system: Article 'Puissance' in Denis Diderot and Jean Le Rond d'Alembert, *Encyclopédie, ou Dictionnaire raisonné* (17 vols., Paris, 1751–65), XIII. 556.

change in the nature of international relations. By the 1760s and 1770s the notion of five states collectively dominating European politics and imposing themselves on the other members of the international system was becoming established.[23] The concept of great power – like the associated emergence of the Pentarchy – belongs to the second half of the eighteenth century and not, as is often still argued, to the Napoleonic era.[24]

This change was rooted in a new and quite different conception of political power. The very notion of 'great powers' underlined the extent to which a state's standing within the international hierarchy was now being assessed both with greater precision and relative to that of other participants. A 'great power' was simply one that could be recognised to be relatively much stronger and therefore to dominate its lesser rivals.[25] The potential of individual monarchies and thus their international standing had always been assessed, but in fairly general terms such as geographical extent, population, wealth and military strength. Success within the early modern system had been measured primarily in terms of military victories and the conquest of new territories to which these led. During the eighteenth century a more modern notion of power came to be developed, particularly in central Europe.[26] This conception was above all relative: a function of one state's strength in relation to that of its competitors. Such measurements were now made with rather greater precision and took account of the available economic, demographic and even geographical resources in order to calculate that country's potential power. This in turn depended upon a related development during the second half of the eighteenth century: the appearance of the distinctively German science of 'statistics' (*Staatenkunde*), which, by collecting reliable quantitative information, facilitated such calculations of relative international strength and which replaced the established juridical framework of public affairs.[27]

[23] See, e.g., Panin's revealing comments in 1774: *SIRIO*, cxxxv. 237.

[24] See, e.g., Karl-Georg Faber, in Brunner *et al.*, eds., *Geschichtliche Grundbegriffe*, III. 930–1. The Congress of Vienna and the settlement it produced were the first occasion upon which the great powers formally assumed international leadership and the responsibilities attached to this: Hinsley, *Power and the Pursuit of Peace*, p. 155.

[25] As Justi explicitly noted: *Die Chimäre des Gleichgewichts*, pp. 19, 86.

[26] See the major study by Harm Klueting, *Die Lehre von der Macht der Staaten: das aussenpolitische Machtproblem in der 'politischen Wissenschaft' und in der praktischen Politik im 18. Jahrhundert* (Berlin, 1986). There is a notable review of this book by Grete Klingenstein in *English Historical Review* 103 (1988), pp. 134–8. It seems to me that Prof. Klingenstein is quite correct to insist that the real origin of the transformation is less cameralist theory, as Prof. Klueting suggests, than books IX and X of Montesquieu's *De l'esprit des lois* (1748). See Grete Klingenstein, '"Jede Macht ist relativ": Montesquieu und die Habsburger Monarchie', in Herwig Ebner *et al.*, eds., *Festschrift Othmar Pickl* (Graz, 1987), pp. 307–24. There is a penetrating discussion of Bielfeld and especially Justi from a rather different perspective in Keith Tribe, *Governing Economy: The Reformation of German Economic Discourse 1750–1840* (Cambridge, 1988), ch. 4.

[27] This connection was underlined by Hertzberg at the very beginning of his *Réflexions sur la force des Etats et sur leur Puissance relative et proportionelle* of Jan. 1782. This is printed in his *Huit dissertations . . . lues dans les assemblées publiques de l'Académie Royale des Sciences et Belles Lettres de Berlin, tenues pour l'anniversaire du roi Frédéric dans les années 1780–1787* (Berlin, 1787), p. 87.

This approach was first elaborated, particularly during the 1750s, by cameralist writers among whom Justi and Bielfeld were the most prominent. Johann Heinrich Gottlieb von Justi (1720–71) was the better known of the two men. He served the governments of Austria, Hanover, Denmark and finally Prussia, and set out his ideas in a series of writings, principal among which were the *Staatswirtschaft oder Systematische Abhandlung aller Oekonomischen und Cameral-wissenschaften* of 1755 and a highly sceptical essay on the idea of the balance of power, *Die Chimäre des Gleichgewichts von Europa*, first published in 1758. Jakob Friedrich von Bielfeld (1717–70) was originally a Hamburg merchant's son. He entered Prussian service, had a brief career as a diplomat and acted as tutor to Frederick the Great's younger brother, Ferdinand, before publishing his *Institutions politiques* in 1760.[28]

Both writers emphasised the centrality of economics to calculations of power, which was a novel development. They also stressed that the international standing of a state ultimately rested upon its internal strength, coherence and organisation: an approach reflected in the widespread efforts at domestic reform and reconstruction, after the destructive Seven Years War.[29] Such assessments were not purely quantitative but possessed a qualitative dimension. The scale and efficiency of government, the extent to which natural resources were exploited and even the moral condition of a ruler's subjects were all important elements in the calculation of a state's potential power.[30] These ideas, moreover, had a considerable and surprisingly rapid impact on practical statecraft. Immediately incorporated into the teaching of cameralism in Austrian and German universities, they influenced internal government and foreign policy. The two individuals who stand at the heart of this present study, the Prussian King Frederick the Great and Austria's leading minister Wenzel Anton von Kaunitz, were both strongly influenced by the new thinking, as was one of Frederick's leading foreign policy advisers, Ewald Friedrich Graf von Hertzberg.[31] The impact of such ideas, and of the notion that power could be accurately calculated, was to be clearly evident during the negotiations which determined the precise annexations from Poland in 1772–3.[32] These were to be

---

[28] The first edition (The Hague, 1760) announced that it would be supplemented by a political gazetteer. This was eventually included in a three-volume edition under an identical title (Leiden, 1767–72), of which it comprised vol. III, in two parts, though it had been completed by 1757, when the exigencies of the Seven Years War forced Bielfeld to take refuge in his native Hamburg: 3rd edn, I. xvi–xvii. All references to the *Institutions politiques* in the present study are to the first edition, unless otherwise indicated.   [29] See below, ch. 3.

[30] See, e.g., the overlapping discussions in Bielfeld, *Institutions politiques*, II. 78–97, Justi, *Die Chimäre des Gleichgewichts*, pp. 27–58, and the article 'Puissance' in Diderot and d'Alembert, *Encyclopédie*, XIII. 556–7.

[31] Klueting, *Die Lehre von der Macht der Staaten*, pp. 138–273; Frederick's Political Testaments of 1752 and 1768 (printed in *Die politischen Testamente*, ed. Dietrich), reflect this approach; for the Chancellor, see below, pp. 78–82. In 1782 Hertzberg provided a succinct introduction to such thinking in his lecture to the Berlin Academy: *Réfléxions sur la force des Etats et sur leur Puissance relative et proportionelle*. The *Institutions politiques* was also translated into Russian (1768–75) and was a significant source of Catherine II's domestic policies, as were the writings of Justi: Claus Scharf, *Katharina II., Deutschland und die Deutschen* (Mainz, 1995), pp. 124–30.   [32] See below, ch. 7.

characterised, on the part of all three participants, by an attempt to calculate and thus to equalise the 'political worth' (*valeur politique*) of each share of the Polish gains. While such ideas were becoming important, during the third quarter of the eighteenth century they overlaid rather than replaced traditional approaches to the conduct of international relations.

In November 1760 France's foreign minister the duc de Choiseul produced a celebrated analysis of the international order which was also an epitaph for an era which was closing:

Colonies, commerce, and the maritime power which accrues from them [he wrote] will decide the balance of power upon the continent. Austria, Russia and the King of Prussia are only second class powers, like all other who can make war only when they are subsidised by the commercial powers, which are France, England, Spain and Holland.[33]

Choiseul's argument was exaggerated and his purpose was polemical: he went on to find one explanation of French failures in the Seven Years War in the fact that 'France bears the brunt of this rivalry and protects the commerce of Europe against English ambition'. His fundamental analysis, however, can be broadly accepted as an explanation of the working of the European states system from the close of the fifteenth century until the mid-eighteenth century. The politically dominant states during the early modern period had mainly been located along the continent's western periphery and had benefited from the access this gave to trade and overseas possessions. Spain's ascendancy during her Golden Age had been heavily dependent upon the wealth of her empire and had also been based upon France's prolonged weakness during the two generations after 1559, while the seventeenth-century emergence of the Dutch Republic had been made possible by the prosperity created by its extensive commercial and financial activities, in Europe as well as overseas. France's hegemony under Louis XIV, like her domination of western Europe under his successor Louis XV, had been founded upon unrivalled demographic and economic strength together with the weakness of Spain and Austria, while Britain's spectacular eighteenth-century emergence was supported by commercial and financial expansion and the wealth and power this conferred. Two exceptions to this general rule were the peripheral states of Poland-Lithuania and Sweden, both of which enjoyed periods of political importance in spite of the limited resources at their disposal. Though Sweden's basic poverty had not prevented her dramatic seventeenth-century rise, her equally rapid decline at the beginning of the eighteenth century highlighted the crucial lack of demographic and economic resources. It was only to be during the third quarter of the eighteenth century that the political leadership exercised by the states along the Atlantic seaboard was decisively overturned, with the emergence of the eastern powers which Jenkinson had highlighted.

[33] This is quoted by Alan Christelow, 'Economic Background of the Anglo-Spanish War of 1762', *Journal of Modern History* 18 (1946), pp. 22–36, at p. 26.

The rise of the eastern powers

I

The political emergence of Austria, Russia and Prussia was part of a wider eighteenth-century evolution which discovered the region and established the idea of eastern Europe.[1] At least since the Renaissance, the continent had been divided conceptually between south and north. During the age of the Enlightenment new fault lines became established, as 'eastern' and 'western' Europe were invented and so became the two areas which made up its land mass. Contemporaries simultaneously incorporated Russia into the new, though geographically imprecise, region designated as 'eastern Europe'. The continental wars of 1756–63 and 1768–74 were important in establishing these new dispensations: exactly as they were to be for the emergence of the eastern powers.[2] By drawing attention to the area and to the important political developments under way, these conflicts highlighted its importance for western Europeans. That emergence, however, was primarily based upon earlier internal and international developments in each of the states which rose so impressively during the third quarter of the eighteenth century.

The first to become a leading European power had been Austria. Unlike Russia and Prussia, who emerged as first-class states only during the decades examined in this book, the Habsburg Monarchy had been a great power in name, if not in fact, since around 1700. This political emergence had always rested on a fragile domestic base. It was not that the extensive though far-flung territories ruled from Vienna were lacking in resources, particularly when compared with the other eastern powers. Austria was always more prosperous than her two rivals and more populous than Prussia, though her economy was also based on agriculture, with much less trade or manufacturing than the more advanced states in western Europe.[3] Vienna's problem had always been that of mobilising sufficient resources to support the extensive commitments which geography, dynastic loyalty and external circumstances imposed upon the central European Habsburgs. By the mid-eighteenth century the lands of the Monarchy were extremely far-flung. No other state was

---

[1] See Lawrence Wolff, *Inventing Eastern Europe: The Map of Civilization on the Mind of the Enlightenment* (Stamford, CA, 1994).   [2] Wolff, *Inventing Eastern Europe*, pp. 171, 196–8, 362.

[3] The most up-to-date survey, albeit rather theoretical in tone, is Roman Sandgruber, *Ökonomie und Politik: Österreichische Wirtschaftsgeschichte vom Mittelalter bis zur Gegenwart* (Vienna, 1996), esp. parts 3 and 4.

involved at so many points on the map of Europe, though Russia's vast empire in Asia created strategic problems of an altogether different order.[4]

Austria's enlarged European role had been a by-product of the struggle against Louis XIV and, to a lesser extent, her own conflict with the Ottoman empire. The fundamental rivalry in early modern Europe had been that between France and the House of Habsburg. The seventeenth-century decline and eventual extinction of the family's Spanish branch had placed their Austrian cousins in the front line against the powerful French monarchy. This rivalry was exploited after 1688 by the Dutch Republic and the British state (together known as the 'Maritime Powers') in their joint search for an ally – and, more important, an army – to put into the field against France, and in this way reduce their own military effort. Dutch and English loans and subsidies helped to finance Austria's involvement in the wars of 1689–1714; these were again to be important during the 1740s.[5] Simultaneously, Habsburg armies had secured an important series of victories over the Ottoman empire during two periods of fighting (1683–99; 1716–18) and thereby recovered control over the Kingdom of Hungary, the greater part of which had been occupied by the Ottoman empire since the first half of the sixteenth century. In 1718 Habsburg possessions in south-eastern Europe had reached an extent which would not be surpassed until shortly before the First World War. These gains, together with Austria's contribution to the Anglo-Dutch struggle against France, elevated her to the front rank of European states. Yet the resources necessary to support such a role could only with difficulty be squeezed from the territories over which the Habsburgs ruled.[6]

This was largely the consequence of the distinctive way in which these lands had been acquired and were now governed. By the mid-eighteenth century Habsburg possessions sprawled through central Europe, with outposts in the distant Austrian Netherlands (most of present-day Belgium and Luxembourg) and in the Italian Peninsula, where Milan was administered directly and Tuscany was ruled personally by Maria Theresa's husband, Francis Stephen, after 1737.[7] A further, small, group of outlying territories was located in western Germany along the Rhine, collectively known as 'Further Austria' (*Vorderösterreich*). The heartlands of the family's power, however, were the central European possessions lying on both sides of the river Danube: principally the Austrian provinces ruled from Vienna, the so-called 'Lands of the Bohemian Crown' (which provided most of the economic and

[4] See below, pp. 14–15.

[5] Gustav Otruba, 'Die Bedeutung englischer Subsidien und Antizipationen für die Finanzen Österreichs 1701 bis 1748', *Vierteljahrschrift für Sozial- und Wirtschaftsgeschichte* 51 (1964), pp. 192–234. Bielfeld considered that this dependence militated against Austria being seen as a first-class power: *Institutions politiques*, II. 80.

[6] The classic study of this is Jean Bérenger, *Finances et absolutisme autrichien dans la seconde moitié du XVIIᵉ siècle* (Paris, 1975).

[7] Upon his death in 1765, the Grand Duchy of Tuscany became a family secundogeniture, being ruled by Joseph II's younger brother, Leopold, from 1765 to 1790.

demographic resources needed to uphold Habsburg power) and the Kingdom of Hungary along with the neighbouring and small principality of Transylvania which was ruled directly.[8] Finally, possession of the imperial dignity – since 1438 in practice hereditary in the family, with the single exception of the period 1740–5 – conferred overlordship, together with some real powers, throughout the Empire.[9]

These territories had been acquired at separate times and in different ways, and remained a dynastic polity: the court and the army, together with loyalty to the House of Habsburg and a culture rooted in the dominance of Counter-Reformation Catholicism, did far more to hold the scattered possessions together than institutional bonds. There was no uniform system of government. Even after the reforms of 1749, which merged the administrations of the Austrian and Bohemian lands, the Monarchy's subjects continued to be ruled through a variety of institutions and Vienna's authority varied significantly from one province to another, while the Kingdom of Hungary enjoyed semi-independent status. Particularism and provincialism had been strengthened by imperfect political and territorial integration which had taken place. In most territories, the traditional élites and the local Estates remained extremely influential during the third quarter of the eighteenth century, and vigorously defended their separate legal systems and distinctive laws. The consequence was that the expansion of central authority and the ability to impose taxation which it conferred were always imperfectly realised, even in the context of the structural limitations upon all government in early modern Europe. In every major continental state during the seventeenth and eighteenth centuries there had been a significant increase in the reach of central authority, and especially its fiscal power, but no such evolution had occurred in the Habsburg Monarchy before the 1740s. The contrast with Vienna's great German rival, Prussia, was particularly striking and proved to be significant during the half century after 1740. This was always Austria's Achilles' heel: as it again proved to be during and after the Seven Years War.

The Habsburg army was a microcosm of the polity which supported it.[10] In the aftermath of the Thirty Years War – mirroring an evolution found in many central European territories – a standing army had grown up, and in the wars around 1700 it had increased significantly in size.[11] These troops had won important victories over Ottoman forces, and had performed respectably in the European wars against

---

[8] The Austrian and Bohemian territories were together known as the 'Hereditary Lands'.

[9] R.J.W. Evans, *The Making of the Habsburg Monarchy 1550–1700* (Oxford, 1979), is the seminal study of this territorial and political consolidation. For the period after 1700, there are some penetrating remarks in Grete Klingenstein, 'The meanings of "Austria" and "Austrian" in the eighteenth century', in Robert Oresko, G.C. Gibbs and H.M. Scott, eds., *Royal and Republican Sovereignty in Early Modern Europe: Essays in Memory of Ragnhild Hatton* (Cambridge, 1997), pp. 423–78.

[10] The best guide is J. Zimmermann, *Militärverwaltung und Heeresaufbringung in Österreich bis 1806* (Munich, 1983).

[11] Figures for its 'official' strength, counting infantry and cavalry in the line army, for the period 1695–1794, are contained in Dickson, *Finance*, ii, Appendix A.

Louis XIV. The Austrian army was always handicapped, however, by shortage of funds, particularly during the wars of 1733–48, and by its own structure. Once again the contrast with its Prussian rival was striking. The rank-and-file was filled up by a mixture of voluntary enlistment and forcible recruiting carried out by the provincial Estates, which together yielded far less impressive results than Prussia's Cantonal System, or even Russia's practice of levying recruits.[12] The officer corps was more cosmopolitan than in any other major European army, reflecting not merely the Monarchy's own diversity but also the extent to which the territorial nobilities appeared to have shunned military service. The shortcomings of leadership from which Austria's army suffered were in stark contrast to the disciplined officer *cadre* provided by Prussia's Junkers. Finally, even in the mid-eighteenth century, the Habsburg forces contained elements of older dispensations, above all the system of regimental proprietorship which recalled the era of military entrepreneurship a century before. The colonel-proprietor (*Inhaber*) retained important judicial, financial and administrative functions, which militated against the establishment of a strict military hierarchy and gave the army the character of a federation of regiments. This was to be found in all eighteenth-century forces, but not to the extent that it existed in the Austrian army. Its poor performance in the wars of 1733–48 had led to significant efforts at reform after the Peace of Aix-la-Chapelle (1748), though at first their impact had been incomplete. The shortcomings of the armed forces epitomised the way in which Austria's international position was always weakened, even in comparison to her eastern neighbours, by the deficiencies of her internal administration.

II

Before the eighteenth century, Russia's impact upon early modern Europe had been very limited. Located on the continent's eastern rim and separated by important religious, cultural and political traditions, contacts with the countries further west had been sporadic. This had been accentuated by her sheer size and diversity. Russia's frontiers, in Asia and in Europe, were far more extensive than those of any other state,[13] and her spectacular territorial expansion exacerbated the problems of defence and government. By comparison with the other two eastern powers, the Russian empire was rich in subjects and especially land. The available resources, however, were spread far more thinly, across an empire which sprawled through much of Asia towards the Far East. Successful expansion, from the sixteenth century onwards, had created an empire which far outstripped any European polity in scale. This vast territory, however, was far from uniform. The Black Earth areas which lay to the south and east of the traditional capital, Moscow, were rich grain-

---

[12] See below, pp. 15–16, 21–2, for these.
[13] This has recently been highlighted by John P. LeDonne, *The Russian Empire and the World, 1700–1917: The Geopolitics of Expansion and Containment* (New York, 1997).

growing regions which were the mainstay of Russian agriculture. Elsewhere the agrarian economy was primitive. Most of the empire comprised steppe, forest or, in Central Asia, desert, while it would be the later nineteenth century before a transport infrastructure was created. The facts of geography which Russia's rulers believed a source of weakness appeared a matter of simple strength when viewed from Europe. Contemporaries were blind to the problems of governing this gigantic land mass, which far eclipsed those of any other continental state, and instead regarded European Russia's relative invulnerability to attack as a special source of her strength.[14] The empire's feet of clay were seldom glimpsed further west.

Knowledge of the vast, mysterious, Muscovite empire, most of which lay across Asia, had been very limited, particularly in western Europe. Eighteenth-century maps distinguished clearly between 'Russia in Europe', which extended as far as the Urals, and 'Russia in Asia'.[15] She long remained – to western observers at least – a semi-Asiatic country, set aside from the European mainstream by her distinctive religion, culture and political system. In 1739 the French foreign office conjured up the danger that Russia's 'troupes barbares' might flood into Germany in a future war, articulating a fear which was to prove particularly tenacious, surviving until the early twentieth century.[16] The clear implication was that she was still a political outsider, not part of Europe's community of nations. Until the important reign of Peter I (1682/96–1725, known as 'Peter the Great'), she had not even been incorporated into the developing network of reciprocal diplomacy. The Russian empire had appeared as peripheral as its Ottoman counterpart. It was 1712 before a European writer – the abbé de Saint-Pierre – definitively included Russia among the European states.[17] Five more years elapsed before the French *Almanach Royal* first included the Romanov monarchy among the 'Kingdoms of Europe'.[18]

This belated inclusion was brought about by Peter I's important victories over the Swedish state during the first decade of the Great Northern War and the growth of Russian power which these signalled. He had destroyed Sweden's military power and with it her empire, and so re-established Russia on the Baltic, making her dominant in northern Europe. His troops had wintered in Mecklenburg in 1716, underlining the new potential of the Russian army. These successes, and the substantial territorial gains to which they led at the Peace of Nystad (1721), had enormously increased Russian power and prestige, and had given Peter's empire a new importance. They had been accompanied by the rapid modernisation of the armed forces, including the creation of a Baltic navy, and of government. These reforms built upon the work of Peter I's seventeenth-century predecessors and especially his own father Alexis (1645–76). Within a decade the army was completely overhauled, with

[14] Schroeder, *Transformation of European Politics*, pp. 14–15, 26.
[15] Wolff, *Inventing Eastern Europe*, pp. 23, 154.
[16] Instructions for the Marquis de la Chétardie, 1 July 1739, *Recueil . . . Russie*, ed. Rambaud, I, pp. 344.
[17] Simon Dixon, *The Modernisation of Russia 1676–1825* (Cambridge, 1999), p. 28.
[18] Wolff, *Inventing Eastern Europe*, p. 152.

new garrison and line regiments and an enlarged and more effective cavalry. Above all, a coherent and unified recruitment system was consolidated, which proved to be a relatively efficient way of establishing and maintaining a large military establishment.[19] Though burdensome upon the peasantry it conscripted and frequently inefficient, it was to provide Russia's eighteenth-century armies with relatively abundant manpower, one important ingredient in their success. Central government was modernised and expanded, though there were important limitations upon what was achieved. The shortage of trained personnel and the sheer vastness of the areas to be administered meant that central authority was vestigial in the more remote regions, while Peter I's impressive achievements had been highly personal in nature and did not prove enduring during the generation of political instability (1725–62) which followed his death.

Peter's successes had been accompanied by a significant expansion in economic and diplomatic contacts with Europe. Reciprocal permanent representation between Russia and the other European states – one of the hallmarks of modern diplomacy – began in the early eighteenth century.[20] Until then, her rulers had sent individual and short-term embassies for specific purposes and had only maintained a permanent representative in neighbouring Poland-Lithuania. The exigencies of the Great Northern War and Russia's enhanced international status under Peter I had led to a rapid increase in the number of diplomats sent and received and to the establishment of the first permanent Russian missions in central and western Europe. By 1701 Russian representatives were to be found in Vienna, The Hague and Copenhagen. There were more or less permanent embassies in Britain and Prussia from 1707, in France from 1720 and in Spain from 1724.[21] By the time of Peter I's death in the following year, Russia had been incorporated into the network of permanent, reciprocal diplomacy which linked the various European capitals.

This was not immediately accompanied, however, by an enlarged role within the European states system, underlining that though the two overlapped, they were not identical.[22] There was a clear distinction between Russia's rise as a military power under Peter I and her emergence as a great power, which was only achieved after the Seven Years War.[23] He had given his state a new importance in northern and eastern Europe, but he had not pushed Russian influence very far into central Europe: that would not be accomplished for another half century.[24] This was later recognised by

---

[19] D. Beyrau, *Militär und Gesellschaft im vorrevolutionären Russland* (Cologne, 1984), parts I and II; John L.H. Keep, *Soldiers of the Tsar: Army and Society in Russia 1462–1874* (Oxford, 1985), chs. 6–8.

[20] See D. Altbauer, 'The Diplomats of Peter the Great', *JGO* NF 28 (1980), pp. 1–16; and Avis Bohlen, 'Changes in Russian Diplomacy under Peter the Great', *Cahiers du monde russe et soviétique* 7 (1966), pp. 341–58.   [21] M.S. Anderson, *The Rise of Modern Diplomacy 1450–1919* (London, 1993), p. 70.

[22] See above, p. 2.

[23] See the comments of George E. Munro, the editor and translator of Soloviev, *History of Russia* XLVII. xii.

[24] Manfred Hellmann, 'Die Friedensschlüsse von Nystad (1721) und Teschen (1779) als Etappen des Vordringens Russlands nach Europa', *Historisches Jahrbuch* 97/8 (1978), pp. 270–88; cf. below, pp. 253–4.

Nikita Panin, Catherine II's foreign minister, who wrote on one occasion that 'In leading his people out of ignorance, Peter the Great considered it a tremendous achievement to make them equal to powers of the second rank.'[25] Russia's military might was recognised by the time of his death in 1725, and she was henceforth to play a more significant role in eastern Europe, concluding important alliances with Austria and, for a time, Prussia.[26] But the Russian empire was not seen in London, Versailles or even Vienna as a leading state for another generation, until the Seven Years War. On the eve of that struggle Kaunitz still did not regard his ally as a state of equal standing to Austria, viewing her as an 'auxiliary power' which needed foreign subsidies if her military potential were to be mobilised.[27]

There were several reasons for this. Sweden's defeat and the partition of her Baltic empire had been attributed not only to Russia's new power but to her own weakness. Swedish human and economic resources had been seriously over-extended, while the King, Charles XII (1697–1718), had pursued a mistaken and even foolhardy strategy. Petrine Russia was viewed as the agent as much as the fundamental cause of her eclipse. Fifty years later, the situation would be quite different. Prussia, with her formidable military machine, efficient administration and remarkable ruler, was clearly emerging as a leading continental state and this would magnify the impact of the Russian performance during the Seven Years War.[28] Neither Peter nor his successors secured admission to the ranks of Europe's leading states, not least because throughout the first half of the eighteenth century, Anglo-French rivalry in western Europe continued to dominate European diplomacy and alliances were shaped principally by fear of France. It was unclear to contemporaries exactly what assistance the distant and remote Russian empire could give against the French monarchy. Twice during the first half of the eighteenth century – in 1735 and 1748 – Russian troops had made the long march across Europe in an attempt to influence a struggle against Bourbon power. On both occasions these contingents arrived too late to play any active part in the fighting, reinforcing the widespread scepticism about her value as an ally.[29] The disintegration of an international system shaped by Anglo-French rivalry was essential to the emergence of Russia as a great

---

[25] Soloviev, *History of Russia*, XLV. 109.

[26] There is a notably intelligent discussion of Russia's eighteenth-century impact on Europe in Martin Malia, *Russia under Western Eyes: From the Bronze Horseman to the Lenin Mausoleum* (Cambridge, MA, 1999), pp. 17–84. This process is examined in the exhaustive and exhausting study by Walther Mediger, *Moskaus Weg nach Europa: der Aufstieg Russlands zum europäischen Machtstaat im Zeitalter Friedrichs des Grossen* (Brunswick, 1952), a study which, paradoxically, demonstrates at considerable length Russia's *limited* impact until Catherine II's reign. See also Reiner Pommerin, 'Bündnispolitik und Mächtesystem: Österreich und der Aufstieg Russlands im 18. Jahrhundert', in Johannes Kunisch, ed., *Expansion und Gleichgewicht: Studien zur europäischen Mächtepolitik des ancien régime* (Berlin, 1986), pp. 113–64, and Jeremy Black, 'Russia's Rise as a European Power, 1650–1750', *History Today* 36 (August 1986), pp. 21–8, which seriously exaggerates Russia's impact.

[27] Pommerin, 'Bündnispolitik und Mächtesystem', p. 131.   [28] See below, pp. 42–51.

[29] This was shared by Kaunitz: Lothar Schilling, *Kaunitz und das Renversement des Alliances: Studien zur aussenpolitischen Konzeption Wenzel Antons von Kaunitz* (Berlin, 1994), p. 121 and, more generally, pp. 97–121.

power. A further obstacle to full integration was Russia's failure, until Catherine II's reign, to adopt the distinctive diplomatic culture which was one foundation of the European states system.[30]

There was a final reason for her limited international impact before the Seven Years War: the narrow and at times blinkered policies pursued by Russian rulers and their advisers during these decades. Eighteenth-century great power status was not simply a matter of resources and relative power. Military muscle was an essential requirement, but did not itself secure that position, which possessed an ideological and qualitative dimension conferred by the conceptual sophistication of a country's leadership. This was most clearly appreciated by the late Andrew Lossky:

> This quality of greatness had little to do with manpower, resources or other quantifiable elements of strength. To put it crudely, it consisted in the ability of statesmen to count beyond three. Any statesman who is not mentally deranged can count up to three: my country, my country's enemy, and the enemy of my country's enemy, who is my ally. On this basis, it is quite possible to carry on an adequate foreign policy, but it will always have an air of simplistic provincialism about it. A statesman who can count to four will also be able to count beyond four; he will perceive an infinity of possible variations in the degree of hostility or alliance as well as the possibility of limited alliance with one's enemy or of limited hostility with one's ally. His mind's eye will also be able to take in at a glance the entire diplomatic chessboard in all its complexity. Such a statesman will have an inestimable advantage over his provincial-minded opposite numbers.[31]

While Lossky's undervaluing of the importance of resources may be questioned, his approach is illuminating. In the eighteenth century, statesmanship consisted of the ability to see the entire international system and the diplomatic possibilities it offered, rather than one dimension of it, and this conceptual sophistication in turn was a precondition of true great power status.

This suggests why Russia only became a leading European power during Catherine II's reign. The Petrine legacy to Russian foreign policy had been a preoccupation with three Baltic problems, all essentially dynastic in nature, and a corresponding neglect of the wider European issues.[32] This was accompanied by a failure to sustain the political momentum created by Peter I. Until the Seven Years

---

[30] See below, pp. 151–61, for a fuller analysis.

[31] This formulation of Andrew Lossky's *dictum* comes from his *Louis XIV and the French Monarchy* (New Brunswick, NJ, 1994), p. 62; an earlier version is to be found in his essay 'France in the System of Europe in the Seventeenth Century', *Proceedings of the Western Society for French Historical Studies* (1974), pp. 32–48.

[32] See the illuminating essay by Hans Bagger, 'The Role of the Baltic in Russian Foreign Policy, 1721–1773', in Hugh Ragsdale, ed, *Imperial Russian Foreign Policy* (Cambridge , 1993), pp. 36–72; the episodic and very detailed study by Mediger, *Moskaus Weg nach Europa*, confirms these dynastic preoccupations; the survey of the period 1725–62 by Michael G. Müller, 'Das "petrinische Erbe": Russische Grossmachtpolitik bis 1762', in Klaus Zernack, ed., *Handbuch der Geschichte Russlands, II:i – 1613–1856* (Stuttgart, 1986), pp. 402–44 – which assumes that Russia became a great power by 1725 – underlines the dominant place of these Baltic issues at this time and in fact demonstrates Russia's limited impact upon the European states system prior to the Seven Years War.

War, St Petersburg's diplomatic outlook was dominated by the political legacies of Peter I's treaties with Courland, Mecklenburg-Schwerin and especially Holstein-Gottorp. Relations with other states were viewed through this narrow Baltic prism, which was one reason why efforts to conclude alliances with Britain and France immediately after 1725 had been unsuccessful. The ministry of A.P. Bestuzhev-Riumin after 1744 saw a broadening of this perspective and began the process which would culminate in Russia's emergence as a great power.[33] The Chancellor sought to establish and maintain alliances with Britain, Saxony (whose Elector was also King of Poland) and especially Austria, and to direct this grouping of states against the rising power of Prussia, who appeared a rival in north-eastern Europe. This amounted to the creation and maintenance of a glacis, a region under St Petersburg's control beyond the western frontier which kept Russia's enemies at bay, and it became an enduring aim of her foreign policy. These objectives were apparent in the 1746 alliance with Vienna, renewing one concluded two decades earlier. But even Bestuzhev's foreign policy during the 1740s and 1750s had still been strongly influenced by the legacies of these dynastic problems and especially the Holstein-Gottorp issue.[34] The political sophistication demanded of a true great power would only be provided by the Empress and Panin after 1763.[35]

Russia's hesitant emergence as a naval power exactly paralleled her political evolution. During the second decade of the Great Northern War she had emerged as a major Baltic naval state, though the impetus had not been sustained, partly due to recurring financial problems. The 1730s had seen a rapid decline in this fleet and, though the Swedish War of 1741–3 and the heightened international tension of the later 1740s saw some improvement, it had been followed by a further sharp deterioration which continued until the very end of the 1760s. Throughout the first seven decades of the eighteenth century, the Russian navy had not even been the Baltic's largest fleet. Until the 1770s it had usually been smaller than that of Denmark, and only marginally larger than that of Sweden. Its purpose had been essentially defensive: that of protecting the Gulf of Finland and particularly the vulnerable new capital, St Petersburg, from attack. There were in any case formidable obstacles to Russia's emergence as a major naval power. Personnel was an enduring problem. Though serfs, sometimes provided with a year of basic training at sea, could be used to man the vessels, many of the officers had to be found abroad: Russia's officer corps was the most cosmopolitan of any major eighteenth-century navy. The material problems were even more serious, and they were to be magnified by the increased range and scale of the fleet's operations under Catherine II. Since they were built of larch and pine rather than oak, Russian ships had the shortest life-span of any

---

[33] His decisive impact upon Russian policy is apparent from Mediger, *Moskaus Weg nach Europa*, pp. 247–95, 582–627. See also the detailed and at times overblown study by Francine-Dominique Liechtenhan, *La Russie entre en Europe: Elisabeth Iʳᵉ et la Succession d'Autriche (1740–1750)* (Paris, 1997). [34] This would remain important in Catherine II's foreign policy: see below, pp. 125–9.
[35] See below, pp. 125–8, for a fuller account of this dynastic imbroglio.

contemporary navy. Until the war with the Ottoman empire after 1768, Russia would not be a significant European naval power and this inhibited her wider political evolution.

III

Prussia's emergence was quite different in nature. The Hohenzollern monarchy was a minor state which, during the middle decades of the eighteenth century, rose spectacularly in stature, rather than a powerful but peripheral empire which moved closer to the centre of the international system. When Frederick William I (1713–40) died, Brandenburg-Prussia was – in her new King's precise formulation – an hermaphrodite, being a kingdom in name but an electorate in fact. This expressed her relative insignificance when her best-known eighteenth-century ruler, Frederick II (1740–86; usually known as 'Frederick the Great') came to the throne. When her subjects in the Kingdom of Prussia are included, she was the most populous German territory after the Habsburg Monarchy. Since 1697 Brandenburg-Prussia had been the leader of the *corpus evangelicorum*, the Protestant party within the Holy Roman Empire (*Reich*). She was one of the larger electorates – Saxony, Bavaria and Hanover were the others – which were sufficiently powerful to be recognised as of more than German importance. On the European stage, however, she was a third- or, at best, a second-class state in 1740. The Hohenzollerns' acquisition of a royal title – 'King in Prussia' – in 1701 added lustre to the Hohenzollern dynasty, but prestige ran ahead of actual power for at least another half century.

Territorial dispersal, together with limited demographic and economic resources, were significant obstacles to Prussia's political rise. Her provinces were exposed and scattered across half the continent. Until the acquisition of Royal (that is to say, Polish) Prussia in 1772, the state known to historians as 'Prussia' in fact consisted of three widely scattered groups of territories: in the west the Rhineland enclaves of Cleves, Mark and Ravensberg, together with East Friesland, acquired in 1744; the core territories of Brandenburg, Pomerania and Silesia, together with Magdeburg and Halberstadt, lying astride the rivers Elbe and Oder; finally the exposed salient of East Prussia, the source of the dynasty's royal title. The consequent problems of self-defence, in the face of hostile and predatory neighbours, were considerable: the furthermost border of East Prussia lay some 750 miles from the Rhineland possessions, a particularly great distance during an era when communications were slow and unreliable. As Voltaire remarked, Frederick the Great was really 'King of the border strips'.

These problems were intensified by the fact that Prussia lacked the resources to support her commitments and ambitions, as Frederick continually emphasised and exaggerated in his writings in a blatant attempt to magnify his own achievements. Yet Prussia's relative poverty could not be doubted. Her population was around 2.25

million in 1740; by 1786, and largely due to the important territorial gains made during Frederick's reign, it had climbed to around 5.8 million. Her population density was particularly low by European and German standards. All the other continental great powers were much stronger demographically. France at mid-century had around 25 million inhabitants; Russia at Catherine II's accession in 1762 had some 23 million; while in that same year the central European lands of the Habsburg Monarchy had around 14 million. Even the fifth great power, the island kingdom of Britain (excluding Ireland) had between 6 and 7 million inhabitants during the Seven Years War. Prussia was also relatively poorly endowed with economic resources, although the export of agricultural produce to western Europe did raise significant sums in cash. With the exception of the Rhineland territories, however, the Hohenzollern lands were impoverished and backward, and contained little industry. Both in the central provinces and in East Prussia, poor soil together with an inhospitable climate ensured that subsistence agriculture prevailed, with a dependent and sometimes enserfed peasantry and small agrarian surpluses. Commercial activity was at a very low level, with only grain and grain-based products being exported, and was driven largely by the demands of the Prussian state, while geographical location and poor internal communications together ensured that the Hohenzollern territories were by-passed by the major trade routes.

Frederick also inherited significant assets when he became King on 31 May 1740. Principal among these was an army which was unusually large for a country of its size, population and political importance. Successive Hohenzollern rulers, aware of the vulnerability of their scattered possessions, had built up a large military force for self-defence. Its creation has shaped internal developments since the Great Elector's accession in 1640, and during Frederick William I's reign it ordinarily consumed around 70 per cent of annual peacetime revenue. In 1740 the army was some 80,000 strong, impressive on the barrack square but untested in combat. With the exception of some indecisive operations in the Rhineland in 1734, during the War of the Polish Succession, it had not fired a shot in anger since the siege of Stralsund in 1715. Its last important victory had been gained as long ago as 1675, though Prussian contingents had fought impressively in the allied armies during the War of the Spanish Succession.

This powerful army was supported, and to a considerable degree made possible, by a system of conscription which had been given its final shape in 1733.[36] Though neither ubiquitous nor uniform, the famous Cantonal System enabled a first-class army to be maintained on the scanty available resources, while an officer cadre was provided by the territorial nobility: the Junkers had come to dominate the military

---

[36] See the pioneering study by Otto Büsch, *Militärsystem und Sozialleben im alten Preussen 1713–1807* (Berlin, 1962). His thesis of 'social militarisation' has proved controversial and is being seriously qualified by recent research, which is valuably surveyed by Peter H. Wilson, 'Social Militarization in Eighteenth-Century Germany', *German History* 18 (2000), pp. 1–39.

commands and, to a lesser extent, the civil administration.[37] The old King also bequeathed to his son a war-chest (*Staatsschatz*) of 8 million *taler* in gold coin, built up from the annual budgetary surpluses which he created. Finally, Frederick inherited an admired and relatively efficient administrative system, the centrepiece of which was the General Directory, established in 1723. Within the limitations of eighteenth-century government, it was remarkably successful in extracting the men, money and agrarian produce needed to support the army and pay the other expenses of the Prussian state.

The military and administrative foundations laid by 1740, together with the social integration achieved under Frederick William I, would provide the necessary foundation of Prussia's eighteenth-century political emergence. But these advantages, in the estimation of most contemporaries, were insufficient to overcome the drawbacks, above all Prussia's territorial vulnerability and her basic poverty, which preoccupied Frederick the Great throughout his reign. Eighteenth-century Prussia always lacked the resources required to establish herself securely as a great power. The achievement of her rulers, and especially of Frederick himself, was to make her a first-class state on a material base more appropriate to a country of the second or even third rank. Even by the time of his death in 1786 and after the important acquisitions of Silesia, East Friesland and Polish Prussia, the Hohenzollern monarchy remained only the thirteenth largest European state in terms of population and the tenth in terms of its geographical extent, though its army ranked fourth (or even third) in size.

Mid-eighteenth-century Prussia had one further advantage which proved decisive: the personality of her King. Political leadership was always important and could be decisive within the competitive states system of eighteenth-century Europe, and never more so than in Prussia's case. To become a member of Europe's political élite, a state – or rather its ruler and that monarch's advisers – had to think and act like a great power.[38] The crucial moment in this transition for Prussia was Frederick the Great's accession in 1740. His predecessor had accepted a secondary political role, pursuing essentially limited objectives such as Berlin's established dynastic claims to the Rhineland enclaves of Jülich and Berg. Frederick William I's political vision was relatively narrow and traditional, and he had usually been content to follow the lead of the Emperor, Charles VI (1711–40).

The contrast after his son's accession had been striking. From the moment he became King – indeed, from his days as Crown Prince – Frederick the Great thought and acted like the ruler of a first-class power, and within a quarter of a century he had raised Prussia to this status. By his political vision, his military successes and his

---

[37] See in particular Peter-Michael Hahn, 'Aristokratisierung und Professionalisierung: der Aufstieg der Obristen zu einer militärischen und höfischen Elite in Brandenburg-Preussen von 1650–1725', *FBPG* NF 1 (1991), pp. 161–208.

[38] See above, p. 18. This was also true of Russia's political emergence, in which the key point was Catherine II's accession in July 1762: see below, pp. 160–1.

diplomatic skills, he made his scattered possessions into a major state, while remaining aware that the domestic base to sustain this role was probably lacking. His decisive political leadership was based upon remarkable intellectual and political abilities together with an ego to match. Believing that the *status quo* was not an option and that territorial expansion was essential in order to overcome Prussia's poverty and strategic vulnerability, the young King pursued the expansionist aims which he viewed as the logical conclusion of his father's impressive domestic achievements. His political vision was far wider, encompassing the whole European diplomatic chessboard. It was apparent in an immediate enlargement of Hohenzollern aims which went far beyond the purely dynastic and largely German objectives pursued under Frederick William I.

IV

Prussia's upward trajectory was inaugurated by her sudden and wholly unexpected invasion of Silesia in December 1740.[39] This wealthy and strategically located Habsburg province lay to the south and east of Brandenburg. The decision to invade was Frederick's alone, and exemplified the new spirit which guided Berlin's policy. Opportunities were there to be seized, and the King judged that which presented itself in late autumn 1740, on the unexpected death of Charles VI, to be uniquely favourable. Encountering minimal Austrian resistance, he overran Silesia within six weeks. An attempted Habsburg counter-attack in spring 1741 was unsuccessful. In April the well-drilled Prussian infantry won an important if fortuitous victory at Mollwitz which encouraged the formation of a wide-ranging coalition directed against Austria and containing France, Spain, Savoy-Piedmont, Bavaria and Saxony. It was this alliance and especially French military power which was to play the leading role in the subsequent struggle.

The War of the Austrian Succession would not be concluded until October and November 1748, when the Peace of Aix-la-Chapelle was signed.[40] Yet Prussia was actually at war for less than half this time: some three years out of a total of eight. German scholarship, acknowledging this, refers not to the 'War of the Austrian Succession' but to the 'First Silesian War' (1740–2) and the 'Second Silesian War' (1744–5). By spring 1742 Frederick's war-chest was all but exhausted, and in June he signed a unilateral peace with Maria Theresa (Treaty of Breslau, confirmed at Berlin in the following month) by which Prussia withdrew in return for guaranteed possession of Silesia. When this appeared to be threatened by an Austrian recovery, the King re-entered the war in August 1744. Impressive victories at Hohenfriedberg

---

[39] The best survey of Prussia's impact upon Europe is still that contained in the standard life-and-times by Reinhold Koser, *Geschichte Friedrichs des Grossen* (3 vols., 6th–7th edns, Berlin, 1925). Among more recent discussions, that by Schieder, *Friedrich*, pp. 127–224, is particularly noteworthy.

[40] There are recent studies by M.S. Anderson, *The War of the Austrian Sucession 1740–1748* (London, 1995), and Reed Browning, *The War of the Austrian Succession* (Stroud, 1994).

(June 1745) and Soor (September), together with the decisive success won by the veteran Prussian commander, Prince Leopold of Anhalt, at Kesseldorf (December), enabled the King to conclude another unilateral agreement with Vienna. By the Peace of Dresden (December 1745) he withdrew from the struggle for the final time in return for a further guarantee of Silesia. The eventual peace settlement at Aix-la-Chapelle provided an international guarantee, which Frederick greatly valued, for this striking gain. The Hohenzollern monarchy's enhanced European status was evident in the way in which her present ally France and her would-be ally Britain competed for the honour of inserting this clause into the final treaty.

Frederick had secured Silesia by exploiting the wider continental struggle and allowing other states to bear the brunt of the fighting against Austria. Convinced of Prussia's strategic vulnerability and believing that scarce resources forced him to fight what he termed 'lively and short wars' – his father's war-chest had been seriously depleted after only two campaigns – the King pursued an opportunistic and single-minded strategy which gained him a new province and considerably enhanced international standing, at the price of a well-deserved and enduring reputation for faithlessness where international agreements were concerned. The three occasions on which he had deserted the anti-Austrian coalition – first, in October 1741 by the truce of Kleinschnellendorf, then by the unilateral settlements of Breslau-Berlin and Dresden – were not forgotten by his allies, especially France, and would come back to haunt him in the years ahead. Frederick's troops had won some significant victories, though there had been reverses as well: the retreat from Bohemia in the final months of 1744 had been little short of a disaster. Prussia's army, however, had gained considerably in reputation and also in size: it was now approaching 150,000 strong.

Neighbouring states such as Hanover (whose Elector was also King of Great Britain) and Saxony (whose ruling family were also Kings of Poland-Lithuania until 1763) were alarmed by the potential of the Prussian military state. The extent to which its revenues and resources were devoted to the single objective of supporting a formidable army caused particular anxiety. There is no doubt that Prussia's striking gain, which was extremely unusual in the eighteenth century because it had involved seizing territory from an established great power rather than a second-rank or declining state, increased her political standing. Other chancelleries were far more aware of Prussian power than a decade before, and were anxious to understand how such a poor and seemingly vulnerable state could support such a formidable army, collecting and analysing all the information they could about the Hohenzollern monarchy and its remarkable ruler. It is important, however, not to exaggerate what Frederick had achieved during the 1740s. Within the Empire, Prussia's rise had been striking. It was the first occasion on which one of the Electorates had achieved equality with the House of Habsburg, with its much larger territorial power-base and imperial dignity. In the wider context of central European politics the King's achievements were more limited. He had secured territory and prestige for his state, and renown for himself, but he had not made Prussia a great power. Silesia was a considerable territorial gain, particularly for the impoverished Hohenzollern lands. The river Oder which ran through the new province and then Brandenburg on its way to the Baltic was now a potentially important commercial artery. Silesia's thriving linen industry was very significant for the backward Hohenzollern economy while, with state support, woollen production would develop impressively. Its economic importance was evident in the fact that, within a decade, it was providing no less than 45 per cent of Prussia's total exports. It thus brought what the Hohenzollern state had hitherto lacked: a manufacturing region.

It also posed problems for the government in Berlin. The new province had to be integrated into the Prussian administrative system, which proved to be difficult and time-consuming, and its fortifications had to be improved. Its acquisition increased the already extended frontiers which had to be defended, while Austria was quite unreconciled to its loss, which compromised her security and military strategy. The recovery of the province was to be the central Habsburg aim throughout the next two decades and continued to influence Vienna's policy until the very end of the eighteenth century. Prussian possession of Silesia meant that the invasion route from its foothills across the Bohemian plain to the very gates of Vienna lay open, with only Moravia as a defensive barrier behind which Austrian forces could organise. Though such an enterprise was not without its difficulties and even risks, Frederick could invade Bohemia at will from his Silesian redoubt: as he did during the Seven Years War. The province's strategic and material benefits, however, were less important than its symbolic importance. By seizing Silesia, Prussia signalled to her neighbours and to the leading European states that she was a rising political force, and obliged Austria to acknowledge that she faced a formidable rival in Germany.

The Prussian annexation of Silesia drove a wedge between Saxony and Poland, united dynastically under the Wettins, and strengthened that family's enmity towards its powerful neighbour.[41] Graf Heinrich von Brühl, Augustus III's principal adviser, was alarmed by the emergence of Prussia's military power during the 1740s and aware of the vulnerability of the Electorate-Kingdom. Rivalry between the Wettins and the Hohenzollerns, political neighbours as well as two of the more powerful German Electorates, was traditional, and this had strengthened as the power of each had waxed. During the first half of the eighteenth century, however, Prussia's impressive internal consolidation had contrasted starkly with the mounting debts and political weakness of the Wettins, for whom possession of the Polish crown (1697–1763) had not brought the anticipated advantages. The Electorate of Saxony, however, remained one of the leading middle-sized German states. Its population of around 2 million rivalled that of Brandenburg-Prussia, while its economy

---

[41] This is apparent from Aladár von Boroviczény, *Graf von Brühl: der Medici, Richelieu und Rothschild seiner Zeit* (Zürich, Leipzig and Vienna, 1930), which, in spite of the preposterous subtitle, provides an informative political biography of Saxony's leading minister.

was far more advanced than that of its Hohenzollern neighbour. Rich soil was the basis of its agrarian prosperity, while it also contained thriving craft industries, significant mining and an important transit trade. Frederick, in his endless search for new resources, set out to exploit his rich but vulnerable neighbour. The decade before 1756 saw a vigorous customs' war, with Prussia wrecking negotiations which would have encouraged the development of a transit trade. The King continued this commercial antagonism after the Seven Years War.[42] Indeed, he long contemplated annexing his wealthy neighbour, though how realistic an aim this was must be questioned.[43]

The War of the Austrian Succession had also aroused Frederick's hostility and even fear towards Saxony. This was less because of her military potential than the political and strategic threat which she represented. Financial difficulties ensured that her army was now only 25,000 strong, a total which would shrink still further by 1756.[44] The political threat was more serious, since possession of the Polish crown made the Wettins clients of Russia; they were also traditional allies of Austria.[45] Yet it was the strategic threat which had been highlighted by the recent fighting which most concerned Frederick. The Wettins had their own claim to the imperial throne, and so the Electorate had initially been part of the anti-Austrian coalition, but it had then reverted to its traditional support of Vienna. In the Second Silesian War, the danger of an invasion of Brandenburg from Saxony had been evident: in the closing months of 1745 an Austro-Saxon army threatened to attack the Hohenzollern heartlands and was only prevented from doing so by its own slowness. The vulnerable and defenceless frontier with the Electorate was the principal source of Frederick's enduring concern with – and fear of – the threat posed by Saxony, which lay only some fifty miles from his own capital, Berlin. He feared it would be used as an advanced bridgehead for an attack: in 1752 he revealingly described it as a dagger pointing at Brandenburg's heart.[46] Supplies could be moved rapidly down the river Elbe, which flowed through the Electorate before bisecting Hohenzollern territory.

The strengthened hostility towards Saxony was one further legacy of the War of the Austrian Succession for Prussia, and it would prove enduring. Frederick acknowledged the considerable progress his state had made, but recognised that it was incomplete. The King saw, more clearly than many foreign observers, the shortcomings of the Prussian army, upon which his international position ultimately depended. The period of peace after the First Silesian War in June 1742 had seen determined efforts to improve the cavalry and infantry, and these continued after

---

[42] See below, p. 112.

[43] See the 1752 Political Testament: *Die politischen Testamente*, ed. Dietrich, pp. 368–72 *passim*; its successor of 1768 endorsed this objective: pp. 658, 664.

[44] Peter H. Wilson, *German Armies: War and German Politics, 1648–1806* (London, 1998), pp. 252, 264: on the eve of the Seven Years War it was 19,000.

[45] See Frederick's comments in 1752: *Die politischen Testamente*, ed. Dietrich, pp. 334, 342.

[46] Dennis E. Showalter, *The Wars of Frederick the Great* (London, 1995), p. 132.

1745. The next decade saw a significant overhaul and a considerable expansion of the army, personally supervised by the King in a series of inspections, parades and manoeuvres. Prussian government was simultaneously strengthened, particularly its ability to exploit the new province and to encourage state industries. The broader aim was to integrate the economy still further into the military state. Its success was apparent in the increasing proportion of royal income spent on the army. Under Frederick William I this had been around 70 per cent. Between 1740 and 1756 it rose to 83 per cent and, during the Seven Years War, it would reach 87 per cent.[47]

This was undertaken for purely defensive purposes. Domestic consolidation, not further foreign adventure, was the King's priority after 1745. Frederick was acutely aware of Prussia's strategic overextension and of the still-limited resources which would be available to resist an Austrian attempt to recover Silesia: he well understood that Vienna was unreconciled to its loss. He also recognised that Prussia remained a second-class power. In his confidential survey of foreign policy drawn up as part of the first Political Testament in 1752 he did not rank his own Hohenzollern monarchy among Europe's leading states. His analysis recognised that France and Britain, the only two unambiguously great powers, dominated the international system, and that the next most powerful were his arch-enemy Austria and, in a different way, Russia.[48]

Prussia's security depended upon the established alliance with France, which was based upon shared hostility towards the Austrian Habsburgs. Frederick declared on one occasion that the Duchy of Lorraine (from which Maria Theresa's husband, Francis Stephen, had been expelled in 1737 and which would eventually become part of the French monarchy) and Silesia were two sisters. France had married the younger and Prussia the elder, and this forced them to pursue the same policy.[49] These ties, however, had already been weakened by the King's own conduct. During the 1740s he had abandoned France on three separate occasions, by signing unilateral agreements with Vienna in defiance of his treaty obligations. This had secured Silesia, but at the price of worsening relations with Versailles, where his desertion was neither forgotten nor forgiven. In the short term, the War of the Austrian Succession had strengthened the Franco-Prussian axis. This was because the decline of Bavaria, strikingly evident during the 1740s, had made Prussia the principal basis for France's policy within the Empire. Frederick's alliance appeared secure as long as French foreign policy retained its anti-Austrian orientation and in 1748, at the end of the latest attempt to destroy Habsburg power, that seemed unlikely to change.[50] Prussia's essential problem was that her acquisition of Silesia had been made

---

[47] Adelheid Simsch, 'Armee, Wirtschaft und Gesellschaft: Preussens Kampf auf der "inneren Linie"', in Bernhard R. Kroener, ed., *Europa im Zeitalter Friedrichs des Grossen: Wirtschaft, Gesellschaft, Kriege* (Munich, 1989), pp. 35–46, at pp. 39–40.

[48] *Die politischen Testamente*, ed. Dietrich, p. 344 and pp. 330–50 *passim*.

[49] Political Testament of 1752: *Die politischen Testamente*, ed. Dietrich, p. 344.

[50] For the King's confidence on this point, see Political Testament of 1752: *Die politischen Testamente*, ed. Dietrich, p. 346.

possible by the existing diplomatic constellation, but her own rise threatened and eventually destroyed those very patterns upon which she herself depended.

Before long a new direction in Austrian foreign policy posed a challenge to the Prusso-French axis.[51] Its proponent was a member of the Moravian service nobility, Wenzel Anton von Kaunitz, who was one of a group of younger advisers who had emerged during the 1740s and had represented Austria at the Aix-la-Chapelle peace conference.[52] He came to prominence in 1749, during the important debates about future Habsburg foreign policy. Kaunitz appreciated that Prussia's rise within Germany between 1740 and 1745 had made her Vienna's greatest enemy, and sought to realign its priorities to take account of this. Silesia's recovery was seen as the principal objective, and important administrative and military reforms were already under way, in preparation for a future war. They were accompanied by a reorientation of Austrian diplomacy, which now recognised Prussia and not France as its principal enemy. With Maria Theresa's decisive support, Kaunitz argued for and set out to create a *rapprochement* and, if possible, an actual alliance with Versailles. Sent to France as ambassador (1750–2) he unsuccessfully pursued such a treaty: at this point the established diplomatic patterns held firm. In 1753 Kaunitz was placed in charge of Habsburg foreign policy as Chancellor (*Staatskanzler*) and, though for the moment his projected alliance made no obvious progress, Austria's eventual aim was clear.

By the second half of 1755 Prussia's international position was beginning to unravel, against a background of an undeclared Anglo-French war in North America which was heightening tension within Europe and threatened to spread to the continent.[53] Frederick had always feared Russia's potential power and its threat to his East Prussian Kingdom. He knew that the Empress Elizabeth and her leading

---

[51] The classic, though occasionally somewhat deterministic, account remains Max Braubach, *Versailles und Wien von Ludwig XIV. bis Kaunitz: die Vorstadien der diplomatischen Revolution im 18. Jahrhundert* (Bonn, 1952), pp. 360–456; Schilling, *Kaunitz und das Renversement des Alliances*, provides an important and thought-provoking examination of his approach to international relations at this period.

[52] The literature on Kaunitz is surprisingly meagre in view of his quite central importance, though this situation has recently begun to improve. There are two rather inadequate older biographies: Georg Küntzel, *Fürst Kaunitz-Rittberg als Staatsmann* (Frankfurt, 1923), is a rapid and uncritical summary of his foreign policy, while Alexander Novotny, *Staatskanzler Kaunitz als Geistige Persönlichkeit* (Vienna, 1947), is interesting but equally one-sided, concentrating on Kaunitz as a 'man of the Enlightenment'. Grete Klingenstein's superb *Der Aufstieg des Hauses Kaunitz: Studien zur Herkunft und Bildung des Staatskanzlers Wenzel Anton* (Göttingen, 1975) established a new standard for writing on Kaunitz and provided a compelling account (pp. 158–301) of his formation and early career, though it only extends up to 1753. It does contain, however, some perceptive comments (pp. 9–25) on Kaunitz historiography. The Chancellor's approach to foreign policy is the subject of the major study by Schilling, *Kaunitz und das Renversement des Alliances*, while Franz A.J. Szabo, *Kaunitz and Enlightened Absolutism 1753–1780* (Cambridge, 1994), examines his role in domestic policy down to Maria Theresa's death. Finally, many aspects of his career are studied in the important collection of essays edited by Klingenstein and Szabo, eds., *Staatskanzler Wenzel Anton von Kaunitz-Rietberg*.

[53] The King's foreign policy in the critical months from mid-1755 until late August 1756 can be followed in *Pol. Corr.*, XI–XIII passim. Richard Waddington, *Louis XV et le renversement des alliances: préliminaires de la guerre de sept ans 1754–1756* (Paris, 1896), remains unsurpassed as a study of the Diplomatic Revolution and the origins of the Seven Years War.

minister, Bestuzhev-Riumin, were anxious to weaken Prussia, seen as a potential rival in north-eastern Europe and an obstacle to further Russian expansion there. Frederick knew that a renewed Russo-Austrian alliance signed in 1746, the so-called Treaty of the Two Empresses, contained a secret clause which provided for the eventual partition of the Hohenzollern monarchy. Yet until the mid-1750s he believed that Russia's lack of a wealthy ally would protect him from attack, underlining that he did not yet view her as a leading power. He calculated that St Petersburg's own poverty and backwardness were so great that only subsidies could propel the Russian military machine into action.[54] In September 1755, Europe's leading commercial state, Britain, concluded a subsidy convention (that of St Petersburg) putting Russian troops and ships at London's disposal as part of the British diplomatic effort to threaten France's ally Prussia and in this way protect George II's Hanoverian homeland should war spread to Europe. Though this convention was never ratified, it set in motion a series of events which revolutionised European diplomacy and involved Frederick in the new war which he had long dreaded.

The King feared Russia and her threat to East Prussia. This, together with the apparent British-Russian axis, forced Frederick to act to strengthen his own security. He believed – or, more accurately, hoped – that British influence in St Petersburg might weaken Russian antagonism towards Prussia, though this did not prove to be the case. In January 1756, building on some generalised British approaches which had begun in the middle of the previous year, Prussia's King signed a remarkably vague agreement – far short of a treaty of defensive alliance – with Britain, the so-called Convention of Westminster. This provided for joint action to defend the peace of Germany, if the colonial war should lead to a French attack on Hanover. It was a further dimension of London's efforts to protect George II's Electorate through continental alliances. Though this proved a misjudgement on Frederick's part, by the winter of 1755–6 his options were rapidly narrowing and it was an understandable reaction to the Anglo-Russian agreement and Prussia's deteriorating security position.

The Convention of Westminster had a decisive impact at the French court, where it was seen as Frederick's latest and most serious betrayal. This was particularly important as the Franco-Prussian alliance was about to lapse, and Prussia's agreement with London ensured no new treaty would be signed with Versailles. Instead, it breathed new life into the Austro-French negotiations, until then becalmed. Kaunitz's renewed offers of an alliance were accepted and the First Treaty of Versailles was signed on 1 May 1756. This conventional defensive alliance was the centrepiece of the famous 'Diplomatic Revolution' of that year, ending as it did a tradition of political rivalry and open warfare between the Austrian Habsburgs and the French monarchy which went back to the end of the fifteenth century. The Austro-French *rapprochement* was a particularly serious matter for Frederick, since

---

[54] Political Testament of 1752: *Die politischen Testamente*, ed. Dietrich, pp. 334, 348.

it completed the encirclement of Prussia, now isolated in the face of three powerful enemies. The Hohenzollerns' principal foe, Austria, had alliances with France and Russia, and was preparing for a war which – Frederick believed – would be launched in 1757. Indeed, in the late spring of the previous year only Austrian diplomatic pressure had postponed a unilateral Russian attack on her Hohenzollern rival. Against this threatening background, the King seized the initiative and, on 29 August 1756, led his troops into neighbouring Saxony, thereby precipitating the continental Seven Years War.

The invasion of Saxony, like that of Silesia fifteen years earlier, appeared simple aggression. It was also, more importantly, a diplomatic miscalculation. Though Austria's aims were offensive, her alliances with France and Russia were purely defensive in nature and required a Prussian attack to make them operative: as Kaunitz was well aware. If Vienna launched a war in spring 1757, the Habsburgs would have Russia (which had mobilised for an attack on Prussia in spring 1756: one source of Frederick's anxieties at that time, until preparations were suspended) but not France on their side. French armies and subsidies, however, were crucial to Kaunitz's calculations. By invading Saxony, the daughter of whose Elector was married to the French *dauphin* (heir apparent), Frederick ensured that Louis XV's monarchy would fight in the continental war and would eventually commit her considerable resources against Prussia. The King had always believed that his military superiority would enable him to defeat Austria and Russia alone, but he now faced France as well.

Frederick had wanted to avoid a conflict, but once convinced it was inevitable he set out to dictate its shape and nature. The decision to fight was, once again, the King's alone: among his advisers and immediate family only General Hans Karl von Winterfeldt, the rising star of the Prussian military establishment, supported the decision to invade Saxony. By mid-June 1756 the King was convinced that he would be attacked in the following spring, and might even have to face three armies simultaneously.[55] Determined that any war must be as short as possible, to protect Prussia's limited resources, he concluded that he should seize the initiative. Frederick's established anxieties about the strategic threat from Saxony were reinforced by his conviction that the Electorate was, or would soon become, a member of the coalition which menaced him. In these circumstances there was a strong military argument – and as war approached military factors came to predominate over diplomatic considerations in Frederick's own thinking – for a pre-emptive strike. In 1744–5 Prussian troops had violated Saxon territory, when its ruler re-entered the war on Austria's side, in a dress rehearsal for their behaviour after 1756. In the event Frederick's actions in the late summer and autumn of that year enjoyed apparent success. The Elector's army was surrounded and disbanded, and 18,000 soldiers were incorporated into Prussian regiments, though many subsequently deserted.

---

[55] See the correspondence for these months in *Pol. Corr.*, XII.

The Saxon ruler was permitted to withdraw to his Polish Kingdom, where he remained until the end of the intense struggle which now began. The Seven Years War would not be concluded until 1763, by which point it would have transformed the eighteenth-century states system.

2

The Seven Years War and the European states system

I

The fighting after 1756 decisively influenced European diplomacy and its conse-quences were to shape international relations throughout the 1760s and 1770s.[1] Its impact was twofold. It increased the number of great powers from three to five through the addition of Prussia and Russia, and also brought about a swift, dramatic and enduring reordering of the political hierarchy, which made possible the subse-quent dominance of the eastern powers. When the struggle began, France was viewed as the strongest continental state, as she had been for almost a century.[2] Austria occupied second place, although Vienna was already facing a serious chal-lenge within the Empire from the rising power of Prussia; while Russia was widely viewed as peripheral and not especially formidable in European politics. By the time peace was concluded, this hierarchy had been turned upside down. Though Britain's triumphant Seven Years War established her as Europe's most powerful and dynamic nation, Prussia and Russia were now viewed as the leading continen-tal states, while France and Austria vied for the status of weakest great power. Throughout the generation after 1763, they appeared the least formidable of the major powers, whose cautious foreign policies facilitated the dominance of other states. French resources and potential were greater, but so too were the problems of the Bourbon monarchy. This decisive alteration was based primarily upon a con-temporary assessment of relative power and potential. Within a competitive states system where political leadership and military force were crucial, the performance of the leaders, the armies and the home-fronts during the Seven Years War estab-lished the international hierarchy for a generation to come. The fighting's second

---

[1] This chapter is concerned primarily with the war's impact on the relations of the major states, not with its battles and campaigns. There is no completely satisfactory modern study of the conflict. The best remains the incomplete masterpiece of R. Waddington, *La guerre de Sept Ans: histoire diplomatique et militaire* (5 vols., Paris, 1899–1915); the only comprehensive survey is the even older A. Schaefer, *Geschichte des Siebenjährigen Krieges* (2 vols., Berlin, 1867). The best short account is W.L. Dorn, *Competition for Empire 1740–1763* (New York, 1940), pp. 318–84; while the central years of the Anglo-French War have been persuasively re-examined by R. Middleton, *The Bells of Victory: The Pitt-Newcastle Ministry and the Conduct of the Seven Years War (1757–1762)* (Cambridge, 1985).
[2] See, e.g., the emphatic verdict of the Danish foreign minister, J.H.E. von Bernstorff, in January 1757: *Bernstorffsche Papiere*, I. 168. Two years earlier, he had painted an admiring view of French power in the instructions given to Denmark's new representative in Paris, Count E. Wedel-Frijs, 31 Jan. 1755, *Bernstorff Corr.*, I. 111–20, esp. p. 111.

legacy was less direct, though scarcely less important, and lay in the financial and material exhaustion of all the belligerents at the end of a prolonged, intensive and extremely destructive struggle. It was to give a notably cautious and subdued tone to diplomacy after 1763, when domestic reconstruction was everywhere a priority.[3]

The Seven Years War had two distinct, if not totally separate, dimensions. Britain, France and, latterly, Spain fought for colonies and commerce, while simultaneously Prussia was engaged in a desperate struggle for survival against a coalition which encircled her. The first of these was primarily maritime and colonial in nature, with Anglo-French fighting on the high seas and in North America, the West Indies, the Indian sub-continent and West Africa. It was one of a series of such conflicts which had begun in 1688 and would continue until 1815, during the century of the second Hundred Years War. Britain won this latest confrontation by means of a strategy which her leader for most of the war, William Pitt the Elder, subsequently and probably misleadingly described as conquering America in Germany. France was tied down in Europe by her position as a land power, by her commitments to the anti-Prussian alliance, and also by Britain's subsidies to Prussia and a British-financed Army of Observation operating in north-western Germany. The resulting division of French resources contributed significantly to Britain's decisive victory overseas. The Peace of Paris, signed in February 1763, brought considerable territorial gains, principally at Louis XV's expense.[4] France was excluded from the North American mainland, retaining only a precarious foothold in the Newfoundland Fisheries through possession of the islands of Miquelon and St Pierre; her position in India was all but destroyed; only in the West Indies did she avoid substantial territorial losses. During the early stages of the Seven Years War Spain had remained neutral rather than supporting her cousin on the French throne. In 1759, however, the accession of the anti-British Charles III propelled her into the fighting on the side of France, with whom an alliance was signed. In the final stages of the conflict, Madrid concluded the Third Family Compact in August 1761 and entered the war in the following January. This intervention was short-lived and disastrous, and by the peace settlement Spain was obliged to cede Florida to Britain, receiving Louisiana from France as compensation.

The Anglo-Bourbon conflict was linked to the struggle in central Europe only by France's participation in the anti-Prussian coalition, which was to be sharply reduced during the second half of the war, and by Britain's limited financial and military support of Frederick II, until it was abruptly ended in 1762. The separation of continental and colonial issues advanced by the fighting accelerated after the Peace of Paris, and during the next two decades Anglo-Bourbon rivalry overseas exerted only a limited impact on international relations within Europe. The principal factor in this rivalry was the extent of Britain's gains by the Peace of Paris and her commanding position after 1763, which France and Spain were determined to

---

[3] The war's domestic consequences are examined below, ch. 3.
[4] Z.E. Rashed, *The Peace of Paris 1763* (Liverpool, 1951), examines the making of the treaty.

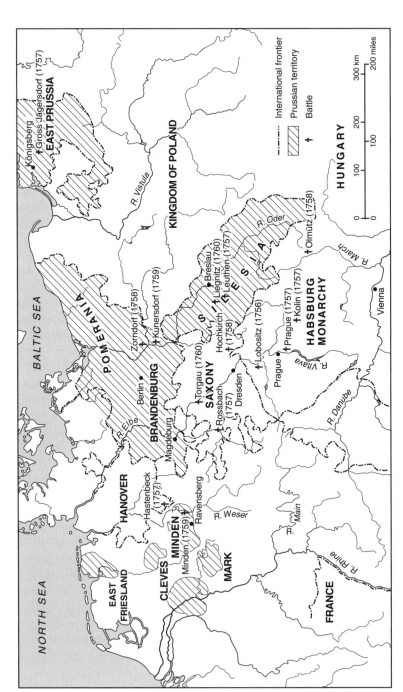

1. The continental Seven Years War

weaken. Their objectives demanded only the continent's neutralisation, while they attacked Britain's world-wide empire. The origins of this strategy, and of the political division of Europe which it furthered, were to be found in the Seven Years War. The fighting on the continent, in complete contrast, produced no territorial changes. The basis of the European peace settlement concluded at Hubertusburg in February 1763 was the return of all territories occupied during the fighting.[5] Prussia, with some limited British assistance, had been able to resist the apparently overwhelming coalition assembled by the Austrian foreign minister, Kaunitz. In 1756–7, an alliance of Austria, France and Russia emerged, and it was subsequently joined by Sweden and supported by substantial contingents of soldiers from the smaller states within the Empire. It was assembled and directed from Vienna, with the aim of recovering Silesia. In spite of the immense disparity in resources, however, Prussia withstood the onslaught of her enemies and emerged without suffering any territorial losses. This had seemed improbable for much of the war, not least to the Prussian King himself.[6] Despite his conviction – evident in his policy during the War of the Austrian Succession[7] – that Prussia's limited resources and strategic exposure demanded short, decisive, campaigns, he found his state trapped in a struggle of attrition and endurance, yet still managed to survive. Frederick himself likened the conflict to a tightrope walk, but by 1763 he had reached the end of this high wire in safety.

There were several reasons for his survival. It was due in part to shortcomings in the opposing coalition. On paper, this alliance appeared to have a massive and perhaps decisive advantage, both in terms of resources and military strategy: Frederick believed in December 1758 that his enemies were collectively so powerful that they could defeat one of Europe's leading states and not merely a minor kingdom such as he declared his own to be.[8] Prussia contained between 4 and 5 million inhabitants when the fighting began, around one tenth of the combined population of her three principal enemies. Her inferiority in troop numbers was less marked, though still striking. In 1756 Frederick had around 143,000 men under arms. Austria alone had 156,000 (a total which approached 200,000 during 1757–61), France at least 100,000 and Russia as many as 172,000 in her field army.[9] Prussia was also encircled, and there was no single frontier which could be defended. This numerical and strategic advantage seemed likely to lead to Frederick's early defeat, but this did not happen. In practice, the coalition proved

---

[5] The only detailed study of the negotiations remains Carl von Beaulieu-Marconnay, *Der Hubertusburger Friede* (Leipzig, 1871).

[6] Important discussions of Prussia's Seven Years War are to be found in: Schieder, *Friedrich*, pp. 182–224; Johannes Kunisch, *Das Mirakel des Hauses Brandenburg: Studien zum Verhältnis von Kabinettspolitik und Kriegsführung im Zeitalter des Siebenjährigen Krieges* (Munich and Vienna, 1978); and the collection of essays edited by Kroener, *Europa im Zeitalter Friedrichs des Grossen*; while Christopher Duffy, *Frederick the Great: A Military Life* (London, 1985), pp. 101–243, and Showalter, *Wars of Frederick the Great* , pp. 135–320, are lively narrative accounts.   [7] Above, p. 24.

[8] *Œuvres*, XXVIII. 154.   [9] See below, p. 48.

far less formidable. The anti-Prussian alliance made temporary partners out of established political rivals, and this hindered its military performance. The fissures were apparent in the contrasting political and territorial aims of its three leading members. Both Austria and Russia expected to be compensated by Prussia with territory when the war ended; while France initially fought in order to uphold its alliances and, in this way, its continental position, but subsequently (under the terms of the Second Treaty of Versailles) looked to make important territorial gains in the Austrian Netherlands and also hoped to secure territory for junior members of the Bourbon dynasty both there and in the Italian Peninsula.

The problem was exemplified by wartime relations between St Petersburg and Versailles.[10] Since the beginning of the eighteenth century, the two courts had been engaged in a struggle for political influence in northern and eastern Europe, where they were established rivals in Sweden, the Ottoman empire and, especially, Poland. France's wider aim was to shut Russia out of Europe. Less than a decade before, in continuation of this strategy, Versailles had barred a Russian representative from the peace conferences which ended the War of the Austrian Succession, in part because of Bestuzhev's anti-French policies. After the Peace of Aix-la-Chapelle, France continued to fear a new Russian attack on her client Sweden, which had been involved in a brief war with its eastern Baltic neighbour as recently as the early 1740s. The Russo-French *rapprochement* which emerged in 1756–7 was both unexpected and entirely fortuitous: it was a by-product of the Diplomatic Revolution, which made Vienna, already linked by treaty to St Petersburg, the partner of Versailles. As Choiseul would later remark, Russia was a French ally only by accident.[11] The bonds between the two states were in some measure strengthened by two treaties in 1757. Such agreements, like the unsuccessful wartime efforts to foster Franco-Russian trade and so solidify political links, could do little to obscure the fundamental clash of interests along Europe's northern and eastern rim. Though this rivalry was necessarily suspended after 1756 in the interest of defeating Frederick II, it was imperfectly achieved, particularly as it became clear that Russia's grip over Poland was being strengthened during the war. The demands of the military struggle made it very difficult for France to resist this extension of Russian power, though it was certainly resented at Versailles, and this increased tension. The Russo-French partnership disintegrated in 1761, amidst mutual recrimination and with little regret on either side. In view of the fundamental clash of interests revealed by the wartime co-operation, the surprising thing is that it lasted as long as it did.

The Franco-Austrian alliance was the most stable and proved to be the most enduring of the new alignments which emerged in 1756–7, yet even this axis was characterised by repeated and severe disagreements, particularly over military strategy and finance.[12] Its vicissitudes exemplified the basic problem: that each member

---

[10] Oliva, *Misalliance*, is a solid study from France's perspective.   [11] Oliva, *Misalliance*, p. 170.
[12] Eckhard Buddruss, *Die französische Deutschlandpolitik 1756–1789* (Mainz, 1995), pp. 70–119.

of the anti-Prussian coalition viewed the struggle in a different light and pursued its own territorial or political objectives rather than concentrating on the single aim of defeating Frederick II. There was an absence of the kind of mortal danger which might have cemented the alliance.[13] This was partly because the Hohenzollern state appeared to lack the material resources to destroy one of its major enemies, far less all three, and so appeared unlikely to win. As a result there was no overriding common purpose to bind Prussia's opponents together, and considerable latent tension between them. The allies anticipated a rapid victory, and its failure to materialise, together with the successes of Frederick's own forces, helped to undermine Kaunitz's alliance. It proved increasingly difficult to prevent individual states pursuing their own interests with scant regard for the overall aim of defeating Prussia. For Austria, it was always a war to recover Silesia. In contrast, Russia's territorial objective was East Prussia, which would probably be exchanged with Poland-Lithuania for the Duchy of Courland.[14] Sweden dreamed unrealistically of reconquering the greater part of western Pomerania and even gaining other Baltic territories, and so re-emerging as a major Baltic power;[15] while France initially hoped and expected that Frederick would swiftly be defeated, but did not wish to see too considerable a weakening of Prussian power and was discouraged by the early reverses her troops suffered and, above all, by the shattering defeat at Rossbach in November 1757. By the end of the following year French attention and resources were being concentrated upon the overseas struggle with Britain.

Versailles' diminished commitment to the continental war was crucial to its outcome. Kaunitz had set great store in securing France's participation in the anti-Prussian alliance, on account of her wealth and military reputation. After Choiseul became foreign minister in December 1758, however, France had concentrated on the colonial and maritime struggle with Britain, and her armies played a much reduced role in the final campaigns, merely engaging in indecisive operations against Prince Ferdinand's 'Army of Observation' in western Germany. Austria was called upon to assume the leading military role, but was now unable to sustain this. By the final months of 1760, the Habsburg home-front and especially the state finances were close to collapse. Only Russia was now in a position to defeat Prussia and so gain a victory for Vienna, and her troops played a leading part in the 1761 campaign. But a complete reversal of St Petersburg's policy during the first half of 1762 following the Empress Elizabeth's death early in January, decided the outcome of the continental war and saved Prussia from defeat. Russia's new ruler was the ardent Prussophile, Peter III, who immediately withdrew from the coalition and set

---

[13] Johannes Kunisch, 'Die Grosse Allianz der Gegner Preussens im Siebenjährigen Krieg', in Kroener, ed., *Europa im Zeitalter Friedrichs des Grossen*, pp. 79–97.

[14] Herbert H. Kaplan, *Russia and the Outbreak of the Seven Years War* (Berkeley and Los Angeles, 1968), pp. 4, 55–6 and 125–6. Various smaller pieces of territory would also be ceded by Poland to Russia.

[15] Klaus-Richard Böhme, 'Schwedens Teilnahme am Siebenjährigen Krieg: Innen- und aussenpolitische Voraussetzungen und Rückwirkungen', in Kroener, ed., *Europa in Zeitalter Friedrichs des Grossen*, pp. 193–212; Michael Roberts, *The Age of Liberty: Sweden 1719–1772* (Cambridge, 1986), p. 45.

about aligning himself with Berlin. In the event, the new Emperor's deposition in July 1762 prevented a Prusso-Russian alliance being formally concluded, but his six-month reign was crucial to Frederick's survival.[16]

Russia's withdrawal exemplified the King's view that chance was an important ingredient in political success. By the beginning of 1762, Frederick II's plight was quite desperate. The Silesian front had collapsed with the Austrian capture of Schweidnitz in the previous autumn, while the loss of the key fortress of Kolberg to the Russians in December 1761 destroyed Prussia's position in eastern Pomerania. The strains of continuous warfare were increasing all the time and the Prussian military state, which had proved more resilient than its rivals, was finally close to collapse: in the winter of 1761–2, for the first time, captains were not provided with the funds essential to prepare their companies for the next campaign.[17] Large tracts of Hohenzollern territory were in enemy hands and Frederick's strategic position had become all but impossible. Elizabeth's death and the diplomatic revolution at the Russian court rescued the King from this predicament. Yet Prussia's survival owed much to her own exertions: the very fact that she was still fighting was a tribute to her remarkable endurance.

Prussia in fact possessed several obvious advantages which did much to nullify her permanent numerical inferiority. Foremost among these was the personality and abilities of the King, who by 1763 was universally known as Frederick the Great, in recognition of his remarkable achievements during the Seven Years War. The Prussian ruler had been the central figure in the fighting, just as his Kingdom's survival as a major state was its principal issue. The unique structure of the Hohenzollern polity, with the King combining political and military leadership in his own person, was an important source of strength. The potential advantages of this integration were recognised in the aftermath of Rossbach by the Cardinal de Bernis, then French foreign minister: 'We must not forget that we are dealing with a prince who is at once his own commander in the field, chief minister, logistical organiser and when necessary provost-marshal. These advantages outweigh all our badly executed and badly combined expedients.'[18] Austrian, or Russian, or French generals never possessed the freedom of action of their principal opponent. Continually obliged to consult their political masters, they suffered the twin handicaps of delay and of divided – and usually cautious – counsels. The coalition's military performance was weakened as much by these divisions between the political leaders and military commanders as by the more fundamental disagreements between the three major allies.

Frederick enjoyed almost complete independence and exploited this to good effect. Prussia's survival was primarily secured on the battlefield, and here superior generalship was crucial. The King actually lost as many battles as he won during the

---

[16] See below, pp. 44–5, for a fuller discussion.
[17] Duffy, *Frederick the Great*, pp. 225–6, 232–3, and more generally, Curt Jany, *Geschichte der Königliche Preussischen Armee bis zum Jahre 1807* (Berlin, 1928), II. 596–624 *passim*.
[18] Quoted by Duffy, *Frederick the Great*, p. 144.

Seven Years War: out of sixteen major engagements, only eight can confidently be identified as victories.[19] Yet twice – in 1757 and 1760 – he retrieved apparently hopeless strategic positions by audacious and decisive military action. The victories at Rossbach and Leuthen gained Prussia a crucial breathing space and ensured that the war's first major campaign would not also be the last, while the later successes at Liegnitz and Torgau ensured that she would not be defeated by the Austrians at least.[20] More important than his victories, however, was his simple survival together with his overall strategic plan. Though Frederick at first took the initiative and even dreamed of new conquests which he believed could alone validate any war,[21] by the beginning of 1759 he clearly stood on the defensive. Yet this posture allowed – indeed, demanded – periodic offensives against his principal enemies, Austria and Russia. These sorties retained the initiative for Prussia and, more important, prevented the effective union of the main Austrian and Russian field armies, which Frederick always feared, until the late summer of 1761. The King was helped by the cautious strategy usually adopted by his opponents and by his own compact position: his celebrated strategy of fighting along interior lines was, in one sense, imposed by the encirclement which confronted him from the outset, but it served him well. The struggle established his reputation as a formidable military commander, certainly the supreme general of his age, and this helped to deter his principal enemy, Austria, from a further war until 1778: the extent of the King's personal dominance after the Peace of Hubertusburg was to be very striking. Frederick had also proved to be an inspiring leader, whose indomitable courage, remarkable resilience and simple refusal to admit defeat had done much to sustain his state during the darkest days of the conflict.

The Prussian army's reputation was also established by the Seven Years War, during which it usually proved superior to the forces of the coalition powers. Some important defeats had been suffered, above all at the hands of the stoically courageous Russian infantry; but these primarily resulted from Frederick's unwillingness and, before long, inability to accept the horrifying numerical losses through which Russia's commanders bought their victories. Prussia's supply of manpower was always severely limited, while Russia's appeared abundant. The Hohenzollern state had also proved better able than its opponents to sustain an intensive and prolonged struggle. The strength and resilience of the Prussian military machine were conclusively demonstrated by the Seven Years War. Its burdens were immense and, by 1761–2, almost overwhelming. A country with Prussia's scanty population could only with difficulty replenish losses on the scale demanded after 1756, and by the war's later stages the ranks were filled up with very young and very dubious

[19] Dorn, *Competition for Empire*, p. 326.
[20] After Liegnitz the King told Britain's representative and his own political confidant, Andrew Mitchell, that defeat would have ended Prussia's resistance: to the Duke of Newcastle, 17 Aug. 1760, printed in *Memoirs and Papers of Sir Andrew Mitchell, K.B.*, ed. A. Bisset (2 vols., London, 1850), II. 202. [21] Schieder, *Friedrich*, p. 218.

conscripts. Serious problems in the supply of new soldiers from the Canton System became apparent in 1758, and these increased with every year of the struggle. Each winter Frederick found rebuilding his shattered army more and more difficult, though he was always able to take the field for the new campaign with replacements for some at least of the losses. The Seven Years War demonstrated the relative effectiveness of Prussia's cantonal conscription, especially by comparison with Austria's traditional and largely haphazard methods of military recruitment. The price, however, was very high: the survival rate for soldiers conscripted into the Prussian ranks after 1756 was perhaps only one in fifteen, confirming the impression that recruitment was close to being a death sentence.[22]

By the conflict's final stages, the internal administrations of Austria and Russia were both in disarray, but Frederick's officials were still managing to scrape together at least some of the men, munitions and money needed for the war effort.[23] This was in itself remarkable. Prussia's resources were limited and also declined further during the fighting, as territory quickly fell into enemy hands: the Westphalian provinces after 1757, East Prussia from January 1758 onwards. Even more remarkably, the salaries of her administrators were often paid only partly in cash (with the balance in supposedly redeemable vouchers), and were suspended altogether in 1757 and again in 1762. Yet these officials stuck to their task and somehow squeezed sufficient resources from Prussia's shrinking territorial base to enable the King to prolong resistance. This exemplified the contribution of superior Prussian morale, something which Frederick deliberately fostered.

The Junkers' role was also important, above all in the officer corps which they monopolised. Nobles were expected to play a full and direct part in the fighting, to an extent that was unusual and even unique in eighteenth-century armies. Their contribution was apparent in the heavy casualties among the officer corps: out of 5,500 in 1756, at least 1,500 were killed and some 2,500 wounded during the war, and still more were captured.[24] No fewer than thirty-three generals died in action between 1756 and 1759.[25] Losses on this scale forced the King to lower the requirements for new officer candidates, and the quality of commanders, at all levels, declined sharply during the second half of the war, which also witnessed the dilution of the noble officer caste through the granting of commissions to commoners, particularly members of the middle class. Nevertheless, the nobility contributed significantly to Prussia's survival, and this was acknowledged by Frederick, whose policies after 1763 favoured the Junkers even more than hitherto, and aimed especially to help them retrieve their shattered economic position.[26]

Britain and Saxony both contributed to Prussia's survival, though in different

---

[22] Duffy, *Frederick the Great*, p. 229.
[23] Walther Hubatsch, *Frederick the Great of Prussia: Absolutism and Administration* (Engl. trans., London, 1973), pp. 112–47, is the best brief survey. See also Simsch, 'Armee, Wirtschaft und Gesellschaft'. [24] Duffy, *Frederick the Great*, p. 230. [25] Schieder, *Friedrich*, p. 184.
[26] See below, p. 86.

ways. Particularly after William Pitt achieved full authority in 1757, London supported Frederick's cause and continued to do so until 1762, when aid was cut off by the new ministry headed by George III's favourite, the Earl of Bute, in an attempt to bring about an early end to the fighting. Britain provided both financial and military assistance.[27] An annual subsidy of £670,000 for four years, from 1758 until 1761, made a significant contribution to Frederick's wartime finances. Paid regularly and in gold, it defrayed almost 20 per cent of the total cost of the war.[28] The British-financed 'Army of Observation' protected Frederick's vulnerable western flank and conferred a significant strategic advantage.[29] Finally, the British partnership – though never, on either side, more than a matter of temporary political expediency – did furnish a measure of psychological support through its demonstration that Prussia was not entirely isolated.

Saxony's contribution was quite different in nature. The Prussian invasion of the Electorate at the very end of August 1756 marked the beginning of the continental war. Though its ruling family was allowed to withdraw unmolested to Warsaw, Saxony was treated as an occupied country throughout the fighting. In November 1760 the battle of Torgau was fought and won in order to enable Frederick to regain control over its resources. It was stripped bare by its temporary Prussian régime, and one estimate is that it contributed around a third of the total cost of Prussia's Seven Years War.[30] Indeed, the Electorate suffered more than Frederick's own possessions, with permanent and heavy taxation and other impositions, forcible recruiting for the Prussian army, and relentless campaigning across its defenceless territories. Large numbers of Saxon cities were completely or partially destroyed, above all Wittenberg, Zittau and the capital, Dresden, which was burnt by Prussian troops in July 1760. Frederick's ruthless and brutal exploitation of Saxony continued the hostility he had exhibited during the 1740s towards this wealthy and potentially strong neighbour. His conduct outraged contemporary opinion and, even in the context of the fluid prevailing notions of international law, was of questionable legality, since the Electorate was never formally a belligerent. But its effectiveness was undoubted. Saxon conscripts and especially revenues did something to make up for Prussia's own shortage of the crucial raw materials for war.

[27] See the authoritative studies of P.F. Doran, *Andrew Mitchell and Anglo-Prussian Diplomatic Relations during the Seven Years War* (New York, 1986), and, on the break-up of the partnership, Karl W. Schweizer, *Frederick the Great, William Pitt and Lord Bute: The Anglo-Prussian Alliance, 1756–1763* (New York, 1991).

[28] See the figures in Bernhard R. Kroener, 'Die materiellen Grundlagen österreichischer und preussischer Kriegsanstrengungen 1756–1763', in Kroener, ed., *Europa im Zeitalter Friedrichs des Grossen*, p. 76, table 17, and in Hubatsch, *Frederick the Great*, 140, together with the standard detailed account by Reinhold Koser, 'Die preussischen Finanzen im Siebenjährigen Kriege', *FBPG* 13 (1900), pp. 153–217 and 329–75.

[29] Its operations are narrated by Sir Reginald Savory, *His Britannic Majesty's Army in Germany during the Seven Years War* (Oxford, 1966).

[30] Schieder, *Friedrich*, p. 223; Kroener, 'Materiellen Grundlagen', p. 76, table 17, suggests a lower total, but this may reflect differences in the way figures are calculated.

These factors together ensured Frederick's remarkable survival and secured peace on the basis of the territorial *status quo* of 1756, which had seemed improbable for most of the struggle. Even more remarkably Prussia – alone among the belligerents – ended the war not with empty coffers, but with no less than 14.5 million *talers* in the *Staatsschatz* (war-chest), a cash surplus which contributed to her future security.[31] The 'miracle of the House of Brandenburg', as Frederick himself termed it immediately after the shattering defeat at Kunersdorf (August 1759), was complete, to the frank astonishment of contemporaries.[32] Prussia, by avoiding defeat, had secured a leading political position. A war which had started as an attempt to partition the Hohenzollern territories and so reduce Frederick's monarchy to its former insignificance ended by decisively establishing its position among the great powers.

The celebrated nineteenth-century German historian, Leopold von Ranke, once remarked that a great power was one that could successfully defend itself against a combined attack by other leading states.[33] By this yardstick, Frederick's state was certainly a great power by 1763, in terms of military strength at least. Eighteenth-century Prussia, rather like seventeenth-century Sweden, owed her greatly enhanced political stature principally to the leadership of her ruler together with the victories gained by a formidable army, supported by a relatively efficient administrative infrastructure. The domestic foundations of this new status, however, were precarious and the essential demographic and economic resources were clearly lacking. Frederick II's achievement was to make Prussia a first-class power on third-class resources. Yet in the view of most contemporaries, the King's own leadership and the power of his army more than compensated for such material shortcomings. Prussia was a permanent and increasingly important factor in European diplomacy after 1763 in a way she had not been even a decade before. In the short term, this was the most obvious political result of the continental Seven Years War.

II

Russia was the other continental state to benefit significantly from the fighting, and her enhanced international status was to be more effectively exploited during the next generation and also appeared more securely based. Though – unusually for its eighteenth-century wars, which brought massive territorial gains – the Russian empire secured no new lands, its standing in Europe was considerably enhanced.[34]

---

[31] Hubatsch, *Frederick the Great*, p. 140. The accumulation of such a reserve for strategic purposes was established Hohenzollern policy: above, p. 22.

[32] See, e.g., the verdict of A.P. von Bernstorff in February 1763: *Bernstorffsche Papiere*, i. 288.

[33] Schieder, *Friedrich*, p. 204.

[34] For a lively account of work on this theme, see Michael G. Müller, 'Russland und der Siebenjährige Krieg', *JGO* NF 28 (1980), pp. 198–219. See also Evgeny V. Anisimov, *Empress Elizabeth: Her Reign and Her Russia 1741–1761* (1986; Engl. trans. by John T. Alexander, Gulf Breeze, FL, 1995), esp. chs. 3, 4, 8 and 9, for a recent Russian view of the struggle; William C. Fuller, Jr, *Strategy and Power in*

Membership of the anti-Prussian coalition was to prove the decisive step towards great power status. After 1763, Russia could never again be ignored by the other major states and especially those in western Europe, as had periodically happened during the first half of the eighteenth century. Though this transformation was facilitated by the broader political changes brought about by the war, it was primarily due to the impressive performance of the Russian army, which for the first time intervened decisively on the battlefields of central Europe.

This intervention was achieved at high cost.[35] There is an important distinction between the long-term political benefits accruing from St Petersburg's involvement in the Seven Years War, and the acute short-term problems which resulted.[36] Yet these problems cannot obscure the enormous increase in Russian power and influence between 1756 and 1763. When the fighting began, Russia was viewed as the third and least important major state in the anti-Prussian coalition. Its architect, Kaunitz, saw a Russian attack on the exposed territory of East Prussia as a useful addition to his military strategy, since it would divert soldiers and resources away from the crucial Silesian theatre-of-war, where he believed the struggle would be decided. But he believed that Russia's participation was impossible without French subsidies, in itself clear evidence that he did not yet view her as a great power.[37] The Chancellor – like most contemporaries – did not expect the Russian army to play a major part in the fighting and clearly underestimated its potential. Indeed, in the spring and early summer of 1756, he postponed an attack on Prussia even though St. Petersburg's support was guaranteed.[38] This was because he feared that Austria and Russia on their own would not be a match for the formidable Prussian army and regarded French military and financial support as essential. At this point, France was still generally viewed as Europe's leading military power, but by the close of the Seven Years War, Russia – like Prussia – had outstripped her.

Russian armies played a minor part in the early fighting.[39] The Empress Elizabeth's troops attacked the exposed and vulnerable prize of East Prussia, winning a notable victory at Gross Jägersdorf (August 1757), and subsequently occupied the territory, which was formally under Russian control from January 1758

Russia 1600–1914 (New York, 1992), chs. 3 and 4, provides an illuminating military survey of Russia's eighteenth-century expansion and of the place of the Seven Years War within this. Considerable detail on the fighting is contained in Soloviev, *History of Russia*, XLI, which provides a narrative of the years 1757–61.

[35] This is emphasised by John. L.H. Keep, 'Die russische Armee im Siebenjährigen Krieg', in Kroener, ed., *Europa im Zeitalter Friedrichs des Grossen*, pp. 133–69, which is fundamental for what follows. I am grateful to Prof. Keep for sending me a copy of his important article.   [36] See below, pp. 71–3.

[37] See Kaunitz's 'Memoir' of July 1756, printed in *Preussische und österreichische Acten zur Vorgeschichte des Siebenjährigen Krieges*, ed. G.B. Volz and Georg Küntzel (1899; reprinted Osnabrück, 1965), pp. 726–39, at p. 728. The whole memoir makes clear the limited place which Russia occupied in the Chancellor's calculations at this point.

[38] See the documents in part two of *Preussische und österreichische Acten*, ed. Volz and Küntzel.

[39] Christopher Duffy, *Russia's Military Way to the West: Origins and Nature of Russian Military Power 1700–1800* (London, 1981), pp. 74–124, provides a campaign narrative of her participation in the Seven Years War.

until the final year of the war. At this stage, however, Russia's armies played no part in the major fighting in central Europe. French and Austrian soldiers bore the brunt of the first two campaigns, though the Russians did stop a Prussian advance in the indecisive and bloody battle of Zorndorf (August 1758). From the conflict's mid-point, however, Russia's role increased. France diverted attention and resources to the struggle with Britain overseas from 1759 onwards, while Austria's own war effort was disappointing. After the twin defeats at Liegnitz and Torgau in 1760, Vienna accepted that Habsburg armies alone could not defeat Prussia. The war's enormous financial and demographic burdens, together with the administrative shortcomings it revealed, reconciled Austria to an unsuccessful end to the conflict, unless victory could be snatched by the Russian armies.

The junior partner of 1756 thus became the leading member of the coalition by 1761–2. Russian armies achieved several notable victories over Prussia, now seen as Europe's leading military power. The campaign of 1759 was Russia's *annus mirabilis* when her forces won striking successes first at Kay (Paltzig) in July and then, the following month, in the great battle of Kunersdorf: the most serious defeat ever inflicted upon Frederick. The next year, Russian troops, accompanied by an Austrian force, reached Berlin for the first time and briefly occupied the Prussian capital, which escaped destruction only at the cost of a large indemnity and damage to its munitions works. During the final two campaigns, the numerical strength and readiness for combat of Russia's army was probably greater than that of any other belligerent. This opportunity was not fully exploited, though the important Prussian bases of Kolberg and Schweidnitz were captured – by the Russians and the Austrians respectively – during the second half of 1761.[40]

By the closing stages of the Seven Years War, Russia had become the arbiter of eastern Europe. This was exemplified by the way in which St Petersburg's reversal of policy in 1762 ultimately determined the conflict's outcome. In that January, the Russian Empress Elizabeth died. Her successor was the notoriously Prussophile Grand Duke, who became Peter III.[41] The new Emperor immediately reversed St Petersburg's established policy, launching a *rapprochement* with Prussia on the very day that he came to the throne.[42] The Russian corps which was fighting alongside the Austrian army was withdrawn, subsequently being transferred to Prussian service, and a truce was signed with Frederick II. This was converted into a full peace treaty, and before long negotiations for a formal defensive alliance between Peter III and his Prussian hero were under way. These were accompanied, from the

---

[40] For the response in Vienna to the capture of Schweidnitz, see HHStA Tagebuch Zinzendorf, vol. 6, 3, 5 and 8 Oct. 1761.

[41] For his short, eventful and controversial reign, see Carol S. Leonard, 'The Reputation of Peter III', *The Russian Review* 47 (1988), 263–92, and the fuller account in the same author's unpublished thesis, 'A Study of the Reign of Peter III of Russia' (Indiana University, 1976), now published in a revised form as *Reform and Regicide: The Reign of Peter III of Russia* (Bloomington and Indianapolis, 1993). These overlapping accounts provide essential detail, but are far too favourable to the Russian Emperor.

[42] Soloviev, *History of Russia*, XLII. 22–3.

end of March 1762 onwards, by clear signs that Russia's energetic new ruler intended to launch a fresh war against Denmark and expected Prussia's support. Peter III was the grandson of Peter I, and the son of that remarkable ruler's daughter, who had married the Duke of Holstein-Gottorp in 1727. Brought up in ducal Holstein, Peter III had only come to Russia in 1743 and retained considerable affection for his homeland. At the end of the Great Northern War, Denmark had occupied parts of the neighbouring Duchy of Schleswig, which belonged to the Holstein family, and this was the ostensible cause of the conflict which, by late May 1762, appeared imminent.

The rapid diplomatic revolution was part of a larger transformation by which Peter III sought an enlarged European role for Russia, and appeared to be abandoning the wartime *rapprochement* with France and the established alliance with Austria, in favour of co-operation with Prussia, Britain and Sweden. There was nothing inherently flawed about this: it anticipated Nikita Panin's 'Northern System', which would guide St Petersburg's policy during the first half of Catherine II's reign.[43] At the time, however, the policy aroused fierce opposition in Russia. Peter III's domestic reforms and especially his foreign policy had alienated all the powerful groups: the Orthodox Church, officials in central government, the nobility and the military establishment. The prospect of a new conflict in Germany, apparently to be fought entirely for Peter III's personal dynastic interests, was especially unpopular, as was the withdrawal from the anti-Prussian coalition: all Russia's sacrifices during the Seven Years War now seemed to have been futile. Resentment and opposition coalesced around the formidable Grand Duchess Catherine, who replaced her husband on the Russian throne in early July 1762. Within a few days, Peter III was dead. The protean Russo-Prussian alliance perished with him. But Catherine II did not, as Austria hoped and Prussia feared, once more reverse St Petersburg's foreign policy. Recognising that pressing financial and other domestic problems demanded peace, the Empress confirmed Russia's withdrawal from the Seven Years War. She ratified Peter III's peace treaty with Prussia but not the alliance he had signed.[44]

Russian troops played little part in the final year of fighting, the thirteen months between Elizabeth's death and the Peace of Hubertusburg. Russia's impact on the war's outcome, however, was decisive. St Petersburg's abandonment of Austria, as it was seen by Maria Theresa, forced Vienna to accept Prussia's peace terms, which were the full restoration of the territorial *status quo* of 1756. Austrian resentment was to prove enduring: five years later Frederick the Great confided to his brother Prince Henry that the 'violent hatred' between Catherine II and Maria Theresa was one foundation of his own alliance with Russia.[45] The final stages of the Seven Years

---

[43] Karl W. Schweizer and Carol S. Leonard, 'Britain, Prussia, Russia and the Galitzin Letter: A Reassessment', *Historical Journal* 26 (1983), pp. 531–56, esp. pp. 546–53; Leonard, 'The Reputation of Peter III', pp. 276–7, 292. For the 'Northern System', see below, pp. 121–4.

[44] For Catherine II's foreign policy during the final stages of the European war, see Waddington, *Guerre de Sept Ans*, v. 349–77.   [45] *Pol. Corr.*, XXVI. 134.

War witnessed another celebrated alienation, that between Prussia and Britain, and this was an element in the diplomacy of the 1760s and 1770s. Scarcely less important, though much less commented upon, was Vienna's resentment at the way she had been abandoned, and especially at Catherine II's refusal to re-enter the war.[46] These memories coloured Habsburg policy towards St Petersburg until Maria Theresa's death in 1780.

Frederick II conceived a lasting dread of Russian military power from his experiences during the struggle, and this was to influence his foreign policy throughout the second half of his reign. Yet the struggle demonstrated both the considerable military potential of the Russian empire and its real limitations, particularly in a war fought in central Europe. Russia's overall military performance had been uneven. In the first place, the quality of her generalship was mediocre. The principal commanders – S.F. Apraksin, Petr Saltykov, V.V. Fermor, A.B. Buturlin – were uninspired and notably cautious. Each, in turn, revealed military abilities which were at best modest. Apraksin, who commanded in 1757, had previous military experience, but was now an ageing *roué* and *bon viveur*: no less than 250 baggage horses were needed to transport his personal possessions to the East Prussian theatre-of-war. His incompetence was apparent in his failure to seek the usual dispensation for his soldiers to be exempt from the Orthodox requirement to fast during Lent, with the consequence that 20 per cent of his army fell ill from malnutrition during the advance towards East Prussia.[47] Fermor, who succeeded the dismissed Apraksin and commanded in 1758, was at best competent and uninspired, though an isolated figure. His Baltic German origins and Lutheran religion alienated him from his colleagues in the Russian officer corps, while Austrian generals who had to deal with him found him surly.[48] Saltykov, who exercised command in 1759–60, was competent but irresolute and unadventurous, and he was laid low by serious illness during the second campaign in which he commanded. A good military administrator, his qualities were those of a regimental officer rather than a commander-in-chief.[49] His successor Buturlin had risen through the bedchamber rather than military command. A favourite of the Empress, he had been made a Field-Marshal before he witnessed a battle, far less won a victory.[50]

These personal shortcomings were exacerbated by the Russian court's unstable politics, which contributed to the rapid turn-over of commanders-in-chief: four in five campaigns, with only Saltykov surviving for more than a year. In 1756 a committee known as the Conference was set up to co-ordinate the war effort. From the very beginning it was divided between the three principal factions: those of the ageing minister, A.P. Bestuzhev-Riumin (until his fall in 1758), of the favourite Ivan

[46] See, e.g., HHStA Tagebuch Zinzendorf, vol. 7, 3 Mar. 1762.
[47] The French ambassador, L'Hôpital, provided a hostile portrait, quoted in Waddington, *Guerre de Sept Ans*, I. 575; Anisimov, *Empress Elizabeth*, pp. 117–24; Fuller, *Strategy and Power*, pp. 109, 123.
[48] Waddington, *Guerre de Sept Ans*, II. 250–1; III. 124.
[49] Waddington, *Guerre de Sept Ans*, III. 128; Showalter, *Wars of Frederick the Great*, p. 239.
[50] Anisimov, *Empress Elizabeth*, p. 141.

I. Shuvalov and of the heir to the throne, the Grand Duke Peter. The last was totally opposed to the war, while the two other groups disagreed as to how it should be waged. In these circumstances it is not surprising that the decisions which emerged from the Conference were often ambiguous and at times contradictory: the instructions given to Apraksin are a case in point.[51]

All four commanders owed their positions to their political connections at court and they often fought with one eye on the changing situation there. Fermor, reappointed temporarily after Saltykov's resignation in autumn 1760, supported and carried out the raid on Berlin in an unsuccessful attempt to strengthen his position in St Petersburg and so secure his command. His successor, Buturlin, habitually consulted Nikita Panin (who in 1760 had been appointed governor of Catherine's son Paul and thus became a member of the court of the Grand Duke) and Zachar Chernyshev before he would conduct any military operations.[52] Elizabeth's own fragile health after the stroke she suffered in September 1757 was a further source of instability. Her growing incapacity during the second half of the war hampered Russian military operations, particularly in the final campaigns. No senior Russian commander wished to be identified with the defeat of the Grand Duke Peter's hero on the Prussian throne. The most notable leaders were in the middle ranks of command – men such as P.A. Rumyantsev – and they never secured real influence. When, in the penultimate campaign of the war, Rumyantsev was given an independent command, he responded by capturing Kolberg in December 1761. Russia's military operations were further hampered by the absence of overall direction from St Petersburg and by the difficulties of co-operation with her war-time partners and especially with Vienna.[53] It proved difficult to co-ordinate military strategy, not least because of Austria's fears of growing Russian influence in eastern Europe and determination to restrict St Petersburg's gains by war.

The fighting also exposed established deficiencies in the Russian supply system and commissariat.[54] Apraksin's advance towards East Prussia in 1757 was delayed by the need to wait for grass to grow for his 92,000 horses. It was to be the first half of August before his forces reached Prussian territory.[55] These logistical problems arose from the country's lack of grain surpluses and of recent experience of fighting beyond the western frontier: Russia's war against Sweden in 1741–3 had been a small-scale affair on the Finnish border, while the previous conflict had been in the south against the Ottoman empire during the later 1730s. Not since the War of the Polish Succession (1733–8) had Russian contingents fought far beyond the empire's own territory. The attempt to do so after 1757 encountered predictable problems of

[51] For these, see Anisimov, *Empress Elizabeth*, p. 119.
[52] Showalter, *Wars of Frederick the Great*, p. 281.
[53] There is an impressive detailed study of the middle years of the war by D.E. Bangert, *Die russische-österreichische militärische Zusammenarbeit im Siebenjährigen Kriege in den Jahren 1758–59* (Boppard-am-Rhein, 1971).
[54] John L.H. Keep, 'Feeding the Troops: Russian Army Supply Policies during the Seven Years War', *Canadian Slavonic Papers* 29 (1987), 24–44.   [55] Soloviev, *History of Russia*, XLI. 18.

supply, which were exacerbated by the poverty of the lands in which Russian armies were forced to operate. In 1760–1 Chernyshev's corps was unable to winter in Pomerania because supplies could not be secured locally and was obliged to retreat. During the previous campaign the Austrians had promised to provide grain for the Russian force which advanced into central Europe and won Kunersdorf. Their failure to do so was one element in the recriminations which followed the victory.[56]

The provision of troops for the Prussian front also proved to be more difficult than might have been anticipated. On paper, St Petersburg had by far the largest army in eighteenth-century Europe, but its political and strategic commitments were larger still, and the resources available to Elizabeth's government were spread thinly over an enormous area.[57] In 1756 Russia's mobilisation was handicapped by a shortage of cavalry, half of which had been sent earlier that year to suppress a rebellion in distant Bashkiria (Orenburg) on the remote Central Asian frontier. This exemplified a wider problem. When the struggle began, Russia had over 300,000 men under arms, with a potential field army of 172,000. But relatively few of these troops were stationed in the Baltic, Pskov and Novgorod provinces: those nearest to the Prussian front. Most regiments were scattered across the vast empire, ensuring that mobilisation in 1756–7 would be slow. Russia was unprepared for the Seven Years War. Bestuzhev's active anti-Prussian diplomacy had not been accompanied by military preparations to match and he seems to have underestimated Prussia as a military power.[58] After over a decade of peace, the Russian army was in no condition to fight a major campaign. Neither the officers nor the rank-and-file had been given the necessary peacetime training.

These difficulties were exacerbated by the fundamental problem of distance, which was magnified by the slow pace at which Russian armies with their unusually large baggage trains habitually moved. Berlin lay 1,000 miles west of Moscow, and even Warsaw was around 700 miles distant.[59] These were vast distances in the context of eighteenth-century warfare. Such Russian military planning as took place before the Seven Years War assumed that no army of any size could be maintained in central Europe for more than a few months. Russia's occupation of East Prussia between 1758 and 1762, together with her exploitation of her Polish client's territory, did something to reduce the resulting problems, but the improvement was far from complete. Even with an East Prussian salient, Russian troops continued to reach the theatre-of-operations relatively late in the campaigning season. In 1759 Saltykov's forces had only reached Posen by mid-July, while two years later Buturlin's contingents crossed the Oder on 12 August and linked up with some Austrian units on the 15th. Combined operations with the Austrians always pre-

---

[56] Soloviev, *History of Russia*, XLI. 146, 151–5, 201.
[57] This has recently been highlighted by LeDonne, *Russian Empire*.
[58] Fuller, *Strategy and Power*, pp. 96–7; Anisimov, *Empress Elizabeth*, pp. 114–17.
[59] Walter M. Pintner, *Russia as a Great Power, 1709–1856* ('Kennan Institute Occasional Papers', 33, Washington, DC, 1976), p. 6.

sented considerable problems, while political ambitions and logistical imperatives alike drew Russian armies towards the Pomeranian and Brandenburg theatres.[60]

In light of these obstacles, the Russian army's performance during the Seven Years War was creditable. It was especially formidable in the context of eighteenth-century warfare in two crucial respects. Its reserves of manpower were considerable. Frederick II, acutely aware of his own state's thinly scattered population and the increasing difficulties of securing satisfactory replacements from the Cantonal System or by 'voluntary' recruitment, was always fearful of her enormous reservoir of potential troops. Russia's vast population, together with the relatively efficient system of military recruitment consolidated by Peter I, ensured that her commanders were relatively well provided with peasant conscripts, though these were untrained and unprepared for the rigours of campaigning, and also arrived after a long delay.[61] This was the real foundation of her notable performance in the Seven Years War. Russian field armies usually enjoyed numerical superiority and this enabled Elizabeth's generals to absorb massive casualties in a way that amazed and appalled contemporaries. Their commanders were prepared to buy victories at the cost of horrific losses: at Kunersdorf, one third of the Russian troops perished (13,500 out of 41,000). At Zorndorf, Prussian casualties were around one third, while the Russians lost almost two-fifths of their own troops.[62]

Numerical strength was enhanced by the stolid courage of the rank-and-file, who always fought bravely and, at times, heroically. The Russian troops, declared Frederick the Great at the end of the campaign during which he had personally encountered them on the battlefield for the first time, were 'aussi féroces qu'ineptes'.[63] The Welshman, Henry Lloyd, who served in the Prussian army during the Seven Years War, declared that Russian soldiers 'cannot be defeated, they must be killed', while Frederick himself exclaimed after Zorndorf that 'it is easier to kill these Russians to the last man than to defeat them'.[64] It is clear that Russia's military power was viewed in an altogether new light by the end of the Seven Years War. Before the fighting began, Frederick had contemptuously dismissed the Russians as 'a heap of Barbarians', and declared that 'Any well-disciplined troops will make short work of them.'[65] After the carnage of Zorndorf and Kunersdorf his view of Russia was

---

[60] In both 1760 and 1761 the military leadership favoured a campaign plan for unilateral operations in Pomerania, and the Conference had to impose military co-operation with the Austrians along the Oder front: Soloviev, *History of Russia*, XLI. 179–85, 253.   [61] See above, p. 48.

[62] Precise figures are given by Christopher Duffy, *The Army of Frederick the Great* (Newton Abbot, 1974), p. 235.   [63] *Œuvres*, XXVIII. 155.

[64] Walter M. Pintner, 'Russia's Military Style, Russian Society and Russian Power in the Eighteenth Century', in A.G. Cross, ed., *Russia and the West in the Eighteenth Century* (Newtonville, MA, 1983), pp. 262–70, at p. 265.

[65] Duffy, *Russia's Military Way*, 74; cf. the King's evident lack of concern with Russian military power in his 'Political Testament' of 1752: *Die politischen Testamente*, ed. Dietrich, pp. 334, 344, 348 and 446. Frederick II's changing attitude towards Russia is incisively discussed by Schieder, *Friedrich*, pp. 225–59; see also Walther Mediger, 'Friedrich der Grosse und Russland', in O.Hauser, ed., *Friedrich der Grosse in seiner Zeit* (Cologne and Vienna, 1987), pp. 109–36.

quite different. Six years after the war ended, in a private letter to his brother Prince Henry, the King went as far as to declare that Catherine II's state was 'a terrible power which will make all Europe tremble'.[66] Though both verdicts were exaggerated – Russia was neither as weak before 1756 as Frederick believed nor as formidable after 1763 – the transformation was real and proved to be of lasting significance.

An established definition of an eighteenth-century great power is that it was a state which possessed the material and moral resources to fight a major war without outside assistance. Resources and the ability to mobilise these, together with military and, where appropriate, naval potential, were crucial to this assessment. By this yardstick, Russia's military performance after 1756 made clear that she now ranked as one of the leading continental states. There was rather more to it than this, however. Great power status also involved an important element of reciprocity: all the other powers had to acknowledge Russia's enhanced position and modify their attitude to the point of negotiating with St Petersburg on a basis of equality, thereby admitting her to the exclusive club of Europe's leading states. This they only began to do during the 1760s and 1770s. Yet it was not enough for the other states to admit the Russian empire to the diplomatic first division. Russia herself had to acquire all the attributes of a major European power, such as a more modern diplomatic service, and had also to begin to think and act like a first-rank state, a process in which Catherine II's personality and ambitions were to prove crucial.[67] It was the way in which the reputation won on the battlefields of the Seven Years War and the European reaction to these victories were skilfully exploited by the Empress which completed Russia's emergence as a great power, a process which continued throughout the next generation.

European observers were certainly aware of this enhanced status. Sir George Macartney, British minister in St Petersburg in the mid-1760s, declared that Russia was 'no longer to be gazed at as a distant glimmering star, but as a great planet that had obtruded itself into our system, whose place was yet undetermined, but whose motions must powerfully affect those of every other orb.'[68] His metaphor well expressed the transformation which had taken place. Before 1756, Russia had been only one factor, and seldom the crucial element, in the diplomatic calculations of the major states, but from the 1760s she occupied a central place in their policies and, at times, consumed all their attention. She was soon recognised as one of the great powers: indeed, Frederick II explicitly declared her to be this in 1768. Russia's potential was clear and it was widely assumed that her strength could only increase, while her size alone alarmed many contemporaries.[69] The extent to which the Russian giant had feet of clay was never fully recognised and, indeed, it was difficult to see clearly behind the imposing façade of Catherine II's empire. During the

---

[66] Duffy, *Russia's Military Way*, p. 124; cf. *Pol. Corr.*, xxviii. 169; the 'Political Testament' of 1768 underlines the King's new-found fear of the Russian army: *Die politischen Testamente*, ed. Dietrich, p. 622.

[67] See below, pp. 151–61.

[68] J. Barrow, *Some Account of the Public Life of the Earl of Macartney* (2 vols., London, 1807), I. 5.

[69] This particularly concerned the Prussian King: see, e.g., *Die politischen Testamente*, ed. Dietrich, pp. 624, 668.

second half of the eighteenth century, Europe's rulers were to be attracted by Russia's evident strength and yet simultaneously fearful of its implications: every state was profoundly ambivalent about the new power in the east. The seeming instability of Catherine's government during the first years of her reign, together with the wild and wholly exaggerated reports circulated by foreign diplomats at her court, did something to undermine the position created by the Seven Years War, but this proved temporary. Russia was a permanent and increasingly important factor in European diplomacy and in the policies of individual states after 1763.

This was especially so in eastern and central Europe, where geographical proximity had made Russia significant for Austrian and Prussian policy at least since the second half of the seventeenth century. Both powers had enjoyed periods of alliance with St Petersburg. In particular, the Russo–Austrian axis had been one of the fixed points of European diplomacy for a generation from 1726 until its dissolution late in the Seven Years War. This co-operation had been based on a common hostility towards the Ottoman empire and, eventually, on a shared opposition to Prussia's rise. The Seven Years War magnified Russia's importance for the two German states and made her the dominant element in their political calculations. This was assisted after 1763 by Britain's insular diplomacy and by Choiseul's determination to neutralise the continent, which made him view the Austrian alliance as a means of upholding the *status quo*.[70] These developments, and the seeming permanence of Austro-Prussian rivalry, ensured that throughout the next generation Russia would usually hold the balance of power in central Europe. For both German states, her alliance and her army appeared the best guarantee of the period of peace each believed essential to carry out domestic reconstruction. In the longer view, St Petersburg's support was deemed essential if a more adventurous policy were to be pursued, and this, too, exemplified Russia's enhanced political importance after the Seven Years War.

III

Prussia's survival and, in a different way, Russia's increased status, were both clear defeats for Austria. Vienna had hoped to recover Silesia and to limit Russian influence, while simultaneously using St Petersburg's army to assist in the defeat of Frederick II. Neither objective had been realised, and the Habsburg failure was complete. Indeed, in the dark winter of 1760–1, when Austria's fortunes were at their lowest ebb, Kaunitz had melodramatically claimed that the very status of great power could soon be lost. Not merely was the Habsburg Monarchy all-but-bankrupt and 'at the mercy of its enemies', but might be on the point of being relegated to the status of a second-class power.[71] The Chancellor's verdict was premature, and

---

[70] See below, p. 62.

[71] Beales, *Joseph II*, p. 91. The whole memoir, dated 9 Dec. 1760, is printed in Friedrich Walter, ed., *Vom Sturz des Directoriums in Publicis et Cameralibus (1760/61) bis zum Ausgang der Regierung Maria Theresias: Aktenstücke (II. Abteilung*, vol. 3 in the series Die österreichische Zentralverwaltung) (Vienna, 1934), pp. 3–10.

partly inspired by his determined campaigns for further administrative reform and against his principal rival Haugwitz, but it contained more than a grain of truth. When peace was concluded, Austria failed to secure any territorial recompense, far less the return of Silesia and Glatz, though these had been the war's principal territorial objectives. The fighting after 1756 was designed to return Prussia to her earlier obscurity, but in the event it accelerated Austria's relative international decline, which would not soon be reversed.

The Habsburg Seven Years War was a series of disappointments and reverses, made the more bitter by the false dawn of 1757.[72] In the first major campaign, the army fought courageously in defeat outside Prague and then won a decisive victory at Kolin (June), inflicting a significant number of casualties on the Prussians. Significantly enough, this was Austria's first important success against Frederick II's troops and testified to improvements in equipment, discipline, morale and tactics since the Peace of Aix-la-Chapelle. This notable recovery was apparent to contemporaries, who anticipated a much-improved Austrian military effort in the new struggle with Prussia.[73] The army and especially its rank-and-file performed significantly better during the Seven Years War, particularly in the early campaigns, while its artillery had become particularly impressive.[74] In the aftermath of Kolin, Habsburg forces reoccupied a large part of Silesia while the Russians won their first victory at Gross Jägersdorf. The rapid victory which these successes appeared to herald and which might have been expected, given the coalition's vastly superior resources, did not materialise. Austria and her allies failed to exploit the victories gained in summer 1757, while Frederick II's swift and effective counter-attack in the final months of the year and, in particular, his successes at Rossbach and Leuthen, negated the coalition's earlier gains.

By the winter of 1758–9, it was clear that France would play a much smaller part in the continental struggle than Kaunitz had expected.[75] Louis XV's forces contributed little, beyond some desultory manoeuvring in Westphalia, to the remaining campaigns. French subsidies to Austria were sharply reduced in March 1759, though they were paid regularly throughout the remainder of the war.[76] The French alliance had been the cornerstone of the new orientation of Habsburg foreign policy, but it certainly did not make the anticipated contribution to the fighting. The role of Austria's other major ally, Russia, was undoubtedly more significant, particularly in the final campaigns. But St Petersburg proved to be a less whole-hearted partner than Kaunitz hoped. Relations were complicated by Austria's attempt to limit

---

[72] The standard full-scale account of the war from an Austrian viewpoint remains Arneth, *GMT*, V–VI. A recent and incisive brief discussion is Szabo, *Kaunitz*, pp. 259–78.

[73] E.g. *Bernstorffsche Papiere*, I. 165. Frederick's testimony to this is in his 'Réflexions sur la tactique et sur quelques parties de la guerre . . .', completed at Breslau during the third winter of the Seven Years War and dated 27 Dec. 1758, *Œuvres*, XXVIII. 155–62. This essay is principally an analysis of Austria's much improved performance in 1756–8.

[74] *Œuvres*, XXVIII. 155, 157, for the Prussian King's view that it was 'prodigious', 'immense'.

[75] This is discussed more fully below, pp. 57–61.   [76] Dickson, *Finance*, II. 173–82 *passim*.

Russia's gains from the fighting and thereby restrict her future political influence in eastern and central Europe. In spring 1760, however, Vienna was forced to promise East Prussia to the Empress Elizabeth once Frederick II had been defeated.[77] This was judged essential in order to keep St Petersburg in the war and its armies in the field. In 1762, however, Russia withdrew from the struggle, thereby delivering a second and, as it proved, fatal blow to the Habsburgs' diminishing hopes of victory. The settlement signed at Hubertusburg was for Vienna a peace of exhaustion.[78]

The failure of her principal alliances was one factor in Austria's defeat. Her war effort was also undermined by her own strategy and especially the preoccupation with Silesia. Vienna's principal objective in the Seven Years War was the recovery of this wealthy and strategically vital province. Maria Theresa and her advisers proved reluctant to undertake any military operations which did not restore another Silesian acre to Habsburg control. This strategy was pursued by a succession of mediocre generals, who remained wedded to the accepted canons of eighteenth-century warfare which prescribed careful, slow, advances, always conducted with due regard for secure lines of communication and the proximity of magazines. It was exemplified by the cautious approach of the leading commander, the victor of Kolin, Field-Marshal Leopold Daun, with his preference for strong defensive positions, which would favour the much-improved Austrian artillery.

After the death of Prince Eugene two decades before, Habsburg commanders were largely mediocrities, and some perhaps did not rise to that level. This desultory pattern largely prevailed during the Seven Years War. There was a culture of exaggerated caution and a defensive mentality throughout the high command. The Empress herself contributed to it through her loyalty to Daun, who embodied many of the defects of Austrian generalship, and by her reluctance to give the enterprising Laudon full authority. Both at court and in the army itself, there were further serious divisions between Laudon's supporters and those of Lacy, the rising star of Habsburg military life, and these also weakened Vienna's war effort. The kind of swift, decisive, stroke or sustained co-operation with Russia essential if Prussia were to be defeated were usually alien to Austrian generals and their political masters. Nothing could be more striking nor, ultimately, more significant than the contrast between Frederick II's necessarily mobile and flexible strategy and Austria's cautious approach and strict adherence to the dictates of an eighteenth-century war of manoeuvre.[79] Vienna, though the aggressor, adopted a defensive and attritional strategy and its relative military inferiority was more evident than ever by 1763.

Shortcomings in generalship and strategy do not completely explain this failure.

---

[77] Arneth, *GMT*, VI. 62–93 *passim*; Soloviev, *History of Russia*, XLI. 203–7.
[78] *Bernstorffsche Papiere*, I. 288.
[79] A point emphasised by Johannes Kunisch, 'Der Ausgang des Siebenjährigen Krieges: ein Beitrag zum Verhältnis von Kabinettspolitik und Kriegsführung im Zeitalter des Absolutismus', *Zeitschrift für Historische Forschung* 2 (1975), pp. 173–222, and in the same author's *Das Mirakel des Hauses Brandenburg*.

The Habsburg war effort was weakened by a diminishing belief in the possibility of victory. Austria did not win, to some extent, because she came to believe that she could not win. Prussian morale was always far superior to that evident in the Habsburg army or at court and in the government. Austrian inferiority had its origins in the reverses suffered during the first major campaign, above all at Leuthen (December 1757), and in Vienna's serious financial difficulties, which were increasingly evident from 1759 onwards and became acute in the following year. In order to finance escalating military expenditure, it was even ordered that all silver plate should be melted down and used to mint more coins.[80] This exhaustion, however, was more than financial. A diminishing belief in the possibility of victory was apparent in 1759–60, though this despondency was briefly relieved by the (Russian) victory at Kunersdorf in late summer 1759. After the defeat at Liegnitz in August 1760 and the bloody reverse at Torgau in the following November, even Maria Theresa, who had personally done so much to sustain the war effort during the preceding two years, finally acknowledged that military victory was impossible for Austria alone. Thereafter, Vienna aimed only to secure the best available peace with, if possible, some limited territorial indemnity at Prussian expense. A variety of circumstances beyond her control – France's desire to end the fighting, Russia's withdrawal, Frederick II's granitic resolution – ensured that the settlement was on the basis of the territorial *status quo ante bellum*. The Peace of Hubertusburg was the complete negation of Habsburg policy since 1748. Silesia, as Maria Theresa conceded, was for the immediate future part of Prussia; its recovery, as she frankly acknowledged in March 1762, a chimera.[81] Habsburg primacy in central Europe was no more. Austria remained as a great power, but her relative position had deteriorated. Prussia was at least her equal in Germany and central Europe, and Russia was an even more threatening presence, while France's place in Vienna's foreign policy and her wider role in continental politics had also been transformed.[82] Inevitably, this political failure exerted considerable – and lasting – influence on the policies and personalities of the Habsburg court, where peace and internal reconstruction were to be the twin priorities for many years to come.

Austria's evident desire for peace and, as a corollary, the recognition that it would not be possible to regain Silesia in the foreseeable future, did not indicate any fundamental change in Habsburg attitudes towards Prussia. On the contrary: the Seven Years War had strengthened Vienna's hostility towards the upstart Hohenzollern King.[83] Austria's political decline, both within the empire and, more generally, in Europe, had been caused principally by Prussia's rise since 1740. Habsburg failure in the Seven Years War had intensified the fundamental rivalry between the two powers. It had also added a new moral tone to this antagonism. One dimension of the fighting had been a propaganda campaign against the Prussian King and his

---

[80] Beales, *Joseph II*, pp. 71–2.   [81] Beales, *Joseph II*, p. 110.   [82] See below, pp. 55–65.
[83] For this hatred see, e.g. HHStA Tagebuch Zinzendorf, vol. 6, 16 Mar. 1761.

state. Central to this had been a distinction, plausible though exaggerated, between the militarism of the Hohenzollerns and the traditional and more pacific societies and states of their opponents.[84] It was argued, in other words, that Prussia's rise had introduced a new and dangerous element into continental politics, that of unrestrained military power. When the fighting began in 1756, Kaunitz had described Prussia's King as 'the monster and tyrant of the North'.[85] This did not prevent a certain grudging admiration for Frederick's achievements. Joseph II in particular came to believe that the Monarchy's salvation lay in a selective emulation of the military and administrative bases of Prussian power, and also personally admired the Hohenzollern King. Yet even he described Frederick and his state as the 'natural enemy and Austria's greatest foe'.[86] Rivalry with Prussia remained absolutely central to Austrian foreign policy after the Seven Years War. Kaunitz, like Frederick the Great, saw Habsburg–Hohenzollern antagonism as structural, that is to say a deep-rooted and permanent feature of central European politics.[87] Austria's recovery could only be completed if Prussia were reduced to her earlier insignificance. The problem was that Vienna's ability to bring this about had been further impaired by the Seven Years War.

IV

In the longer perspective, France can be seen to have lost most by the Seven Years War and to have suffered a more serious setback than even the Habsburgs.[88] Her prestige in 1763 was at its lowest ebb for over a century, as even friendly observers noted.[89] The French defeat in the maritime and colonial war with Britain had been complete, and only London's war-weariness together with Choiseul's skilful diplomacy averted even more concessions than were made to secure an end to the fighting. Louis XV's losses by the Peace of Paris were still substantial, and France now possessed only the remnants of a colonial empire, principally in the West Indies. Britain was more than ever established as her major enemy, and in 1763 British

---

[84] Kunisch, *Das Mirakel des Hauses Brandenburg*, pp. 17–43; Szabo, *Kaunitz*, p. 266.

[85] Quoted by Szabo, *Kaunitz*, p. 266, from a poem composed by the Chancellor in that year.

[86] See the 'Tableau Générale des Affaires de la Monarchie', finalised in March/April 1768, HHStA Familienarachiv Sammelbände 88, fos. 120, 123; cf. fos. 121, 124 and, more generally, fos. 145–53. (I am grateful to Professor Derek Beales for drawing this document to my attention and loaning me his copy of it.)

[87] On the development of his attitude see Schilling, *Kaunitz und das Renversement des Alliances*, pp. 19–52. A valuable guide to the Chancellor's political outlook after the Seven Years War is provided by his 'Anmerkungen über dermahliges Staatssystem des Wiener Hofes', 27 Sept. 1764, printed by Adolf Beer, 'Denkschriften des Fürsten Wenzel Kaunitz-Rittberg', *AÖG* 48 (1872), pp. 63–74.

[88] The vintage study by Pierre Muret, *La prépondérance anglaise 1715–1763* (2nd edn, Paris, 1942), pp. 507–74 *passim*, is still in many ways the best introduction.

[89] Pierre Rain, *La diplomatie française d'Henri IV à Vergennes* (Paris, 1945), p. 249; cf. *Bernstorff Corr.*, II. 7, 114–15, for the views of the noted Francophile J.H.E. von Bernstorff at the end of the Seven Years War. Six short years before he had pronounced France to be Europe's leading power: above, p. 32.

power appeared unassailable. Within Europe too military defeat had dramatically lowered France's international reputation. This decline was highlighted by her absence from the negotiations which concluded the continental war.[90] The Peace of Hubertusburg was the first settlement involving German issues for over a century in which France had not been involved. It appeared as if her established role, created at Westphalia in 1648, of guarantor of the imperial constitution and upholder of the political *status quo* was being abandoned.[91] Indeed, immediately after 1763 the duc de Praslin, French foreign minister and Choiseul's cousin and political subordinate, declared that France might soon slip into the ranks of the second-class states, so reduced were its power and resources.[92]

This eclipse appeared to contradict contemporary analyses of relative international power, which were increasingly made in terms of quantifiable factors, above all human and economic resources.[93] By these yardsticks, the French monarchy remained potentially the strongest state throughout the quarter century after 1763.[94] It was still the most populous European country, and at mid-century contained around 25 million inhabitants. The next generation would see further and spectacular demographic growth: by the eve of the French Revolution, its population was approaching 30 million and dwarfed that of any other state with the single exception of Russia.[95] France's economic strength was equally striking. Its agrarian economy, in spite of periodic and serious short-term fluctuations, was prosperous, while its commercial and colonial sectors were dynamic and buoyant at least until the 1770s. These considerations explain why Bielfeld had unhesitatingly placed it in the first rank of powers during the Seven Years War: unlike Russia, Prussia or Austria, it could fight a large-scale and prolonged war without outside financial support.[96] The economic foundations of French power remained relatively secure until the later 1780s. A further and enduring source of strength was France's compact geographical position and relative invulnerability to attack by a continental state.[97] The significant territorial gains made under Louis XIV and Vauban's impressive fortifications had made the northern and eastern frontiers more defensible, while the establishment of a junior Bourbon branch on the Spanish throne at the beginning of the eighteenth century had removed anxieties about the southern border with Spain. The Austrian alliance concluded in 1756 ensured that an ally and not an enemy was established upon the northern and north-eastern frontiers. Throughout the second half of the eighteenth century, France remained the most geographically compact major state. Its coherence con-

---

[90] As Vergennes would later note: Ségur, *Politique de tous les cabinets*, III. 231.

[91] A.P. von Bernstorff to A.G. von Bernstorff, 18 Dec. 1762, *Bernstorffsche Papiere*, I. 280.

[92] Rain, *La diplomatie française*, pp. 251–2.   [93] See above, pp. 8–10, for this development.

[94] See Vergennes' comments in April 1777: Doniol, *Participation de la France*, II. 430.

[95] Russia had around 36 million inhabitants by 1796.

[96] Bielfeld, *Institutions politiques*, II. 84. France meets all the yardsticks for great power status set out in his chapter devoted to this (Bielfield, *Institutions politiques*, II. 80–1) but is not mentioned explicitly in the text.   [97] See Vergennes' comments in March 1784: Ségur, *Politique des tous les cabinets*, III. 201.

trasted sharply with Prussia's territorial fragmentation and the Habsburg Monarchy's sprawling possessions.

There was far more to state power, however, than abundant resources and favourable geography: if these alone had been decisive, France would never have declined so dramatically. Though the eighteenth-century international system might be beginning to relativise power and thus give greater precision to political calculations, it had a Janus face. Diplomatic relations between what were – with the obvious exception of Britain – still personal absolutisms and therefore pre-modern political structures, also took account of a monarchy's present leadership and of vaguer, more subjective, factors, above all reputation. Assessments of relative political standing gave most weight to what contemporaries styled 'crédit' and 'considération': that is to say (very broadly) a monarchy's reputation and the regard in which it was held in other major capitals, together with the present state of its own power.[98] These in turn depended primarily upon the condition of its army and, where relevant, its navy, and its public finances, together with the assessment of these made by other governments. Judgements of this kind were, to a considerable extent, retrospective. They gave most weight to past performances and existing problems, rather than to present – far less future – prospects.

In the crucial area of military power the Seven Years War had inflicted severe and lasting damage upon France's international position. The fighting had destroyed her reputation, built up during a century of successful warfare, of being Europe's leading military monarchy, which she had remained in the mid-1750s. By the time the conflict ended the French army had dropped to third or even fourth position. The acute if prejudiced eye of Jean Favier, the celebrated publicist and renowned critic of the Austrian alliance, would subsequently declare that France had sunk to fourth place among the continental powers by 1763.[99] This underlined that assessments of relative military potential were fundamental to the European states system. In the same way that the simultaneous rise of Russia and Prussia was brought about by their impressive military performances in the Seven Years War, France's decline was rooted in its defeats and failures on the continent and in the parallel struggle with Britain overseas, and was highlighted by the notably improved performance of Prussian, Russian and even Austrian arms.

The Seven Years War destroyed France as a military power for a generation. It is difficult to exaggerate the French army's eclipse. When the fighting began, Louis XV's monarchy was acknowledged to be Europe's strongest military state. This was why Kaunitz was so anxious to have French soldiers and French subsidies as the

---

[98] See, for these concepts, Favier, 'Conjectures raisonnées . . .', 16 Apr. 1773, in Ségur, *Politique des tous les cabinets*, I. 225; cf. Vergennes, 'Mémoire', 8 Dec. 1774, in Doniol, *Participation de la France*, I, 20. The foreign minister spoke of 'respect' rather than 'crédit', but his approach was almost identical.

[99] In the celebrated 'Conjectures raisonnées . . .', inspired by the then director of the *secret du roi*, the comte de Broglie, and completed in April 1773: this is printed in Ségur, *Politique des tous les cabinets*, I. 222. On Favier, see the important article by Gary Savage, 'Favier's Heirs: the French Revolution and the Secret du Roi', *Historical Journal* 41 (1998), pp. 225–58.

foundations of his alliance against Prussia.[100] The Seven Years War opened with two striking French successes: the duc de Richelieu's capture of Britain's Mediterranean naval base of Minorca in June 1756 and the victory over a Hanoverian army at Hastenbeck in July 1757, followed by the Duke of Cumberland's surrender at Klosterseven in September. At this point, France favoured the swift occupation of George II's Electorate of Hanover, which would then be held as a hostage against any future British gains overseas.[101] Vienna was concerned that this might alarm the Empire's Protestant rulers and drive them to join Prussia. Although it was not a religious conflict in any fundamental sense, the Seven Years War was largely fought along confessional lines, and Vienna's Catholic clients made a significant contribution in contingents of troops to the military struggle with Prussia, particularly in 1756–8.[102] Austria proposed instead and won French approval for a joint campaign in central Europe. The anticipation of a swift and overwhelming victory, after which France could concentrate on the war with Britain, had induced the French government to sign an offensive alliance, the Second Treaty of Versailles. Against this background the almost unbroken series of defeats and failures which followed were all the more striking.

These setbacks were symbolised by the rout suffered at Rossbach on 5 November 1757, during the first full campaign of the Seven Years War.[103] The shattering defeat inflicted upon a Franco–Imperial army led by the duc de Soubise by Frederick's impressive Prussian regiments destroyed French military credibility for a generation: until it was restored by the forces of Revolutionary France in the 1790s. 'Rossbach', declared contemporaries, 'ruined the House of Bourbon'. Voltaire announced that it was a greater humiliation than any of the defeats of the Hundred Years War: Crécy, Poitiers or even Agincourt.[104] It was certainly a shattering reverse, made the more striking because the Franco–Imperialists had been expected to defeat the Prussians, enjoyed a numerical superiority of almost two to one and probably occupied a superior strategic position when the fighting began.[105] In its aftermath France's demoralised army in Westphalia came close to disintegration.[106] The orders sent to the commander in Germany for the following year's campaign reveal

---

[100] There is an important analysis of the *Staatskanzler*'s view of France's power in Schilling, *Kaunitz und das Renversement des Alliances*, pp. 122–202.

[101] Michel Antoine, *Louis XV* (Paris, 1989), pp. 732–3.

[102] The confessional dimension of the struggle is explored in the important study by Johannes Burkhardt, *Abschied vom Religionskrieg: der Siebenjährigen Krieg und die päpstliche Diplomatie* (Tübingen, 1985).

[103] France's immediate reaction is apparent from Paulmy to Soubise, 18 Nov. 1757, and Paulmy to Gayot, 18 Nov. 1757, SHAT A^{1}3444, Nos. 47 and 53. In the battle's aftermath two contrasting and revealing analyses of the disaster were produced by the military administrator de Vault and by the maréchal-duc de Belle-Isle: SHAT A^{1}3444, No. 62, and A^{1}3445, No. 81. For its enduring impact, see the penetrating recent discussion by T.C.W. Blanning, *The French Revolutionary Wars, 1787–1802* (London, 1996), ch. 1.   [104] Blanning, *French Revolutionary Wars*, p. 5.

[105] See the revealing comments of Belle-Isle: SHAT A^{1}3474, No. 59.

[106] There is considerable evidence of this in the correspondence for winter 1757–8: SHAT A^{1}3445, 3446, 3471, 3472 and 3473.

that Versailles' aims in 1758 were to avoid any battle and thus the possibility of a further defeat, to keep the army in existence and so permit efforts to improve its condition, and to use the river Rhine as a defensive perimeter.[107]

France's military decline was to be confirmed by the subsequent fighting, to which her armies made a limited and decidedly inglorious contribution. During the war's four final campaigns (1759–62) Louis XV's army fought in western Germany and Westphalia. France made a significant military effort, sending an army usually around 100,000 strong to the region every spring. Though there was one major victory, that at Bergen in April 1759, the list of defeats was longer and more striking: Krefeld in 1758, Minden in 1759, Vellingshausen in 1761. The shortcomings which had been apparent for a generation became glaringly evident. The French army, imprisoned in its own past achievements, had become an outmoded military machine.[108] Defective leadership, both at high command and battalion level, frequent changes in strategic plans and in the commanders charged with implementing them, inadequate supply and logistical support, the lack of reliable intelligence, an artillery arm which was numerically strong but obsolete in its preference for large field pieces, above all acute financial problems: these and other weaknesses were all starkly highlighted. Only the rank-and-file can escape severe censure, and it lacked the stolid courage of its Russian counterpart, which shared many of the same failings but achieved some significant victories.[109] The decline since the age of Louis XIV was apparent to contemporaries both within France and throughout Europe.[110] It was being extensively analysed within the French military establishment, and reforming initiatives proposed, even before the fighting in Germany had come to an end.[111]

After 1763 action was taken to remedy the situation.[112] The next generation saw a significant overhaul of the army, largely inspired by Prussia's example, and these reforms did much to reduce the shortcomings apparent during the Seven Years War. Restoring the army's reputation, however, proved much more difficult, because of a marked lack of opportunity to demonstrate France's military recovery to other European states. This was because the next major war in which her army took part was in 1792. There was only one occasion during these decades when French troops

---

[107] SHAT A¹3471, No. 107; A¹3473, Nos. 84 bis and 89.

[108] There is an informative study by Lee Kennett, *The French Armies in the Seven Years' War: A Study in Military Organization and Administration* (Durham, NC, 1967); Jean Delmas, *Histoire militaire de la France, II: de 1715 à 1871* (Paris, 1992), pp. 1–149, provides the best introduction to the eighteenth-century army. The French nobility's failure to become a Prussian-style military caste is emphasised, and probably exaggerated, by Bernhard R. Kroener, 'Militärischer Professionalismus und soziale Karriere: der französische Adel in den europäischen Kriegen 1740–1763', in Kroener, ed., *Europa im Zeitalter Friedrichs des Grossen*, pp. 99–132. [109] See above, pp. 47–9.

[110] Frederick the Great was especially disdainful: see his comments in late Dec. 1758, *Œuvres*, XXVIII. 155.

[111] See, e.g., SHAT A¹3631, which contains correspondence and memoirs on this topic for 1760–3.

[112] The central dimension of these reforms is the subject of a detailed study by Claudia Opitz-Belakhal, *Militärreformen zwischen Bürokratisierung und Adelsreaktion: das französische Kriegsministerium und seine Reformen im Offizierskorps von 1760–1790* (Sigmaringen, 1994).

actually fought within Europe: the brief and not altogether successful Corsican campaign of 1768–9.[113] France's thinly disguised purchase of Corsica from the Republic of Genoa involved her in the island's reconquest and a struggle with the Corsican insurgent movement led by Pasquale Paoli. French troops suffered some setbacks in their efforts to defeat an enemy composed of irregulars who fought skilfully using guerrilla tactics and made good use of their knowledge of the island's terrain. The Corsicans inflicted a severe reverse upon French regulars at Borgo in October 1768, and during the following winter it seemed that they might be capable of resisting Louis XV's forces. Though infinitely superior resources ensured that France eventually defeated the Corsican insurgents, the military performance of her troops had been far from outstanding and did little – if anything – to repair her tattered military reputation. Indeed, it may have further tarnished it, given the skilful way in which Corsicans exploited the potential for propaganda and the evident sympathy of Enlightened Europe for their struggle.[114]

The notion of French decline was strengthened by a simultaneous and quite fundamental transformation in France's strategic outlook, which suggested that she had disengaged from Europe. It was rooted in the mid-century wars with Britain and had, in its essentials, taken shape by 1763. Throughout the long eighteenth century France's strategic position was fundamentally flawed. By history and tradition the Bourbon monarchy was a continental power with a record of fighting the rival House of Austria which went back to the end of the fifteenth century and remained alive into the mid-eighteenth century: the War of the Austrian Succession had been at one level simply the latest attempt to inflict a decisive defeat upon the Habsburgs. During the decades after 1688 this fundamental rivalry had been overlaid by a new struggle overseas with the rising British state. Until the Seven Years War, France had divided her abundant resources between the continental and the colonial theatres of war and had avoided making a permanent choice between the competing demands of each. As Britain had often been the ally of France's enemy Austria between 1688 and 1756, this merged the two wars into one. The celebrated Diplomatic Revolution of that year, the centrepiece of which was a Franco-Habsburg *rapprochement* through the first Treaty of Versailles, transformed international rivalries and, before long, French strategic priorities.[115]

The Seven Years War underlined that even France's abundant economic and demographic resources were insufficient to support both a continental war and the

---

[113] Thadd E. Hall, *France and the Eighteenth-Century Corsican Question* (New York, 1971), pp. 183–213, provides a brief introduction.

[114] There is a detailed and informative account of this, from an Italian perspective, in Franco Venturi, *Settecento riformatore, v: l'Italia dei lumi (1764–90)*, part 1 (Turin, 1987), pp. 3–220.

[115] This has recently been brought into sharp focus by Daniel A. Baugh, 'Withdrawing from Europe: Anglo-French Maritime Geopolitics, ca. 1750–1800', *International History Review* 20 (1998), pp. 1–32. See also the old and rather general article by Dietrich Gerhard, 'Kontinentalpolitik und Kolonialpolitik im Frankreich des ausgehenden ancien régime', *Historische Zeitschrift* 147 (1933), pp. 21–31.

world-wide struggle with British power. This tension had been apparent during the previous struggle, that of the Austrian Succession. During the 1740s, however, the fighting overseas had been on a far smaller scale than would be the case after 1756, while French armies had won significant victories in the continental struggle. The Seven Years War was quite different in both respects. The defeat at Rossbach and the unsuccessful allied campaign against Prussia in 1758 together made clear that a swift victory within Europe would not be achieved. Simultaneously the war over-seas began to turn against France. By the winter of 1758–9 it was clear that a choice had to be made between the conflicting demands of the two theatres. Against this background, and under Choiseul's energetic leadership, a fundamental reassess-ment of French strategic priorities was carried through. It subordinated the conti-nental conflict to the colonial and commercial rivalry with Britain, and concentrated French resources upon the latter struggle: this was the purpose of the third Treaty of Versailles.[116] Though it did not avert a decisive defeat both in Europe and over-seas by 1763, it shaped France's foreign policy until the early 1790s.

Between the 1750s and 1792 Britain became France's principal enemy. The shift was apparent in a wider change in French attitudes.[117] During the first half of the eighteenth century British hostility towards France had been far greater than French animosity towards her rival. This changed with surprising speed in 1755, when – before war had formally been declared – the British navy seized some French ships. Encouraged by official propaganda, there was an upsurge of anti-British feeling, which proved enduring. When, in the mid-1760s, a play on the siege of Calais in 1346–7 was performed in Paris and many provincial towns, it was an enormous success.[118] The images it presented of French bravery and resilience, at the unsuccessful outset of a struggle in which France would ultimately gain the upper hand, were apposite at what was the nadir of her fortunes in this second 'Hundred Years War'. Throughout the next generation, there was to be consider-able public hostility in France towards England and the English.[119]

Official policy ran in parallel to this change in attitudes. England, declared Choiseul in 1765, is and will always be the declared enemy of France.[120] Vergennes was to be no less emphatic.[121] The scale of Britain's victory, as measured by the Peace of Paris, was a permanent obstacle to future good relations. It became France's

---

[116] For the negotiations and terms of the treaty, see Waddington, *La guerre Sept Ans*, II. 415–85 *passim*; III. 452–4. The reversal of priorities was evident in the French proposals for the coming campaign, in late 1758 and early 1759: SHAT A^{1}3511, No. 2.

[117] This has now been illuminated by the impressive and large-scale study of Edmond Dziembowski, *Un nouveau patriotisme français, 1750–1770: la France face à la puissance anglaise à l'époque de la guerre de Sept Ans* (Oxford, 1998).

[118] François Crouzet, 'The Second Hundred Years War: Some Reflections', *French History* 10 (1997), pp. 432–50, at pp. 434–5; Dziembowski, *Un nouveau patriotisme*, pp. 472–86.

[119] F. Acomb, *Anglophobia in France, 1763–1789* (Durham, NC, 1950).

[120] *Mémoires de Choiseul*, ed. Calmettes, p. 393.

[121] Notably in the 'Réflexions', which were inspired by him: these are printed in Doniol, *Participation de la France*, I. 243–9.

central purpose to secure revenge. Immediately after 1763, resources and energy were concentrated upon the navy, which would have a crucial role in any future war. Though Choiseul was unable to rebuild France's decaying fleet with the speed he initially hoped and his own strategy demanded, his energetic work re-established French sea power during the next two decades: the War of American Independence was to be the one eighteenth-century conflict during which the Bourbon powers competed effectively at sea.

These new priorities were apparent in the different purposes of France's alliances during the generation after 1763. France possessed two principal allies: Austria and Spain. Both were legacies of the Seven Years War and neither – rather unusually for eighteenth-century treaties – contained any time-limit upon its duration. The original treaty with Vienna, signed in 1756, theoretically remained in operation until the beginning of the Franco-Austrian War in 1792, while the Third Family Compact concluded with Madrid in August 1761 also survived until the early stages of the French Revolution. France's new strategic priorities were apparent in the changed roles of the two alliances after 1763. That with Austria was a simple defensive alliance which accorded perfectly with France's aim of stabilising and neutralising Europe in any Anglo-Bourbon war: Choiseul and his successors were determined that in future they would not be drawn into simultaneous continental and maritime conflicts.[122]

The alliance with Madrid was central to French strategy after 1763.[123] Choiseul spoke for the next generation when, in 1765, he styled Spain 'an indispensable power' and, as a fellow-Bourbon monarchy and also an enemy of Britain, a natural ally: in contrast to the Austrian treaty which was simply 'an uncertain alliance' which, for the moment, it was 'more advantageous than detrimental to support'.[124] Links with Vienna were now less important in the overall structure of French foreign policy than the ties which bound Louis XV to his cousin Charles III on the Spanish throne. This was not simply a matter of Bourbon monarchical solidarity, though this could be significant. It principally reflected Spain's intended role in the next war against Britain. Her navy, rebuilt at France's urgings and with some French help, was crucial to creating a maritime balance with the formidable British fleet. The far-flung Spanish empire could be exploited economically by French traders and, during war-time, would provide a tempting target for British strategy.

The Franco-Spanish alliance was not always harmonious. Madrid resented French assumptions of diplomatic leadership and economic dominance, and had its own political priorities which were not automatically compatible with Versailles' assumed ones. Tension was caused by France's failure to support Spain in the second and more serious clash over the Falkland Islands in 1770–1, which forced

---

[122] See Buddruss, *Die französische Deutschlandpolitik 1756–1789*, pp. 120–53.

[123] The best study is the vintage book by Lionel Blart, *Les rapports de la France et de l'Espagne après le pacte de famille, jusqu'à la fin du ministère du duc de Choiseul* (Paris, 1915), though it only deals with the first decade of the alliance. [124] *Mémoires de Choiseul*, ed. Calmettes, p. 389.

Madrid to yield to British pressure. It was followed by a few years of distant and at times acrimonious relations, which lasted until the early stages of the War of American Independence. Throughout the generation after 1763, a strong bond of mutual interest – that of shared opposition to Britain – made the Franco-Spanish alliance remarkably stable and enduring. Spain was the weaker partner, and needed French naval and diplomatic support to protect her far-flung and vulnerable empire against Britain's seeming dominance. This ensured that the Family Compact was usually available to serve Versailles' wider aims.

France's image as a failing power was strengthened by her preoccupation with colonial rivalry with Britain and the accompanying determination to neutralise the continent, rather than aim at leadership. Yet Versailles could not turn its back completely upon Europe, however much its own priorities were dominated by maritime and colonial issues. Other states were accustomed to treat France as a leading continental power, albeit one in decline, and the obligations of reciprocal diplomacy ensured that she remained an element in European politics: particularly for Austria, who saw her French alliance as the basis of her international system at least until the later 1770s. Within France both past traditions and present priorities suggested the need for a continental policy. The aim of neutralising Europe in itself required a degree of involvement. During the preceding century the French monarchy had grown accustomed to exercising political and military leadership, a tradition kept alive both within the foreign office establishment and in military circles. The foreign minister, the cardinal de Bernis, had articulated these assumptions when he declared in 1757 that France's objective was 'to play in Europe that superior role which suits its seniority, its dignity, and its grandeur'.[125] The French diplomatic service remained the envy of its rivals and its professionalism was unsurpassed. Its traditions and assumptions, however, were still grounded in the age of Louis XIV, when France had been Europe's leading power. It was very difficult for a state simply to abstain from European involvement, especially after a century of domination. Choiseul's emphasis on the struggle with Britain overseas did not exclude an enduring conviction that France remained a leading – if not *the* leading – continental state. It is instructive that, immediately after 1763, Praslin should remark to a British diplomat that France and Britain must dominate the European states system, as they had always been the leading powers.[126] In the early 1770s d'Aiguillon's foreign policy was underpinned by the same assumption of Franco-British diplomatic ascendancy, coupled with a growing recognition that this had been undermined,[127] while Vergennes' own background as a career diplomat ensured that he shared the same assumptions about French leadership.

France's decline contained a political dimension which contributed to the

---

[125] Orville T. Murphy, *The Diplomatic Retreat of France and Public Opinion on the Eve of the French Revolution, 1783–1789* (Washington, DC, 1998), p. 15.
[126] PRO SP 78/258, fos. 188–9. J.H.E. von Bernstorff at first shared this view: to St Saphorin, 23 Mar. 1765, *Bernstorff Corr.*, II. 208–9.   [127] See below, chs. 7 and 8.

diplomatic realignment underway. The Seven Years War saw the collapse of her traditional position in eastern Europe and, above all, her influence in Poland. Eighteenth-century French foreign policy had increasingly aimed to create and maintain a *barrière de l'est* against Russia's westward expansion. This had involved support for Sweden, the Ottoman empire and Poland, three apparently declining states which lay across Russia's road to Europe and which Versailles' diplomacy had aimed to strengthen. After 1756, however, this traditional policy had been suspended, since Russia was at least temporarily a partner, and the resulting damage to France's standing in the region proved to be permanent.[128] This was particularly evident in Poland, where successive French foreign ministers after 1756 accepted the slow but inexorable loss of their traditional influence as the price of wartime co-operation.[129] By the end of the Seven Years War, the *rapprochement* with Russia together with France's poor military performance had seriously undermined France's influence in Polish politics.

This was not, however, the end of the matter. There existed, side-by-side with her official foreign policy, a separate, private, diplomacy – the so-called *secret du roi* – directed by the comte de Broglie in the name, at least, of Louis XV.[130] Poland had been the occasion, if not the real origin, of the *secret* and also the main focus of its activities hitherto. In the mid-1740s, the ambitions of Louis XV's cousin the prince de Conti, in pursuit of a traditional aristocratic family strategy, to become King of Poland, had brought into existence an organisation designed to further this aim. For the next decade the *secret*, under Louis XV's benign patronage and, sometimes, active direction, had tried to prepare the way for Conti's election when the elective Polish throne was next vacant. The prospects of a French-backed candidate, far less a native-born Frenchman, in any election were very poor, but from the outset a grasp of political reality was not a noticeable feature of the *secret*'s activities. Conti had quarrelled with the King at the very beginning of the Seven Years War, being effectively replaced as its director by Broglie. The network's original purpose remained, however, since Louis XV was still determined to have a say in the next Polish election.

The Seven Years War had seen an intensification of *secret* activity in Poland, directed by the anti-Russian Broglie and aimed at combating St Petersburg's increasing influence.[131] Considerable effort, and not a little money, had been devoted

---

[128] Oliva, *Misalliance*, pp. 107–8, 155–9, 168–9, 183, and *passim*; see above, p. 36.

[129] For Choiseul's recognition of this, see the 'Instructions' for Paulmy, 7 Apr. 1760, *Recueil: Pologne*, ed. Farges, II. 216–29, esp. pp. 217–20.

[130] The most satisfactory introduction to the endless complexities of the *secret du roi* is the introduction to *Correspondance secrète du comte de Broglie avec Louis XV (1756–1774)*, ed. D. Ozanam and M. Antoine (2 vols., Paris, 1956–61), I. xi–cxiv; Rohan Butler, 'Paradiplomacy', in *Studies in Diplomatic History and Historiography in Honour of G.P. Gooch*, ed. A.O. Sarkissian (London, 1961), pp. 12–25, provides some illuminating comments.

[131] M. Antoine and D. Ozanam, 'Le secret du roi et la Russie jusqu'à la mort de la Czarine Elisabeth en 1762', *Annuaire-bulletin de la Société de l'histoire de France* (1954–5), pp. 69–93.

to an attempt to rebuild the 'French' party, but the operations of the *secret* were on too small a scale to be of enduring importance. Though it no doubt reinforced Russian fears of lingering French influence, to Polish observers it principally revealed the weakness and confusion of French policy. Paradoxically, Louis XV's private diplomacy appeared to confirm the impression created by his official policy: that France was no longer able to influence events in Poland, could only with difficulty do so in Stockholm and in Constantinople, and was therefore ceasing to be a political force throughout central and eastern Europe. This French decline was to contribute to the new diplomatic pattern which became established during the next decade.

V

The war's principal legacy for future diplomacy was the system of five great powers. It was a fundamental transformation. The fighting brought to an end a century during which international relations had been dominated by fear of French power and by efforts to combat the threat, whether real or imaginary, of French hegemony. The Seven Years War was the first full-scale conflict since 1648 which had not been primarily about France's place in Europe. The emergence of Prussia during the 1740s had been a significant breach in the established pattern of international relations. Yet even the War of the Austrian Succession had been initially dominated by France's unsuccessful attempt to destroy Habsburg power once and for all, and in this way recover her own former predominance. The fighting in Europe after 1756, however, had centred on Prussia's position and had revealed the extent of French decline.

This shift was crucial, and had profound consequences for both the western and eastern halves of the continent. The conclusion of the Franco-Austrian alliance in 1756 and the ending of Bourbon–Habsburg antagonism neutralised large areas in western and southern Europe which traditionally had been arenas for the military conflicts which had accompanied this rivalry. Between the Seven Years War and the struggle with the French Revolution, the established cockpits of the Southern Netherlands, the Rhineland (which alone had seen fighting after 1756) and the Italian Peninsula were put into political cold storage. As recently as the 1740s these regions had all seen significant military operations, but this role came to an end after 1756. For a generation after the Seven Years War the western half of Europe was to be peaceful and stable, unlike the situation during earlier decades. Its neutralisation resulted from the new direction of French strategy which emerged during the fighting and the alliance with Vienna which accompanied it. This stability and peace were highly unusual, in the history of early modern Europe, and also contrasted sharply with the situation further east.

The emergence of Prussia and Russia as first-class powers was a decisive development. There were now five major states who collectively dominated Europe almost completely. By the third quarter of the eighteenth century, there was a larger gap between these great powers and the other countries, who were often political clients lacking a fully independent foreign policy. After the Seven Years War, no second-rank state played the kind of independent role which countries such as Savoy-Piedmont and Bavaria had traditionally played, and indeed had attempted as late as the 1740s. The fighting after 1756 had demonstrated the political chasm which now existed between the leading states and the rest. This was exemplified by Sweden's disastrous war, which forced her to accept the permanent status of a second-rank power. Spain's relative weakness had been equally clearly demonstrated after she entered the fighting. The brief Anglo-Spanish War of 1762–3 saw a series of disasters for Spain and reconciled Charles III and his advisers to a generation of political dependence upon Versailles. This was also to be Copenhagen's fate during the half century which followed the signature of the Russo-Danish alliance in spring 1765, during which it was St Petersburg's client.[132] The dominance in practice exercised by the leading states here ran in parallel with the theoretical developments which were producing the very notion of 'great powers'.[133]

The new dominance of the great powers was particularly evident within the Holy Roman Empire, which now appeared to be at the mercy of Austria and Prussia.[134] The election of Archduke Joseph as King of the Romans in spring 1764 was an early illustration of the all-powerful axis between Vienna and Berlin.[135] In several ways the Seven Years War had decisively altered imperial politics. The Austro-French alliance had fractured the Empire's cohesiveness, which had hitherto depended upon Habsburg-led hostility towards France, and this was accelerated by the Austrian offensive against Prussia whose ruler was a leading Elector. The fighting which followed pitted Protestant Prussia against Catholic Austria and France, and so re-confessionalised imperial politics. Frederick's influence was increased by his survival, despite the fact that he had launched the war by invading the territory of the Saxon Elector. Prussia's enlarged role after 1763 in turn contributed to a further weakening both of the machinery of the Empire and of Vienna's control over it: as Joseph II would soon discover.[136] The slow disintegration of the imperial structure, together with the new power of Prussia and the relative decline of Austria, strengthened the marginalisation of the smaller German territorial states. The Empire's unimportance for the relations of the great powers, until the onset of the Bavarian Succession issue in the second half of the 1770s, explains its neglect in this study. Poland and the Ottoman empire were to be far more important issues than the stale backwaters of imperial politics.

---

[132] See below, p. 129.   [133] See above, pp. 7–8, for these.

[134] The most recent survey, incorporating its author's distinctive approach, is Karl Otmar Freiherr von Aretin, *Das Alte Reich 1648–1806* (3 vols., Stuttgart, 1993–7), vol. III: *Das Reich und der österreichisch-preußische Dualismus (1745–1806)*, pp. 87–167 covers the Seven Years War and its aftermath. See also Tadeusz Cegielski, *Das Alte Reich und die erste Teilung Polens 1768–1774* (Stuttgart and Warsaw, 1988), esp. pp. 18–66.   [135] For which see Arneth, *GMT*, VII. 70–87.

[136] See Beales, *Joseph II*, ch. 5.

The Seven Years War and the European states system

The emergence of two leading powers in eastern Europe gave this region a wholly new importance after the Seven Years War. This would be apparent in the major diplomatic issues of the 1760s and 1770s. Poland, Sweden and the Ottoman empire would attract most attention, and in the settlement of the problems they posed, the eastern powers were to play the decisive roles. The age of Anglo-French diplomatic leadership was over, though this did not immediately become apparent. Rivalry between Britain and France continued and even accelerated after 1763, but no longer was it the predominant influence upon continental diplomacy. The political division of Europe would only be completed in the early 1770s, but its origins were to be clearly glimpsed during the Seven Years War and in the separate peace settlements which concluded the fighting. The changed political pattern did not immediately become apparent, partly due to the uncertainty in the alliances of several great powers. Only two of the five partnerships which had waged the Seven Years War were still in existence when it ended: the Franco-Austrian alliance of 1756 and the Franco-Spanish Third Family Compact of 1761, and both were under considerable strain, mainly due to military and naval failures. France's co-operation with Russia ended amidst mutual recrimination in 1761, as in the following year did Britain's partnership with Prussia and Austria's with Russia. The resulting uncertainty and instability dominated the political horizon when the peace treaties were signed. These structural changes in the European states system, however, were less important than the widespread exhaustion and a universal desire for a period of peace and recuperation, in order to tackle the internal reconstruction which was everywhere deemed essential.

3

The domestic legacies of the Seven Years War

I

The scale and intensity of the fighting had far eclipsed Europe's most recent conflict, that over the Austrian Succession. Not since the War of the Spanish Succession at the beginning of the eighteenth century had the leading states been involved in such a prolonged and wide-ranging struggle. Its political and financial legacies had strongly influenced international relations during the generation after the Peace of Utrecht. In exactly the same way, the quarter century after 1763 was lived out under the shadows cast by the Seven Years War. The fighting had established new priorities, and these were everywhere pursued during the 1760s and 1770s. The serious domestic problems revealed and also considerably intensified everywhere became the focus of government attention. Peace, retrenchment and reform were the keys to the post-war epoch, objectives which were set by the empty treasuries and enlarged debts. Frederick the Great explicitly declared that this general financial exhaustion was the main reason both for the conclusion of the Peace of Hubertusburg and for the subsequent tranquillity of the international scene.[1] This verdict was not without an element of smugness, as Prussia was the only belligerent with a cash reserve and no substantial debts when the fighting stopped. The King had raised some small domestic loans during the Seven Years War, but always refused to have recourse to foreign borrowing, which would have infringed his principle of autarky. A similar situation existed in Russia, which only began to borrow abroad during the war of 1768–74; an attempt to do so during the Seven Years War was unsuccessful.[2] This did not mean that Prussia and Russia lacked economic problems after 1763. These were of a different nature, however, to those of France and Austria, where the war had largely been funded by internal and international borrowing, with lasting consequences.

This was especially so for France, where the impact upon state finances was extremely serious, both in the short term and in the longer perspective.[3] The

---

[1] *Œuvres*, VI. 3–4, 9; cf. *Pol. Corr.*, XXV. 268.
[2] James C. Riley, *International Government Finance and the Amsterdam Capital Market, 1740–1815* (New York and Cambridge, 1980), pp. 109, 153–7.
[3] The fundamental, if occasionally controversial, work is James C. Riley, *The Seven Years War and the Old Regime in France: The Economic and Financial Toll* (Princeton, 1986), which should be read in conjunction with the same author's article, 'French Finances, 1727–1768', *Journal of Modern History* 59 (1987), pp. 209–43.

fighting after 1756 cost Louis XV's monarchy approximately twice the earlier conflict over the Austrian Succession: between 189 and 225 million *livres* annually on
average, compared to a yearly figure of between 90 and 100 million *livres* during the
1740s.[4] Interestingly enough, this proportion was almost identical to the increased
military costs of the Habsburg government during the Seven Years War.[5] Though
France entered the war with her finances in a reasonable condition, it was soon
proving difficult to support the level of expenditure necessitated by the fighting
against Britain and on the continent.[6] By the winter of 1757–8, the navy was facing
acute financial problems, and these subsequently increased. Finance, or rather the
lack of it, was also an ever-present problem for the French army. The solution was
not found, as might have been expected, in increased taxation. Indeed, taxes were
not much heavier after 1756 than they had been during the 1740s.[7] Louis XV
appears to have believed that his subjects were already overtaxed, while increases in
direct taxation would have involved confronting the whole matrix of privilege and
fiscal exemption which dominated eighteenth-century France. Instead, the decision
was taken to pay for the war mainly by a massive expansion of borrowing: around
60 per cent of the total cost was met in this way.

The long-term consequences were enormous. By 1764, the state debt had climbed
to some 2,350 million *livres*, an increase of almost 1,000 million *livres* on the figure a
decade before and a serious problem for a power whose annual income of 300 million
livres was only some one eighth of the borrowing. By the end of the 1760s, the cost
of servicing these loans amounted to around 60 per cent of annual expenditure,
approximately double the proportion in 1753.[8] In the aftermath of the Peace of Paris,
France was saddled with a large and seemingly permanent peacetime deficit, while
simultaneously trying to rebuild her navy and reform her army. The massive financial problems inevitably slowed Choiseul's efforts at naval and military reconstruction and were one source of the pacific foreign policy pursued after 1763. France,
like all the other belligerents, recognised that the material and especially financial
costs of the Seven Years War demanded peace at almost any price. The situation confronting Louis XV was, however, especially acute. This was because of the link
between state finances and the monarchy's other considerable domestic problems.

Many contemporaries had believed in 1756 that these internal difficulties were at
least as urgent and serious as the war which France was entering. A weakened monarchy and a divided government faced increasingly assertive and vocal opposition,
above all from the *parlements* in Paris and in the provinces. This clash acquired a
religious dimension when a small but well-organised and influential Jansenist
minority within the *parlements* began to attack their sworn religious adversaries, the
Jesuits, who were entrenched at court.[9] This dispute had far reaching implications

[4] Riley, *Seven Years War*, pp. 138–9, 160.   [5] See below, p. 74, for the Austrian figures.
[6] Antoine, *Louis XV*, p. 703.   [7] Riley, *Seven Years War*, p. 144.
[8] Riley, *Seven Years War*, pp. 182–4.
[9] The classic account of this is Dale Van Kley, *The Jansenists and the Expulsion of the Jesuits from France, 1757–1765* (New Haven, CT, 1975).

for the all-important question of finance. The *parlements* were, in general, opposed to any redistribution of the fiscal burden which might increase state revenues and simultaneously distribute taxation more in accordance with ability to pay; more important, they could obstruct and, perhaps, prevent any such changes, while further borrowing might depend upon their support. The crown's financial plight, by the war's mid-point, was acute and in 1759 Choiseul in effect abandoned the Jesuits to the *parlements* in return for promises of backing for his fiscal measures. Within three years, the expulsion of the Jesuits from France had begun. But the gains to the ministry were less than had been anticipated, and the *parlements* remained a formidable barrier to financial reform, as became evident after 1763.[10]

France's prestige would suffer further blows during the 1760s and 1770s from both unfavourable domestic developments and new diplomatic reverses. Serious and mounting financial problems, and the accompanying publicity, were the principal sources of the former. To these difficulties could be added the recurring strife with the *parlements*, especially that of Paris, periodic and sometimes acute ministerial instability, and a series of colourful scandals at court.[11] These episodes were widely reported by diplomats whose despatches influenced the attitudes of the other powers and thus France's relative international standing.[12] The details of these setbacks and scandals also filled the expanding periodical press. This was a period when the number and circulation of journals and newspapers were increasing, particularly throughout western and southern Europe, and the news and rumours which they contained indirectly confirmed the prevailing view of French decline.[13] The *parlement* of Brittany boasted correctly in November 1770 that its struggle with Louis XV's monarchy had become 'known to all of Europe'.[14]

Reports by diplomats and journalists confirmed the impression that France was a divided and declining state.[15] The personal failings of Louis XV and his successor after 1774, Louis XVI, strengthened this picture of a once-great monarchy faltering. The new King's foreign minister Vergennes himself recognised the damage

---

[10] Julian Swann, *Politics and the Parlement of Paris under Louis XV, 1754–1774* (Cambridge, 1995), chs. 5–7, provides an informative account.

[11] See the lively article by T.C.W. Blanning, 'Louis XV and the Decline of the French Monarchy', *History Review* 22 (1995), pp. 20–4.

[12] See, for example, the reports of the British ambassador Lord Stormont during the final months of 1774 and early 1775, when the clash with the *parlements* was at its height, in PRO SP 78/293–5 *passim*, or the very strong (and probably exaggerated) picture of domestic confusion and court intrigue given by the despatches of the Prussian resident Sandoz Rollin during the six months which followed Choiseul's fall in December 1770, which can be found in GStAPK Rep. 96.27.C.

[13] See, for example, the reports – principally from the *Notizie del mondo* – which are the basis of Franco Venturi's account of the problems of the French monarchy in his great odyssey through the eighteenth century: *The End of the Old Regime in Europe, 1768–1776: The First Crisis*, trans. R. Burr Litchfield (Princeton, NJ., 1989), ch. 11; *The End of the Old Regime in Europe, 1776–1789*, trans. R. Burr Litchfield (2 vols., Princeton, NJ, 1991), I, ch. 4, and II, ch. 10.

[14] Venturi, *The End of the Old Regime in Europe, 1768–1776*, p. 355.

[15] These problems were predictably emphasised by British diplomats in Paris: see especially Rochford to Shelburne, Secret and Confidential, 7 May 1767, PRO SP 78/272, fos. 256–9.

to France's international reputation, and the obstacle which weakness and division at home represented to recovery abroad.[16] With the exception of Britain, all Europe's great powers were absolute monarchies in which ministers encountered little or no meaningful criticism, far less opposition to their policies or exercise of power, which depended entirely upon the royal will, or whim. To observers whose point of reference was a political system of this kind, the rise of criticism and eventually opposition in Europe's leading absolute monarchy was disconcerting and became alarming.[17] These domestic problems did not, in any real sense, cause France's decline. That proceeded from far more fundamental developments, over which French policy-makers could exert surprisingly little control. But the acute financial problems and their political repercussions, together with the upheavals at court, confirmed the growing assumption that France was no longer the power it once had been. Its 'crédit' and 'considération' were both damaged, seemingly beyond repair.

The impact of the Seven Years War upon Russia was also to be distinctive. Unlike the situation of the other two eastern powers, the fighting between 1757 and 1762 had not taken place across Russian territory, and so the extent of devastation and economic dislocation was considerably less than for either Austria or Prussia.[18] St Petersburg's participation in the anti-Prussian coalition had been costly, however, as Catherine II discovered when she seized power in July 1762. It was by far the longest and most intensive conflict which Russia had waged since the Great Northern War, and its domestic legacies were considerable. The struggle had caused immense material destruction. One indication of its scale was the loss of artillery. In 1756, the Russian army had 13,160 guns at its disposal; by 1763, no less than 9,558 of these – over two-thirds – required to be replaced.[19]

The government's financial problems were also acute.[20] Since Russia did not borrow either at home or abroad during the Seven Years War, the sharply increased wartime spending had to be met from the country's own resources. Indirect taxation was increased, with higher levels of alcohol excise and salt gabelle in particular, while a new tariff introduced in 1757 on foreign goods entering Russia was partly a revenue-raising initiative.[21] The Seven Years War also saw the debasement of the copper coinage, with a consequent devaluation of the currency. The costs of the fighting, however, ran far ahead of the government's ability to raise money. Though reliable figures do not exist, it is clear that the financial problems were always serious and, by the closing stages, had become overwhelming: one estimate is that the army and the extravagant court together cost 43.4 million rubles during the first four

---

[16] 'Mémoire', 8 Dec. 1784, in Doniol, *Participation de la France*, I. 15, 17–18.

[17] These and related themes have been illuminated by the last generation of historians; their work is surveyed by Vivian R. Gruder, 'Whither Revisionism? Political Perspectives on the Ancien Régime', *French Historical Studies* 20 (1997), pp. 245–85.   [18] See below, pp. 73–5, 84–5, for this.

[19] Arcadius Kahan, *The Plow, the Hammer and the Knout: An Economic History of Eighteenth-Century Russia* (Chicago, IL, 1985), p. 100.   [20] Kahan, *The Plow*, pp. 54, 109, 238, 319, 321–3 and 327.

[21] There was effective consumer resistance to the increase in the salt gabelle: Kahan, *The Plow*, p. 329.

years of fighting, almost three times the annual revenues of the empire.[22] Taxation was not collected, debts mounted, troops and military suppliers went unpaid, and officials in the central administration were judged fortunate if they received even half salary. Catherine II subsequently wrote that, at her accession, 'The finances were exhausted to the point that every year there was a deficit of seven million rubles . . . The army had not been paid for eight months.'[23] A year later the Empress identified the restoration of the state finances to be the principal task facing her and believed this would not speedily be accomplished.[24]

Russia's financial plight mirrored that of the other participants and would contribute to a cautious and pacific foreign policy in the early years of peace. The fighting had also highlighted established shortcomings in the administration, particularly at the local level.[25] By 1760s, if not earlier, Russian government had been close to collapse. The energetic though ill-judged domestic policies pursued by Peter III during his brief reign had created a further series of urgent problems for the new Empress. Foremost among these were her predecessor's secularisation of the lands of the Orthodox Church and his manifesto granting the nobility freedom from the service obligations imposed by Peter I, while the Church peasants were in uproar at the possibility that they might be transformed into state peasants, whose conditions and obligations were far worse.

These various problems dominated Catherine II's early years on the throne.[26] The inexperienced Empress tackled the pressing financial problems, and launched an important series of administrative initiatives. Local government was strengthened, her own supporters were placed in key posts in the central administration, while control over the Baltic Provinces and over Little Russia was tightened. She also confirmed the secularisation of Church lands, securing much-needed income, and tacitly accepted her predecessor's manifesto on the nobility. These domestic priorities mirrored Austrian and Prussian objectives at this period. Yet Catherine II also had one special priority which had no counterpart in any major state: that of consolidating her own régime after the *coup* which had propelled her to power.

Peter III's deposition and murder cast a long shadow over Catherine II's early years. The Empress's hold on the throne was not completely secure and the situation at court remained confused for several years. Many of her subjects felt that her

---

[22] Leonard, 'A Study of the Reign of Peter III', pp. 190, 192–3.

[23] Isabel de Madariaga, *Catherine the Great: A Short History* (New Haven, CT, 1990), p. 40. Cf. Soloviev, *History of Russia*, XLII. 106–7 and 110–11, for the financial problems at her accession. In November 1760, the Chancellor, M.L. Vorontsov, had told the Conference, in the course of a plea for the war to end, that the four years of campaigning (1757–60) had cost 40 million rubles and that the government had a deficit of 8.5 million rubles: Leonard, 'A Study of the Reign of Peter III', p. 192.

[24] Soloviev, *History of Russia*, XLIII. 64.

[25] David L. Ransel, *The Politics of Catherinian Russia: The Panin Party* (New Haven, CT, 1975), p. 38.

[26] The best account is Madariaga, *Russia*, parts I–III. Informative upon all aspects of government is John P. LeDonne, *Ruling Russia: Politics and Administration in the Age of Absolutism, 1762–1796* (Princeton, NJ, 1984), though its value is weakened by the author's ideological preconceptions.

son, the Grand Duke Paul, might be a more desirable ruler.[27] There was also wide-spread peasant unrest, industrial as well as rural, during the 1760s. The serious domestic difficulties which she faced were urgent matters, and Catherine clearly wished to concentrate upon securing her régime at home while avoiding commitments abroad.[28] In one final respect, moreover, the Empress's position was unusual. She only became ruler in the final year of the fighting. Though membership of the 'Young Court' had placed her close to the centre of the Russian war effort, while her own government confronted its legacies, Catherine II had been less directly involved than her counterparts in Austria, France or Prussia, and so was to be less influenced by her own memories of the Seven Years War.

II

The two German powers had borne the brunt of the fighting, and for each the legacies were to be not merely enduring but far more extensive than for either Russia or France. The struggle was to leave a permanent imprint upon an entire political generation. Leadership in Prussia and Austria was to be exercised by three individuals who had together sustained the struggle: Frederick the Great, who would survive until 1786; Maria Theresa, who would reign until 1780; and Kaunitz, who would be the most long-lived, remaining in office until 1792. For each the conflict had been a formative experience, shaping their subsequent attitudes and policies. It was not simply a matter of the war's destructive legacies, important as these were. The new doctrine of power which was emerging at this period and which clearly influenced King and Chancellor, contained an important internal dimension.[29] There was a general appreciation that international strength was directly related to available human and economic resources and the effectiveness with which they could be mobilised. If these could be increased, a state's relative position could be enhanced. This approach had been strengthened by the experience of the Seven Years War. It was why both Kaunitz and Frederick gave a novel priority to domestic government and especially economic consolidation after 1763. This preoccupation rested ultimately upon a desire to enhance their state's international power.

Austria had strained every sinew in the attempt to recover Silesia, and her territories had borne a terrible burden which in certain regions was comparable to and may even have exceeded that endured by the central Prussian provinces.[30] The army had lost slightly over 300,000 men killed or seriously wounded, and this was only

---

[27] Paul was probably the son not of Catherine's husband, Peter III, but of her lover S.V. Saltykov: Madariaga, *Russia*, pp. 10–11; Roderick E. McGrew, *Paul I of Russia 1754–1801* (Oxford, 1992), pp. 24–7.
[28] Catherine to Chancellor M.L. Vorontsov, 1 Nov. 1762 (OS), Martens, *Recueil des traités*, IX(X). 216; *SIRIO*, XXII. 15–16. [29] See above, pp. 8–10.
[30] Dickson, *Finance*, II. 125. For the situation in Prussia, see below, pp. 84–5.

the most obvious cost.[31] The military and fiscal pressure after 1756 exacerbated an already serious situation, created by the wars of the 1730s and 1740s, but was on a wholly new scale. The consequent burdens did not fall evenly throughout the Habsburg Monarchy. Hungary escaped very lightly, due to her fiscal privileges and semi-independent position, though she did provide some loans and Hungarian regiments fought in the early campaigns. The Kingdom and especially her powerful nobility paid only a small fraction of the increased taxation imposed by Vienna, and even benefited from the opportunities created by the fighting for the profitable export of grain and horses. In contrast, Bohemia and Moravia were the front line of the war effort and suffered accordingly.[32] In every single year except 1762 the Hereditary Lands provided more than half of the money raised to fight Prussia.[33] Considerable destruction was caused by military operations, the march of armies and the forced levying of supplies, and it was exacerbated by the fighting's indirect impact. The activities of the recruiting sergeant and the tax collector left the Bohemian provinces prostrate by 1763, while the situation in the Austrian lands was only marginally better. As a result of the war, commerce and manufacturing were collapsing, agriculture was at a low ebb, while in parts of Bohemia peasant depopulation was becoming a problem for the nobility.[34] The contrast with Hungary's continuing prosperity was striking, and was to be one source of efforts after 1763 to make the Kingdom contribute more effectively to Habsburg finances.

In the Hereditary Lands, the burden of higher taxation and forced loans had been enormous.[35] The total cost of the Seven Years War was 392 million florins, of which only 144 million florins had been raised by ordinary taxation. By 1761 the fighting was costing 64 million florins annually. Expenditure on this scale ensured that the war's impact on the public finances was both immense and enduring. During the fighting, military expenditure had risen sharply to over 40 million florins; a comparable figure for the War of the Austrian Succession is difficult to calculate because of wildly fluctuating campaign costs, but the annual average had been 18 million florins during the 1740s.[36] Particularly in the final campaigns of the Seven Years War, taxation was sharply increased. In 1761–3, the fiscal screw was turned especially in the Austrian and Bohemian provinces. Even more important than such taxation, however, were the loans which were raised. Vienna principally funded the attempt to regain Silesia by extensive borrowing and this brought about a dramatic rise in debt, which increased by more than 150 per cent from a pre-war level of some 113

---

[31] This is suggested by Christopher Duffy, *The Army of Maria Theresa* (London, 1977), p. 205.

[32] Dickson, *Finance*, II. 139–41.   [33] Dickson, *Finance*, II. 125.

[34] For one example of the war's destructive impact, see Herman Freudenberger, *The Industrialization of a Central European City: Brno and the Fine Woollen Industry in the 18th Century* (Edington, Wilts., 1977), pp. 185, 192.

[35] Dickson, *Finance*, II. 124–47 and *passim*. The following section depends almost entirely on Professor Dickson's great work, which brings a degree of precision to the study of Habsburg public finances which is wholly lacking for those of Prussia and Russia. I have presented his figures in rounded totals. See also the account in Szabo, *Kaunitz*, ch. 4.   [36] Dickson, *Finance*, II. 36, 123.

million florins to almost 285 million florins by the time peace was concluded.[37] This figure was seven or eight times the annual revenue at this point. In 1763, interest payments consumed no less than 41 per cent of net income, while a further 50 per cent was committed to the military budget. The financial expert Ludwig von Zinzendorf believed that only the signature of the Peace of Hubertusburg had prevented a total breakdown of public finances.[38]

The Monarchy's parlous financial situation was examined at length by the government between May and July 1763, and a series of palliative measures introduced in the following month.[39] It was recognised that the levels of borrowing, and thus the cost of servicing this debt, must be reduced. The obvious problem was that the proposed reforms involved sharp increases in peacetime taxation, at a time when the Hereditary Lands in particular hoped for and expected some relief from fiscal burdens and when such income was itself reduced due to the mortgaging of future revenues during the fighting. Throughout the 1760s and 1770s Habsburg policy was to be dominated by the struggle's financial legacies, with the continuation of wartime fiscal burdens throughout the next decade and a half, and a series of initiatives to ameliorate Vienna's plight. Some success was achieved: the net peacetime revenue in the Monarchy's central lands was to be increased by 40 per cent between 1763 and 1780, from around 35 million florins to some 50 million florins.[40] The burden of interest payments was slightly reduced during the same period, with an important restructuring of the debt, though the level of borrowing at Maria Theresa's death was approximately the same as it had been at the conclusion of the Seven Years War.[41]

The implications for Austria's foreign policy were considerable. The exorbitant interest payments, together with the high cost of the military establishment deemed essential, imparted a cautious tone to her future diplomacy. In the first year of peace Kaunitz expressed the hope that, if war could be avoided until 1780, at least loans contracted in the Austrian Netherlands might be cleared off by then.[42] This underlined the scale of the problem. Though Vienna's financial difficulties were similar to those faced by the other belligerents, they proved to be rather more fundamental, with the single exception of France. The war's enormous cost in itself made for a period of peace and retrenchment. The inevitable bitterness of failure was intensified by the enormous and enduring burdens of an unsuccessful struggle; together, these factors contributed to the generally pacific tone of future foreign policy. Yet it was not simply a matter of financial exhaustion, important as this was. The inability to sustain the war effort once more highlighted a fundamental problem.

---

[37] Szabo, *Kaunitz*, p. 132, suggests a slightly higher figure (118 million florins) for the debt on the eve of the Seven Years War.   [38] Szabo, *Kaunitz*, p. 130.

[39] Dickson, *Finance*, II. 38–48. Christine Lebeau, *Aristocrates et grands commis à la cour de Vienne (1748–1791)* (Paris, 1996), is in part a study of the financial specialist Ludwig von Zinzendorf.

[40] Dickson, *Finance*, II. 77.

[41] Dickson, *Finance*, II. 77 *et seq.* and table 2:6. There was, in fact, a significant reduction in the debt in the mid-1770s, but it was again pushed sharply upward by the high levels of expenditure made necessary by the War of the Bavarian Succession in 1778–9.   [42] Dickson, *Finance*, II. 282.

A central theme of Austria's eighteenth-century history had been the growing divergence between the role as a great power which she was called upon to assume and the limited resources which could be mobilised to sustain this. Habsburg armies had always depended to a considerable extent on foreign paymasters.[43] In an age when fiscal strength was one foundation of military power, Austria was always at a considerable disadvantage. Her fundamental financial and military weakness had been sharply revealed by the disastrous defeats suffered against the Turks in the later 1730s and at the hands of the Prussians and their allies in the 1740s. The fighting after 1756 was the latest and also the most serious failure, apparent as early as the second campaign of the war. It had been most evident in the decision to reduce the numerical establishment of the army in 1761, when actual bankruptcy threatened. Though the military struggle continued, the nominal strength of Habsburg military units for the final campaign of the Seven Years War was reduced by almost one eighth.[44] This was not simply a question of the shortage of human and economic resources. Austria was not especially wealthy when compared to a western commercial state such as France or the Dutch Republic, but she was potentially far more prosperous than either Prussia or Russia. Vienna's fundamental problem had long been that of extracting sufficient resources from the Monarchy's various territories to pay for a modern, professional, army, and it was to this perennial task that attention was again devoted after 1763.[45]

This preoccupation with finance was closely linked to a whole range of domestic reforms. These involved not merely continuing administrative reorganisation but a series of important military, religious, educational, agrarian and economic initiatives, which were Vienna's primary concern after the Seven Years War.[46] The competing priorities inspired divergent views. While the increasingly influential Joseph II favoured extra expenditure on the military, with the aim of expanding the army, Kaunitz believed that the wider economic growth of the Monarchy should be promoted, since this would eventually make possible higher fiscal yields. The significance of these reforming measures for the present study is the official time and energy they consumed. During the 1760s and 1770s, foreign policy ceased to be as dominant as it had been traditionally. Full attention tended to be given to diplomatic issues when problems arose; at other times, external policy frequently took second place to internal reconstruction. Crucially, both Maria Theresa and, to an even greater extent, her principal minister, Kaunitz, were both more concerned with domestic affairs than hitherto.

---

[43] See above, pp. 11–12.

[44] Figures in Dickson, *Finance*, II, Appendix A; Beales, *Joseph II*, p. 93. Whether this had any impact upon actual troop strength – as distinct from the army's nominal establishment – has been doubted: Showalter, *Wars of Frederick the Great*, pp. 317–18.

[45] In Aug. 1763 the military budget was set at 16.5 million florins; by 1770 it was almost 18 million and eight years later, 20 million: Dickson, *Finance*, II. 46.

[46] The best full-scale account of these for the period down to 1780 is now that contained in Beales, *Joseph II*. A lively brief survey is provided by T.C.W. Blanning, *Joseph II* (London, 1994), while Szabo, *Kaunitz*, is a detailed and scholarly study from the Chancellor's perspective.

The domestic legacies of the Seven Years War

The first decade of peace was a time of considerable sorrow for Maria Theresa.[47] Worn out by perpetual child-bearing (she had given birth to sixteen children, the last in 1756) and by the strains and disappointments of the Seven Years War, she was now confronted by a seemingly endless series of personal tragedies. Two of her children had died in the closing stages of the struggle: Karl Joseph in 1761, Johanna in 1762. The first year of peace brought the death of Joseph II's wife, the enchanting Isabella of Parma (November 1763). Two years later came the heaviest blow of all: the sudden and unexpected death in August 1765 of her husband, the Emperor Francis Stephen of Lorraine. The traumatic effects on Maria Theresa are well known: her repeated threats, never carried out, of abdication; the increase in the extent of her private devotions; her appearance permanently thereafter in mourning, familiar from the well-known portrait by Joseph Ducreux, painted *c.* 1769.[48]

The year 1767 brought fresh tribulations. The imperial family fell victim to a smallpox epidemic, which carried away her daughter Josepha and her son Joseph's second wife.[49] Another daughter, Elisabeth, and Maria Theresa herself were also infected and, though both eventually survived, the Empress was for long despaired of, received the last rites, and recovered slowly. Three years later Joseph II's only child, his daughter by his first marriage, Maria Theresa, died. The Emperor's lack of a male heir, and his refusal to re-marry after 1767, highlighted the threat to the Habsburg succession, about which there was considerable anxiety. Maria Theresa had only one other surviving adult son, Leopold (who had become Grand Duke of Tuscany on his father's death), and it was not until February 1768 that his first male child was born: an event which was celebrated with especial warmth in Vienna since it appeared to secure the succession in the male line, seen as particularly important in the context of the crisis which followed Charles VI's death in 1740 with only daughters as heirs. The first decade of peace also saw the passing of a generation of ministers, the men who had shared the tribulations of the previous quarter century with the Empress and with whom they had come to enjoy an unusual degree of familiarity.[50] Koch died in 1763, Haugwitz two years later, Daun in 1766, Bartenstein in 1767, Silva Tarouca in 1771, Gerard van Swieten in 1772. The sense of increasing isolation, amounting almost to loneliness, was considerable and increased Maria Theresa's melancholy. The loss of so many family and close friends and advisers indirectly contributed to the generally restrained, quiescent, nature of Austrian foreign policy after the Seven Years War.

---

[47] Maria Theresa has been the subject of numerous biographies and certainly her life offers ample opportunity for the romantically inclined. The most satisfactory account remains E. Guglia, *Maria Theresia: ihr Leben und ihre Regierung* (2 vols., Munich and Berlin, 1917), II. 171–89, 228 *et seq.*, is relevant for the post-Seven Years War period. Of subsequent biographies, only H. Kretschmayr, *Maria Theresia* (Gotha, 1925), repays study. Beales, *Joseph II*, proved a cooler and more persuasive account of the Empress than any of her biographers. Illuminating insights can be obtained by reading her correspondence in *KuF*, I–IV, much of which – as her family gradually dispersed – dates from the 1760s and 1770s.

[48] This is reproduced, e.g., in Ernst Wangermann, *The Austrian Achievement, 1700–1800* (London, 1973), at p. 78.   [49] Joseph had married Maria Josepha of Bavaria in Jan. 1765.

[50] Friedrich Walter, *Männer um Maria Theresia* (Vienna, 1951), provides cameos of the more important members of Maria Theresa's circle.

Personal tragedy, however, did not deflect the Empress from family and state pre-occupations. She still had a large family – in 1763, eleven of her sixteen children remained alive – and she took her maternal obligations very seriously: particularly, of course, after her husband's death.[51] Their future well-being – domestic and spir-itual – and happiness were major priorities, and these had important political and international repercussions. By the 1760s, her children were of an age when they had to be provided for: either a suitable consort and establishment or, as a consola-tion prize, a position in the Roman Catholic Church had to be found. Securing suit-able marriage partners was no easy matter. All Protestant candidates were, of course, excluded. The search was further complicated by the problem of *mésalliance*, for members of the imperial family could not marry too far beneath themselves, and by the difficulties of marriage within the prohibited degrees, given the extensive scale of earlier Habsburg marital diplomacy. Saxony, Bavaria and, above all, the Bourbon courts were the most obvious sources of prospective partners, the Italian Peninsula the most promising area for advantageous matches.

This concern inevitably influenced Vienna's external policy. Royal marriages were political actions and were, traditionally, arranged by diplomats. Inevitably, these reinforced Austria's links with the Bourbon courts, both because these were Catholic and in order to buttress Vienna's diplomatic system, based as it was upon the French alliance. These ties were strengthened by five marriages. Maria Theresa's family concerns after 1763 helped to reduce her own involvement in the day-to-day conduct of foreign policy. She retained in theory the final word, and she was certainly kept informed and occasionally intervened decisively. She was largely content, however, to entrust the direction of policy to her Chancellor, Kaunitz. Maria Theresa was a strong supporter of his French alliance, even when it had been weakened by the new diplomatic pattern of the early 1770s, and she believed an extended period of peace was essential.[52] She remained at heart distrustful and even hostile towards Prussia and especially her King, and was scarcely less antagonistic towards Russia. These attitudes made it more difficult for her to adjust to the realignment of Austrian policy during the Russo-Ottoman War of 1768–74,[53] but they qualified rather than over-turned her reliance upon her leading minister during the second half of her reign. This revealed her absolute confidence and growing dependence upon him. It also reflected her priorities: the family preoccupations, involvement in internal reform and sheer exhaustion after the dispiriting failure of the Seven Years War. Kaunitz ran foreign policy during the 1760s and 1770s, though (as will be seen) Joseph II, who became Emperor and Co-Regent on his father's death, exerted significant if sporadic influence, particularly after the outbreak of the Russo-Ottoman War.

Though foreign policy had brought Kaunitz to power, the failure of his diplo-matic schemes did not diminish his authority. Indeed, the Seven Years War had increased his importance, particularly after the death of several senior advisers left

---

[51] See, e.g., her rather dramatic expression of this preoccupation in March 1766: *KuF*, IV. 37–8.
[52] E.g. *MT–MA*, I. 61, 79–80; III. 150, 161–2.   [53] See below, chs. 7–8.

him as the only minister of real experience and stature. It was to the Chancellor that Maria Theresa increasingly turned for advice and assistance. She was well aware of his growing eccentricity and his increasing slowness in discharging business, yet she tolerated him out of a conviction that his perception and political wisdom more than compensated for his human frailties.

Kaunitz's involvement in internal government in any case had been significantly increased by the Seven Years War.[54] In mid-1756, before the fighting began, a new advisory body had been established to co-ordinate the military struggle. Chaired by the Chancellor, this War Cabinet directed Austria's efforts to regain Silesia. Kaunitz shouldered a massive workload, and came to appreciate the way in which Habsburg government could be bogged down by inter-departmental disputes. As early as two years after the war began, he had put forward a proposal for a new body – styled, at this stage, the *Conferenz in Internis* – to provide co-ordination and direction. Though initially rejected, it was renewed two years later: by which point the failure of the Haugwitz reforms and thus of the military struggle was apparent.[55] The result was the Council of State (*Staatsrat*), which began to meet early in 1761 and which was the first body to consider each and every part of the far-flung Habsburg Monarchy. Though there remained separate administrative bodies for each province or group of provinces, there was now more co-ordination in internal policy. The Council of State was Kaunitz's creation; after Daun's death in 1766, he was the only minister to sit on it; it came to be filled by his protégés; and it formally confirmed his enlarged role in internal government. This was in any case quite logical given his ideas on state power and the importance of economics to this.[56] Kaunitz thus assumed a much larger role in domestic policy after the Seven Years War. He ceased to be solely a foreign minister and became a first minister for whom diplomacy constituted only one element in his portfolio. His personal preoccupation with domestic reform mirrored Austrian concerns at this time, while his enhanced authority made him almost the Monarchy's third ruler.[57]

---

[54] Szabo, *Kaunitz*, pp. 51–60, an account which modifies in important ways the article by Friedrich Walter, 'Kaunitz' Eintritt in die innere Politik: ein Beitrag zur Geschichte der österreichischen Innenpolitik in den Jahren 1760–61', *Mitteilungen des Instituts für österreichische Geschichtsforschung* 46 (1932), pp. 37–79.

[55] See Kaunitz's paper of 9 Dec. 1760, printed in Walter, ed., *Vom Sturz des Directoriums*, pp. 3–10.

[56] This is emphasised and probably exaggerated by Klueting, *Die Lehre von der Macht der Staaten*, pp. 167–84. The Chancellor's economic ideas and their origins are examined with great penetration by Grete Klingenstein, 'Between Mercantilism and Physiocracy: Stages, Modes, and Functions of Economic Theory in the Habsburg Monarchy, 1748–63', in Charles W. Ingrao, ed., *State and Society in Early Modern Austria* (West Lafayette, IN, 1994), pp. 181–214.

[57] Professor Szabo goes much too far when he argues that, after the Seven Years War, Kaunitz became an advocate of the 'primacy of domestic policy' and in foreign affairs abandoned territorial ambitions in favour of a peaceful maintenance of the balance of power (*Kaunitz*, pp. 349–50). The consolidation of the Monarchy's domestic base was viewed by the Chancellor as an essential preliminary to a further attempt to recover Silesia, though he believed that this might have to be postponed until Frederick the Great died, while his willingness to seize lands from both Poland and the Ottoman empire during the 1770s (below, chs. 7–8) is difficult to reconcile with Professor Szabo's claim that Kaunitz had abandoned such territorial ambitions.

The Chancellor's personality has always been an enigma. Kaunitz, commented a British traveller in the 1780s, was 'a man of superior abilities, and one of the first statesmen that ever existed; but he is at least as much distinguished for his singularities and oddities as for his genius and talents'.[58] There is certainly no shortage of anecdotes, though many seem to have gained considerably in the telling. Kaunitz's morbid fear of death, the apotheosis of his hypochondria, has always attracted particular attention, and anecdote has all too often been a substitute for analysis.[59] His celebrated idiosyncrasies have certainly received more attention than they merit. This is not to deny that Kaunitz was vain, neurotic, irascible, petty, pathologically jealous of political rivals against whom he could, on occasions, intrigue ruthlessly; nor is it to gainsay his unattractive egoism, his lack of consistent application to the business before him, his *hauteur* and renowned touchiness, often over the most trifling of matters. His increasing slowness and periodic inaction were sources of particular irritation to those around him.[60] In late January 1772, at the critical moment for the first partition of Poland, Joseph II complained bitterly that everything was waiting on the Chancellor, 'who goes to the play and the riding school every day . . . I am told that the prince [Kaunitz] does not want to be hurried, that all geniuses are like that . . . in the end we shall find ourselves, as they say, up the creek without a paddle.'[61]

The Emperor's irritation revealed the highly charged atmosphere in Vienna during the later 1760s and 1770s. After Francis Stephen's death Joseph became not merely Emperor but also Co-Regent.[62] The vague and ill-defined authority conferred by this position was one source of the endemic guerrilla warfare, with periodic set-piece battles, between the three principal figures and their clients and supporters, clashes which would continue until Maria Theresa's death in November 1780.[63] The peaks were the prolonged ministerial crisis of 1766 and the moment in December 1773 when all three sought simultaneously to withdraw from public life, while these years saw a succession of attempted abdications and resignations by one or other. The very distinctive personalities involved contributed significantly to the tension. The Empress was by turns overbearing, autocratic, maternal and martyred and, in any case, intermittent in her own attention to government business; her son

---

[58] Quoted in *Memoirs and Correspondence of Sir Robert Murray Keith*, ed. Mrs Gillespie Smyth (2 vols., London, 1849), II. 197; cf. A.R. Vorontsov's similar verdict a quarter of a century earlier: *AKV*, v. 50–1.

[59] See, e.g., Maria Theresa to Mercy Argenteau, 25 May 1774 (*MT–MA*, II. 151) for the Chancellor's hysterical reaction to Louis XV's death. Habsburg foreign policy was temporarily paralysed by Kaunitz's refusal to mention the French King's demise, far less to discuss its implications. Cf. AAE CP (Autriche) 308, fo. 36, for his hysterical reaction to the news that Maria Theresa had caught smallpox. Even after she recovered, it was several weeks before he would go to see her: Stormont to Conway, 10 June 1767, PRO SP 80/204.   [60] E.g. *MT–JII*, I. 332, 370.

[61] To Leopold, 26 Jan. 1772, not in *MT–JII*, vol. I, but printed and translated from the copy in HHStA in Beales, *Joseph II*, p. 216. See below, ch. 7, for Vienna's policy at this point.

[62] The best introduction is Derek Beales, 'Love and the Empire: Maria Theresa and her Co-Regents', in Oresko *et al.*, eds., *Royal and Republican Sovereignty*, pp. 479–99.

[63] The surest guide is Beales, *Joseph II*, chs. 6–7.

youthful, energetic, impatient, often unrealistic, a root-and-branch reformer resentful that his authority was circumscribed; the Chancellor aloof, isolated, determined to retain and even expand his own power and skilled in political in-fighting. This struggle primarily concerned domestic issues and had little direct impact upon the conduct of Austrian diplomacy. Yet it formed an essential backdrop to events in Vienna and to the formulation of all policy at this period.

Kaunitz's abilities and his political achievements were both considerable.[64] His real talents as a minister are obvious enough: high intelligence and openness to the new ideas of the Enlightenment and to the commercial doctrines of western Europe, considerable political perception and intuition, and unusually wide-ranging knowledge of continental issues, which overcame a certain mental inflexibility and a dogmatic certainty about the rectitude of his own judgements. He always found it particularly difficult to accept that he might have miscalculated. Kaunitz is chiefly remembered for his advocacy and, at times, his practice of a new and more rational style of diplomacy, that of 'political algebra' with its roots in Cartesianism.[65] This was a mathematical approach to international relations, which he claimed gave greater precision to political calculations. His education had given especial prominence to the mathematical deductive rationalism of Christian Wolff, whose influence had been reinforced by the young Kaunitz's period of study at the University of Leipzig in the early 1730s.[66] It was the origin of his rational, deductive, mode of conducting foreign policy. He believed that geometrical reason could be applied to diplomacy. His approach embodied the conviction that international power was relative and that the new science of statistics enabled this to be calculated precisely. It followed that the trajectory of individual states and their responses in particular situations could be predicted. Calculations of this kind, rather than emotions such as hatred, should be the basis of all political decisions. This distinctive approach was set out in numerous memoranda and other state papers, produced throughout his long career and all characterised by clear, logical argument: there are moments when the historian of eighteenth-century Habsburg foreign policy might be forgiven for believing its director to have been a professor of philosophy rather than a practical statesman.[67] The Chancellor's perception was sometimes less logical and mathematical than he himself

---

[64] Surprisingly little has been written on his foreign policy after the Seven Years War since the pioneering narratives of Arneth and Beer during the second half of the nineteenth century and so all judgements must in some degree remain provisional. Several studies cast considerable light on this topic, however: see Helmut Mathy, *Franz Georg von Metternich: der Vater des Staatskanzlers* (Meisenheim-am-Glan, 1969); Paul P. Bernard, *Joseph II and Bavaria* (The Hague, 1965); Karl Otmar Freiherr von Aretin, *Heiliges Römisches Reich 1776–1806*, vol. I (Wiesbaden, 1967); two books by Karl A. Roider, Jr, *Austria's Eastern Question 1700–1790* (Princeton, 1982), and *Baron Thugut and Austria's Response to the French Revolution* (Princeton, 1987); and, above all, Beales, *Joseph II*.

[65] The latest discussion is Klueting, *Die Lehre von der Macht der Staaten*, pp. 167–235; for the decisive importance of his period at Leipzig, see Klingenstein, *Aufstieg des Hauses Kaunitz*, pp. 170–1; cf. above, pp. 8–10, for the wider European evolution.

[66] Klingenstein, *Aufstieg des Hauses Kaunitz*, pp. 158–219, is an illuminating study of his education.

[67] The most important of these writings were edited by Adolf Beer, 'Denkschriften des Fürsten Kaunitz-Rittberg'.

believed, yet his political realism was unquestioned. Sound common sense, though this might periodically be obscured, together with a pragmatic acceptance that there were limits to what could be achieved in any given situation, were probably his greatest political assets.

Kaunitz's distinctive approach to international relations has generally been appreciated. His equally distinctive handling of actual negotiations and his unusual ability to view bilateral relations as dimensions of his own broader diplomatic strategy have been rather neglected, though the latter was a corollary of his 'political algebra'. In its simplest terms, the Chancellor pursued a coherent overall policy into which Vienna's diplomacy towards individual powers such as Russia or France was integrated. All foreign ministers or rulers no doubt possessed or acquired broad diplomatic objectives, and sought to relate relations with one state to these overall aims. This was often attempted and sometimes achieved, but usually within a loosely conceived framework of policy. Specific objectives were only imperfectly integrated into the overall strategy. What was exceptional in Kaunitz's case was the degree of coherence between strategic ends and tactical means. This ensured that his conduct of diplomacy was distinctive in a second respect because of the unity achieved between the broad goals of policy and the tactical management of particular negotiations. This linkage was made more consciously and logically by the Chancellor than by any of his contemporaries, with the single exception of Frederick the Great.

Kaunitz possessed a remarkable aptitude to view the international system as a whole and to use the relations of the other powers to the Monarchy's advantage. This was an important practical consequence of his theoretical approach. At the same time, however, his policy was less perfect in operation than it appeared in state papers or diplomatic instructions, where it was set out with seemingly flawless logic. Historians have perhaps been too impressed by his capacity to argue with compelling certainty on paper, and have given insufficient attention to the course of actual negotiations and to the way policy objectives were pursued in practice. This has led to an unfair neglect of the Chancellor's real skills as a negotiator. He took personal charge of all the important negotiations, and usually preferred to deal directly with foreign representatives in Vienna, rather than work through Austrian diplomats in other courts. Kaunitz's style of diplomacy was highly personal and, while it was far from universally successful, it was more important than has hitherto been recognised.

The institutional means by which his personal dominance was exercised was the *Staatskanzlei* which had been set up as recently as 1742 and was the formal mechanism for the direction of Austrian diplomacy.[68] Its secretary (*Referendar*), Friedrich

---

[68] For the development of which, see Friedrich Walter, *Die Geschichte der Österreichischen Zentralverwaltung in der Zeit Maria Theresias (1740–1780)* (Vienna, 1938), 77–80, 239–41 and 313; the two important articles by Grete Klingenstein, 'Kaunitz kontra Bartenstein: zur Geschichte der Staatskanzlei, 1749–1753', in H. Fichtenau and E. Zöllner, eds., *Beiträge zur neueren Geschichte Öster-*

The domestic legacies of the Seven Years War

Binder Freiherr von Kriegelstein, carried out much of the routine work – the drafting of despatches and so forth – and by a remarkable devotion to duty compensated for his superior's renowned laziness. Binder's rise illustrated the Chancellor's practice of surrounding himself with able subordinates whose careers he carefully advanced. The future *Referendar* had been a close friend since the 1730s and had been employed first in Kaunitz's own private office and then in the administration of his family patrimony of Rietberg. When Kaunitz became Chancellor in 1753, Binder was appointed to be his deputy, responsible for running the *Staatskanzlei*. By the mid-1760s the *Referendar*'s ability to carry out this post's extensive workload had been undermined by his own declining health. In the ministerial reorganisation of 1766 he was replaced by Johann Anton, Graf Pergen, and transferred to a seemingly less onerous position as a member of the Council of State. He was, however, given access to *Staatskanzlei* files and seems to have continued to advise and assist Kaunitz over foreign policy. Binder actually resumed his former post in 1771, when Pergen was demoted in a further re-shuffle, and he continued in office until the end of that decade, when his infirmities were so great that he had to retire. Though at times as temperamental as Kaunitz, he was hard-working and thoroughly professional at a period when this was less common than it subsequently became. For a generation he was the Chancellor's most important adviser and a loyal and wholly indispensable right-hand man.[69]

Policy was laid down by Kaunitz, with occasional and sometimes decisive interventions by Maria Theresa and, increasingly, by Joseph II. At times there were to be significant clashes between the 'three sovereigns' over Austrian policy: these were to be especially important during the Russo-Ottoman War after 1768 and over the Polish partition in the early 1770s.[70] Yet there was also considerable agreement over future Habsburg policy. It was recognised that the legacies of the Seven Years War were unfavourable to Austria, above all the swollen public debt and the need for a period of recuperation, during which the army could be built up and reforms implemented. The central problem after 1763 was that of recruitment, since the conflict had demonstrated the shortcomings of traditional methods of filling up the ranks, while it was recognised that Austria's peacetime military establishment would have to be increased.[71] Joseph II, with the important support of Lacy, argued that the best solution would be to establish Prussian-style cantons. This was strongly opposed by Kaunitz, but finally adopted in February 1770. The establishment of military

reichs (Vienna, 1974), 243–63, and 'Institutionelle Aspekte der österreichischen Aussenpolitik im 18. Jahrhundert', in *Diplomatie und Aussenpolitik Österreichs: Elf Beiträge zur ihrer Geschichte* (Vienna, 1977), pp. 74–93; and Szabo, *Kaunitz*, 38–51. The major recent study by Michael Hochedlinger, *Krise und Wiederherstellung: Österreichische Großmachtpolitik zwischen Türkenkrieg und 'Zweiter Diplomatischer Revolution' 1787–1791* (Berlin, 2000), pp. 44–80, provides a stimulating and informative commentary on these developments from the perspective of the later eighteenth century.

[69] Szabo, *Kaunitz*, pp. 17, 48, 62–7, 71. When Kaunitz (above, p. 80 n. 59) was paralysed by Louis XV's death from smallpox, Binder stepped into the breach: *MT–MA*, II. 151.   [70] See below, chs. 7 and 8.

[71] Szabo, *Kaunitz*, pp. 278–95.

recruiting districts began in the next year though it proceeded very slowly.[72] These initiatives sought to fill up the ranks with a plentiful supply of recruits, though success was incomplete. Simultaneously, shortcomings in leadership were addressed, with efforts to forge a far closer bond between the nobility and the officer corps, of the kind that existed in Prussia and was viewed as central to that state's military power.[73] Fundamental reforms such as these demanded a generous time-scale, particularly given the overwhelming financial problems. It would be a decade or more before Austria's army could be overhauled and built up, as Joseph II certainly intended. These priorities appeared to make peace essential. This was certainly the consistent view of Maria Theresa, whose overriding aim – frequently expressed during the 1760s and 1770s – was to avoid any more fighting. This objective was usually shared by Kaunitz and by Joseph II, who both recognised that an extended period of peace was imperative.

III

The war's impact on Austria's principal enemy had also been immense. Prussia in 1763 was described by her King as being 'like a man with many wounds who has lost so much blood that he is on the point of death'.[74] This graphic metaphor conveyed the conflict's destructive legacy, particularly in the central Hohenzollern provinces – Silesia, Brandenburg, Magdeburg, Pomerania – which had seen most of the fighting.[75] Frederick subsequently declared that peace had been even more essential for Prussia than for the other belligerents simply because she alone had borne most of the burdens of the struggle.[76] The King was prone to exaggerate material destruction and Prussia's scanty resources, in order to magnify his own achievements. In this case, however, the verdict was justified by the devastation left by the Seven Years War. Agriculture and commerce had been disrupted by the ceaseless campaigning. Farms lay abandoned, their peasants either dead, or refugees or permanent settlers in neighbouring territories: as many as 90,000 may have fled during the conflict. The fighting had severely affected the region's trade and its few urban centres, depriv-

---

[72] The Habsburg adoption of recruiting districts remains to be properly studied, surprisingly for such a crucial initiative. Research in progress by Dr Michael Hochedlinger on army recruitment will clarify the whole topic.

[73] See the informative article by Michael Hochedlinger, 'Mars Ennobled: The Ascent of the Military and the Creation of a Military Nobility in Mid-Eighteenth-Century Austria', *German History* 17 (1999), pp. 141–76.

[74] Quoted by C.B.A. Behrens, *Society, Government and the Enlightenment: The Experiences of Eighteenth-Century France and Prussia* (London, 1985), p. 81; cf. *Œuvres*, VI. 4. On the war's aftermath, see the fundamental study of Ingrid Mittenzwei, *Preussen nach dem Siebenjährigen Krieg: Auseinandersetzungen zwischen Bürgertum und Staat um die Wirtschaftspolitik* ((East) Berlin, 1979), esp. ch. 1.

[75] The old article by Ludwig Beutin, 'Die Wirkungen des Siebenjährigen Krieges auf die Volkswirtschaft in Preussen', *Vierteljahrschrift für Sozial- und Wirtschaftsgeschichte* 26 (1933), pp. 209–43, remains informative. [76] *Œuvres*, VI. 4.

ing them of their life-blood of commerce, while individual towns had been bombarded and lay in ruins: Küstrin in particular had been devastated. The demographic losses were enormous throughout the Hohenzollern monarchy. Pomerania lost some 70,000 inhabitants, one fifth of its entire population, Silesia 45,000, the Neumark and the Kurmark together 114,000. Even those territories where the fighting had been less intense had suffered: East Prussia had 90,000 fewer inhabitants when the war ended, and the western provinces 65,000. Overall it is estimated that around 400,000 had died during the Seven Years War, some 10 per cent of Prussia's total population.

Demographic losses on this scale were especially serious for a country so thinly populated and for a King who believed that a numerous and prosperous population was the very foundation of international power.[77] One principal objective after 1763 was to replenish these losses and to increase Prussia's population. The second *Rétablissement*, as the recovery measures are known, aimed not merely to repair the ravages of the war, but, more fundamentally, to create a stronger domestic base to support Prussia's newly won position as a great power. One principal way this was attempted was by attracting immigrants, primarily from other German territories. Potential colonists were lured by promises of land, cash bounties and tax exemption for a period of years, together with assurances of religious toleration. Prussian immigration offices operated in large towns such as Frankfurt-am-Main, Hamburg and Regensburg, as well as in Amsterdam and Geneva. They searched ceaselessly both for agricultural colonists and for the more highly prized skilled craftsmen. Their efforts enjoyed considerable success: around 250,000 immigrants arrived in Prussia during Frederick's reign, the majority after 1763. These colonists were directed towards the regions which had been particularly devastated by the fighting: eastern Pomerania was resettled especially energetically and successfully.

The Seven Years War had highlighted Prussia's basic poverty, particularly when measured against the resources available to all her great power rivals. Here, too, established policies came to be more systematically and extensively pursued after its conclusion, and also to be brought under tighter central control.[78] Frederick's overall aim was autarky – which had guided Prussia's economic policies since Frederick William I's reign – to be achieved principally through protectionism and increased state control of all economic activity. Efforts to improve internal communications were redoubled, mainly by building canals and by making rivers more navigable. Road communications were relatively neglected, because the King feared they might be used by his enemies in wartime and because he suspected transit trade could deprive him of revenue and undermine autarky: an illustration of his primitive but deeply held economic principles.

Though Prussia was an overwhelmingly agrarian economy and a rather poor one, the King's personal interest in this area was limited. He sponsored the setting up of

---

[77] *Die politischen Testamente*, ed. Dietrich, p. 494.   [78] Mittenzwei, *Preussen*, p. 134.

model farms, and he encouraged efforts to import the latest techniques from the Dutch Republic and England to improve yields, alongside the publication of journals to disseminate such new ideas. More fundamental social initiatives were not attempted. Though Frederick in his writings made much of his own opposition to serfdom, which he viewed as an affront to the doctrine of natural rights and an obstacle to economic modernisation, he made only one half-hearted and unsuccessful attempt at reform. The key question of serf reform was broached immediately after the Seven Years War, in the first instance for Pomerania. The prompt and entrenched opposition from the province's noble Estates convinced him that any amelioration in the peasantry's condition would undermine the social, economic and military foundations of the Prussian state, which was unthinkable.

The treatment of the serfs contrasted sharply with the considerable help given to the nobility in the central provinces to assist them to recover from the Seven Years War. Frederick intended that the Junkers would continue to provide the backbone of the Hohenzollern state, serving primarily in the officer corps of his expanded army and, to a lesser extent, in the upper levels of the administration, and he was alarmed at the nobility's weakened condition in 1763. Estates had been ruined and abandoned during the fighting, families had become burdened by massive debts and by the loss of many adult males on the battlefield. To assist their economic recovery, and also to prevent noble estates (*Rittergüten*) from passing into the hands of the middle class, the King proclaimed a moratorium of five years on the repayment of all debts owed by the nobility. He then sponsored the establishment of rural credit institutes, known as *Landschaften* and established first for Silesia in 1769 and then for Brandenburg (1777) and Pomerania (1781).[79] These institutions were to provide cheap and guaranteed credit for nobles restoring their estates and rebuilding their family finances. They could raise cash through mortgages of up to half or even (in some provinces) two-thirds of the value of their landholdings. This credit was less expensive than normal borrowing, because it was backed by the state and by the entire nobility of a particular province. The *Landschaften* had one immense advantage: they protected the principle that the nobility alone should own land while securing funds from the middle class, who in turn received stable and guaranteed returns from their loans.

Efforts were also made to build up Prussia's manufacturing sector, through subsidies to individual entrepreneurs and through the establishment of a favourable, protectionist tariff regime.[80] In the depressed economic aftermath of the Seven Years War, Frederick was obliged to bale out and take over several manufacturing enterprises, and this set the pattern of increasing state involvement, to generate much-needed income and to direct Prussia's economic development. Silk manufacturing was especially favoured by the King, being both supported by subsidies and

---

[79] East Prussia, which Frederick chose to believe had collaborated with its Russian occupiers during the Seven Years War, did not receive its *Landschaft* until two years after his death.

[80] Mittenzwei, *Preussen*, esp. chs. 2–3, is important for the discussion which follows.

protected by tariffs. Woollen and textile production were also encouraged, while Friedrich Anton von Heinitz presided over an important expansion of mining and iron production. The state's growing role in the economy – and its ceaseless search for income – were also evident in a whole series of initiatives: the setting up of the Berlin Bank (1765) and the Overseas Trading Company (1772), together with the establishment of monopolies for tobacco (1766) and for coffee (1781), and of a state lottery. These enhanced central control over important areas of the economy and generated much-needed income, though whether they were beneficial to longer-term development is much less certain.

The very limited extent of Prussian borrowing during the Seven Years War ensured that Frederick did not face the problems of debt repayment which afflicted Austria and France after 1763. The fighting, however, had been immensely costly, and the demographic and economic resources available to support Prussia's new position as a great power were limited. One main preoccupation after the Seven Years War was to increase tax income, to fund the build-up of the army and the wide-ranging state activities such as land reclamation, settlement and manufacturing. This lay behind the celebrated experiment of the *Régie*, the most unpopular initiative of these years but also the most successful, if judged in terms of the fiscal motives for its introduction. Against the background of declining revenues from taxation and an especially alarming fall in the urban Excise in the depressed post-war economic climate – in 1763 tax payments had had to be remitted in certain provinces – Frederick demanded an annual increase of two million *taler*. When the General Directory replied that this was impossible, and in so doing further weakened its own vulnerable position, Frederick put five French tax experts, headed by de la Haye de Launay, in charge of indirect taxation, though the actual collection was always undertaken by Prussian officials. The *Régie* was established in 1766 and remained responsible for the indirect taxation system (but not for the rates at which it was levied) for the next twenty years. Though it aroused considerable criticism and resentment, its success was evident in the sums raised for the royal coffers. These were also boosted by income from economic initiatives exemplifying the extent to which Prussia's survival as a great power dictated domestic policy throughout the second half of Frederick's reign. The consequence was that, according to one established estimate, total revenues increased from 13.8 million *taler* in 1768 to 21.7 million two years before the King's death.[81] These measures, moreover, were the King's main priority after the Seven Years War. He subsequently wrote that – exactly like Austria – internal reconstruction consumed all his attention after 1763.[82] Though this was a characteristic exaggeration, it expressed the reversal of royal priorities which had taken place.

The fighting had also exerted a profound and enduring impact on Frederick himself. This was crucial because, throughout the rise of Brandenburg-Prussia, the

[81] Koser, 'Die preussischen Finanzen', esp. pp. 119–21.   [82] *Œuvres*, VI. 4.

link between the state's development and the ruler's personality had been particularly close: as it was to be after 1763. The King had worn himself out in the defence of his realms, and contemporaries who had not seen him for seven years were amazed by his physical decline on his return from the war. He had departed in 1756 as a reasonably vigorous man of forty-four; he returned as a prematurely aged and increasingly cranky old despot of fifty-one. Already known behind his back as 'Old Fritz', *der alte Fritz*, he had been broken in health by his exertions during Prussia's struggle for survival. He never allowed anyone – above all himself – to forget this. With a pronounced stoop, and now permanently clothed in an old and roughly patched blue army great coat, which was stained by the snuff which he took ceaselessly and was only replaced every few years, the King's elderly appearance presented a sharp contrast to the halcyon days before the Seven Years War. It was also an accurate guide to his declining health. Frederick's own constitution had never been especially robust and throughout his life he suffered periods of ill-health, which became more frequent and serious during the second half of his reign. By now his teeth were falling out, his face was drawn and pale, his body increasingly emaciated. During the autumn of his life the King suffered from a series of ailments which included gout, piles, chest-pains, stomach cramps, fits of choking and bouts of fever.[83] He almost died in 1775, when his life was despaired of for many months.

The King was also an even more isolated figure than he had been before 1756. The Seven Years War had taken a heavy toll of his immediate family and his closest military collaborators. Among the latter the fighting had seen the deaths of the senior commander, Field-marshal Kurt Christoph Graf von Schwerin, of the rising star of Prussian military life, General Hans Karl von Winterfeldt, and of the dependable Field-Marshal Jacob Keith. Within his own family his mother and his beloved sister Wilhelmina had died. So too had the heir to the childless King, his younger brother Augustus William, who had been brutally banished from the army and from Frederick's presence after his military blunders and, by implication, his cowardice during the retreat from Bohemia in 1757. He had died in internal exile less than a year later. This highlighted the problem of the succession, which now rested on the flabby shoulders of the King's nephew, Augustus William's son, the adolescent Frederick William. The Hohenzollern succession was a particular concern in view of the increasingly personalised nature of the Hohenzollern monarchy,[84] and throughout the second half of his reign Frederick brooded frequently on the problems which he believed would arise when the fat, stupid, bovine, Crown Prince (as he viewed his successor) ascended the throne. Yet the King's devotion to the principle of male primogeniture was so complete that he never seriously contemplated any alteration in the Hohenzollern line of succession.

The change in Frederick was more than merely physical. His greatest German

---

[83] Hubatsch, *Frederick the Great* p. 124.   [84] See below, pp. 89–90.

biographer, Reinhold Koser, described him on his return from the Seven Years War as being 'gloomy, cold and hard, like a sunless winter day'.[85] Personal traits apparent during the first half of the reign now became more pronounced. The loss of so many family and collaborators contributed to the increasingly sombre tone. The royal dinner parties at which especially favoured *literati* and military men were entertained at Potsdam soon were a pale shadow of the convivial gatherings before 1756 and, before long, became much reduced in scale. The King's solitude reflected the extent to which his overpowering sense of duty now dictated his whole life. It made him fiercely protective of his own time, and unwilling to squander it on anything he believed unnecessary. His day was structured by military precision and an invariable timetable of work, with limited opportunities for leisure. He rose at daybreak and began with foreign affairs, going on to consider domestic and financial policy and concluding with reports from military inspectors. Royal decisions were dictated and then turned into written directives, and these were duly signed in the afternoon or early evening. This routine only varied when Frederick was ill, and it enabled a vast amount of business to be transacted.[86]

The ageing Frederick grew more remote, misanthropic, caustic and capricious. Administrators and officials suffered the King's wounding sarcasm, and received much simple rudeness and open ridicule. His frank contempt for his subordinates rested upon a profoundly unattractive view of human nature. Frederick believed, as he wrote in his second Political Testament of 1768, that 'Human beings move if one drives them, and stop the moment one ceases to drive them forward.'[87] His constant theme was that orders must not merely be issued; their execution must be supervised. The royal martinet reinforced precept with example, through tongue-lashings to summary dismissal and even legal prosecution. Prussia's army bore the brunt of the King's displeasure precisely because it occupied the central place in his policies. Officers were demoted and whole regiments lost seniority when their deportment in parades and manoeuvres did not come up to scratch. Royal actions, in the military as in other spheres, often appeared to rest on the whim of the moment, as Frederick became increasingly harsh and arbitrary. In the short term his towering personality papered over the cracks which were appearing between the ruler, and the army and administration upon which Prussia's great power position ultimately depended. During the King's final decade these divisions would become increasingly apparent, and their legacies were to be one source of the problems facing his successor after 1786.

The Seven Years War also exerted a decisive influence upon Prussian government and especially the monarch's role, and this had important if indirect implications for foreign policy. Eighteenth-century Prussia was always a strongly personal monarchy

---

[85] Quoted by Gerhard Ritter, *Frederick the Great* (Engl. trans., London, 1968), p. 185.
[86] For the King's daily pattern of work at this time, see Dieudonné Thiébault, *Mes souvenirs de vingt ans de séjour à Berlin* (3rd edn, 4 vols., Paris, 1813), I. 179–94 *passim*.
[87] Quoted by Hubatsch, *Frederick the Great*, p. 232.

and not a protean bureaucracy.[88] Her kings, in other words, ruled as well as reigned, and were always the mainspring of government. The task of rebuilding and strengthening the Prussian state was one which Frederick was determined to shoulder himself. Prussia's ruler was an egoist who carried belief in his own superior abilities almost to the point of megalomania. He delegated less and less after 1763, and personally directed more and more of the key activities. Although there was some decentralisation and delegation in specialised fields as diverse as justice, education and mining, where Frederick could identify reliable subordinates capable of providing initiative, the general trend was increased centralisation and rigid monarchical control.[89]

Whatever the situation in practice, the theory was quite clear: Frederick, alone and unaided, ruled Prussia and made all the important decisions, demanding unquestioning obedience. Military hierarchy and discipline were applied to the administration, while the nobility's dominance in its higher levels assisted the creation of a military ethos in civilian government. A leading administrator, the mining expert Heinitz, significantly commented that Prussia's ruler 'believes that through experience he is strong enough to rule without advice and to follow the plan he has made, to remain true to it and through it to give [the state] order and strength'.[90] These reforming activities automatically increased because of the need to restore the shattered fabric of the Prussian state, and this in turn increased the personal nature of government after 1763. This had two closely related dimensions. The first is that Frederick now resided permanently at Potsdam; the second is his greater degree of control over the entire administrative machine.

The ruler's physical location was crucial within a strongly personalised monarchy. After the Seven Years War the King withdrew permanently to Potsdam, a garrison town (containing 8,000 soldiers) and a significant manufacturing centre, located some fifteen miles to the south-west of the capital Berlin. It had originally been a hunting lodge and had been used by rulers at least since the Great Elector's reign; before 1740, it had been Frederick William I's favoured residence. Frederick the Great's own preferences had already become clear during his first decade on the Prussian throne. Around the time of the second Silesian War (1744–5), he seems to have decided to live principally at Potsdam, though this decision only became fully effective some two decades later. The later 1740s had seen the transformation of the *Stadtschloss* ('Town Palace') and the construction of the little palace of Sans Souci. Both were carried out by Frederick's principal architect, Georg Wenzeslaus von Knobelsdorff, though Sans Souci had been designed by the King himself and would quickly become his favourite residence.

Once these buildings had been completed, Frederick the Great had lived at

---

[88] There are some interesting reflections in Eberhard Naujoks, 'Die Persönlichkeit Friedrichs des Grossen und die Struktur des preussischen Staates', *Historische Mitteilungen* 2 (1989), pp. 17–37.

[89] See the King's comments in 1768: *Die politischen Testamente*, ed. Dietrich, p. 612.

[90] Quoted by Hubatsch, *Frederick the Great*, p. 226.

Potsdam for an increasing proportion of the year, spending Brandenburg's cold, bleak, winters in the *Stadtschloss* and migrating in the warmer months to his beloved Sans Souci.[91] But before the Seven Years War Potsdam had not been his permanent residence. In the first place, he had been frequently on the move. Eighteenth-century Prussia's monarchy and government were in important respects more peripatetic than has sometimes been appreciated. The King commanded his armies in person and this meant that he was absent on campaign for more than a quarter of his entire reign. During peacetime too he was frequently travelling, conducting army reviews, carrying out manoeuvres with his regiments, or putting the civil administration through its paces.[92] Inspection tours through the provinces were undertaken annually in May, June and August. After 1763 Frederick maintained a punishing schedule of journeys and reviews, though the pace slackened after the 1770s as he grew older and, eventually, infirm. These reviews were crucial to his system of government, enabling him to interview officials and even ordinary subjects, examine local conditions and the work of provincial administrations, and in this way make himself less dependent upon the written reports which flowed into his Potsdam study. Whenever Frederick travelled, moreover, the nucleus of government and officials to staff it moved with him.

Potsdam was not merely the principal royal residence. After 1763 it also came to be the main centre of government. Until the Seven Years War, Frederick had continued to stay in Berlin, and his ministers and officials had enjoyed relatively easy access to their royal master, from whom decisions could readily be secured. After the conclusion of the fighting, it was to be a very different story. The ageing ruler spent less and less time in his capital and cut himself off entirely from all except a handful of key subordinates, such as his brother Prince Henry (though his influence rose and fell), the foreign ministers Karl Wilhelm von Finckenstein and Ewald Friedrich von Hertzberg, and favoured administrators like Ludwig Philipp von Hagen and Heinitz. Even these men had no guaranteed role in the making of policy, which remained the King's sole responsibility. Apart from a handful of ceremonial occasions, usually with distinct political purposes, there were only two annual occasions when the King went to Berlin: for the festivities at Carnaval (December–January), designed primarily to entertain members of the rural nobility who came to the capital at that time of year,[93] and for the public army manoeuvres in the second half of May.[94]

---

[91] *Pol. Corr.*, XXVI. 106, for the King's wish to see the 'first smile' of spring before leaving his town palace. K.H.S. Rödenbeck, *Tagebuch oder Geschichtskalender aus Friedrichs des Grossen Regentenleben (1740–1786)* (3 vols., Berlin, 1840–2), and for the first half of the reign, Hans Droysen, 'Tageskalender Friedrichs des Grossen, von 1. Juni 1740 bis 31. März 1763', *FBPG* 29 (1916), pp. 95–157, provide information on the King's movements. The pattern which these reveal can be verified by checking the King's location given at the head of all letters in the volumes of the *Pol. Corr.*: these confirm, with only minor discrepancies, the pattern revealed by Rödenbeck and Droysen.

[92] This is apparent from the volumes of *ABB* and *Pol. Corr.*, which record the King's movements in the headings of individual cabinet orders or letters.

[93] Schieder, *Friedrich*, p. 52; Thiébault, *Mes souvenirs*, II. 18.

[94] These normally took place around the 21–3 May: AAE MD (Prusse) 8, fo. 89.

The ceremonial obligations of monarchy were more and more observed in the breach by the ageing Frederick. The retreat under way was epitomised by the King's failure even to celebrate his own birthday during the final third of his reign. The ruler's birthday was an important annual event for early modern monarchies, and at most courts was the occasion for elaborate and costly festivities. In Frederician Prussia it was usually celebrated, albeit in a more modest way. The King's birthday fell on the 24th of January, shortly after the end of the Carnaval season. During the first half of his reign, when Frederick was at or near to Berlin, he had normally celebrated his own birthday in his capital and in person. In the last winter before the Seven Years War, for example, the King arrived shortly after 18 December, and remained in his capital until the final week of January, thereby playing his part in the celebrations.[95] During the early years of peace after 1763, this remained Frederick's practice, but towards the end of that decade a different pattern began to emerge. In 1768, he left Berlin at the end of Carnaval and before 24 January.[96] In the following year, and again in 1770, the King actually travelled back to Potsdam on his birthday, though in the second of these years he had a brief lunch with the royal family before he set out! Thereafter the only two years when he remained in Berlin for the birthday celebrations were 1772 and 1780.[97] In every other year, these festivities took place in the absence of the principal guest and were instead presided over by another member of the royal family, such as the ill-used Queen Elisabeth Christine (who had lived in exile at Schönehausen since immediately after her husband's accession) or Prince Henry who gave an annual masked ball to celebrate his royal brother's birthday.[98]

Prussia's ruler ensured that his *Residenzstadt* came to be further from Berlin than its relative geographical proximity might suggest. In the 1770s a French diplomat declared this distance to be 'immense', given the limited communications between the two towns, while his successor claimed that nothing less than an 'impenetrable barrier' separated them.[99] The King erected a *cordon sanitaire* around Potsdam. When he was living there, soldiers guarded the walls and gates (which were closed every evening) and controlled access. Everyone arriving was obliged to give not merely their name but the details and purpose of their journey.[100] Visitors seem to have required a pass, which could be secured only in Berlin, in order to visit the

[95] *Dreissig Jahre am Hofe Friedrichs des Grossen: Aus den Tagebüchern des Reichsgrafen Ernst Uhasverus Heinrich von Lehndorff, Kammerherrn der Königin Elisabeth Christine von Preussen* ed. Karl Eduard Schmidt-Lözen (1 vol., with 2 vols. of *Nachträge*, Gotha, 1907–13), I. 233–47.

[96] PRO SP 90/87, fo. 33.

[97] In January 1776, he was still too ill to come to the capital, while in 1779 the War of the Bavarian Succession was in progress and the King was at Breslau with the army.

[98] This can be worked out from the information in Rödenbeck, *Tagebuch*, II. 227 *et seq.*, III *passim*. The British minister Mitchell reported that in both 1768 and 1771 the Queen received the compliments upon the King's birthday: PRO SP 90/87, fo. 37; PRO SP 90/90, fo. 17.

[99] AAE CP (Prusse) 193, fo. 54; 198, fo. 370.

[100] For the security measures see Thiébault, *Mes souvenirs*, I. 93; for the view that for everyone except the King, Potsdam was 'une sorte de prison', Thiébault, *Mes souvenirs*, II. 18.

town, far less to see the King himself. Relatively few made the difficult journey, and far fewer actually secured admittance to the royal presence.

One who did both was the insatiable traveller and Habsburg official Karl Graf von Zinzendorf.[101] His visit in August 1770 took place at an opportune moment. Prussia's King was seeking to improve relations with Vienna and was soon to meet Joseph II for the second time, on this occasion at Neustadt and in the company of Kaunitz.[102] He therefore went out of his way to see Zinzendorf, especially since the latter was a protégé of the Chancellor. The logistical difficulties surrounding this interview, however, were still considerable and also very revealing. Zinzendorf was obliged to leave Berlin on the previous evening and to travel throughout the night,[103] changing horses *en route*. Arriving at 6 o'clock in the morning, he sent a letter of introduction, which Finckenstein had provided before he left the capital, not to a member of the royal household but to the commander of the Potsdam garrison. The latter arranged for Zinzendorf to see the marshal of the court, who calmly informed him that he would have to wait until that evening, when he would be invited to have supper with the King. When the meeting eventually took place, Frederick went out of his way to be personally gracious to his visitor. Zinzendorf's experiences, however, underline the formidable obstacles in the way of securing an audience.

It was partly a question of logistics. Communications were slow and difficult, and the region between Potsdam and Berlin bleak and uninhabited: one British visitor declared that 'the intermediate country is almost a wilderness'.[104] The journey ordinarily took no less than five hours: this was the scheduled time of the daily public post-coach. The royal couriers (*Feldjäger*) who regularly carried state papers on horseback could cover the distance in half that time. Characteristically Frederick – or so it was claimed – could travel even faster: using the eight-horse coach favoured by his father, he could apparently complete the journey between Potsdam and Berlin in just over an hour.[105] After the Seven Years War, it was a road down which the King was less and less inclined to travel.

This growing and, before long, almost complete isolation was crucial for the changed nature of government. The King, its focal point, might be at Potsdam, but all the central administrative departments – *Kabinettsministerium* (foreign office), General Directory, Departments of Justice and Ecclesiastical Affairs, military agencies and so forth, together with the personnel who staffed them and the officials who headed them – were permanently located in Berlin. This physical separation was crucial for the more personalised monarchy which emerged after 1763. It built upon earlier developments. The new structures had their origins during the first half of

[101] See his account in HHStA Tagebuch Zinzendorf, vol. 15 (1770), fos. 91–7, on which this paragraph is based.   [102] See below, ch. 7.

[103] This seems to have been quite common: see e.g. Mitchell to Holdernesse, 27 May 1756, PRO SP 90/65.

[104] N.W. Wraxall, *Memoirs of the Courts of Berlin, Dresden and Vienna in the Years 1777, 1778 and 1779* (2 vols., London, 1799), I. 102.   [105] Hubatsch, *Frederick the Great*, p. 38.

Frederick's reign, particularly in the administration of Prussia's diplomacy. From his accession the King had reduced the role of the *Kabinettsministerium* and its officials in foreign policy and had personally handled not merely the most important negotiations but much of the day-to-day correspondence.[106]

In order to cope with the volume of paper generated by this direct royal control of foreign policy and by the ruler's wider role in government, the so-called *Kabinett* had grown quite significantly.[107] It was quite distinct from the *Kabinettsministerium* and indeed from all the formal structures of eighteenth-century Prussian administration. The *Kabinett* was really a team of secretaries, often of lowly and invariably non-noble birth – in contrast to Prussia's ministers, who were almost always noblemen – who were in direct and daily contact with the King.[108] The increased role and importance of these secretaries were apparent in their subsequent elevation to the rank of cabinet councillors. Unlike the various ministers and their subordinates, who remained in Berlin, members of the *Kabinett* accompanied Frederick when he was travelling or campaigning. Indeed, its influential head for much of the King's reign, August Friedrich Eichel, had suffered the indignity of being captured by the Austrians after the Prussian victory at Soor in 1745, though he was soon repatriated through the usual exchange of prisoners of war. The *Kabinett* provided essential copying services. Its members turned royal decisions into formal instructions to subordinates, the famous cabinet orders through which government was increasingly conducted.

The *Kabinett*'s role had expanded notably during the Seven Years War when the King had visited Berlin only once. Before Frederick departed for the 1757 campaign, he had issued an order conferring an unusual degree of initiative upon the General Directory, making it solely responsible for raising money for the struggle. This decision, and the administration's growing independence, have been seen as a crucial point in the relationship between ruler and civil service, and in the growing autonomy of Prussia's bureaucracy.[109] What has been less appreciated, though in the longer perspective it would be more significant, is the *Kabinett*'s enhanced role during the fighting.[110] Throughout the Seven Years War, the centre of Prussian

---

[106] There is a detailed study by Meta Kohnke, 'Das preussische Kabinettsministerium: ein Beitrag zur Geschichte des Staatsapparates im Spätfeudalismus' (PhD thesis, Humboldt University, Berlin, 1968), which is informative and solidly based on manuscript material, though the ideological framework is – inevitably – that of the DDR in the later 1960s. A substantial summary was published under the same title in *Jahrbuch für Geschichte der Feudalismus* 2 (1978), pp. 313–56. See also H.M. Scott, 'Prussia's Royal Foreign Minister', in Oresko *et al.*, eds., *Royal and Republican Sovereignty*, pp. 500–26.

[107] There is a brief, authoritative introduction by Otto Hintze, which forms part of his magisterial survey of Prussian government: *ABB*, VI:1. 59–66.

[108] See the informative article by Hermann Hüffer, 'Die Beamten des ältern preussischen Kabinetts von 1713–1808', *FBPG* 5 (1892), pp. 157–90.

[109] H.C. Johnson, *Frederick the Great and his Officials* (New Haven, CT, 1975), esp. ch. 6.

[110] This is apparent from *ABB* vols. IX–XII *passim*. It is noted by Hubatsch, *Frederick the Great*, pp. 113–14.

government continued to be where the King was. Aided only by Eichel and a handful of secretaries, Frederick personally handled all the details of troop movements and supply, maintaining a remarkably extensive correspondence and accomplishing what would later occupy an entire general staff. The King also devoted some attention to broader administrative issues. This enhanced both the importance of the *Kabinett* and the personal standing of Eichel, now the key figure in government.

The more executive style of monarchy created by the Seven Years War was continued from Potsdam throughout the second half of Frederick's reign, considerably strengthening his personal control over domestic government.[111] He alone united the diverse, overlapping and frequently confusing elements in Prussian administration. Only the King and the *Kabinett* could take a general view of the Hohenzollern monarchy. This process, and the resulting administrative reorganisation, were facilitated by demographic accident. The era of the Seven Years War saw the deaths of a number of prominent officials who had begun their careers – often in the General Directory – under Frederick William I and had remained influential throughout the first two decades of Frederick's own reign.[112] The King was then able to appoint younger, hand-picked top officials who helped reshape central government after 1763.

Prussia's ruler had always been critical of the General Directory, its slowness and the collegial principle which it embodied and which provided opportunities for exactly those ministerial disagreements he detested. Though – exactly like his father – he had become President of the General Directory in 1748, the same year in which he had issued an important new Instruction to guide its operations,[113] he became increasingly suspicious of this key body and, eventually, downgraded it. The establishment of the *Régie* in 1766 removed one principal function, collecting taxation, while its decline was accelerated by the creation of more specialised ministries and the way powerful individuals such as Hagen, Heinitz and Schulenburg acquired personal administrative fiefdoms.

The practice of by-passing the nominally responsible central department was extended throughout domestic government. The *Kabinett* gradually replaced the General Directory, as Frederick more and more ruled from Potsdam through a team of secretaries. The General Directory and the other departments were sidelined as the King corresponded directly with his provincial administrators and army commanders. After 1763 cabinet orders increasingly were sent directly to officials in the provinces, rather than being routed through the General Directory and then the

---

[111] The final volume of *ABB* contains a brief but suggestive survey by Peter Baumgart, 'Tendenzen der spätfriderizianischen Verwaltung im Spiegel der Acta Borussica': vol. XVI:II, pp. xxi–xxxvii.

[112] These men are listed in Johnson, *Frederick the Great*, pp. 160–1. It must be remembered that, ordinarily, there was no retirement age: Prussian officials served until they died or, occasionally, they were released because they had become too decrepit to continue.

[113] This is notably detailed, and is illuminating on the King's views on government: it is printed in *ABB*, VII. 572–655.

responsible departments in Berlin.[114] Provincial administrators were in turn expected to reply directly to the King. Up to twelve cabinet orders a day were being issued during the King's later years.[115] The greater workload which resulted led to a rise in the number of *Kabinett* secretaries and clerks: after 1768, when Eichel died, the total doubled from three to six. These men provided a small and highly flexible executive at the apex of the administrative pyramid, responsible only to the King. Simultaneously, the *Kabinett* was formally divided into three sections: foreign policy, domestic administration and military affairs.[116] The vital role of the *Kabinett* secretaries was apparent in Frederick's recommendation – in his Personal Testament of January 1769 – to his successor that 'They have a good knowledge of affairs and they can, at the beginning of the reign, advise the King on many things of which they have knowledge and which are unknown even to Ministers.'[117] To facilitate royal decision-making, Frederick insisted that the reports he received each day from his immediate advisers should be no longer than two pages. In this way, he extended his personal control of military and external policy.

The King's domestic priorities, together with the exhaustion of both Prussia and her ruler, reinforced the search for peace. Frederick's overriding aim was now to secure his state's position among the great powers: this determined both foreign and internal policy after 1763. Prussia had become a member of Europe's political élite, yet she apparently lacked the resources to sustain such a role. The King was uncomfortably aware of the narrow margin of survival in the Seven Years War and recognised that a further conflict might well destroy his state and his own life's work. Where others were awed by Prussia's military strength and admired her remarkable ruler, Frederick saw only the scanty resources and strategic vulnerability, which he believed were real obstacles to her remaining a great power. The King's analysis was too pessimistic: his own state was probably stronger, and his rivals certainly weaker, than he believed. In particular he overestimated Russian power, because of his serious reverses at their hands in 1758–9. His new-found respect for Austria's military might, evident in his collecting detailed and up-to-date information on her army and finances, was also carried to exaggerated lengths.[118] Though the Habsburg army had performed much better during the Seven Years War, it long remained inferior to that of Prussia. But the King's analysis, and the problems of resources and strategic vulnerability which underpinned it, helped to shape policy after 1763.

Frederick characteristically joked about Prussia's central problem, remarking more than once that the Hohenzollern coat of arms should contain not a black eagle

---

[114] This shift was becoming apparent by the early summer of 1763: in April and May the majority of cabinet orders were being sent to the General Directory; by June and July these were mainly going to provincial administrators and administrative bodies: see *ABB*, XIII *passim*.

[115] Schieder, *Friedrich*, p. 298.

[116] On the reorganisation in February 1768 after Eichel's death, see *ABB*, XIV. 449–52.

[117] Quoted by Hubatsch, *Frederick the Great*, p. 223.

[118] See GStAPK Rep. 96.46.F1, fos. 18–23; cf. Rohde to Frederick II, 1 Jan. 1768, Rep. 96.46.K.

but a monkey: all Prussia could do was ape the great powers.[119] The fundamental problems of exiguous resources, territorial dispersal and incomplete political integration, evident during the period of political emergence, had been starkly highlighted during the Seven Years War. The western enclaves had been occupied by the French and Austrians, and such loyalty as these territories possessed to the King in far-away Berlin had been attenuated, as older regional identities re-emerged.[120] Much more seriously, East Prussia had been occupied and governed by Russia after January 1758, and had only been returned to Hohenzollern control in June 1762.[121] Frederick the Great believed that the Kingdom's political élite had collaborated with their Russian occupiers, and seldom visited the province during the rest of his reign.[122] His capricious attitude, however, could not disguise the fault lines revealed by the conflict, when a permanent Russian take-over of East Prussia had seemed possible.

Frederick's earliest important initiatives on returning from the Seven Years War was the construction of the *Neues Palais* (New Palace) at the far end of the park at Potsdam, for which he had been planning before 1756. It was not completed until 1769, and was on a wholly new scale to any previous Hohenzollern palace, consuming scarce funds needed for the social and economic reconstruction which was essential. It was a vast, architecturally resplendent, palace where Frederick never lived for any length of time, though he occasionally held concerts there: it became the principal royal residence only after his death. Its construction was a deliberate act of policy, intended to reinforce Prussia's shaky great power position and project an image of strength. It was meant to impress political rivals, being used to house and to entertain the privileged foreign visitors permitted direct access to the King in his Potsdam redoubt. The *Neues Palais* was representational monarchy on a quite massive scale. Impressive and ornate, it dwarfed the classical simplicity of Sans Souci at the other end of the park.

Prussia's international position, however, was to be primarily defended by military power and by avoiding war. The fighting had raised the reputation of the Prussian army and of its commander-in-chief to new heights, a model to be emulated by its rivals: during the next two decades the army reforms undertaken in Austria, France and Russia were all partly inspired by Prussia's example. Admiring foreigners made the pilgrimage to Berlin hoping to see at first hand the famed blue-coated regiments put through their paces and, if they were especially fortunate, to catch a glimpse of the Great Frederick, now one of the wonders of the age. The potential of this was quickly appreciated by the King, who welcomed foreign military experts and

---

[119] For example to Luccesini in 1781: Schieder, *Friedrich*, p. 259.

[120] There is an excellent study by Horst Carl, *Okkupation und Regionalismus: die preussischen Westprovinzen im Siebenjährigen Krieg* (Mainz, 1993).

[121] For some account of this, see Stefan Hartmann, 'Die Rückgabe Ostpreußens durch die Russen an Preußen im Jahre 1762', *Zeitschrift für Ostforschung* 36 (1987), pp. 405–33.

[122] In 1768 he wrote that its nobility had been 'more Russian than Prussian' during the Seven Years War: *Die politischen Testamente*, ed. Dietrich, p. 588.

curious civilians to Berlin's annual May parades and exercises. His soldiers and their officers drilled with parade ground efficiency, underlining to an admiring Europe the continuing strength of Hohenzollern military power. This, like the *Neues Palais*, was also a form of propaganda aimed at Prussia's political rivals. Its military significance was negligible: the important manoeuvres took place away from the capital and prying foreign eyes, often in Pomerania and Silesia and usually in the autumn.

Despite the army's reputation, Frederick believed that Prussian military power needed to be rebuilt, refined and perfected, and he devoted considerable energy to this task during the second half of his reign.[123] The means was hierarchical control imposed by an increasingly demanding and arbitrary King, reinforced by strict and frequently harsh discipline and incessant drilling, as officers and men became mere cogs in a great military machine. The long-term consequences were deleterious, as became evident in Frederick's final campaign, the brief and strategically barren War of the Bavarian Succession (1778–9), during which he successfully prevented Austria from annexing the Electorate. This would demonstrate how initiative at all levels of command had been eroded by a decade and more of royal dictatorship, exercised by a remote King: in sharp contrast to the close personal links which had done so much to maintain army morale during the first half of the reign. In the short term, however, the twin gods of drill and discipline maintained Prussia's forces at an impressive level of readiness.

The King's efforts to overhaul the army began at the top. Behind the well-known and successful efforts to hound middle-class officers out of regiments, to which they had been commissioned during the emergency of the Seven Years War, lay not merely an established social preference but a distinct military purpose. Frederick believed that only men of noble birth possessed the attributes essential to exercise command, and he set out to establish an overwhelmingly Junker officer corps.[124] Simultaneously determined efforts were made to improve the professional training available to young noblemen intent upon military careers. The *Académie des Nobles*, set up in 1765, in which Frederick took a personal interest, had a curriculum intended to provide the best training for officers anywhere in Europe. The composition of the rank-and-file was similarly subjected to royal scrutiny, though with fewer immediate results. During the second half of the Seven Years War in particular Frederick had been forced to rely more heavily upon the diminishing supply of native conscripts than he wanted: the problem inherent in the much-admired Cantonal System was that it could weaken the crucial agrarian base of Prussia's economy by diverting peasants into his regiments and, in wartime, permanently reducing the numbers available to labour on the land. The King's efforts to increase

---

[123] There are up-to-date introductions by Dennis Showalter, 'Hubertusburg to Auerstädt: The Prussian Army in Decline', *German History* 12 (1994), pp. 286–307, and the same author's *Wars of Frederick the Great*, ch. 7. The standard, full-scale, account remains that of Curt Jany, *Geschichte der Königliche Preussischen Armee bis zum Jahre 1807* (Berlin, 1929), III.

[124] This was obviously linked to his efforts after 1763 to assist the nobility to rebuild its economic position: see above, p. 86.

the proportion of non-Prussians in his forces were aided by his army's high reputation after the Seven Years War, though success was incomplete. By 1786 out of a total effective force of around 195,000 men (itself 40,000 more than in 1763) no less than 110,000 were recruited from outwith the Hohenzollern lands, primarily from other German territories.

Behind the extension of hierarchical control over the Prussian army lay a broader purpose. Frederick's experiences during the fighting had convinced him that Prussia's security demanded an enlarged army ready for immediate war: it was henceforth to be maintained as 'a front-loaded military deterrent'.[125] As the King wrote in his 1768 Political Testament, 'This state cannot maintain itself without a large army, [since] we are surrounded by enemies more powerful than ourselves against whom we may at any moment have to defend ourselves.'[126] The Hohenzollern army must be able to intimidate its rivals and, if war broke out, to win early victories, thereby preventing a repetition of the kind of life-and-death struggle which the Seven Years War had become. It was therefore increased in size after the conclusion of peace, in sharp contrast to the reductions evident in the armies of her enemies. During the decade after 1763, the Russian field army was some 20 per cent below wartime levels, while its Austrian counterpart was also scaled down with the ending of fighting. Prussia's army, however, was deliberately expanded, from around 150,000 when the war ended to 187,000 by 1777 and almost 195,000 by the time of Frederick's death.[127]

It was also kept in a higher state of preparedness than the forces of Prussia's enemies. To this end military supplies were stockpiled: by the eve of the War of the Bavarian Succession, Prussian arsenals housed no less than 1,376 recast artillery pieces and a staggering 140,000 muskets, while the magazines contained sufficient grain to feed two armies 70,000-strong for two campaigns.[128] The storage of grain had begun in 1746, and it was vigorously undertaken during the second half of the King's reign. Though these stores could be used to feed the civilian population during periods of dearth, their real purpose was always military. This impressive build-up was accomplished at the cost of severe economising in the army's day-to-day functioning: at times the cavalry was forced to graze its horses, rather than feed them, and to perform its exercises on foot. But it achieved Frederick's aim of raising military preparedness to a wholly new level. That objective was also evident in the determined and successful efforts to create an annual budgetary surplus and in the huge war-chest built up in the *Staatsschatz* as a consequence. By the King's death this was over 51 million *taler*, over twice the figure in 1756 (around 20 million *taler*)

---

[125] Showalter, 'Hubertusburg to Auerstädt', p. 344.

[126] Quoted by Behrens, *Society, Government and the Enlightenment*, p. 36.

[127] Precise figures for the official strength of the armies of the eastern powers are provided by Wilson, *German Armies*. p. 388 n. 94; Dickson, *Finance*, II. Appendix A; John P. LeDonne 'Outlines of Russian Military Administration 1762–1796. Part I: Troop Strength and Deployment', *JGO* NF 31 (1983), pp. 321–47, at p. 322.

[128] Christopher Duffy, *The Army of Frederick the Great* (2nd edn, New York, 1996), p. 311.

and more than six times that in 1740.[129] This remarkable total was clear evidence of the importance Frederick attached to maintaining a cash reserve.

IV

Prussia's army was intended to support and reinforce a foreign policy with one over-riding objective after the Seven Years War: the preservation of peace which, in turn, meant establishing and maintaining good relations with Vienna. Frederick believed that any further fighting would imperil his state's very existence because of its relative weakness. His priorities thus mirrored those of his rival Austria, where Kaunitz explicitly declared that, in order to concentrate upon essential internal reconstruction, good relations must be established with Prussia.[130] Though the fundamental rivalry remained, it had been put into cold storage by the need to restore the domestic bases of their power. This was immediately apparent when diplomatic relations, broken off in autumn 1756, were restored after the Peace of Hubertusburg.

The importance which Frederick now attached to relations with Vienna was evident in the person initially chosen for the mission and in the level at which the post was eventually filled. The King's first choice was one of Prussia's most senior and trusted diplomats, Freiherr Dodo Heinrich zu Inn- und Knyphausen, who had served in France (1754–6) and then in Britain (1758–63).[131] Knyphausen, however, was reluctant to take on a third diplomatic mission and, more importantly, the costs involved, declaring that he had 'eaten up' one estate while in Paris and another in London, and had only one left, which he was anxious to preserve.[132] This exemplified a more general problem. It was an established complaint of all eighteenth-century diplomats that they were poorly and belatedly paid, but it seems as if Prussian representatives suffered most of all in this respect. Money was always in short supply in Frederick's Prussia, and what there was was ruthlessly husbanded by the miserly King; very little found its way into the pockets of those who served abroad.[133] Frederick's personal direction enabled him to economise quite ruthlessly upon his diplomatic service.[134] Salaries and expenses were paid irregularly and seldom completely, and Frederick's subjects were often reluctant to accept diplomatic missions because of the costs involved.[135] Indeed, the King appears to have regarded such service as a form of covert taxation of the nobility.[136] Yet there were

[129] Hubatsch, *Frederick the Great*, pp. 138, 147; cf. above, p. 22, for the earlier total.
[130] 'Denkschriften des Fürsten Kaunitz-Rittberg', ed. Beer, p. 67.
[131] *Pol. Corr.*, XXIII.17; *Repertorium*, II. 296, 297.
[132] Thiébault, *Mes souvenirs*, III. 142–3; AAE CP (Prusse) 71, fos. 163–4.
[133] Thiébault, *Mes souvenirs*, III. 142–3.
[134] A. Schaefer, 'Urkundliche Beiträge zur Geschichte des siebenjährigen Krieges', *Forschungen zur Deutschen Geschichte* 17 (1877), pp. 95–106, for the stringent economies during the Seven Years War.
[135] Cf. Bielfeld, *Institutions Politiques*, II. 75.
[136] See his revealing letter to Minister von Borck, 27 Nov. 1754, *ABB*, X. 122–3.

limits to such impositions, particularly if a state servant was involved. In spring 1763 Knyphausen was permitted to decline the Vienna mission and was instead appointed to an important post in the General Directory: though only after repeated threats to retire altogether from Prussian service.[137]

A senior member of the East Prussian administration, Graf Jakob Friedrich von Rohde, was immediately named envoy extraordinary to Austria.[138] The King's refusal to receive – and thus to send – ambassadors, because of the cost and because of the disputes over rank and ceremonial which he believed would result, was well known.[139] Most Prussian diplomats were given a lowly character, that of resident or secretary of embassy, and pay to match. This highlighted the King's determination to conduct all the major negotiations himself and, as a corollary, his view that Prussian diplomats were primarily appointed to gather information. The fact that Rohde was given the relatively exalted status of envoy extraordinary (only ministers and ministers plenipotentiary outranked him in Prussia's diplomatic service) indicated the importance of his mission in Frederick's eyes. This was also apparent in the fact that he received his instructions in a private interview with the King.[140] Rohde was provided with an experienced secretary of embassy. Though he possessed considerable diplomatic experience, first in the Empire and then in Sweden, he had more recently been a senior administrator and enjoyed the relatively exalted rank of Minister of State.[141] In the first week of August 1763 Prussia's new representative took up his post in Vienna;[142] simultaneously his Austrian counterpart Freiherr Josef von Ried reached Berlin.[143]

The reception accorded Rohde perfectly indicated the *détente*, strengthened as it was by Prussia's promise in the Peace of Hubertusburg to vote for Joseph in the forthcoming election of a King of the Romans. Fêted as he travelled through Habsburg territory, he was welcomed in Vienna with a warmth which was only partially contrived.[144] In particular Kaunitz immediately gave him a long and extremely revealing audience in which, as was his wont, he treated the new arrival to a political tutorial.[145] Behind the formal expressions of Austria's desire to re-establish good relations, the necessity of a period of peace and recovery shone through: as

---

[137] *Pol. Corr.*, XXIII. 23.

[138] Rohde (sometimes spelled 'Rohd') was to serve in Vienna from August 1763 until November 1771: *Repertorium*, III. 324.

[139] See his remarks in 1752: *Die politischen Testamente*, ed. Dietrich, p. 330; cf. F. Masson, ed., 'Berlin il ya cent ans', *Revue d'histoire diplomatique* 5 (1891), pp. 28–65, at pp. 44–5.

[140] *Pol. Corr.*, XXIII. 23. [141] *Repertorium*, II. 294, 298, 299, 301, 307; *Pol. Corr.*, XXIII. 51.

[142] After an unsuccessful attempt to extract payment from the King of the salary he was owed for the period December 1757 until 1762!: *Pol. Corr.*, XXIII. 57–8. After further complaints he eventually received some of the arrears in January 1765, but contined to plead poverty and was permitted to return to Prussia for an extended period in the following year in order to attend to his family finances: see the correspondence in GStAPK Rep. 96.46.G1 and Rep. 96.46.H.

[143] Ried was to be envoy extraordinary and minister plenipotentiary in Berlin from August 1763 until December 1764: *Repertorium*, III. 86. [144] See his despatches for August in GStAPK Rep. 96.46.E

[145] Rohde to Frederick II, 10 Aug. 1763, GStAPK, Rep. 96.46.E.

Frederick did not fail to note.[146] Ried's warm and friendly reception when he arrived at Berlin mirrored that of his Prussian counterpart.[147] Vienna's real desire for peace and even a measure of reconciliation were quite genuine: it was now recognised that no further attempt to recover Silesia could be made until Frederick died.[148] Yet the fundamental hostility remained and was apparent in the shared belief of Maria Theresa and Kaunitz that Vienna's attitude to other states should be governed by their relations with Prussia.[149]

Rohde's early weeks in Vienna were relatively uneventful. He was to prove a diligent but decidedly uninspired diplomat,[150] though even at this early point in his mission his own status as an envoy denied him access to the highest level of Vienna's diplomatic society, which was open only to those with the rank of ambassador.[151] In any case Rohde was at the Habsburg court not to conduct negotiations but to gather information, particularly on Austrian finances and the state of the army, and this he sought to do.[152] Two months after his arrival, however, the death of the Polish King, Augustus III, presented a serious challenge to the peace which had been so recently restored and which was the principal aim of all those states which had fought the Seven Years War. The ubiquitous concern with domestic reconstruction was now challenged by the very real threat of a new war over Poland.

[146] Frederick II to Rohde, 20 Aug. 1763, *Pol. Corr.*, XXIII. 89–90.

[147] *Pol. Corr.*, XXIII. 85–6, 96, 99–100.

[148] Arneth, *GMT*, VIII. 26–7; cf. pp. 541–2 for an extract from Ried's Instructions.

[149] Arneth, *GMT*, VIII. 25.

[150] As the French ambassador was noting a mere fortnight after Rohde's arrival. Châtelet went on to claim that Kaunitz appeared to view the Prussian envoy as a very inconsiderable figure and would, for that reason, conduct relations through Ried: to Praslin, 24 Aug. 1763, AAE CP (Autriche) 295, fos. 223–4. For a later, even more dismissive, verdict by Châtelet see AAE MD (Autriche) 38, fo. 178.

[151] Cf. below, pp. 141–2, for more on this.

[152] His interest in military affairs was evident in his very first despatch: 6 Aug. 1763, GStAPK Rep. 96.46.E.

4

The stabilisation of Europe, 1763–1766

I

In January 1763, the final month of the Seven Years War, the Polish King Augustus III became seriously ill. Though he recovered, his health again worsened in the autumn and he died, on 5 October. His death, unexpected at least in its suddenness, confronted Europe's leading states with a difficult and perhaps dangerous problem little more than six months after peace had been restored. Poland's throne had been elective since the sixteenth century, and vacancies had usually provoked an international crisis and sometimes actual fighting. The last royal election, that of 1733, had been accompanied by a full-scale conflict, the War of the Polish Succession. By the mid-eighteenth century, the country's archaic constitution, weak monarchy and powerful magnate class had made it an arena for great power rivalry. Poland's powerful neighbours had come to support one or more of the noble factions which dominated political life and were anxious for the foreign backing which might enable their own ambitions to be realised.[1]

In 1763, however, all the leading states were exhausted, preoccupied with domestic reconstruction, and therefore reluctant to confront the situation created by Augustus III's death. On hearing the news, Frederick the Great caustically observed that he could not stand the Poles; they were always doing things at the wrong moment.[2] The King's real fear of a new war was widely shared. The early months of peace had been marked by considerable political uncertainty, mingled with caution. Prussia and Russia, the two leading continental powers, were both diplomatically isolated, as was Britain. Among the major states, the only stable alliances were France's treaties with Austria and Spain. The accompanying diplomatic fluidity was to be removed by the events which followed the Polish King's death. Most previous accounts have highlighted the way in which the great powers determined the outcome of the royal election.[3] What has been less studied until now is the Polish interregnum's crucial importance for the future relations of the leading

---

[1] J.T. Lukowski, 'Towards Partition: Polish Magnates and Russian Intervention in Poland during the Early Reign of Stanislaw August Poniatowski', *Historical Journal* 28 (1985), pp. 557–4, esp. pp. 559–64 and 572–74 for this development.

[2] To Prince Henry, 9 Oct. 1763, quoted by Beer, *Erste Theilung Polens*, I. 134.

[3] This is certainly true of what is still the best study of events over Poland in 1763–4, the vintage book of Simon Askenazy, *Die letzte polnische Königswahl* (Göttingen, 1894).

states.[4] Developments following Augustus III's death influenced European alignments until the later 1770s. This was principally because they created the most
important alliance of the post-war period, that between Prussia and Russia, which
would dominate European diplomacy throughout the next fifteen years. Its signature in spring 1764 underlined the interaction between internal reconstruction and
external policy, since the international stability it provided facilitated the widespread preoccupation with domestic reform.

Poland had been ruled since 1697 by the Electoral House of Saxony.[5] The first
Wettin King had been the legendary Augustus the Strong, who had reigned in
Poland as Augustus II (1697–33), and he had been succeeded by his son, Augustus
III (1733–1763). Augustus II had dreamed of creating a new power in central
Europe and tried to establish a viable union, rather than a merely dynastic connec-
tion. His goal had been a consolidated and fully integrated Kingdom of Saxony-
Poland, ruled by the Wettins as hereditary absolute monarchs. Opposition from
Poland's neighbours, above all Russia, and to a lesser extent domestic resistance had
forced Augustus II to abandon his schemes. The idea of a Polish–Saxon union had
died with him. Augustus III instead sought to exploit the Kingdom in the interests
of the Electorate. Poland was a convenient source of revenue for Saxony (whose
public finances were in disarray), and also provided the Wettins with the prestige of
a royal title which exalted them above almost all the other rulers of the Empire.
Augustus III and his advisers governed from Dresden until the Seven Years War
forced them to seek reluctant sanctuary in Warsaw: significantly enough this exile
was the longest unbroken period spent by either Wettin in his Polish lands.[6] The last
Saxon King had in fact spent no more than two out of the first twenty years of his
reign actually in Poland.[7]

Saxon rule had been accompanied by Russia's growing influence and ultimately
domination at Warsaw. Ever since Peter I's reign, Russian rulers had enjoyed the
status of 'protector' of Poland and had not hesitated to intervene to prevent developments which threatened their own interests. Poland's independence and sovereignty were ignored by successive rulers, for whom the perpetuation of this
informal empire was a central aim. During the eighteenth century, St Petersburg
came to regard its western neighbour as a satellite. In 1764 Nikita Panin would
declare that, 'We shall lose a third of our strength and advantages, if Poland does not

---

[4] The principal exception to this generalisation is Frank Spencer, in his edition of *The Fourth Earl of Sandwich: Diplomatic Correspondence 1763–1765* (Manchester, 1961): see esp. pp. 25–42.

[5] Jörg K. Hoensch, *Sozialverfassung und politische Reform: Polen im vorrevolutionären Zeitalter* (Cologne, 1973), and the more recent Jerzy Lukowski, *Liberty's Folly: The Polish-Lithuanian Commonwealth in the Eighteenth Century 1697–1795* (London, 1991), are valuable syntheses, while a distinguished short introduction to the 'The Saxon period, 1697–1763/4' is provided by E. Rostworowski, in S. Kieniewicz, ed., in *History of Poland* (Warsaw, 1968), pp. 272–312. For Saxony, see above, pp. 25–6.

[6] Lukowski, *Liberty's Folly*, p. 175.

[7] W. Konopczynski, 'Later Saxon Period, 1733–1763', in W.F. Reddaway, J.H. Penson, O. Halecki and R. Dyboski, eds., *The Cambridge History of Poland 1697–1935* (Cambridge, 1941), p. 29.

remain dependent on us.'[8] The Kingdom was an invaluable buffer state which protected a long stretch of Russia's exposed western frontier from direct attack yet at
the same time provided easy passage for her own troops as they moved westwards:
it was the glacis which her rulers craved.[9] Its strategic value had been made clear by
the fighting after 1756. After her occupation of East Prussia two years later, Russia
had established a series of forward bases in Great Poland (*Wielkopolska*) in preparation for an attack on the Hohenzollern heartland of Brandenburg.[10] In retaliation,
Frederick had launched raids against these bases, which the Poles had been powerless to prevent. The Seven Years War had made clear the extent to which Poland was
at the mercy of her neighbours. The fighting had also seen an intensification of St
Petersburg's control and marked the origins of an enduring Russian military presence on Polish soil, though this would only become evident in retrospect.

Russia's interests demanded that the Polish King should be responsive to her
pressure, in order that the country be kept weak and divided. Yet Augustus III's
deteriorating health came at an especially inopportune moment for Catherine II.[11]
Her own hold on the throne was not completely secure, the situation at court was
confused, while she also faced urgent and serious domestic difficulties. The new
Empress had had a troubled apprenticeship in foreign policy as Grand Duchess, and
came to power determined to uphold Russia's political independence, which she
believed both Elizabeth and Peter III had failed to do. She therefore wished to secure
her régime at home and avoid commitments abroad.[12] By the early weeks of 1763,
however, it was evident that Russia faced a serious problem in foreign policy.

In mid-February Augustus III's ill-health led Catherine and her closest advisers
to consider their attitude to any vacancy.[13] They were clear that there could be no
question of another Saxon King: the danger of quasi-hereditary monarchy inherent
in a third successive Wettin triumph was certainly appreciated. Publicly, Russia only
declared her preference for a *piast*, i.e. a native-born Pole, and for the exclusion of all
foreign candidates. Privately, Catherine was already determined that the next King
would be her former lover, Stanislas Poniatowski, a middle-ranking Polish nobleman
and member of the powerful and extensive Czartoryski aristocratic lineage, whom
she believed would be an admirable vehicle for continued Russian control.[14] Since

---

[8] J.T. Lukowski, *The Szlachta and the Confederacy of Radom, 1764–1767/68: A Study of the Polish Nobility* (*Antemurale*, XXI; Rome, 1977), p. 33.　　[9] See above, p. 19.
[10] Lukowski, *Liberty's Folly*, p. 175.　　[11] See above, pp. 71–2.
[12] Catherine to Chancellor M.L. Vorontsov, 1 Nov. 1762 OS, Martens, *Recueil des traités*, IX(X). 216; *SIRIO*, XXII. 15–16.
[13] Madariaga, *Russia*, p. 189; Russia's general objectives were made apparent by Panin in a conversation with the Prussian resident, Solms: see his despatch of 22 Feb. 1763, *SIRIO*, XXII. 25–8. For Russian aims in Poland, see more generally, Lukowski, *The Szlachta and the Confederacy of Radom*, pp. 31–45 *passim*.
[14] This had been communicated to Poniatowski in August 1762: Michael F. Metcalf, *Russia, England and Sweden Party Politics 1762–1766: The Interplay between Great Power Diplomacy and Domestic Politics during Sweden's Age of Liberty* (Stockholm and Totowa, NJ, 1977), p. 14. The Empress' reserve candidate was Adam Czartoryski.

his expectations for the throne had been negligible, it was assumed in St Petersburg that he would be especially grateful to his benefactress. To secure his election, the Empress announced her willingness to mobilise 80,000 troops and to spend up to half a million rubles.[15] This decision implied a shift away from Russia's traditional system of alliance with Austria, Saxony and Britain, which was still advocated by Bestuzhev.[16] Instead it made co-operation with Prussia, which Panin was urging, more likely.

The need for international support was certainly recognised. Though Poniatowski's elevation would be a difficult and perhaps dangerous task, the anticipated benefits for Russia were even greater.[17] Foreign intervention had usually accompanied elections and the Saxon royal family were unlikely to renounce the Polish throne without a struggle. Despite the long period of Russian control, the Wettins retained powerful friends in Versailles and Vienna, principally through their skill in concluding dynastic marriages. A Saxon princess was married to Louis XV's son and heir, while Augustus III had himself married a Habsburg, the daughter of the Emperor Joseph I (1705–11). In any Polish election French opposition was to be anticipated. Catherine was particularly afraid that France might use her influence at Constantinople to incite the Ottoman empire to attack Russia: as Choiseul, in fact, attempted unsuccessfully in 1763–4. The spectre of such an attack when Russia was deeply committed in Poland was to be a recurring anxiety for the Empress.[18] Austria would be at best sullenly indifferent, at worst openly antagonistic. A full-scale war could certainly not be ruled out. The previous election had involved Russia in two years' bitter fighting to impose her candidate and memories of this remained alive in St Petersburg.

In the face of this opposition, Russia was dangerously isolated: in contrast to 1733, when she had enjoyed important support from her Habsburg ally. This isolation was a legacy of Peter III's foreign policy. By switching sides during the final stages of the Seven Years War, the Emperor had seriously alienated Russia's traditional ally, Austria, and had also delivered the final blow to the wartime *rapprochement* with France.[19] Catherine II's only potential supporters among the major powers appeared to be Britain and Prussia. The initial British response, when the question of aid in Poland was first raised in the winter of 1762–3, had been discouraging. London was certainly anxious to conclude an alliance, but both now and in the future would not countenance the substantial subsidy Russia was demanding as the price of a formal treaty. Bland expressions of good-will could not disguise Britain's basic indifference to St Petersburg's interests in eastern Europe.[20]

[15] Lukowski, *Liberty's Folly*, p. 178.

[16] At the February meeting, he unsuccessfully argued for the choice of a Saxon prince as Russia's candidate: Soloviev, *History of Russia*, XLIII. 64–5.

[17] *SIRIO*, XLVIII. 216, 242–3, 299–300. On Russian policy in Poland in 1763–4, see more generally Soloviev, *History of Russia*, XLIII. 63–89, 144–78.   [18] E.g. *SIRIO*., XLVIII. 312, 389, 602–3; LI. 24.

[19] See above, p. 45.

[20] For the negotiations in 1762–4, see H.M. Scott, 'Great Britain, Poland and the Russian Alliance, 1763–1767', *Historical Journal* 19 (1976), pp. 62–9.

Prussia appeared to be the most promising source of support, though Frederick the Great was too much of a rival in Poland to be an ideal partner. Co-operation with the King had obvious attractions and these had become evident barely six months after Catherine II's accession. Early in 1763, Prussian support had contributed to the first political success of the Empress' reign: the restoration of Ernst Biron as ruler of the Duchy of Courland and the reimposition of the Russian protectorate.[21] Biron, the favourite of the Empress Anna (1730–40) and the regent for Ivan VI (1740–1) had ruled the Duchy since the 1730s, but in 1741 had been exiled to Siberia when Elizabeth seized power. During the Seven Years War, Augustus III had attempted to transfer Courland, which was technically a Polish fief, to his own son, but this had subsequently been resisted by Peter III. The Duchy was a Protestant salient in the eastern Baltic, but the proposed Wettin ruler was of course Catholic. Shortly after her own accession, Catherine II forced Biron to accept an agreement which made him totally subservient. In spring 1763 he was forcibly restored to the Duchy, which was now completely under Russian influence.

This episode was viewed in St Petersburg as a crucial test of its control over Poland, which would be important when Augustus III finally died.[22] Frederick's formidable military reputation after the Seven Years War could be used to intimidate Russia's opponents, and his state temporarily appeared to be the continent's strongest power. Although Catherine II certainly hoped to secure Prussian support over Poland, she does not seem to have intended to conclude a formal alliance at this time. This was the objective of Panin, who was emerging as the Empress' principal adviser and who believed that Russian security should be based on close co-operation with Frederick.[23] There were, however, influential voices who favoured a restoration of the traditional alliance with Austria, and as yet Panin's predominance was uncertain. It would be difficult for a ruler who had so recently and effectively exploited Russian resentment at Peter III's pro-Prussian policies to conclude an early treaty with Frederick. Catherine's manifesto when she seized power in July 1762 had denounced Prussia as the 'mortal enemy',[24] and immediate alliance negotiations with a state which had been Russia's foe during the Seven Years War were problematical. The Empress, who retained control over Russian diplomacy, clearly appreciated this. Above all, St Petersburg was traditionally suspicious of treaty commitments to foreign powers and this was initially a significant dimension of Catherine II's foreign policy. The Empress' need for support over Poland was balanced by a determination to sign no treaties, at least for the present.

By contrast, Frederick was always determined to secure a formal alliance and viewed the Polish situation entirely in these terms. The King had emerged from the

---

[21] E. Seraphim, *Geschichte Liv-, Est- und Kurlands* (2 vols., Reval, 1895–6), II. 606–30, provides a brief account. Cf. *SIRIO*, XXII. 31, 32–3.

[22] This emerges clearly from *SIRIO*, XLVIII: see esp. pp. 546–50, 552–4.

[23] K. Rahbek Schmidt, 'Wie ist Panins Plan zu einem Nordischen System entstanden?', *Zeitschrift für Slawistik*, 2 (1957), pp. 406–22.

[24] Karl Elias, *Die preussisch-russischen Beziehungen von der Thronbesteigung Peters III. bis zum Abschluss des preussisch-russischen Bündnisses vom 11. April 1764* (Göttingen, 1900), pp. 40–1.

Seven Years War fearful of Russian military power and, even more, political potential, and was convinced that Prussia's future security must be based on a treaty with St Petersburg. He was opposed to links with either Britain or France, believing that these could only involve him in further fighting: he anticipated that a new Anglo-French war might soon break out.[25] The restoration of diplomatic relations with Vienna in summer 1763 would reveal that Prussia's desire for peace was fully shared by the Habsburgs and that a period of good relations was possible.[26] Yet the King recognised that alliance or even reconciliation with Austria was, for the moment, unthinkable. There remained only Russia among the great powers,[27] and he had been seeking her alliance since the closing stages of the Seven Years War. One reason why Frederick had been prepared to support Peter III's planned attack on Denmark in spring 1762, at a time when his own country was exhausted, was his belief that such co-operation would produce a formal treaty. The Russo-Prussian alliance signed in June 1762 had not been ratified before Peter III was swept from the throne and his successor had refused to ratify it. Yet this did not deflect the King from his quest. When a new Prussian agent, Ewald Friedrich Graf von Solms, was sent to St Petersburg in autumn 1762, an alliance was declared to be the only important purpose of his mission.[28] Frederick the Great's conduct during the final winter of the Seven Years War had been designed to improve relations with Catherine II, and as soon as peace had been signed, he began to press for a treaty.

Negotiations formally began in February 1763.[29] The deterioration in Augustus III's health made the Empress more inclined to listen to the Prussian overtures, while the ending of the fighting enabled Frederick to concentrate on securing the prized alliance. The King was content to play a waiting game, confident that St Petersburg's need for support over Poland would produce an agreement sooner or later. This belief was accompanied and reinforced by a conviction that Panin would soon assume the direction of Russian foreign policy and would conclude a treaty.[30] An exchange of personal letters between the two rulers soon confirmed that their priorities in Poland were the same: or, rather, that Catherine's wishes would imme-

---

[25] A particularly strident statement of this concern is in Frederick's letter to Prince Henry, 24 Feb. 1763, *Œuvres*, XXVI. 270. [26] See above, pp. 100–2, for this.

[27] As Frederick subsequently was honest enough to admit: see the Political Testament of 1768, *Die politischen Testamente*, ed. Dietrich, p. 648.

[28] His 'Instructions', dated 20 Sept. 1762, are summarised and partially printed in *Forschungen zur Deutschen Geschichte* 9 (1869), pp. 60–2. Cf. 'Supplément à l'Instruction du Comte de Solms', 29 Sept. 1762, *Pol. Corr.* XXII. 242–3. In addition, Solms had a private interview with the King *en route* to Russia and it seems reasonable to assume that it was primarily concerned with a future alliance, though no formal record of this meeting has apparently survived: *Pol. Corr.*, XXII. 190–1, 194.

[29] The negotiations which led to the treaty of April 1764 are a familiar enough story and only a brief outline is provided here. Elias, *Die preussisch-russischen Beziehungen*, pp. 72 *et seq.*, and Georg Küntzel, 'Friedrich der Grosse am Ausgang des siebenjährigen Krieges und sein Bündnis mit Russlands', *FBPG* 13 (1900), pp. 97 *et seq.*, provide fairly detailed narratives; the best account, if inevitably rather brief, is Koser, *Geschichte Friedrichs des Grossen*, III. 281 *et seq.* The week-to-week progress of discussions can be followed in *SIRIO*, XX (correspondence of Catherine and Frederick) and XXII (reports of the Prussian Minister in St Petersburg), and in *Pol. Corr.*, XXIII. [30] E.g. *SIRIO*, XXII. 11.

diately become Frederick's political objectives. Augustus III's recovery in spring 1763 removed one pressing reason for Russia to sign an alliance, and a prolonged crisis at the Russian court in the summer was a further barrier to negotiations. At this stage, Prussia's King remained confident that a treaty would be concluded, and was repeatedly assured by the Empress that this was so. Substantial progress appeared to be made in August when St Petersburg finally agreed to receive a Prussian draft of a defensive alliance, which was immediately submitted: within a month Frederick was confidently proclaiming that a treaty was 'near enough'.[31] In view of the King's remarkable willingness to allow Catherine to dictate its terms, and the repeated assurances he received that the treaty project would soon be returned, his optimism appeared justified.

During the next few months, however, this confidence was to be steadily eroded by Russia's failure to return the Prussian draft. The precise reasons for this hiatus are unclear. Though any diplomacy at St Petersburg was likely to involve impenetrable delays, the period when the Prusso-Russian negotiations were stalled saw considerable activity, if not actual progress, in parallel Russo-British discussions. This suggests there was more to it than ordinary dilatoriness. The delay probably reflects Catherine II's continuing desire to avoid signing any formal alliance.[32] While it may be that Russia always intended to ally with Prussia, the Empress was determined to dictate the timing and the terms of any agreement. For his part, the King was increasingly concerned at the lack of progress and sceptical about the sincerity of the assurances he continued to receive. Frederick was all too aware that while he was Catherine II's political partner, he was not yet her formal ally. These anxieties were increased when it became apparent that developments over Poland were undermining his whole diplomatic strategy. Augustus III's death early in October, far from forming the expected alliance, seemed likely to deprive him of any such treaty.

Frederick's problem had always been how to turn Russia's need for support into an actual alliance. This was why he had been so willing to concur with Catherine's wishes. He had always assumed that, when the Polish King died, the Empress would have to sign a treaty to secure his support. The Prussian King's uncharacteristic patience during the spring and summer of 1763 sprang from his conviction that in all probability nothing could be done until Augustus III died. His immediate response to this event was to declare that the time was ripe for a determined attempt to conclude the alliance.[33] It clearly indicated his expectations but, little more than a month later, Frederick was beginning to realise that a treaty might well slip through his fingers.[34]

---

[31] *Pol. Corr.*, XXIII. 112. For the Russian response to the receipt of the treaty-project promising a reply 'soon', see *SIRIO*, XLVIII. 599.

[32] See, e.g., the Empress' remarks to Keyserling in late July: *SIRIO*, XLVIII. 550–1.

[33] Frederick to Solms, 11 Oct. 1763, *Pol. Corr.*, XXIII. 145; 'Unterredung des Königs mit dem Etatsminister Graf Finckenstein', 20 Oct. 1763, *Pol. Corr.*, XXIII. 152.

[34] For his attitude in the weeks after Augustus III's death, see *Pol. Corr.*, XXIII. 141 *et seq.*

This was principally because events over Poland proved less threatening than Catherine II had feared. Even the Ottoman empire seemed unlikely to intervene actively, though Russia remained anxious on this point.[35] The Empress' concerns about Austria and France were soon reduced, though they did not disappear altogether. The ill-will of both states was evident, but their exhaustion and fear of a new war were pre-eminent and neither was willing to oppose Poniatowski's election actively. Both at Versailles and in Vienna a desire to remain at peace soon overcame sympathy for the Saxon cause and hostility to growing Russian control in Poland. Catherine was correct to judge that Choiseul was her enemy, at Warsaw as elsewhere. But she did not fully appreciate that France was exhausted and all but bankrupt, and in any case had new priorities.[36] The Polish election of 1763–4 made clear that Louis XV's leading minister was concentrating on preparations for a future war against Britain and would not, for the moment, pursue an active policy in eastern Europe. Choiseul recognised France's diminished influence in Poland and was unwilling to spend her scanty financial resources on electioneering, especially when the prospects were so poor. Though he saw the risk of a subsequent partition, he believed the established rivalry of her neighbours would prevent this. Choiseul all along seems to have recognised that Russia could only be successfully opposed by direct military intervention, which was unthinkable. In May 1763, French policy when Augustus III should die had been laid down in a memoir approved by the King's council.[37] France, this declared, would not intervene in a Polish election but pursue what had earlier been described as 'une système de neutralité et d'indifférence'.[38] This was exactly the policy pursued after Augustus III's death.

There remained the question of France's traditional links with the Wettins and the *dauphin*'s marriage to a Saxon princess. When Augustus III died, Choiseul immediately announced that France wanted to see a free election, which revealed that the French would play no direct part, and also voiced his hopes that a Saxon candidate might be successful. The declaration went on to express the wish that Poland's territorial integrity would be respected; the spectre of annexations by her powerful neighbours, above all Russia, was already worrying French observers. There was also the question of the *secret*'s attitude which, unusually, proved to be almost identical to official French diplomacy. Louis XV gave verbal backing to Prince Xavier, who was the favourite brother of the *dauphin*'s wife and became the Saxon candidate upon the death in December 1763 of the new Elector, Frederick Christian. But the King's pacifism and dread of a new war, together with his

---

[35] See, in particular, the analysis of A.M. Obreskov (Russian resident in Constantinople) of the Ottoman reactions and Panin's response: *SIRIO*, LI. 140–2. Cf. *SIRIO*, LI. 173–4, for Russian concessions in a dispute with the Porte, with the intention of cultivating Ottoman good-will because of the critical situation in Poland.

[36] The French attitude is examined by H.M. Scott, 'France and the Polish Throne, 1763–1764', *Slavonic and East European Review* 53 (1975), pp. 370–88, on which the following discussion is based.

[37] It was drawn up by Praslin and is printed in duc de Broglie, *Le secret du roi* (2 vols., Paris, 1879), II. 73–82. [38] Praslin to Breteuil, 12 Oct. 1762, *SIRIO*, CXL. 93.

appreciation of France's own reduced standing in Polish politics, led him also to favour abstention. In this way, France's official and *secret* diplomacies converged. Both accepted that there was little or nothing they could do in practice to influence the forthcoming election. On the other hand, French ill-will was considerable and Choiseul sought unsuccessfully to incite the Ottoman empire to intervene in Poland.[39] France's leading minister was reduced – now and during the rest of his ministry – to opposing Russia by proxy: exactly as had been done during the era of the *barrière de l'est*.

France also ignored Vienna's repeated pleas for her to act over Poland or to subsidise any opposition which might emerge. Austria was even more hostile to Catherine II's growing influence and to the emerging axis between Russia and the Habsburgs' arch-enemy, Prussia.[40] Vienna's own interest in Poland was considerable. Austria had a long common frontier and this had always led her to watch developments there particularly closely. There were also established links between the Habsburg court and the Wettin family, and Maria Theresa made no secret of her personal support for a Saxon candidate. Austria was the sole Catholic state among the eastern powers and naturally backed a dynasty which had converted to secure the Polish throne. Kaunitz's attitude was dictated by purely political considerations, however, and proved to be decisive. He disliked the emerging Russo-Prussian protectorate and also feared that the new partners might accompany the election of a King by making territorial gains at Poland's expense. This would further tilt the balance of power in central Europe against the Habsburgs and would also advance Russian influence westwards. Austrian policy was dictated, however, by the absolute necessity of avoiding a further war. This was why, in summer 1763, Vienna made clear to St Petersburg that it would not intervene in any future election, and would expect the Poles themselves to choose their next King.[41] Kaunitz's reaction to Augustus III's death was to declare that Poland now lay in Russia's hands.[42] The kind of armed intervention which alone might prevent Russia and Prussia imposing their candidate was unthinkable immediately after the burdensome and destructive Seven Years War. Without powerful outside support, Austria could play no part. The formula in which this impotence was expressed was identical to that employed by France. On 10 October 1763, less than a week after Augustus III's death, a circular despatch to Habsburg diplomats announced Vienna's attitude to the vacancy: this blended hopes for a free election and verbal support for the Saxon candidate with fears for Poland's territorial integrity and a frank acknowledgement that Austria could do little to prevent Poniatowski becoming King.[43]

---

[39] For these efforts, see L. Bonneville de Marsangy, *Le Chevalier de Vergennes: son ambassade à Constantinople* (2 vols., Paris, 1894), II. 224–59, and Murphy, *Vergennes*, pp. 143–50. France used the phantom of a later marriage between Catherine II and Poniatowski and a subsequent political union between Russia and Poland, in this attempt to alarm the Porte.

[40] Askenazy, *Die letzte polnische Königswahl*, pp. 24–5, 30–3, sketches Vienna's attitude, while Arneth, *GMT*, VIII. 28–92, provides a fuller analysis.   [41] *SIRIO*, XXII. 89.   [42] Arneth, *GMT*, VIII. 51.

[43] Arneth, *GMT*, VIII. 35–6.

The inability of France and Austria to oppose Russia actively reduced Catherine II's anxieties, though she still feared Ottoman intervention. The Empress was also assisted by the waning fortunes of the Saxon ruling family, whose hopes of effective international support were soon dashed. Without it, the Wettins were unlikely to secure election, especially in view of the outright opposition of Russia and Prussia. The ending of the dynastic union with Poland was a decisive moment for Saxony, whose diminished resources forced her to scale down her ambitions. The new Elector, Frederick Christian, realistically sought a *rapprochement* with Frederick the Great, though the extent of this was limited because the King's intended ally, Russia, was now hostile towards Dresden. A further blow was the unexpected death of Frederick Christian at the end of December. His heir was only thirteen, and his widow assumed control in the Electorate, while his oldest surviving brother, Prince Xavier, briefly became Dresden's new candidate. Xavier's appeals for international support also went unheeded. The brave words and good wishes he received from Vienna and Versailles were no match for the Russian troops who were beginning to move into Poland. He therefore withdrew from the contest early in 1764. Subsequently, Saxony was to give her support to the aged Grand Hetman, Branicki, who was Poland's ruler during the interregnum and who emerged as an actual candidate for the throne when it became clear that only a *piast* would be elected. Dresden's hope was that, on his death, a Wettin restoration might be possible.

By early 1764 it was clear that the regency government in Saxony could take no active part in the Polish election. Henceforth the Electorate's fate was to be that of all minor states, particularly one located so close to the powerful Prussian monarchy. Saxony was to be a pawn in the relations of the great powers during the 1760s and 1770s.[44] Her passivity over the Polish election further strengthened Russia's position, though Catherine II's belief that Poniatowski's imposition might be less hazardous than she had feared was based principally on the attitudes of Austria and France. Their passive stance encouraged the Empress' hope that her candidate might triumph without the formal Prussian alliance which Panin contined to recommend.[45] This remained her view at least until the end of 1763. Catherine's confidence was evident in the lack of progress in her negotiations with Prussia, and it was apparent to Frederick.

The King rightly concluded that there would be no fighting over Poland, that Russia would impose her candidate and therefore would not be forced into an immediate alliance.[46] Underlying and reinforcing this analysis was his innate distrust of St Petersburg's intentions and his fear that Austria would always be a more natural

[44] O. Schulze, *Die Beziehungen zwischen Kursachsen und Friedrich dem Grossen nach dem Siebenjährigen Krieg bis zum Bayrischen Erbfolgekriege* (Jena, 1933), pp. 4–5, 28–9, and chs. 1–5 *passim*.
[45] Soloviev, *History of Russia*, XLIII. 84.
[46] *Pol. Corr.*, XXIII. 141 *et seq*. An important series of despatches from Rohde in Vienna, before and after Augustus III's death, confirmed Austria's financial weakness, preoccupation with the forthcoming election of Joseph as King of the Romans, and therefore powerlessness over Poland: 3 Sept., 12 and 15 Oct. and 19 Nov. 1763, all in GStAPK Rep. 96.46.F.

ally for Russia.[47] He was uncomfortably aware of the extent to which, in his rush to support Catherine II, he had already committed himself in advance of any treaty and in this way effectively removed her need for a formal agreement. During the second half of November, however, Frederick produced a new and inventive strategy. By skilfully exploiting the opportune presence in Berlin of an Ottoman diplomat, Ahmed Resmi Efendi, he convinced St Petersburg that nothing less than an improbable Prusso-Ottoman alliance was on the point of being concluded.[48]

This first Ottoman embassy to Berlin took place at the end of a decade during which there had been a significant improvement in relations. The potential value to Prussia of an alliance with Constantinople was obvious: in any war against Austria, the threat of an Ottoman attack on Hungary would seriously compromise Habsburg strategy.[49] It was why, during the desperate struggle for survival after 1756, Frederick had pursued such links and in 1761 had actually concluded a treaty of friendship and commerce. Ahmed Resmi's mission was ostensibly the conventional follow-up to the Prusso-Ottoman agreement. At this period there was some interest in a full political alliance in Constantinople, but rather less in Potsdam. Frederick had been disillusioned about the Ottoman empire's value as an ally by its failure – as he unreasonably viewed it – to come to Prussia's aid in 1761–2,[50] and he was in any case determined to conclude an alliance with Russia. Negotiations with the Sultan were always a useful means of putting pressure on Austria, particularly at a moment when Vienna's own truce with the Porte which dated from 1739 was about to expire.[51] In the closing weeks of 1763, however, such discussions came to play the crucial role in his quest for a Russian alliance.

St Petersburg had been anxious about Ahmed Resmi's mission long before he reached Berlin.[52] Its representative in Constantinople had procured a copy of his Instructions, which revealed the Porte's interest in a Prussian alliance, and forwarded these to his superiors.[53] Russia was in any case worried about potential Ottoman intervention over the Polish election and, even before the embassy reached Berlin, had ordered her own representative there to dissuade Frederick from any alliance. The unusually warm welcome which Ahmed Resmi received during the second half of November and December 1763 and, in particular, his extended stay with the King at Potsdam – a privilege accorded to very few diplomats – suggested

[47] Wolfgang Stribrny, *Die Russlandpolitik Friedrichs des Grossen (1764–1786)* (Würzburg, 1966), pp. 28, 36.

[48] For the decisive Ottoman dimension, see Virginia H. Aksan, *An Ottoman Statesman in War and Peace: Ahmed Resmi Efendi 1700–1783* (Leiden, 1995), pp. 65–99, and H.M. Scott, 'Frederick II, the Ottoman Empire and the Origins of the Russo-Prussian Alliance of April 1764', *European Studies Review* 7 (1977), pp. 153–75, on which the following account is based.

[49] This was why there had been tentative Prusso-Ottoman contacts during the 1740s.

[50] See, e.g., his savage comments to Finckenstein, 9 Sept. 1762, *Pol. Corr.*, XXII. 204–5.

[51] This may have been Frederick's initial intention over Ahmed Resmi's embassy: see, e.g., the King's despatch to Rohde, 24 Aug. 1763, GStAPK Rep. 96.46.E.   [52] *SIRIO*, XLVIII. 627–8, 634; LI. 22–4.

[53] *SIRIO*, XLVIII. 626–7. This account of Ahmed Resmi's instructions corresponds with the summary of these provided by Hammer, *Histoire de l'empire Ottoman*, XVI. 116–17.

that serious alliance negotiations were in progress: which was, of course, exactly what Frederick intended. The discussions with the Ottoman diplomat were deliberately shrouded in secrecy. Though a treaty-project was given to Ahmed Resmi it was deliberately made unacceptable by including Austrian wars with Prussia while excluding a conflict between Russia and the Ottoman empire.[54] The appearance of alliance negotiations was what mattered to Frederick, not their content. This impression was strengthened by Resmi's reception at the Prussian court, where extreme parsimony usually prevailed: Andrew Mitchell commented, with lingering incredulity, on 'the great distinctions that are here paid to the Turkish Internonce'.[55] Prince Henry gave a ball in Ahmed Resmi's honour; a special meeting of the Berlin Academy was held to welcome him; while he was also permitted to attend manoeuvres by the Prussian army.

Simultaneously, the King increased the diplomatic pressure on Russia. Though privately convinced there would be no war over Poland, Frederick repeatedly expressed his concern to the Russian government that the forthcoming election was a real threat to peace.[56] As part of the same general strategy of intimidation he eagerly spread exaggerated rumours of Austrian mobilisation with the clear intention that these would reach Catherine II.[57] At the same time – belatedly and quite cynically discovering the scruple that Prussia had no legal basis for interference in Poland – the King made it very clear indeed that he would give Russia no further support at Warsaw until an alliance had been concluded.[58] The message conveyed by these various stratagems was the corollary of the reception given to Ahmed Resmi.

Russia was represented in Berlin by Prince Vladimir Sergeevic Dolgorukov, a diplomatic novice who had taken up his post – his first mission – in the previous February and was inexperienced in the by-ways of the Prussian capital and of diplomacy.[59] He was quite unable to penetrate the web of deceit spun by Frederick, and his patently naïve reports further alarmed observers in St Petersburg. Fear of Ottoman involvement in Poland was central to Russian policy; the Empress came to believe that there was no alternative to a treaty with Prussia. Her reluctance to sign a formal alliance was overcome less by her need for support in Poland than by her anxiety that a treaty between the Ottoman empire and Prussia might frustrate her schemes. While in retrospect it may appear surprising that Russia should have believed that such an improbable union would be concluded, at the time Catherine

[54] *Pol. Corr.*, XXIII. 201–2.
[55] To Sandwich, 24 Dec. 1763, PRO SP 90/82, fo. 406, a view which contrasted sharply with his earlier emphasis on the surly way in which Prussian ministers accepted the necessity of the embassy. For Ahmed Resmi's own account of the way he was fêted in Berlin, see Aksan, *An Ottoman Statesman*, pp. 88–90.   [56] *Pol. Corr.*, XXIII. 226, 230, 234.   [57] *Pol. Corr.*, XXIII. 210, 213.
[58] See especially Frederick II to Solms, 23 Dec. 1763, *SIRIO*, XXII. 175–80.
[59] For his inexperience, see *SIRIO*, LI. 22–4; PRO SP 90/82, fos. 369–70. Once the treaty had been signed, Dolgorukov read it out in its entirety (including the secret article on Poland!) to Mitchell: Soloviev, *History of Russia*, XLIII. 165.

and Panin were forced to take the King's posturing seriously because of the errone-ous reports which they were receiving from Berlin. Indeed, by mid-January 1764 the Russian government actually believed a draft treaty had been signed.[60] Reports from Poland were beginning to suggest that the extent of opposition there was rather greater than Russia had anticipated, while Catherine and Panin both believed that Frederick's support was essential if Poniatowski were to be elected. They there-fore concluded that they had no alternative to concluding a formal treaty.[61]

Alliance with Prussia was, as Frederick had always intended, the price of Russian success in Poland, though the exact route to an agreement was different from that initially anticipated. Negotiations were resumed towards the end of January 1764, when the Prussian treaty-project of the previous August was resurrected, amended by the Empress and her leading minister, and given to Solms.[62] The path to the final alliance was remarkably smooth.[63] Prussia's King was not about to throw away his hard-earned triumph by haggling over detailed terms: what mattered was the sig-nature of the treaty, not the fine print of its clauses. The modifications which Frederick requested to the Russian counter-project were therefore so trifling that St Petersburg readily agreed to them. By early spring the definitive treaty was ready for signature, and this duly took place in St Petersburg on 11 April 1764. The Russo-Prussian agreement was a conventional defensive alliance, initially to last for eight years.[64] Both rulers promised assistance if the other were to be attacked. In the case of an Ottoman offensive against Russia, or an invasion of Frederick's Rhineland territories, such aid could be restricted to a subsidy, a provision which clearly favoured Prussia. The two states also pledged themselves in effect to main-tain the weakness and division of Poland by upholding the existing constitutional arrangements, and also to defend the Swedish Constitution of 1720, with its severe restrictions on monarchical power.[65] A separate, secret convention provided for joint action to secure Poniatowski's election as King of Poland.[66] It was accom-plished in September 1764, when this co-operation decided the issue at Warsaw. Both the Polish nobility and the other European powers accepted, especially after the formal Russo-Prussian alliance, that they could do nothing to challenge St Petersburg's candidate. The various stages in the election were now carried through. The limited Polish opposition which emerged was easily overcome and on 6 September, under the shadow of Russian bayonets, Stanislas Poniatowski was duly elected King.[67]

---

[60] *SIRIO*, LI. 176–8, on the basis of an erroneous report from Dolgorukov. This probably referred to the treaty-project given to Ahmed Resmi.   [61] *SIRIO*, LI. 142, 174, 177, 259.
[62] *Pol. Corr.*, XXIII. 273.
[63] Elias, *Die preussisch-russischen Beziehungen*, pp. 106 *et seq.*, provides an account of these negotiations.
[64] It is printed in Martens, *Recueil des traités*, VI. 11–25.
[65] Sweden's importance for the diplomacy of these years is analysed below, pp. 129–36.
[66] Printed in Martens, *Recueil des traités*, VI. 25–33.
[67] Askenazy, *Die letzte polnische Königswahl*, pp. 97–131, provides a convenient account of the election's final stages.

The election was saluted by contemporaries as the most peaceful in Poland's history. The threat of a general European war had evaporated, as the desire for peace everywhere neutralised hostility towards Catherine and her new ally. Success in Poland set the seal on the Russo-Prussian treaty. Both partners judged they had gained considerably from its conclusion. The Empress had secured important support over the election, and believed she had averted a projected alliance linking Berlin and Constantinople. It would be several years before the high cost of Russia's triumph, the acceptance of the Prussian King's almost equal influence in Poland, would become evident. This was something which Frederick deliberately sought. In 1763–4 the King, who was the target of Protestant appeals for support, was careful to secure Russia's agreement to his right to intervene to protect Poland's religious dissidents. In this way he secured leverage in Polish affairs which would be important in the years to come.[68] For the time being, King Stanislas Augustus (as he now became) reigned in Warsaw, and St Petersburg's continuing control seemed to have been assured. Within several years, however, the intrinsic instability of these arrangements in Poland would become clear.[69]

Frederick had gained even more than Catherine. Though Prussia was clearly the weaker partner,[70] the King had secured his primary objective: a defensive alliance with Russia. During the second half of 1763, St Petersburg had hoped to avoid a definite choice between Prussia and Austria as an ally, but this had proved impossible.[71] Russia might well have concluded a treaty with Frederick II eventually, and this was certainly Panin's goal. Any such alliance, however, would have been on terms laid down by the Empress. The Prussian King's skilful exploitation of the situation in Poland, together with his willingness to make concessions when these were necessary, secured a treaty on the basis of strict reciprocity. This imparted an aura of political equality to the alliance, which was not fully justified by the relative strengths and weaknesses of the two signatories, but which would only slowly dissolve. Frederick's skilful exploitation of Russia's temporary need of Prussian support successfully disguised his own fundamental weakness and concealed the basic fact that he had far more to gain. Though Austria was, for the moment, pacific, she was still a more formidable opponent for Prussia than the Ottoman empire was for Russia, and the King had secured a Russian alliance to guard against the Habsburg threat. He rightly believed that this would deter Vienna from attacking him, since Catherine II now held the balance of power between the two German rivals. The King was, at first, to be the leading spirit in the partnership. By the later 1760s, however, Russia had gained in strength and self-confidence and Catherine II slowly assumed the dominant role. This was facilitated by a deliberate attempt by St Petersburg to damp down Prusso-Austrian antagonism, which was already muted after 1763, and to establish an independent position for Russia between the

---

[68] *SIRIO*, XXII. 129–30, 257–8 and 310–11. For Frederick's use of this, see below, pp. 177–8.
[69] See below, pp. 174–82, for developments after Poniatowski's election.
[70] Cf. Stribrny, *Die Russlandpolitik*, pp. 16–17. [71] Madariaga, *Russia*, p. 192.

two German powers.[72] The success of this strategy inevitably weakened Frederick's position within the alliance.

The extended period of peace which Frederick deemed essential, in order to repair the ravages of the Seven Years War, appeared to be guaranteed by the alliance. Prussia's possession of Silesia and her new status as a great power were also apparently confirmed by this treaty, which understandably aroused considerable fear and anxiety in Vienna.[73] It was a reaction which the King took every opportunity to reinforce. In June 1764 when the Russo-Prussian agreement was formally communicated to Austria, Frederick went out of his way to see that Kaunitz was given a copy of the entire treaty, including the secret article concerning Poland and Poniatowski's election, rather than the summary of its provisions which would have been more conventional.[74] His clear intention was to leave the Chancellor in no doubt as to the real political advantages Prussia had secured little more than a year after the Peace of Hubertusburg.

These were in any case quite apparent to Kaunitz. The Russo-Prussian treaty decisively affected the third eastern power, reinforcing the most important legacies of the Seven Years War for Habsburg foreign policy. It strengthened Vienna's dependence upon its French alliance and underlined that, for the foreseeable future, Russia was not a potential ally, while simultaneously making clear that St Petersburg was now the key to Austro-Prussian rivalry. It also reinforced the Chancellor's pacific outlook. Prussia's success in securing the alliance made a new war even more unthinkable, since the 1764 treaty would bring Russian aid if Frederick were to be attacked. This was exactly the same calculation which the King himself made in reverse. International relations in eastern Europe, like Kaunitz's own political horizon, were to be dominated between 1764 and 1781 by the Russo-Prussian alignment. It ensured that France was Vienna's only possible ally among the great powers. External circumstances thus reinforced his own established preference to make the French alliance the basis of his post-war foreign policy and the very 'foundation of the Monarchy's security'.[75]

This alignment was not without its difficulties and tensions. It tied Vienna to a state which had been defeated both in Europe and overseas, with enduring damage to its international standing.[76] Nevertheless, the French treaty long remained central to Austria's foreign policy.[77] Though it had failed to produce victory over

---

[72] Scharf, *Katharina II.*, p. 274.
[73] Stribrny, *Die Russlandpolitik*, p. 11; Rohde to Frederick II, 23 May 1764, GStAPK Rep. 96.46.F1.
[74] Rohde to Frederick II, 9 June 1764, GStAPK Rep. 96. 46.F1.
[75] This was the description of the shrewd and well-informed Sardinian minister in Vienna, Count Canale: see his despatch of 20 June 1764, quoted by Ada Ruata, *Luigi Malabaila di Canale: Riflessi della cultura illuministica in un diplomatico piemontese* (Deputazione subalpina di Storia Patria, Turin, 1968), p. 188.   [76] See above, pp. 55–65.
[77] One of the best guides to the Chancellor's post-war diplomatic strategy and France's place within it is the immensely detailed and wide-ranging Instructions for the new ambassador in London, Seilern, 3 Sept. 1763, HHStA England-Korrespondenz 109.

Prussia, Kaunitz remained personally devoted to the new alliance which he always regarded as his political masterpiece. As Canale emphasised, 'it is his [Kaunitz's] achievement; he idolises it, and congratulates himself on having by this striking success changed the political face of Europe'.[78] The Chancellor continued to advance his established arguments in its support: that it enabled the Monarchy to concentrate upon its principal enemy, Prussia, and that it protected outlying Habsburg possessions in the Italian Peninsula and the southern Netherlands from French expansion.[79] Within the Empire the Franco-Austrian alliance did something to reduce French opposition to Vienna, but the *détente* with Prussia did rather more to strengthen the Habsburg position there. Austria's French connection also produced some income, in the form of subsidy arrears from the Seven Years War, and this was far from negligible when Habsburg finances were in a very poor state.[80]

It soon became clear, however, that his ally's policies threatened the continuation of peace, which was Kaunitz's central aim. The main difficulty was Choiseul's aggressive attitude and seemingly bellicose intent. Though France now intended to fight Britain overseas, while neutralising the continent, this was little reassurance. Observers in Vienna appreciated that Britain's continuing naval superiority might force the French monarchy after early defeats to seek to recover lost ground in Europe, where George III's Electorate of Hanover would be a tempting target. In this way, Austria through the 1756 treaty might be drawn into new Franco-British hostilities on the continent.[81] Choiseul's actions certainly appeared threatening when viewed from a Habsburg perspective. Under his energetic leadership, France was preparing for a war of revenge, and by the mid-1760s she was adopting a belligerent tone in a series of colonial disputes. In fact, this aggression was more apparent than real: France's hostility towards Britain was undoubted, but her ability to fight and win was less evident.[82] The essential moderation of French policy, and its complex nuances, however, were not fully appreciated in Vienna, and consequently Choiseul's actions aroused apprehension there. This was to be increased by the active anti-Russian strategy launched by the duc in 1766.[83] Despite these concerns Austria's foreign policy after the Seven Years War rested upon her French alliance, a dependence which was strengthened by the Russo-Prussian treaty.

Kaunitz had feared such an axis ever since the reversal of St Petersburg's policy

---

[78] Ruata, *Canale*, pp. 188–9.
[79] See his 'Anmerkungen über dermahliges Staatssytem des Wiener Hofes', 27 Sept. 1764, printed in 'Denkschriften des Fürsten Wenzel Kaunitz-Rittberg', ed. Beer, pp. 63–74, esp. pp. 63–5. Kaunitz's views are, for the most part, followed by Joseph II in the foreign policy sections of the 'Tableau Générale', finalised in March–April 1768: HHStA Familienarchiv Sammelbände 88, fos. 118–244; cf. Beales, *Joseph II*, pp. 273–7.
[80] For the importance Kaunitz attached to them, see his letter to Starhemberg (ambassador in France), 13 May 1763, HHStA Frankreich 125, fos. 71–3; for the settlement reached in October of that year and its subsequent implementation, Dickson, *Finance*, II. 174–84 *passim*.
[81] See Joseph II's later comments: 'Tableau générale', HHStA Familienarchiv Sammelbände 88, fo. 127. This anxiety had been heightened by the danger of an Anglo-Bourbon war in 1766.
[82] See below, pp. 165–6. [83] See below, pp. 168–73.

during the closing stages of the Seven Years War. Though Peter III's treaty with Frederick had not been ratified by his successor, the Chancellor had been concerned that Catherine II might ally with Prussia.[84] His attitude to the Polish election assumed co-operation between the two other eastern powers, which he recognised Vienna was powerless to oppose. The formal alliance, communicated to Austria in June 1764, signalled that St Petersburg had ceased to be a potential ally. The intensity of Russo-French hostility during the first decade of peace ensured that this would be so. Russia and France could not simultaneously be Austria's allies, as the Chancellor recognised, and after 1763–4 he believed there was no prospect of a Russian treaty and no alternative to a French alliance. This reinforced one further consequence of St Petersburg's change of rulers at the end of the Seven Years War. During the preceding generation Austria's ally in eastern Europe had been Russia, whose role in the anti-Prussia coalition had increased as the war progressed. Russia's withdrawal in 1762 and signature of a Prussian alliance two years later moved her decisively out of Austria's political orbit.

Kaunitz's own attitude at this point remains problematical.[85] Whereas Maria Theresa's hostility towards Russia and especially her ruler was considerable and Joseph's interest in a future alliance was real, the Chancellor's approach was much more ambiguous. He certainly appreciated the political potential of a Russian alliance. During the debates in 1749 over the future direction of Habsburg policy, he had emphasised the permanent value of such links and – as with his approach to the French alliance – this attitude was enduring.[86] In April 1763 he described Russia as Austria's most useful and natural ally, though he admitted that no treaty could be signed for the present.[87] The Seven Years War had underlined Russia's military potential and simultaneously increased her power to a point where it rivalled the Habsburg Monarchy: during the later 1760s and 1770s this challenge would be particularly serious in south-eastern Europe. A desire to keep Russia at a distance and therefore to maintain Poland's territorial integrity were one dimension of the Chancellor's attitude. He also questioned the stability of Catherine II's régime, and this concern was increased by the exaggerated reports he was receiving from

---

[84] E.g. AAE CP (Autriche) 294, fos. 245–55.

[85] There are relatively few explicit statements on this theme by the Chancellor during the early years of peace. It is striking that Russia is not even mentioned in the best-known and most valuable memoir on post-war foreign policy: 'Denkschriften des Fürsten Wenzel Kaunitz-Rittberg', ed. Beer, pp. 63–74. The problem is compounded by the fact that the Austrian diplomatic correspondence from St Petersburg for this period, printed in *SIRIO* vols. XLVI and CIX, included only the reports from the Russian court (*Berichte*) and excluded the instructions (*Weisungen*) drawn up by the Chancellor. The principal source for his policy is the material in Arneth, *GMT*, VIII, chs. 2–7 *passim*. A comprehensive modern study of Austro-Russian relations during and after the Seven Years War, based on the abundant archival material, is badly needed.

[86] *Aufzeichnungen des Grafen William Bentinck über Maria Theresias*, ed. Adolf Beer (Vienna, 1871), pp. xlvii–lxix (which prints substantial extracts from Kauniz's famous memorandum); Alfred Ritter von Arneth, 'Biographie des Fürsten Kaunitz: Ein Fragment', *AÖG* 88 (1899), pp. 1–201, at pp. 168–9.

[87] Arneth, *GMT*, VIII. 24.

Austria's representative in St Petersburg.[88] The final element in Kaunitz's diplomatic strategy was a wish to do nothing which might impede an eventual *rapprochement*.[89] While the Russo-Prussian treaty made this, for the present, unthinkable, he appreciated that the political fault lines which increasingly separated the two halves of Europe had made Russia the arbiter between the two German powers. Any restoration of Austria's international position, which remained the Chancellor's eventual aim, would only be possible in partnership with Catherine II and, in the early years of peace, he did what he could to ensure that the lines to St Petersburg remained open.[90] For the present, however, Austria's foreign policy was based upon her French alliance, a preference which had been strengthened by Frederick's success in securing the crucial treaty with Russia.

II

The Russo-Prussian alliance was decisive in a second and more important way for international stability. The future orientation of St Petersburg's diplomacy was made clear by developments over Poland. Throughout the first year of Catherine II's reign, disagreements over foreign policy had been integral to the confused court politics. The main division was between advocates of a return to Russia's traditional alliance with Austria and spokesmen for co-operation with Prussia. The first group were headed by the ageing minister of the Empress Elizabeth, A.P. Bestuzhev-Riumin (whom Catherine had recalled to favour), and by the Chancellor, M.L. Vorontsov; while Nikita Panin was the principal advocate of links with Frederick II. This was part of a larger struggle for influence and power at the beginning of Catherine II's reign. A crucial stage was reached in late July 1763 when Vorontsov was given leave to travel abroad for two years, a thinly disguised way of dismissing him.[91] Augustus III's death finally clarified St Petersburg's future foreign policy and who would shape it in co-operation with the Empress. At an informal meeting of Catherine's closest advisers on 17 October, Bestuzhev made a final attempt to commit Russia to co-operation with Austria and support for a Saxon candidate in Poland.[92] Both proposals were anathema to the Empress, convinced of the implacable hostility of Vienna's ally France and determined to impose Poniatowski. It marked the effective end of Bestuzhev's influence. Less than a month later, Panin was appointed senior member of the College of Foreign Affairs, which had been set

---

[88] These are printed in *SIRIO*, XLVI and CIX.   [89] AAE CP (Autriche) 294, fo. 68.

[90] See the comments of the French ambassador, Châtelet, in Aug. 1765: AAE CP (Autriche) 303, fo. 68.

[91] *SIRIO*, XLVIII. 554–5. M.L. Vorontsov had remained loyal to Peter III at least until the *coup* of 1762 and his niece had been the Emperor's mistress, two circumstances which made him suspect to Catherine II. In September 1764, he wrote to the Empress declaring his health to be restored, but she replied that he should prolong his stay abroad, and he soon resigned: D.M. Griffiths, 'Russian Court Politics and the Question of an Expansionist Foreign Policy under Catherine II, 1762–1783' (PhD thesis, Cornell University, 1967), pp. 11, 15–16.

[92] Madariaga, *Russia*, p. 189; cf. *SIRIO*, LI. 5–11, for this meeting.

up in 1719 and controlled Russian diplomacy, and he began to act as *de facto* foreign minister. He was never to be Chancellor, the title which hitherto had usually been assigned to a leading minister and to the head of the College of Foreign Affairs, but one which Catherine II allowed to lapse until the very end of her reign.[93] His supremacy was soon apparent, however, and he was to be the dominant ministerial influence on Russian diplomacy for the next fifteen years. Pleasure-loving and often slow in discharging official business, he nevertheless brought real knowledge of Europe and its diplomatic *mores* to the conduct of St Petersburg's foreign policy.[94]

Panin advocated a network of alliances known as the 'Northern System'.[95] It envisaged treaties with Prussia, Britain and Denmark, while Poland, Sweden and even Saxony were to be passive members of the projected league, which was intended to provide a period of peace during which pressing domestic problems could be tackled. This programme was to guide Russian policy until the later 1770s, when it was superseded by the more aggressive ideas of southern expansion championed by Grigory Potemkin. Its aims were succinctly defined in the formal instructions given to Count Ivan G. Chernyshev when he set out in summer 1768 to be ambassador in London:

By the Northern System [Panin wrote] we have in mind and mean the largest and closest possible union of northern powers in a direct focal point for our common interest, in order to oppose to the Bourbon and Austrian Houses a firm counter-weight among European Courts, and a northern peace completely free from their influence, which has led so often to harmful effects.[96]

Catherine II would later comment that her minister 'had a great love of general principles, though less attracted to working them out in practice'.[97] It is certainly true that his grandiose schemes were not to be fully realised, yet the goals he set for

---

[93] Panin was, of course, never to hold the post of 'foreign minister', since this office did not exist in Russia until the nineteenth century. After 1773, he was described in official minutes as 'Minister of Foreign Affairs', but this title was honorific and descriptive: Griffiths, 'Russian Court Politics', pp. 16–19.

[94] See the comments of Solms, written at the end of his mission to Russia: G.B. Volz, ed., 'Katharina II. und ihr Hof 1779–80: Zwei preussische Denkschriften', *Zeitschrift für Osteuropäischen Geschichte* 7 (1933), pp. 193–229, at p. 207.

[95] The best introductions are Michael G. Müller, 'Nordisches System-Teilungen Polens-Griechisches Projekt: Russische Aussenpolitik 1762–1796', in K. Zernack, ed., *Handbuch der Geschichte Russlands*, vol. II:ii, *1613–1856* (Stuttgart, 1988), pp. 567–623, and Madariaga, *Russia*, esp. chs. 12–15. D. M. Griffiths, 'The Rise and Fall of the Northern System: Court Politics and Foreign Policy in the First Half of Catherine II's Reign', *Canadian-American Slavic Studies* 4 (1970), pp. 547–69, is a convenient summary, while a fuller account of its creation can be had from the same author's thesis, 'Russian Court Politics', esp. pp. 28–53. Among the more specialised studies, those of Otto Brandt (below, n. 109), and Erik Amburger, Michael F. Metcalf and Michael Roberts (below, n. 127) are far superior to Ljubow Jacobsohn, *Russland und Frankreich in den ersten Regierungsjahren der Kaiserin Katharina II. 1762–1772* (Berlin and Königsberg, 1929), which is based solely upon printed material but does at least provide an outline of events. The German dimension of Russian policy is re-examined in the important and large-scale study of Scharf, *Katharina II.*, esp. pp. 272–429.

[96] 26 July 1768 OS, quoted by N.N. Bolkhovitinov, *The Beginnings of Russian–American Relations 1775–1815* (Engl. trans., Cambridge, MA, 1975), p. 5.

[97] Quoted by Griffiths, 'Russian Court Politics', p. 31.

Russian diplomacy were shared by the Empress.[98] Their partnership, and with it Panin's complete authority, was sealed by Poniatowski's election.[99]

Catherine II always played an active role in the formulation of foreign policy, reading despatches and debating diplomatic objectives with her advisers. She possessed considerable knowledge of European affairs and had a clear set of political priorities. Distinguishing between her contribution and that of her minister is difficult and perhaps impossible. This is partly because the 'Northern System' was, to a significant extent, imposed on St Petersburg by the shift in European alignments in the mid-1750s. Russia had been more fundamentally affected by the Diplomatic Revolution than any other major power.[100] Traditionally, her foreign policy had been based on friendship with Austria, Saxony and, to a lesser extent, Britain, and on hostility towards France. Yet the 'reversal of alliances' had made Russia the temporary ally of France and placed her on the opposing side to Britain. The continuation of the Franco-Austrian alliance after 1763 created a major problem for Russian policy-makers. St Petersburg's principal enemy was the Ottoman empire, yet an Anglo-Prussian system was of very limited utility in a war with the Sultan, against whom the preferred ally was Vienna. However, this could not be secured without abandoning hostility to the arch-enemy, France. This predicament contributed to the incomplete nature of the Northern System. It was why Peter III's foreign policy had anticipated in important respects that subsequently adopted by the Empress and Panin.[101] Both rulers were aware that their strategy was a return to the policy pursued during Peter I's final years, that of alliance with Prussia and dominance over Poland. The first half of 1762 had seen efforts to create a nascent 'Northern System', based on alliances with Prussia, Britain and Sweden and on ascendancy at Warsaw. The Emperor intended to use it in an aggressive manner to expand Russian territory, initially at the expense of Denmark. This distinguished Peter III's policies from those later adopted.

Panin's Northern System aimed only to strengthen Russia's western frontier and to provide defence, especially against French influence in Poland and Sweden. He shared Catherine II's view that Russia's existing territory was sufficiently extensive, especially in relation to its thinly scattered population, and that no further annexations were desirable, at least for the moment. The Northern System was intended to provide stability and security, and thus make possible a concentration upon Russia's pressing internal problems: the connection between foreign policy and the domestic situation was very clear during the first phase of the Empress' reign, as it

---

[98] Catherine II subsequently wrote to the Vice-Chancellor, A.M. Golitsyn, that Panin would control Russian foreign policy because 'le système que j'ai établi et dont M. de Panine a seul la parfaite connaissance, exige cet arrangement': quoted by Griffiths, 'The Rise and Fall of the Northern System', p. 550.   [99] Soloviev, *History of Russia*, XLIII. 153.

[100] Griffiths, 'The Rise and Fall of the Northern System', 547–9.

[101] A point emphasised, and perhaps exaggerated, by Leonard: see, e.g., 'A Study of the Reign of Peter III', pp. 1–2, 191; cf. the comments in an article she wrote jointly with Schweizer, 'Britain, Prussia, Russia and the Galitzin Letter', esp. pp. 546, 547, 553.

was in the other two eastern powers. Yet Panin's projected alliance provided very little protection against the most likely source of a new war: the Ottoman empire. This was its principal flaw, and it was a drawback upon which critics at the Russian court would increasingly concentrate.

Panin's strategy was based on unquestioned opposition to France, which he believed was the principal threat to Russian dominance throughout the eastern half of the continent. Though the diplomatic programme it embodied had long been his objective, the phrase 'Northern System' does not seem to have been employed until March 1764. It was then launched in an attempt to capitalise on reports that Austro-Bourbon negotiations were in progress and would produce strengthened links between Austria, France and Spain.[102] The Northern System was thus a deliberate response to Choiseul's 'Southern System' (*Système du Midi*). Yet while Panin correctly identified French hostility, he failed to appreciate that this was now tempered by the decline of Louis XV's state during the Seven Years War and by its preoccupation with the rivalry with Britain overseas. The *secret*'s continuing anti-Russian activities accomplished very little, but they did reinforce St Petersburg's fears of France. Relations were also exacerbated by the revival of the established dispute over the imperial title, which Catherine II was determined to claim and France was equally determined to deny her. When a new French representative arrived in St Petersburg in spring 1764 bearing credentials which did not include the word 'imperial', he was refused an audience and diplomacy downgraded to the level of *chargé d'affaires*.[103]

These clashes worsened relations. Russia's anxiety, however, rested more upon memories of previous French policy than on an assessment of Versailles' real potential after the Seven Years War. These fears were strengthened, in the early years of peace, by Russia's knowledge of the negotiations underway to establish stronger ties between Austria and the Bourbon powers. Though these failed, they suggested that a powerful diplomatic axis might be created, an effective Southern System to rival the Northern System.[104] France had traditionally been Russia's opponent and had intervened in the three critical border zones for St Petersburg: Sweden, Poland and the Ottoman empire. During the 1760s and even the 1770s, the Empress and her adviser continued to fear French influence in these perennial problem areas, and aimed to neutralise this through the Northern System. Panin had witnessed this struggle at first hand, during the thirteen years he had spent as a Russian diplomat in the Baltic region, initially in Copenhagen (1747–8) and then Stockholm

---

[102] Metcalf, *Russia, England and Swedish Party Politics*, pp. 46, 50–1. In the early years of peace, there were several unsuccessful attempts to create a Triple Alliance out of France's alliances with Austria and Spain.   [103] Madariaga, *Russia*, pp. 195–6. For more on the imperial title, see below, p. 155.

[104] See, e.g., his revealing conversation with Solms in mid-October 1763, occasioned by news that Choiseul's political confidant Grimaldi (who had been ambassador in Paris and an architect of the Family Compact) had become Spain's foreign minister, in which Panin's anxieties about such a triple alliance were articulated: *SIRIO*, XXII. 126–9; cf. Solms to Frederick II, 13 Mar. 1764, *SIRIO*, XXII. 220–1, for a subsequent expression of concern.

(1748–60).[105] The first eight years in Sweden had placed the future foreign minister in the front line against French intrigues, and this significantly influenced his own thinking about Russia's future policy.

The Russo-Prussian treaty became the first plank in the Northern System. From spring 1764 onwards, Panin set about trying to conclude a series of alliances to complete his planned league. His success was incomplete, and certain of the intended members of the Northern System were to prove elusive. This was to be the case with Britain, originally regarded as one of its twin foundations. Panin believed that British gold and British naval power would be valuable to Russia and naturally complement her military might. The foreign policies of both states were based upon opposition to France and this appeared to be a good foundation for an alliance. Ministers in London, however, exhibiting that peculiar blend of stubbornness and sagacity which characterised Britain's diplomacy after the Seven Years War, consistently refused to join the Northern System on the terms which were available. Negotiations for a political treaty took place intermittently throughout the first decade of peace, but always foundered on one of two obstacles: London's refusal to pay a peacetime subsidy and its rejection of the so-called 'Turkish clause'.[106] This was the requirement that in any defensive alliance, the exclusion of a Russian war with the Ottoman empire must be balanced by a British concession, such as the granting of a subsidy. If this was refused, support must be promised against the Sultan. Such a provision had been part of the Russo-Prussian treaty, and Frederick II successfully insisted that any future ally must also promise at least financial aid if the Ottoman empire attacked: as Denmark would do in 1765. The terms for entry, moreover, were to be raised as Russia's own international position improved and her self-confidence increased. In 1763–4 Catherine II and Panin would have concluded an alliance in return for a substantial peacetime subsidy or aid over Poland. Thereafter both financial assistance in Sweden and the 'Turkish clause' were viewed in St Petersburg as essential elements in any treaty, which must be concluded on a near-equal basis as befitted a new great power. Britain was not yet prepared to negotiate on the basis of political equality and this ensured that all attempts to conclude an alliance would fail, though the quest for such a treaty was to be the will o' the wisp of British diplomacy throughout the 1760s and 1770s.

This was not the end of the matter. The interests of the two states coincided to a considerable extent and relations were generally good throughout this period. They were sustained by a mutually advantageous commercial connection, embodied in a formal trade treaty first signed in 1734 and renewed (not without considerable difficulty) in 1766. This Commercial Treaty was, in Panin's eyes at least, seen as a way

---

[105] There is a sketch of his time in Sweden in Ransel, *Politics of Catherinian Russia*, pp. 16–27, and a fuller account in Werner Krummel, 'Nikita Ivanovic Panins aussenpolitische Tätigkeit 1747–1758', *JGO* 5 (1940), pp. 76–141.

[106] For Russo-British relations at this period, see Scott, *British Foreign Policy*, 55–61, 80–4, 94–8, 107–12, 127–36, 156–9.

of attaching Britain to the Northern System. London was also dependent upon Russia as the principal source of the naval stores upon which British sea power was dependent. More importantly, shared hostility towards France ensured that Russo-British relations quickly became and long remained harmonious. By the mid-1760s an *entente* was coming into existence, exemplified by the co-operation in Sweden.[107] In time, its maintenance came to be the limit of St Petersburg's policy. As Panin very sensibly pointed out to the Empress, why should Russia undertake the formal commitments embodied in an alliance, given the degree of co-operation she had already secured from London. This made Britain into an honorary member of the Northern System, a state whose support could usually be exploited, at least to a limited extent, in Russia's interest: as it was to be in Sweden and during the early stages of the Russo-Ottoman War.[108]

The absence of formal political links with London ensured that the Northern System would always possess a rather lop-sided appearance. With the exception of the original alliance with Prussia, the only full member was Denmark, with whom treaties were signed in 1765 and 1767.[109] Though in no sense a major power, Copenhagen possessed the largest fighting navy in the Baltic throughout most of the eighteenth century and its support in northern Europe was certainly to be prized. Only during the 1780s did Russia's Baltic fleet achieve first parity with and then supremacy over its Danish counterpart. Denmark's naval potential was reduced by the need to recruit additional sailors to crew her ships in any emergency, though she always possessed a strong nucleus of experienced officers and men.[110] This, together with her strategic location on one side of the Sound and willingness to co-operate in upholding the 'tranquillity of the North', primarily by intervening in Sweden, made Denmark's alliance attractive to St Petersburg.

Copenhagen's support was secured by means of a settlement of a complex dispute over ducal Holstein, a strategically vital territory which lay to the south of Denmark and was part of the Holy Roman Empire.[111] It was the southern of two Duchies; the northern, Schleswig, had been occupied by the Danish monarchy since the Great Northern War of 1700–21. The senior branch of the House of Oldenburg ruled in Copenhagen, while cadets were established in several territories in northern Germany and, most importantly, in Holstein-Gottorp. Russian involvement dated back to the reign of Peter I, whose eldest daughter had married its reigning duke.

[107] See below, pp. 134–6.

[108] Martens, *Recueil des traités*, IX (X). III, for Panin's testimony to this; Martens, *Recueil des traités*, IX (X) 241, makes clear that his view dated from *c.* 1766.

[109] For Russo-Danish relations see in particular Otto Brandt, *Caspar von Saldern und die nordeuropäische Politik im Zeitalter Katharinas II.* (Erlangen and Kiel, 1932), esp. ch. 3.

[110] Jan Glete, *Navies and Nations: Warships, Navies and State Building in Europe and America 1500–1860* (2 vols., Stockholm, 1993), I. 295–305, esp. Diagram 23: 3, p. 299; cf. Glete, *Navies and Nations*, I. 74–6, for his measurement system of 'displacement tonnage'.

[111] See the detailed monograph by Eckhard Hübner, *Staatspolitik und Familieninteresse: die gottorfische Frage in der russischen Außenpolitik 1741–1773* (Neumünster, 1984).

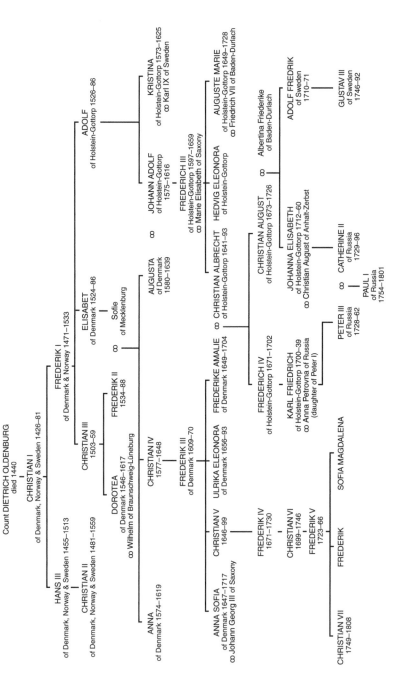

The Holstein Succession

Their son, Charles Peter Ulrich, had been summoned to Russia soon after the Empress Elizabeth seized power in 1741 and named heir to the throne. The Grand Duke Peter (as he now became) had converted to the Russian Orthodox faith. An already complex dynastic dispute was further complicated by the fact that a member of the ducal House of Holstein-Gottorp, Adolf Frederik, had become King of Sweden in 1751. Though he had renounced his claim to Holstein the year before he became Swedish monarch, it was feared in Copenhagen that he might revive it if he were able to strengthen his powers as King and free himself from control by Sweden's diet.[112]

Denmark had for some time been trying to promote an exchange by which the Grand Duke Peter gave up Holstein while, in return, the two small principalities of Oldenburg and Delmenhorst (which were under Danish control) would pass to a minor branch of the Holstein-Gottorp family: a scheme known in Danish as *Mageskiftet*. The existence of a regency government for the heir to the Russian empire in Holstein, which might potentially be claimed by the King of Sweden, was obviously an uncomfortable problem for the Danish monarchy, especially as Elizabeth's illness from an early stage of the Seven Years War appeared to bring closer Peter's accession to Russia's throne. There were also potential rival claims to Schleswig, since Copenhagen's extended occupation had never been fully accepted. This had been the ostensible source of the war against Denmark planned by Peter III and cynically supported by Prussia.[113] The first half of 1762 underlined Danish vulnerability in the face of the threatened Russian attack: despite her powerful navy, Denmark wholly lacked land power and feared her territories would be overrun.[114] In the event, Peter III's deposition saved Denmark from invasion, occurring as it did just as her ill-matched army prepared to advance to meet the attackers, but the problem posed by the link between Holstein and St Petersburg had been graphically highlighted. Upon Peter III's death, moreover, his Holstein salient together with the claim to Schleswig had passed to his heir, Paul, who had been born in 1754.

Panin recognised that Holstein was an obstacle to a close relationship with Copenhagen and to its incorporation into the Northern System. Yet it also presented an opportunity: as he wrote, 'through Holstein we might draw Denmark into a permanent alliance with us'.[115] This became his strategy, and he quickly secured the Empress' support for the Duchy's formal transfer to Danish sovereignty. Panin argued, interestingly enough, that continued possession of a fief in Germany, and the homage this technically involved to the Holy Roman Emperor, was not appropriate for an emerging great power such as Russia. The cession of this territory

---

[112] For the constitutional situation in Sweden, see below, pp. 131–3.   [113] See above, p. 45.

[114] See the correspondence for these months in *Bernstorff Corr.*, II. 1–80, *passim*; Danish anxieties are even clearer in J.H.E. von Bernstorff's letters to his nephew, A.P. von Bernstorff, at this time: *Bernstorffsche Papiere*, I. 430–1, 437, 451, 458–9, 460, 462, 463.

[115] Soloviev, *History of Russia*, XLV. 110, and more generally pp. 108–10. No date is given, but it clearly belongs to the early part of Catherine II's reign.

would also deprive the Grand Duke Paul of an independent power-base outside Russia, and this may have helped to persuade Catherine II to support the projected exchange, which might strengthen her own position in Russia.[116]

The carrot of Holstein proved sufficient for Denmark to abandon finally her traditional French alliance. This had been severely weakened by Copenhagen's neutrality during the Seven Years War, and by France's inability and, increasingly, reluctance to pay the subsidies which bound the two states together.[117] Danish foreign policy between 1751 and 1770 was in the very capable hands of J.H.E. von Bernstorff, whose diplomatic objectives now mirrored those of Panin.[118] Bernstorff was a member of a prominent north German family and had entered Danish service as long ago as 1731. An extended diplomatic career had been crowned by six years (1744–50) as ambassador to Paris, where he worked to strengthen the partnership created by the Franco-Danish alliance of 1742 and also befriended the future duc de Choiseul. He returned to Copenhagen to become foreign minister. Bernstorff's approach to diplomacy was shaped by his own dislike of war, on religious and philosophical grounds. It also embodied an attempt to chart an independent line for Denmark, to the extent that this was possible for a small power with a respectable navy but a negligible army. The threatened Russian attack in 1762 had made clear the need to secure an alliance with a major state for purposes of self-defence and to carry through the Holstein exchange. That state could only be Russia, whose new power was apparent to the Danish foreign minister.[119]

By the 1760s Bernstorff's policy had three principal aims.[120] He wanted to uphold peace around the Baltic. To this end he believed the Swedish Constitution of 1720 should be maintained, since it made Sweden less of a threat to her neighbours and to the peace of the region. Any strengthening of the Swedish monarchy might also imperil Denmark's rule over Norway. Finally, he desired to bring about the Holstein exchange, both as a preliminary to improved relations with Russia and to remove the potential threats to Denmark's own back door from Stockholm and St Petersburg. Underlying these objectives was Bernstorff's disillusionment with France, to whom Denmark had been closely allied for two decades but who had refused all aid when

---

[116] Madariaga, *Russia*, p. 192.

[117] For the subsidy question and its eventual settlement, see Eduard de Barthélemy, *Histoire des relations de la France et du Danemarck sous le ministère du comte de Bernstorff 1751–70* (Paris, 1887), chs. 3–10; cf. *Bernstorff Corr.*, II. 177–9, for the way France's refusal of subsidies changed the situation in northern Europe.

[118] For a brief introduction see Lawrence J. Baack, 'State Service in the Eighteenth Century: The Bernstorffs in Hanover and Denmark', *International History Review* I (1979), pp. 323–48, esp. pp. 329–36. His foreign policy can best be approached through the material printed in *Bernstorff Corr.*, I–II, and *Bernstorffsche Papiere*, I–III, *passim*. There are some illuminating comments in Michael Roberts, 'Great Britain, Denmark and Russia, 1763–70', Ragnhild Hatton and M. S. Anderson, eds., in *Studies in Diplomatic History: Essays in Memory of David Bayne Horn* (London, 1970), pp. 236–67.

[119] For Bernstorff's recognition that Russia's military victories in the Seven Years War had made her the dominant power in northern Europe, see his despatch to Osten, 26 June 1760, *Bernstorff Corr.*, I. 339; cf. *Bernstorff Corr.*, I. 363–9, and *Bernstorffsche Papiere*, I. 420–5.

[120] Cf. Roberts, 'Great Britain, Denmark and Russia, 1763–70', pp. 238ff.

Peter III threatened in 1762 and had been laggardly over subsidy payments. Denmark's foreign minister also recognised, more clearly than some observers, the extent of France's decline by the end of the Seven Years War. Choiseul, for his part, was equally disillusioned, disliking Denmark's neutrality during that conflict, and was determined to extract value for what he saw as exorbitant subsidies.

While the duc was reassessing France's entire Baltic policy during the early years of peace, Denmark moved decisively out of the French orbit, as Bernstorff and Panin together brought about a Russo-Danish *rapprochement*.[121] This was another success for Panin's broader objective of curbing French influence. It was accomplished in two stages. In March 1765, a conventional defensive alliance was signed between Russia and Denmark.[122] Two years later, this was followed by a provisional agreement to transfer ducal Holstein to Danish rule.[123] The exchange, however, was not to take place until Paul reached his majority in six years' time. This second treaty retained Copenhagen in St Petersburg's orbit into the early 1770s and beyond. Denmark provided important support for Russia around the Baltic and especially in Sweden.[124] But it was always a very one-sided partnership, with Copenhagen aware of its own weakness and generally content to follow the Russian lead. Bernstorff had sought political independence for his adopted country, but in practice Denmark exchanged France's diplomatic leadership for that of Russia. The great disparity between the two states in resources and power made this inevitable, and exemplified the increasing dominance of the great powers within the international system.

The alliances with Prussia and Denmark, the less formal co-operation with Britain and the perpetuation of control over Poland all contributed to Russia's sense of security and her notable diplomatic recovery during the early years of peace. The Northern System was also strengthened by less formal ties and especially by two royal marriages sponsored by Bernstorff, those of George III's youngest sister, Caroline Mathilda, to the future King of Denmark, Christian VII, and of Crown Prince Gustav of Sweden to a Danish princess. These dynastic marriages reinforced Panin's diplomatic system, which by the mid-1760s had reached its fullest extent.

III

Sweden's incorporation as a passive member of the Northern System had always been Panin's objective, though he recognised it would take 'some years' to

---

[121] See the 'Instructions' for Osten, 7 Apr. 1763, *Bernstorff Corr.*, II. 122–9; the new policy towards Russia, in the aftermath of Catherine II's accession, had first been set out in Bernstorff to Haxthausen, 8 Sept. 1762, *Bernstorff Corr.*, II. 84–95; a copy of this crucial despatch was given to Osten as part of his Instructions.

[122] The treaty of 11 Mar. 1765 is printed in *Danske Tractater*, pp. 183–202.

[123] Treaty of 22 Apr. 1767, printed in *Danske Tractater*, pp. 229–60.

[124] See Panin's very interesting assessment of the alliance's value: to Korff, 20 Oct. 1765, *SIRIO*, LVII. 386–97.

accomplish.[125] In the meantime, he believed that her massive financial problems would make her outlook completely pacific and remove any threat to Russia, at least for the present. Immediately after the Seven Years War, Poland dominated St Petersburg's foreign policy, and developments in Stockholm were a secondary issue. This was apparent in the fact that the Russian agent there, Count I.A. Ostermann, does not seem to have received a single despatch from Panin between late May and mid-November 1764, a period of almost six months during which Russia's attention was fixed upon Warsaw.[126] During the final weeks of that year, however, these priorities were reversed. Poniatowski's formal election in September consolidated the Russian protectorate over Poland, while in Sweden the party strife was approaching its climax. In the same month as Poland's new King was elected, the Swedish government finally accepted that its pressing financial problems required the summoning of an extraordinary *riksdag* (Sweden's Diet) for January 1765. That *riksdag* would also be dominated, as Swedish politics were coming to be, by discussions about constitutional reform.

During the next two years, Stockholm was to occupy a more prominent place in St Petersburg's foreign policy and in the wider relations of the great powers.[127] Developments there were to consolidate the Northern System, while simultaneously revealing its real limitations. Panin's own role in the evolution of Russia's Swedish strategy was quite central. The dozen years he had spent as a diplomat in Stockholm established him as the government's expert on that country, and in 1762–4 he had done more than anyone to shape Russian thinking. From late in 1764, moreover, he appears to have secured Catherine II's full support for his strategy, a development which contributed to the emergence of an active policy in Sweden. In the mid-1760s, minister and ruler together determined Russia's policy. During the closing months of 1764, they began to grapple with a complex and rapidly evolving situation which presented a serious threat to Russia's strategic position around the Baltic. Once again, St Petersburg's attitude was guided by opposition to France, who was also Sweden's traditional ally and patron. The Seven Years War had weakened the Franco-Swedish alignment, and Panin intended to complete its destruction. In time, Russia's leading minister came to be even more concerned with the nature of Sweden's internal government.

Eighteenth-century Sweden was a country living on fading memories of a glorious imperial past, while simultaneously struggling to adjust to the often-harsh realities of her new status as a minor power.[128] The loss of most of the trans-Baltic

---

[125] Metcalf, *Russia, England and Swedish Party Politics*, p. 58.   [126] Roberts, *British Diplomacy*, p. 72.

[127] Developments in and over Sweden in 1764–6 are examined in Michael Metcalf's dense but important monograph, *Russia, England and Swedish Party Politics*, and in Michael Roberts' magisterial biography of Sir John Goodricke, *British Diplomacy*, pp. 38–232. These two studies have largely superseded the vintage survey by Erik Amburger, *Russland und Schweden 1762–1772: Katharina II., die schwedische Verfassung und die Ruhe des Nordens* (Berlin, 1934; repr. Vaduz, 1965), chs. 2–3, and my debt to them throughout this section is considerable.

[128] The best non-Scandinavian surveys are now Roberts, *The Age of Liberty*, and Claude Nordmann, *Grandeur et liberté de la Suède (1660–1792)* (Paris, 1971).

territories by the Peace of Nystad had been accompanied by a dramatic change in Sweden's system of government. The long and ultimately unsuccessful campaigns waged by Charles XII, and the burdens these imposed on his exhausted country, had discredited the absolute monarchy established by his father, Charles XI, after 1680. Charles XII's death without an heir in 1718 enabled Caroline absolutism to be swept away in a bloodless revolution. The Constitution of 1720 established the sovereignty of the *riksdag*, restored elective monarchy and made the King the prisoner of the Estates. Eighteenth-century Sweden was ruled during its 'Age of Liberty' (1719–72) by the *riksdag* and its committees, and increasingly by the dominant Council of State and the powerful central bureaucracy. Further restrictions were placed on the monarchy after an unsuccessful royalist *coup* in 1756. These included the manufacture of a name stamp, in order that the signature of the King, Adolf Frederik (1751–71), could simply be added to official documents if the ruler again tried to go on strike by refusing to exercise his functions. The events of 1756 were a unique example of decisive action by Sweden's weak and irresolute ruler. Though Adolf Frederik was a cypher, his formidable wife, Lovisa Ulrika – sister of Frederick the Great – emerged during the later 1750s as the effective leader of the Court, and their son, Crown Prince Gustav, became the focus of royalist ambitions. Attempts by the Court party to strengthen the monarchy's powers were to be an increasingly important dimension of Sweden's domestic politics.

During the 1760s the Court provided an uncertain but important third factor in the political equation. The second half of the Age of Liberty had witnessed fierce rivalry between two competing alignments, the Hats and the Caps. This 'rage of party' had emerged quite suddenly after 1740, and it was at first more a clash of personalities than of fundamental political principles. Only in the very twilight of the Age of Liberty, the later 1760s, did these alignments begin to acquire the rudiments of modern party organisation, which deepened the fundamental political divisions. The Hats had dominated the *riksdag* and formed the government for a quarter of a century from the end of the 1730s, but by the early 1760s their hold on power was slipping. This resulted primarily from Sweden's disastrous intervention in the Seven Years War. Throughout the Age of Liberty, the government had faced serious financial problems, and these had been made acute by the campaigns in Pomerania: between 1757 and 1762, the budget deficit had increased no less than tenfold.[129] The Seven Years War had been even more disastrous for Sweden than for the other belligerents: by its mid-point, a potential state bankruptcy threatened. The situation was exacerbated by the Hats' inflationary policies and by France's failure to pay the promised subsidies in full, either during the fighting or when it ended. This was ostensibly in retaliation for Stockholm's separate peace with Prussia in May 1762, when Sweden had withdrawn from the war, but was also linked to France's own acute financial difficulties. Sweden's financial chaos was highlighted by the complete failure of the war effort, and these two factors together did most to weaken the Hats' hold on power.

---

[129] Roberts, *The Age of Liberty*, p. 20.

The clash of parties had been accompanied and, to some extent, sustained by the intervention of foreign states, in a way that was broadly comparable to Poland. At Stockholm, this intervention had been in the form of substantial financial contributions to one side or the other. Sweden had long been part of France's own Northern System, and from the 1730s the Hats had been supported by French diplomacy and French money. The Caps, in their turn, were backed by Britain and Russia after the 1740s. Foreign funds were used less for outright corruption, though there was undoubtedly some open bribery and buying of proxy votes, than for paying the living expenses of the impoverished nobility and members of the other Estates who came to Stockholm periodically for meetings of the *riksdag*, which could be lengthy: that of 1765–6 lasted for twenty-one months and was the longest in the entire eighteenth century. Great power support for one or other alignment continued until the very end of the Age of Liberty, though its precise impact is difficult to establish. Swedish politics were certainly more independent of the foreign paymasters than was sometimes imagined in St Petersburg or London. Diplomats exerted some influence on party objectives, but their main role was to provide the essential lubricant of Swedish political life: money. Such payments – like the foreign subsidies received by the government for some two-thirds of the period 1721–72[130] – attested to Sweden's innate poverty and weakness. International involvement in her domestic politics was motivated not by commercial considerations but by geography and strategy. Russia, Britain and France all believed that their wider interests could be furthered at Stockholm.

Russia's concern was always most pressing. It was rooted in an established and well-grounded awareness of her own vulnerable north-western frontier. This anxiety was reinforced by memories of the campaigns of Charles XII, Sweden's famous warrior-king, who during the Great Northern War had penetrated deep into Russia. Observers in the Russian capital equated absolutism with Swedish revanchism and for this reason always feared and opposed any strengthening of the monarchy's powers. Article seven of the Peace of Nystad could plausibly be interpreted as conferring on Russia the position of guarantor of Sweden's Constitution of 1720, and it provided a convenient justification for intervention in her political life.[131] The final source of Russian concern was Sweden's traditional role as a client of the arch-enemy, France: she had been part of the famous *barrière de l'est*. These three anxieties had merged in the early 1740s, when a French-backed Hat government attacked Russia in a vain attempt to reconquer the territories ceded two decades before at Nystad. The war of 1741–3 had been a disaster for Sweden. It highlighted her military and financial weakness, and by the Peace of Åbo the Hat government was forced to hand over more Finnish territory to secure an end to the fighting. This gain did something to strengthen Russia's defensive position at the eastern end of the Gulf of Finland, but little to calm her anxieties about Swedish revanchism. This

---

[130] Roberts, *The Age of Liberty*, p. 26.   [131] Metcalf, *Russia, England and Swedish Party Politics*, p. 2.

was because her concern was part of a broader preoccupation with the security of her western frontier, which the Northern System was intended to address, and her continuing efforts to maintain a glacis behind which Russia could be secure from attack. What was especially feared was that Sweden might strike when Russia was at war with the Ottoman empire, or fighting in central Europe, or even both.[132] These concerns were strengthened by the permanent military confrontation along the Russo–Swedish border in Finland, which had effectively been partitioned in the settlements of 1721 and 1743.[133]

The further restrictions on the King's authority imposed after the failed *coup* of 1756, together with the personality of Adolf Frederik, appeared additional safe-guards against a resurgent Sweden. Yet the Seven Years War had also witnessed two developments which seemed to threaten Russian interests, and both had been viewed at first hand by Panin, then a diplomat in Stockholm. The first was the emer-gence of a distinct Court alignment led by the resolute and able Lovisa Ulrika. The constitutional implications of Sweden's intervention in the Seven Years War were even more serious. This had been carried through as a *coup* by the Hat party which dominated the Council of State, and the *riksdag*'s approval had not been sought, as the Constitution required. This unlawful action was a reminder that guarding against Swedish revanchism was not simply a matter of curbing the power of the King. Only the accident of the Diplomatic Revolution, which made France the ally of Austria and thus Russia, had ensured that Sweden fought in the Seven Years War in the unusual position of St Petersburg's ally and not her more normal role as its enemy.

These various strands came together in the final months of 1764, when Sweden replaced Poland as the principal Russian problem in foreign affairs. The crippling financial legacy of the Seven Years War, and the inflation which followed its conclu-sion, together with widespread revulsion against Hat corruption, led to a change of government. The elections for the three lower houses of the *riksdag* (Clergy, Burghers and Peasantry) saw sweeping Cap gains, and the meeting of the Estates scheduled to open in January 1765 would evidently mark the end of a quarter century of Hat ascendancy. Panin's approach was exactly the one which he himself had pursued as a diplomat at Stockholm during the 1750s. It was guided by his wish to restore the balance between King and *riksdag* established in 1720, and thereafter to prevent further constitutional change. It was also influenced by the broader demands of his foreign policy. In December 1764 he produced a plan to stabilise – or, rather, immobilise – Sweden's politics and government for the foreseeable future. It envisaged the erection of insurmountable barriers to any future reform of the constitution. This would have to be approved unanimously and by two succes-sive meetings of the *riksdag*, with a general election in between. Panin calculated

---

[132] Roberts, *British Diplomacy*, p. 44.
[133] Kari Tarkiainen, 'The Finland of Gustav III and of Catherine II', in *Catherine the Great and Gustav III* (Helsingborg, 1999), pp. 128–31.

that this mechanism would prevent any attempt to strengthen the authority of either the Estates or the crown, and in this way would render Sweden less of a danger to her neighbours, above all Russia. This was his ultimate aim during the *riksdag* of 1765–6, with its complex political strife, but he was willing to be flexible in his pursuit of its objective. In its early stages, he clearly toyed with support for the Court, in order to curb any future Council-led aggression. His well-founded suspicions about Lovisa Ulrika's aims produced a breach with the royalists in summer 1765. Throughout the *riksdag*, however, Panin continued Russia's traditional policy, that of supporting the now-victorious Caps.

The situation in Sweden influenced in varying degrees St Petersburg's relations with three of the intended members of the Northern System: Prussia, Denmark and Britain. Frederick the Great had promised on several occasions to provide support not merely in Poland but also in Sweden, which had been envisaged by the alliance signed in April 1764. His assistance at Stockholm, however, proved to be very limited, though it was none the less significant. Panin used the Prussian King to exert influence on Lovisa Ulrika. Frederick corresponded regularly with his sister, and this was an obvious means of trying to steer the Court faction in Russia's interest and, in particular, to stop it forming too close links with the French party.[134] This was the limit of active Prussian involvement, though Berlin's minister in Stockholm was given general instructions to co-operate with his Russian counterpart. The penny-pinching Frederick would not provide funds for electioneering and subsistence, and he was less directly threatened by developments in Sweden than any other power. Denmark's interests at Stockholm coincided to a remarkable extent with those of Russia. Copenhagen also feared Swedish revanchism, especially since Danish-ruled Norway was a vulnerable and attractive prize for an absolute monarch seeking to inaugurate his rule with a striking military success. The Russo-Danish alliance of March 1765 opened the way to significant co-operation at Stockholm, both during the *riksdag* of 1765–6 and beyond. Though there was some initial reluctance to abandon traditional Hat allies, Denmark's support was soon given to the Caps and, very broadly, to Panin's scheme for the stabilisation of the constitutional arrangements, while Bernstorff even provided some belated financial support.

Britain's involvement in Sweden, and Russia's intentions regarding her precise role there, were much more complex. London's approach was now governed entirely by a belief that co-operation in Sweden might be the way to secure the prized Russian alliance and to overcome the barrier represented by its own refusal to make concessions over a subsidy and the 'Turkish clause'. In the first two years of peace, when the navy-minded Earl of Sandwich was responsible for British diplomacy in northern Europe, the wish to prevent Sweden's fleet being at France's disposal was for a time a secondary motive, until detailed enquiries established its poor condition.[135] But British ministers always viewed developments in Stockholm

---

[134] For Russia's view of co-operation at Stockholm, see *SIRIO*, XXII. 357–9.
[135] Roberts, *British Diplomacy*, p. 125.

primarily in terms of their relations with St Petersburg and their wish for a political alliance. Panin, by contrast, saw a formal treaty as a means of securing London's support rather than an end in itself. He intended that Britain should assist Russia in two distinct ways. First, her seemingly abundant wealth should be drawn on to underwrite Russian policy in Sweden. St Petersburg's own poverty was a potential barrier to success, but this could be overcome by a British paymaster. Even more important, Britain could assume a role which Russia herself could only play with considerable difficulty. Russia's earlier responsibility for the destruction of Sweden's Baltic empire and her victory in the war of 1741–3 had made hostility towards her a dominant sentiment in eighteenth-century Swedish political life. This made it difficult for a Russian diplomat to intervene effectively in the party struggle. Panin intended that Britain would act as a proxy for Russia and take on the part which his own ambassador could only with difficulty play. He was aware of the Anglophilia of many of the leading Caps and, recognising that a Russo-Swedish alliance was impossible for the present, looked towards a Swedo-British treaty as the way France's dominance at Stockholm would be ended. Russia's policy always distinguished between promoting a change in Sweden's foreign policy, which was to be Britain's task, and establishing a new constitutional dispensation, which she would handle herself.

St Petersburg's second aim was never fully appreciated in London. British ministers instead concentrated upon the question of financial support at Stockholm. Successive governments, now and in the future, were prepared for some expenditure if this would smooth the path to a Russian alliance. These funds, however, were never to be provided on the scale that Russia had hoped for, nor with the regularity she had expected. It has been calculated that Britain spent around £17,000 during the *riksdag* of 1765–6, and in addition gave two pensions of £800 *per annum*. The comparable figure for Russia was £100,000, and even Denmark – albeit grudgingly – spent £20,000 at Stockholm.[136] Sweden thus revealed both the possibilities of Russo-British co-operation and the real problems it had to surmount. Foremost among these was an enduring British suspicion that Russia was trying to pass on the main part of the cost of her own policy in Sweden: as, indeed, she was. Yet in 1764–6 the extent and importance of joint action were considerable. It rested primarily on the close and harmonious co-operation between the respective diplomats in Stockholm. Russia's minister, the shrewd and resourceful Ostermann, and the newly arrived British representative, Sir John Goodricke, quickly established a *rapport*, and their partnership survived the baffling vicissitudes of British policy during the next few years. This co-operation was first evident at the time of the *riksdag* elections, when it contributed to the resounding Cap victory. It was due to their strategic grasp and tactical flair, rather than the limited financial resources at their disposal. The French ambassador, Breteuil, spent more in his support of the defeated Hats than his British and Russian colleagues did together on behalf of the

---

[136] Roberts, *British Diplomacy*, p. 229.

triumphant Caps.[137] This fact underlines that Swedish party politics were more independent of foreign paymasters than sometimes imagined.

Developments over Sweden in 1764–6 did much to confirm Britain's emerging role as an honorary member of the Northern System, while simultaneously revealing the considerable barriers in the way of any formal alliance. Though forced to abandon his idea of restoring the constitutional balance established in 1720, Panin was eventually able to secure some of the changes for which he had long been pressing. The *riksdag* of 1765–6 was dominated by Cap attempts to solve the fundamental economic and financial problems which were paralysing the country and its government, but in its final stages Russia's allies secured the passage of an *Ordinance for the Better Execution of the Laws*.[138] Panin's original scheme, now supported by Denmark, was taken up and carried through by the Caps leaders. The resulting *Ordinance* institutionalised the principle of unanimity between King, *riksdag* and Council in any constitutional amendment, which also had to be approved by two successive meetings of the Estates, with an intervening general election. This had long been Panin's principal aim in Sweden, and the passing of the *Ordinance* seemed to have removed most of Russia's anxieties. The conclusion of a Swedo-British treaty of friendship by the Cap *riksdag* in February 1766, though unimportant in itself, signalled the end of Stockholm's commitment to France and was a further boost to Russia's position.[139] By the second half of 1766, St Petersburg's interests appeared to be protected by its new alliances with Prussia and Denmark, by the *entente* with Britain and finally by the constitutional amendment in the closing stages of the *riksdag*. Catherine II's own position, initially so fragile, had also been transformed. The Empress' régime was now securely established at home and abroad, her hold over Poland seemingly assured and her anxieties over Sweden significantly reduced, so that more attention could be given to fundamental domestic reforms in the next few years.

Developments over Sweden in 1764–6 had revealed the coherence and stability of the new international pattern established by the Seven Years War and the Polish election which followed. The two new great powers, the leading continental states after 1763, were now effective allies. This alignment had the support, important within a Baltic context, of Denmark, and received limited financial aid and diplomatic backing from Britain. The Russo-Prussian axis was clearly dominant in northern and eastern Europe, and enjoyed a limited ascendancy over the continent as a whole. It faced the *Système du Midi*, Choiseul's parallel alliances with Madrid and Vienna. In a European context, however, this was a purely defensive alliance which aimed only to preserve peace and the political and territorial *status quo*. Its

---

[137] Metcalf, *Russia, England and Swedish Party Politics*, pp. 140–1; cf. Roberts, *The Age of Liberty*, p. 157.

[138] For the *riksdag* see Metcalf, *Russia, England and Swedish Party Politics*, pp. 142–70; for the constitutional issue at it, Metcalf, *Russia, England and Swedish Party Politics*, pp. 171–203.

[139] Its negotiation and conclusion are examined by Metcalf, *Russia, England and Swedish Party Politics*, pp. 204–33.

inability to challenge its rival had been evident over Poniatowski's election, and would continue to be apparent in the years ahead.

The period immediately after the Seven Years War witnessed one further development of enduring importance: Britain's political marginalisation. The overwhelming victory of the British state over its Bourbon adversaries had created a leading position for it among the great powers by 1763. Within a few years that ascendancy had been undermined, as it became clear that ministers in London would not assume the dominant European role which Britain's successes and her wealth had created for her.[140] This was what Panin meant when he commented in 1768 that the British state was no longer a 'land power', that is to say it had ceased to be a full participant in the continental states system.[141] At the end of the Seven Years War Britain had been an attractive ally. Her wealth and power were widely admired, not least by the Empress and Panin. This was why they sought unsuccessfully to conclude an alliance and thus secure British aid over the Polish election. By the second half of the decade it was to be a very different story: Panin, who had sought a subsidy over Poland in 1763, was by 1766 demanding one over Sweden on pain of an immediate end to all negotiations.[142] Though his threat was not carried out, the new tone in relations was evident.

Britain's growing insularity in these years, as ministers proclaimed their indifference to continental issues and saluted their own good fortune in living in an island-kingdom, quickly undermined the admiration of her power created by the triumphant Seven Years War. Her ministers, as the Russian ambassador in London sourly remarked during the Polish crisis of 1763–4, were more concerned with the election in Essex than with that in Warsaw.[143] In fact Britain faced considerable domestic problems of her own, with the ending of the Seven Years War. Its principal legacies were an inflated National Debt, which alarmed fiscally prudent contemporaries, and the difficulties of administering and defending the enlarged colonial empire which had been created. The 1760s also saw considerable ministerial instability, with a series of short-lived governments. Frederick the Great was predictably quick to sneer: George III, he declared, changed his ministers as often as he changed his shirts.[144] Yet behind this malicious sally lay an important point. Foreign observers, used to considerable stability in government and to ministries which were long-lasting because they depended only upon the absolute ruler's continuing support, found it particularly difficult to comprehend the frequent changes of personnel in London, where there were no less than eight alterations at the Northern Department (responsible for Britain's diplomacy in northern Europe) between 1763 and 1772. This soon diminished the regard in

---

[140] For this evolution see Scott, *British Foreign Policy*, pp. 53–124 *passim*.
[141] To I.G. Chernyshev, 27 Oct. 1768 OS, Martens, *Recueil des traités*, IX (X). 274.
[142] Scott, *British Foreign Policy*, pp. 111–12.
[143] Michael Roberts, *Macartney in Russia* (*English Historical Review*, Supplement 7; London, 1974), p. 38.   [144] *Pol. Corr.*, XXV. 353.

which Britain was held on the continent. So too did the emergence of serious urban radicalism in the Wilkite agitation and, during the second half of the decade, new problems in Britain's North American colonies and with the East India Company. The inexperienced and frequently inept ministers responsible for foreign policy in London found it difficult to focus upon European issues, as problems at home and in the colonies crowded in on them, and this strengthened the notion of British insularity.

Britain's eclipse as a factor in continental politics was surprisingly swift. By the mid-1760s it was coming to be recognised that there was no place for her in the new political pattern. An ill-considered approach to Austria during the winter of 1763–4 had immediately foundered on Vienna's attachment to its French alliance, while ministers in London were always unwilling to pay the full price of membership of Panin's Northern System: a peacetime subsidy, the 'Turkish clause', or possibly both. They mistakenly believed that no such inducements were needed to secure a political treaty. The continuation of Anglo-Bourbon rivalry – the early years of peace had seen a series of small-scale clashes in the colonial sphere – was a further obstacle to Britain's acquisition of a continental ally and, with it, a European role. Its consequence, as Bernstorff shrewdly pointed out, was that any state allying with London immediately became the target of Bourbon enmity yet secured next to nothing in return, given Britain's unwillingness to pay subsidies in peacetime.[145] The fundamental causes of the political marginalisation of Britain, however, were her own increasing insularity, together with the wider international changes set in motion by the Seven Years War. By the mid-1760s Britain was being squeezed out of Europe, which was now dominated by Russia and her ally Prussia. London's withdrawal was ultimately Frederick's and Catherine's gain.

There was, however, a single threatening cloud upon St Petersburg's horizon. In July 1766, Goodricke handed to his Russian colleague two French diplomatic despatches intercepted by the authorities in Hanover.[146] These revealed a significant change in France's policy in Stockholm. This was now nothing less than the full restoration of absolutism, in the hope that this might once again make Sweden an effective French ally. Choiseul had been meditating such a change at least since the closing stages of the Seven Years War, but it was only announced once he had returned to the foreign office in April 1766. Hitherto, France had broadly continued its established support for the Hats, while simultaneously exploring the possibilities of co-operation with the Court. The decision to work actively for a restoration of absolute monarchy in order to make Sweden a more valuable ally had long been anticipated by Panin at least, and it did not immediately threaten Russia's position in the Baltic. But it was part of a wider transformation of French policy carried out by Choiseul when he exchanged the naval portfolio for direct control of

---

[145] *Bernstorff Corr.*, II. 391–2.
[146] PRO SP 95/109, fo. 13, 28; cf. Metcalf, *Russia, England and Swedish Party Politics*, pp. 198–99, and Roberts, *British Diplomacy*, p. 219.

French diplomacy. This was, in turn, one of a series of linked developments which, during the next three years, would first threaten and then destroy the peace restored between 1763 and 1766, and the stability which it seemed to promise and which was widely desired.

5

Diplomacy and the eastern powers

I

By the third quarter of the eighteenth century the nature of ancien régime diplomacy was well established.[1] During and immediately after the long personal rule of Louis XIV (1661–1715) the reciprocal exchange of diplomats had become more widespread and a network of resident ambassadors and ministers had spread across southern, western and central Europe, while the customs and practices of modern international relations simultaneously took shape. These decades had given a new formality to the content and conduct of relations between states, with France serving as the model. Ceremonial, protocol, diplomatic instructions and the negotiations actually undertaken: all became more formalised during and immediately after the Sun King's reign. France's contribution to the development of resident diplomacy was apparent in the fact that French became the diplomatic language *par excellence* of eighteenth-century Europe. Half a century after Louis XIV's death, France's diplomatic service remained pre-eminent. Her ambassadors were more polished and also more subtle, her infrastructure more extensive, her negotiating techniques more advanced than those of other states.[2] Though Austria had been part of the European diplomatic network from the very beginning,[3] the other two eastern powers only joined during the eighteenth century. While Vienna by this period closely resembled the kind of diplomatic society to be found in every major capital, the situations in Berlin and, in a different way, St Petersburg, were distinctive and were important for their states' political rise. The emergence of the eastern powers influenced the nature of international relations as well as their content.

By the mid-eighteenth century diplomats, mostly drawn from a common social caste, the high nobility, were becoming a distinct society at almost every European court. This development had been assisted by the growth of large-scale peace con-

---

[1] The best introduction is Anderson, *Rise of Modern Diplomacy*, pp. 41–102, while Lucien Bély, *Espions et ambassadeurs au temps de Louis XIV* (Paris, 1990) is an important detailed study of the crucial decades around 1700. Valuable background is provided by the wide-ranging collection edited by Lucien Bély, *L'invention de la diplomatie: Moyen Age – temps modernes* (Paris, 1998).

[2] For French diplomacy, see Claire Béchu, 'Les ambassadeurs français au XVIIIe siècle: formation et carrière', in Bély, ed., *L'invention de la diplomatie*, pp. 333–48.

[3] For Austria's involvement in the emergence of resident diplomacy, see Klaus Müller, *Das kaiserliche Gesandtschaftswesen im Jahrhundert nach dem Westfälischen Frieden (1648–1740)* (Bonn, 1976).

gresses after 1648, above all that at Utrecht in the closing stages of the War of the Spanish Succession, and by the emergence of French as the language of diplomacy.[4] By the mid-eighteenth century if not actually before, the diplomatic round had become established.[5] Ambassadors and envoys met their counterparts, together with the ministers, military commanders and leading noblemen of the host country, at an endless series of social yet semi-official engagements: receptions, formal dinners, balls, and musical and theatrical entertainments of all kinds.[6] These occasions were reciprocal: they were given by foreign diplomats as well as by the high officials and court nobility. The political function of the diplomatic round, with its elaborate and formalised social intercourse, was to permit the exchange of information. Diplomats traded scraps of intelligence as a commodity and in this way secured much of the news which filled their despatches.[7] Its anticipated benefits had been succinctly set out by François de Callières, a French foreign ministry official who in the 1690s had written the best-known diplomatic manual of the age:

A good table is the easiest and best way of getting intelligence of what passes, when the people of the country are at liberty to go and dine with the ambassador . . . It is the natural effect of good eating and drinking to beget friendships, and to create a familiarity and frankness among those who eat and drink together; and when people begin to be a little warmed with wine, they often discover secrets of importance.[8]

This was certainly the situation in Vienna.[9] There, as in most capitals, the diplomatic corps constituted one part of a much larger social universe. This world centred upon the Habsburg court and imperial family, together with the individual courts of the leading ministers and great aristocrats. During much of the year the town palaces of the dynasty and of the aristocracy provided an elegant setting for an unbroken series of social and cultural gatherings. The leading foreign ambassadors were admitted as of right to these events, and provided reciprocal hospitality in return. Their own social status, as members of the high nobility, together with the standing of the rulers whom they represented, guaranteed access to a very hierarchical and regulated world of assemblies, dinners and cultural events, and enabled them to return the compliment. Prussia's diplomats in Vienna were here at a real disadvantage. Usually drawn from the lesser nobility and lacking the high diplomatic rank and resources of their fellow representatives, who were frequently ambassadors, they were on the very fringes of the Habsburg capital's diplomatic

---

[4] Bély, *Espions et ambassadeurs*, pp. 373–410 *passim*.

[5] For its significance, see *François de Callières: The Art of Diplomacy*, ed. H.M.A. Keens-Soper and Karl W. Schweizer (Leicester and New York, 1983), pp. 112–14 *passim*.

[6] For its importance: Bielfeld, *Institutions politiques*, II. 222.

[7] Anderson, *Rise of Modern Diplomacy*, p. 43.

[8] *François de Callières: The Art of Diplomacy*, ed. Keens-Soper and Schweizer, p. 116.

[9] Though official correspondence offers occasional glimpses, this informal diplomatic society is difficult to reconstruct in any detail. An unparalleled source for the Habsburg capital is the diary of Karl von Zinzendorf: HHStA Tagebuch Zinzendorf, esp. vols. 8–9.

round.[10] Remarkably, this world of regular dinners and entertainments had continued in Vienna almost unabated during the desperate struggle of the Seven Years
War.[11] It was always on a far more lavish scale than diplomatic society in Berlin and
even St Petersburg, and became even more opulent with the return of peace after
1763.

Austrian diplomacy was also closer to the western European pattern, and no
major innovations were evident during the period covered by this study. A secure
and much more professional institutional structure had been established in the early
1750s, with the reconfiguration of the *Staatskanzlei*.[12] A minor dimension of
Kaunitz's important reform proved to be of enduring significance. In 1753 the
Oriental Academy was established.[13] Its purpose was to train young men in the language and customs of the Ottoman empire, where they would then be sent to serve
as secretaries and translators in Austria's diplomatic mission. Hitherto such training had been undertaken in Constantinople itself, but it was now moved to Vienna
and made more extensive and systematic. The Chancellor's initiative did something
to compensate for Austria's relative political decline and gave her diplomacy at the
Porte particular expertise. One problem facing all European states in
Constantinople was their own ignorance of the country's language, though Italian
seems to have been something of a *lingua franca*. A steady supply of qualified lin-
guists may have given Austrian diplomacy a relative advantage over Russia and
Prussia in the crucial south-eastern European sector. The Habsburg representative
in Constantinople during the Russo-Ottoman War of 1768–74, Thugut, was one of
the Oriental Academy's first graduates.[14]

The nature and purpose of resident diplomacy – at Vienna as elsewhere – had
become established by the beginning of the eighteenth century. Callières had
declared that 'The functions of a minister who is sent into a foreign country may be
reduced to two principal heads: the one is, to negotiate there the affairs of his own
Prince; and the other is to discover those of others.'[15] This encapsulated a diplomat's
duties.[16] Though ambassadors, envoys and ministers were expected periodically to
conduct negotiations, their routine functions were to submit regular assessments of
the political objectives of the court to which they were accredited and to report with

---

[10] It is revealing how very seldom Karl von Zinzendorf encountered Rohde, as he moved through the
upper levels of Vienna's social world: HHStA Tagebuch Zinzendorf, vols. 8–9 *passim*.
[11] See the astonished remarks of A.R. Vorontsov: *AKV*, v. 51–2. His impression is confirmed by the sections of the Zinzendorf Diary for 1761 to early 1763, substantial extracts from which have been published as *Karl Graf von Zinzendorf – Aus den Jugendtagebüchern 1747, 1752–1763*, ed. Maria Breunlich
and Marieluise Mader (Vienna, 1997), pp. 184–314. The full version is in HHStA Tagebuch
Zinzendorf, vols. 6–8.   [12] See above, pp. 82–3.
[13] Karl A. Roider, Jr, 'The Oriental Academy in the *Theresienzeit*', *Topic* 34 (1980), pp. 19–28, provides
an accessible introduction.   [14] See below, p. 204.
[15] *François de Callières: The Art of Diplomacy*, ed. Keens-Soper and Schweizer, p. 110.
[16] The best discussion of diplomatic practices in the mid-eighteenth century is that contained in
Bielfeld, *Institutions politiques*, II. 143–262. It was extremely derivative, acknowledging a predictable
obligation to the well-known handbooks of Wicquefort, Callières and Pecquet.

any intelligence they could assemble. Prussia's spectacular rise had made this second task especially important for diplomats posted to Berlin. From the 1740s onwards other European governments had sought to collect information on her distinctive political and military system and her remarkable King.[17] The situation throughout the Hohenzollern territories, however, placed considerable obstacles in the way of diplomats seeking such information. The internal security measures which were routine in Prussia made the kind of intelligence activities which were commonplace elsewhere a high-risk undertaking, while the systematic and large-scale interception of foreign diplomatic correspondence also impeded the transmission of such information as could be gleaned.[18] Since Frederick expected his own diplomatic agents to act in effect as spies, he assumed that their foreign counterparts would do likewise and therefore ensured that diplomats in Berlin were closely watched.[19] The veil of secrecy behind which Prussian diplomacy was conducted extended to all the political and military activities of the Hohenzollern state.[20] Enlightened thinkers rightly praised the real freedom of thought and expression which prevailed at Berlin, but – as they were careful to note – this liberality did not extend to questions of security and defence. On the contrary: eighteenth-century Prussia was a very difficult place in which to assemble reliable political and military intelligence, and this was more and more true the longer Frederick the Great's reign lasted.

This problem was compounded by the King's retreat from active diplomacy after 1763.[21] Before the Seven Years War, he had observed many of the necessary formalities, though even at this period he economised severely over the time he was prepared to spend on such events. His dislike of ceremonial and the disputes it created, which made him extremely reluctant to send or receive agents of the highest rank, that of ambassador, together with his desire to keep diplomats at arm's length, had been evident from a very early point in his reign.[22] The foreign representatives had been squeezed out almost from the moment he began to rule.[23] They had audiences with the King when they arrived and departed, though remarkably little was usually said on such occasions. Frederick was always noticeably taciturn and ended such interviews as quickly as he could: unless, of course, such audiences had distinct political purposes, as that given to Ahmed Resmi in late 1763 clearly did, when the King would go out of his way to be gracious to his diplomatic guest.[24] One well-placed

---

[17] See, e.g., AAE MD (Prusse) 2, which contains several memoirs on these subjects.

[18] See the account in NLS 12944, fo. 70; cf. Thiébault, *Mes souvenirs*, III. 16–17.

[19] 'Political Testament' of 1752, *Die politischen Testamente*, ed. Dietrich, pp. 360, 658; Bielfeld, *Institutions politiques*, II. 215. Hugh Elliot noted in 1777 that 'a jealous eye is kept over all those who form any particular connection with [foreign diplomats] at Berlin': to Suffolk, 3 May 1777, PRO SP 90/101.

[20] See, e.g., Wraxall, *Memoirs*, I. 117, on the extreme security measures which surrounded the secret military manoeuvres at Potsdam. On the absolute imperative of secrecy in the conduct of Prussian foreign policy, see Bielfeld, *Institutions politiques*, II. 76. [21] See above, p. 90.

[22] See the 'Political Testament' of 1752: *Die politischen Testamente*, ed. Dietrich, p. 330.

[23] Valori to Amelot, 7 June 1740, AAE CP (Prusse) 110, fo. 380.

[24] Aksan, *An Ottoman Statesman*, p. 86, for his reception; cf. above, pp. 113–15, for the Ottoman embassy and the use made of it by Prussia.

contemporary remarked that Frederick regarded all such ceremonial occasions as 'a species of forced labour'.[25] Though he went on to claim that the King performed such duties with good grace, few foreign diplomats would have endorsed this view, as they were rushed through brief audiences. A good illustration had been the perfunctory interview given to Sir Charles Hanbury-Williams in 1750.[26] Britain's envoy was not lacking in self-confidence, and turned up to present his credentials – the formal inauguration of a mission – fully expecting an extended political discussion, during which he could pass on his own accumulated political wisdom to the King. What happened was the exact opposite: to his lasting chagrin, he was forced to wait for an hour, and his audience then lasted precisely five and a half minutes from the point at which he entered the royal chamber until he left it. It was more and more to be the experience of diplomats who were posted to Berlin.

After 1763 Frederick became even less accessible to the diplomatic corps, a circumstance which was strengthened by his retreat to Potsdam.[27] Obsessed with restoring the shattered fabric of his state and buttressing his international position, he devoted less and less time to diplomatic formalities. At some point – probably in the 1760s – audiences for the foreign envoys became generalised rather than individual, as they were at every other court. A diplomat, instead of seeing the King privately, would find himself one of a group waiting upon Prussia's ruler in the audience chamber and might exchange a few snatched words with the King, if he were fortunate.[28] All of this saved Frederick considerable time.[29] It was, however, a further obstacle to effective negotiation and even routine diplomacy in Berlin. Indeed, it was plausibly claimed that there were diplomats who had been in the Prussian capital for many years, but who had not exchanged a word with the King since their first, formal interview.[30] This was less of an omission than it might seem, however, in view of Frederick's notorious willingness to embarrass foreign representatives during the occasional audiences he granted, usually by asking pointed and often playful questions.[31]

The situation was exacerbated by Berlin's attenuated diplomatic round, which contrasted sharply with the situation in Vienna and even in St Petersburg. Political high society was to be found in almost every European capital, but it scarcely existed in the Berlin of Frederick the Great: 'dull and insipid' was Hugh Elliot's decisive verdict.[32] A basic diplomatic round had existed under his predecessors and, despite Frederick's efforts, it continued throughout his reign, albeit on an infinitely smaller

[25] Thiébault, *Mes souvenirs*, II. 207.   [26] To Newcastle, 22 July 1750, PRO SP 88/71.

[27] See above, pp. 90–3.   [28] AAE CP (Prusse) 191, fos. 193–4.

[29] As did the practice of not invariably giving returning diplomats a formal audience at Potsdam: AAE CP (Prusse) 193, fo. 316.   [30] AE CP (Prusse) 192, fo. 22; cf. PRO SP 90/93, fo. 2.

[31] For a good example, see Mitchell to Rochford, 31 Dec. 1768, PRO SP 90/87, fo. 175.

[32] *A Memoir of the Right Honourable Hugh Elliot*, ed. Countess of Minto (Edinburgh, 1868), p. 202. Upon his appointment he had been warned by a friend from his time at Regensburg (where he had earlier served) that this would be so: *A Memoir of Hugh Elliot*, ed. Minto, pp. 105–6.

scale than at other courts: as newcomers invariably commented.[33] Karl von Zinzendorf declared when he visited Prussia's capital in 1770 that the social round was far less extensive than at any major court through which he had passed: a significant verdict given his wide-ranging travels during the previous decade.[34] While in Prussia, he himself usually dined alone at his inn or with a single acquaintance. Two decades earlier, Hanbury-Williams was believed to have declared, and probably did say, towards the end of his own stay, that 'a man might as well make his court to a parcel of hogs as to the court of Berlin'.[35] This characteristically trenchant verdict underlined the absence of a court society for much of the year.[36] Ministers and members of the Hohenzollern family were actively discouraged from having links with foreign representatives.[37] Indeed, after the death of the Queen Mother in 1757 an attempt was made to bar diplomats from the separate courts maintained by members of the royal family, and this seems to have been partially successful.[38]

The absence of diplomatic society was also due to the poverty of the country and its nobility,[39] as well as to the royal disfavour towards such contacts which radiated out from Potsdam. In 1780, Graf Spiridion von Lusi, who was about to be named as Prussia's representative in London and for this purpose was learning English, found it prudent to avoid all contacts with the diplomatic corps in Berlin. This, reported a British observer, 'is known to be a means of paying court to His Prussian Majesty, and a precaution almost necessary for those who have the prospect of being employed in His service'.[40] Finckenstein and Hertzberg, the two ministers formally responsible for foreign policy after the Seven Years War, gave relatively few dinners for diplomats, perhaps no more than five or six a year, and only occasionally opened their own houses in the evenings.[41] This contrasted sharply with Kaunitz, who held open house at least once a week, welcomed visitors on a large scale and regularly gave more intimate dinners.[42] In Vienna leading aristocrats and other officials and military commanders also offered hospitality liberally: in contrast, their Prussian

---

[33] E.g. James Harris's strictures: *Diaries and Correspondence of James Harris, First Earl of Malmesbury*, ed. Earl of Malmesbury (4 vols., London, 1844), I. 97–8; cf. the views of Robert Liston, who was successively secretary to Hugh Elliot (British Envoy Extraordinary 1777–82) and *chargé d'affaires* during the latter's absence in 1779–80: *A Memoir of Hugh Elliot*, ed. Minto, pp. 193–4, 202, 217.

[34] HHStA Tagebuch Zinzendorf, vol. 15 (1770), fos. 86 *et seq.*

[35] Quoted by D.B. Horn, *Sir Charles Hanbury-Williams and European Diplomacy (1747–58)* (London, 1930), p. 66 n. 1.   [36] Cf. above, pp. 91–2.   [37] AAE CP (Prusse–Supplément) 7, fos. 157–8.

[38] AAE CP (Prusse) 204, fos. 211–12.

[39] AAE MD (Prusse) 8, fo. 84; *A Memoir of Hugh Elliot*, ed. Minto, p. 107.

[40] Robert Liston to Benjamin Langlois, 11 Mar. 1780, NLS 5819, fo. 55. Lusi was to serve in London from 1781 to 1789: *Repertorium*, III. 329.

[41] Masson, ed., 'Berlin', p. 38. This substantially prints the Chevalier de Gaussen's account of diplomacy in the Prussian capital.

[42] This emerges from HHStA Tagebuch Zinzendorf, vols. 8–9 and 15–17 *passim*. A.R. Vorontzov, who visited Vienna during the Seven Years War, claimed that the Chancellor gave dinners (which in the eighteenth century were held in the early afternoon) for a small group of specially invited guests (including favoured foreign diplomats) every day at 2.00 p.m.: *AKV*, v. 51.

counterparts gave only three or four dinners annually.[43] There were only occasional exceptions. One came in late May 1779, when Frederick returned from the War of the Bavarian Succession almost as a conquering hero and the diplomatic corps were included in the celebrations in the Prussian capital.[44] Yet even these were not without a calculated snub to the foreign representatives, who waited for five hours for the King to arrive, in order to pay their compliments, only to find that he ignored them and went into another room to speak to his military commanders.[45] Such festivities were very rare, particularly during the second half of the reign.

Prussia also did not possess the kind of aristocratic society which flourished at Vienna or Versailles and was an essential component of the diplomatic round. This reflected the distinctive structure of the Prussian nobility, which completely lacked the sizeable aristocratic élite which existed elsewhere by this point, and also its relative poverty. The notoriously poor soil throughout most of the Hohenzollern territories, the smallness of many Junker estates and the continuing importance of partible inheritance all militated against the kind of stratification familiar elsewhere in Europe.[46] It is striking that only one family in later eighteenth-century Brandenburg (the von Arnim-Boitzenburg) had an annual income of between 50,000 and 100,000 *taler*; in the Habsburg Monarchy no less than 100 noble families enjoyed a yearly revenue of this size.[47] This relative impoverishment was one reason why such noblemen who attended court in Berlin did so only for the period of Carnaval, which lasted for some five weeks annually in December and January.[48]

One explanation widely advanced by foreign observers was Prussian poverty.[49] It was especially evident after 1763, when retrenchment was rigorously pursued. Frederick personally spearheaded the economy drive. During the King's final decade a British traveller commented, with mingled awe and admiration, that England's Good Queen Bess 'was not more frugal of the public purse'.[50] In 1767, James Harris, who in the next decade was to be Britain's minister to Prussia, visited Berlin in the course of his travels. He was startled to see the King personally supervising the distribution of candles before the marriage celebrations of a Prince of Anhalt-Dessau could begin: only the main rooms were allowed more than one, and elsewhere a Stygian gloom prevailed. Harris's surprise turned to disdain when the wine quickly ran out, and he was offered only tea.[51] Yet for a Prussian minister such as Finckenstein, poverty was also a convenient cloak behind which he could shelter. Royal disfavour towards contacts with foreign diplomats, together with his own

---

[43] Masson, ed., 'Berlin', p. 36.   [44] NLS 5819, fo. 3.
[45] *A Memoir of Hugh Elliot*, ed. Minto, p. 188.
[46] Edgar Melton, 'The Prussian Junkers, 1600–1786', in H.M. Scott, ed., *The European Nobilities in the Seventeenth and Eighteenth Centuries* (2 vols., London, 1995), II. 71–109, especially pp. 76, 81, 109.
[47] James Van Horn Melton, 'The Nobility in the Bohemian and Austrian Lands, 1620–1780', in Scott, ed., *European Nobilities*, II. 124.   [48] See above, p. 91.   [49] Masson, ed., 'Berlin', p. 38.
[50] Wraxall, *Memoirs*, I. 122.
[51] *Diaries and Correspondence of James Harris*, ed. Earl of Malmesbury, I. 4–5; for another example of royal miserliness, *Diaries and Correspondence of James Harris*, ed. Earl of Malmesbury, I. 133.

ignorance – whether real or feigned – made him anxious to restrict formal and informal contacts with the diplomatic corps. It was aided by the extremely limited etiquette at Berlin between foreign representatives and the Ministers of State: in 1756 the French ambassador the duc de Nivernais had been surprised to discover that, although Podewils received his first visit – the essential inauguration of an embassy – he was unwilling to return it as would have happened at almost every court, and this practice seems to have been general.[52]

The life of a foreign representative in Prussia during this period was thus as bleak as Brandenburg's weather. The relative openness of diplomacy under Frederick William I[53] had given way after 1740 to a situation where the diplomats lived within a laager in Berlin and only occasionally sallied out beyond their compound. The only regular dinners and receptions were those laid on by other envoys and there were (according to the French *chargé d'affaires* in the 1770s) no more than one or two of these a week. At most, the enterprising diplomatic *bon viveur* might find – if he was fortunate or merely determined – three houses where he could be received in the evening. For most of the year, the principal relaxation was provided by interminable games of cards. Diplomats habitually dined at home, and grasped at the earliest opportunity to leave the Prussian capital. Formal contacts with officials and with the King were kept to an absolute minimum: one observer explicitly declared that the diplomatic corps were kept behind a *cordon sanitaire* in Berlin.[54] Remarkably, at least by the 1770s, the Prussian ministers did not appoint a regular day and time at which they were available to see foreign diplomats, who were forced to ask for a special interview if they had anything to discuss.[55] Once again, this was in sharp contrast to the situation in every other major capital. In any case, such meetings only revealed the ignorance of the Ministers of State. The French minister, the marquis de Pons, spoke for all his fellow diplomats when he complained that these were 'purely mechanical instruments who tried to hide their own unimportance under an air of discretion'.[56]

After 1763, as throughout Frederick's reign, the *Kabinettsministerium* contained two ministers who were formally responsible for Prussian diplomacy.[57] The senior was the King's youthful companion, Graf Karl Wilhelm Finck von Finckenstein (1714–1800), who had been given early diplomatic experience and had been marked out for rapid promotion, becoming minister in June 1749.[58] After the veteran Podewil's death in 1760, he alone handled affairs until the end of the Seven Years War. He was joined in 1763 by Graf Ewald Friedrich von Hertzberg (1725–95), who had studied law at Halle, had a special expertise in German affairs and was to prove

[52] Nivernais to Rouillé, 13 Jan. 1756, AAE CP (Prusse) 181, fos. 103–4; AAE MD (Prusse) 8, fo. 115.
[53] See the comments of the British representative Melchior Guy Dickens: PRO SP 90/47, fo. 11.
[54] Thiébault, *Mes souvenirs*, II. 358–9.   [55] AAE CP (Prusse) 195, fos. 61–2.
[56] AAE CP (Prusse) 195, fo. 255.   [57] The only periods when this was not so were 1740–1 and 1760–3.
[58] *ABB*, VII. 248; Finckenstein had served for short periods in Sweden, Denmark, Britain and Russia. This varied experience, which recalled that of Podewils, was clearly intended to prepare him for a career in the *Kabinettsministerium*: for his diplomatic posts, see *Repertorium*, II. 291, 297, 304, 306.

shrewd and notably hard-working: he was later to be very influential under Frederick William II (1786–97). Both Finckenstein and Hertzberg came to acquire royal respect and even a degree of influence, and this increased during the 1770s and 1780s. The volume of correspondence and negotiations was far too great even for Frederick to transact, especially as the King grew older and more infirm. His need for information and for advice on matters of detail gave some power to his foreign ministers. For much of the time, however, the two men were reduced to handling unimportant issues and matters that were minor or routine. Their downgrading was apparent in the fact that, due to Frederick's strict economising, they were at times forced to make their own copies of despatches and state papers.[59] While both came to be trusted subordinates, they were always subordinates, and they were occasionally kept in the dark or even deceived as to the real aims of Prussia's policy and the negotiations their master was actually pursuing.[60] Their principal task remained that of routine liaison with the foreign diplomats posted to Berlin.[61] The corollary of absolute royal control of all important negotiations was that the ministers were stripped of any initiative and were also unable to influence diplomacy.

The King alone – together with the trusted and invisible Eichel – was aware of Prussia's real objectives. A diplomat could, of course, always ask for an interview with Frederick. It was not without its dangers. Private audiences with the King were extremely difficult to secure and, perhaps, dangerous to request. In the first place it was necessary to ask for a formal meeting and for this request to be granted: something which could not be assumed,[62] and which involved a diplomat explaining why it was essential for him to see Frederick personally, with a consequent gain of information to Prussia. This system prevented the kind of freewheeling interviews and private insinuations which were the meat and drink of eighteenth-century ambassadors elsewhere. For most of the year, these audiences would take place at Potsdam, and they were usually seen by the King as an intrusion: diplomats who troubled him unnecessarily could expect a frosty reception, as Britain's Sir Andrew Mitchell found to his cost in 1766.

In that summer, a new ministry took office in London. Its leader was William Pitt, now ennobled as Earl of Chatham, and its first objective was to revive the alignment

---

[59] Thiébault, *Mes souvenirs*, III. 142; cf. AAE CP (Prusse) 204, fo. 26, for one example of Finckenstein acting as a glorified clerk and himself taking dictation.

[60] See the decisive verdict of Sir Andrew Mitchell, written after more than a decade's service in Berlin: to Stormont, 12 Oct. 1768, BL Add. MSS 6810, fo. 173. James Harris, with less experience of the Prussian capital, was inclined to exaggerate, though he made the same basic point: PRO SP 90/93, fo. 62, 125. It was apparently fairly common for ministers to be ignorant of the formal Instructions which were given to Prussian diplomats: e.g. AAE CP (Prusse) 205, fo. 38. In 1755 Podewils had been forced to admit to France's representative in Berlin that he did not know the King's attitude to the Prusso-French alliance, though this would soon lapse!: AAE CP (Prusse) 179, fo. 167.

[61] See the King's extremely revealing letter to Finckenstein, 14 Aug. 1775, *Pol. Corr.*, XXXVII. 166–7. This was exactly the role Frederick had prescribed for the senior official in the *Kabinettsministerium*, Heinrich von Podewils, in the first year of his reign: *Pol. Corr.*, I. 198.

[62] PRO SP 90/82, fo. 309; Wraxall, *Memoirs*, I. 133–4.

with Prussia which had existed during the Seven Years War.[63] Frederick was resolved to avoid any British alliance in the future, believing that he had been exploited during that conflict and that new links would only involve Prussia in the Anglo–French conflict which he deemed inevitable.[64] He believed in any case that his own security was guaranteed by the Russian treaty signed in April 1764. This was apparent to Mitchell, though not to his superiors in London, who were intent upon a new alliance. In autumn 1766, he returned to Berlin, where he enjoyed a privileged relationship with the King. Mitchell had first been appointed in 1756 and had shared the burdens of the Seven Years War with Frederick, being admitted to his inner circle.[65] Yet even this did not protect him from the King's notoriously sharp tongue, though it may have reduced the number of insults which he received. In early September and again at the beginning of December, Mitchell went to Potsdam to broach a new alliance. On each occasion he received only barbs, sarcasm and outright rejection.[66] His experience mirrored that of other foreign envoys who dared to disturb Frederick in his lair, though – lacking Mitchell's special status – they usually received a more brutal and certainly more caustic rebuff. Indeed, the French minister, Guines, went as far as to claim that few diplomats possessed the necessary courage even to ask for an audience at Potsdam.[67]

The corollary was that invitations to stay at Potsdam were used to honour and flatter visiting diplomats when the King wanted something – usually an alliance or some other form of political co-operation – from their state, or was engaged in important negotiations with it. There had been two particularly clear illustrations of this in 1756. Frederick faced a menacing situation, with a hostile alliance taking shape against him in Europe and an unofficial Anglo–French colonial war threatening to spread to the continent.[68] His response had been to sign a Neutrality Convention for 'Germany' with Britain in mid-January.[69] It was difficult to reconcile this with Prussia's existing French alliance, which would expire in May.[70] France's new minister, the duc de Nivernais, arrived in Berlin at the beginning of the year with instructions to renew the previous alliance, which Frederick was also anxious to do. The diplomatic red carpet was laid out for Nivernais, who was fêted in Berlin, invited to Potsdam for an extended stay and given unparalleled access to the King.[71] This included the singular distinction of being allowed to reside with the monarch at his winter residence, the *Stadtschloss*. His mission, however, was

---

[63] Scott, *British Foreign Policy*, pp. 33–6, 93–4, 97–101, provides an account of these efforts and their context.   [64] See above, p. 108.   [65] See the exemplary study by Doran, *Andrew Mitchell*.
[66] His accounts of these interviews are in *Correspondence of William Pitt, Earl of Chatham*, ed. W.S. Taylor and J.H. Pringle (4 vols., London, 1838–40), III. 67–71 and 139–43, and PRO SP 90/85, fos. 223–7.
[67] To Choiseul, 11 Mar. 1769, AAE CP (Prusse–Supplément) 7, fo. 157. In 1777, Hugh Elliot declared that foreign diplomats 'dare not approach' Frederick's *Residenzstadt*: to Suffolk, 3 May 1777, PRO SP 90/101.   [68] See above, pp. 28–9.   [69] The Convention of Westminster, signed on 16 Jan. 1756.
[70] AAE CP (Prusse) 179, fos. 65–6.
[71] See his despatches for the second half of January and February 1756: AAE CP (Prusse) 181, *passim*.

soon aborted. France, already suspicious of Prussia's good faith, was outraged by Frederick's signature of the Convention of Westminster.

The conclusion of the Austro-French defensive alliance on 1 May 1756 surprised and isolated Prussia, and made relations with London crucial. This was evident in the special treatment accorded to Mitchell when he first arrived in Berlin in May 1756. Between then and the final week of August (when Frederick invaded Saxony), Britain's minister made no less than six visits to Potsdam.[72] There was an element of Frederick's personal convenience in all this: it was a natural consequence of his own isolation at Sans Souci. Such invitations were sparingly bestowed, especially after 1763, and were primarily a way of honouring particular diplomats and cultivating – or appearing to cultivate – their states: as it had been for Ahmed Resmi.[73] In December 1775, when the King was seeking improved relations with France, her new ambassador was invited to Potsdam. This had a secondary purpose: to demonstrate Frederick's supposed recovery after a serious and prolonged period of illness.[74] It highlighted the way in which such visits by a foreign envoy also came to be the principal means by which the diplomatic corps could discover the present state of the King's health: something that was periodically important during the second half of the reign.[75]

Too much should not be claimed for this distinctive method of conducting Prussia's external policy and of the singular position of diplomats at Berlin. It was one of a number of factors which enabled Frederick's state to have such a dramatic impact upon Europe. During the quarter century of political emergence between 1740 and 1763, skilful diplomacy had contributed something to Prussia's rise, but it was less important than military power, administrative efficiency, social cohesion and the quality of political leadership provided by the King. Diplomacy contributed far more to securing and buttressing her vulnerable position as the weakest of Europe's great powers after the Seven Years War, in terms of position and resources though not her political standing. The distinctive characteristic of Frederick the Great's diplomacy was less its highly personal nature than its genuine secrecy. Eighteenth-century diplomacy enjoys the popular reputation – due to the title, though not the contents, of a celebrated work by Karl Marx – of being above all secret.[76] In other words, it was conducted behind a veil of confidentiality and often in a way that was subterranean, hidden from all but a handful of well-placed individuals. In fact the conduct of foreign policy and of actual negotiations was remarkably open, at least to members of the political élite. While this last qualification is important, it remains true that much diplomacy was conducted in public and its contours were clearly visible to experienced and well-placed observers: this was the

---

[72] See his correspondence for these months in PRO SP 90/65–66; cf. Doran, *Andrew Mitchell*, pp. 50–89.
[73] See above, pp. 113–14.   [74] AAE CP (Prusse) 193, fos. 410–18.
[75] In December 1766, for example, after his second interview at Potsdam, Mitchell was interrogated by the Austrian minister Nugent: PRO SP 90/85, fos. 232–4.
[76] Karl Marx, *Secret Diplomatic History of the Eighteenth Century* (London, 1899 edn).

situation in Vienna and also St Petersburg. The arrival and departure of couriers, meetings between foreign ambassadors and the ministers and even rulers of the host state, the existence of important negotiations, finally the rumours that seeped out from council chamber and bed chamber: all this made it difficult to conceal negotiations completely. In many states, the ruler's court, which provided the context for diplomacy, was also the principal source of the disclosures, which other envoys speedily transmitted to their superiors.

Berlin was the principal exception, and herein lies the broader importance of these arguments. Prussia's King ran his state's foreign policy through the *Kabinett*, from Potsdam or wherever he happened to be at that moment, while the diplomatic corps, the court and even his own ministers remained in the capital and in ignorance. Superficially, diplomacy in Berlin resembled the situation in all the other major European capitals. In practice, however, foreign representatives were always at a very considerable disadvantage. The potential benefits to Frederick of shrouding all his important political activities in secrecy are obvious, yet they are also difficult to quantify with any precision. The advantages to Prussia were to be most clearly evident during the negotiations in 1771–2 which led to the partition of Poland.[77] As a general rule, this enabled him to retain the initiative in diplomatic negotiations and to observe the cards – or at least some of them – held by the other players in the game, while at the same time keeping his own hand, with its feeble suit of trumps, hidden from view. In other words, it was one of a number of structural factors which did something to make up for Prussia's strategic diffusion and limited resources, and in this way helped to disguise her vulnerable international position after the Seven Years War.

II

The 1760s and 1770s were to be a crucial period for Russia's political integration. By 1763, her new power was evident, though the seeming fragility of Catherine II's régime was also recognised by contemporaries. Its pride and even arrogance, together with its new-found independence and tenacity in all political transactions, were a consistent diplomatic refrain. Britain's Sir George Macartney spoke for his fellow envoys when he remarked in November 1765 that 'this Court rises hourly higher and higher in her pride, and dazzled by her present prosperity looks with less deference upon other powers and with more admiration on herself'.[78] Poniatowski's election significantly boosted Russia's self-confidence, which increased still further during the next few years. By summer 1766, Britain's representative was moved to write: 'Vain of past success, giddy with present prospects, blind and incredulous to the possibility of a reverse, this Court becomes every day more intoxicated with pride, more contemptuous towards other powers, more elated with her own.'[79]

---

[77] See below, ch. 7.   [78] *SIRIO*, XII. 232.   [79] *SIRIO*, XII. 270; cf. *SIRIO*, XXII. 274.

While it is true that Macartney was stung to these – and similar – outbursts by the reverses and humiliations he was experiencing at the Russian court, his verdict was endorsed by other observers.[80] Such judgements reveal the final stage in the process by which Russia became a great power.

There is an important distinction between European awareness of Russia's power and potential, which had been evident for decades before 1756 – particularly in neighbouring eastern Europe[81] – and her emergence as a full member of the family of great powers, which determined the continent's political destiny. The leading states treated one other as equals: this was the key to their collective dominance of the international system. In Russia's case, this equality of treatment only began after the Seven Years War, and even then was incomplete. Britain in particular was reluctant to base relations upon strict equality and continued to assume St Petersburg's inferiority during prolonged alliance negotiations, which ensured that these would fail.

The fighting had been a watershed for Russia's own self-image. In spring 1756, anxious for hostilities to begin against Prussia, St Petersburg had suspended military preparations when Austria made clear that she did not intend to attack until the following year. Eighteenth-century thinking demanded that, to be considered a great power, a state should possess sufficient resources to fight and win a major war without outside support.[82] By this yardstick the Russia of Elizabeth and Bestuzhev was not yet a leading European power, while that of Catherine and Panin was. Though Russia's military performance in the Seven Years War was here important, the personality and political goals of her ruler after July 1762 were crucial. Catherine II's own position was not beyond challenge and she was conscious that it could be strengthened by Russia's new-found international prestige. From her first weeks on the throne, she was determined that her foreign policy should be free from the external control which she believed had influenced her predecessors' diplomatic strategy and so relegated Russia to a subordinate role.[83] She always appreciated the importance of reputation, sought to assert her political independence, and gave Russian diplomacy a new sense of purpose and direction.[84] The Empress was willing to take the initiative, to demand complete equality in all negotiations and insist that any Russian concessions must be matched by any prospective ally. This was most clearly demonstrated over the 'Turkish clause'.[85] Catherine and Panin

---

[80] E.g. Solms, in Aug. 1766: *SIRIO*, XXII. 471–2; cf. J.H.E. von Bernstorff, in the previous September: *Bernstorffsche Papiere*, II. 235–6.   [81] See above, p. 17.

[82] E.g. Bielfeld, *Institutions politiques*, II. 118–19.   [83] See above, p. 107.

[84] For an early example, see Catherine II to H.C. Keyerling, 6 Feb. 1763, *SIRIO*, XLVIII. 293; *SIRIO*, CXVIII. 280; cf. the comments of France's representative, Bérenger: to Praslin, 23 July 1763, *SIRIO*, CXL. 207. Panin wrote in the mid-1760s of the need to lay 'a real and firm foundation of our own independent system'; quoted in Soloviev, *History of Russia*, XLV. 109. In 1773 he would write that only after the Seven Years War did Russia begin 'to act independently and according to its own policy': Soloviev, *History of Russia*, XLVIII. 150; cf. LeDonne, *Russian Empire*, p. 41, for a similar verdict on Russian policy in Poland-Lithuania after July 1762.   [85] See above, p. 124.

believed that the exclusion of aid in any Ottoman war was a symptom of Russia's inferior political position, and therefore insisted that future allies must provide assistance if the Sultan attacked. Both Prussia (1764) and Denmark (1765) had agreed to do so.[86] Britain always refused to accept the 'Turkish clause', and this was one significant reason for the failure of extended alliance negotiations after the Seven Years War.

It has been suggested that the 1750s and 1760s saw Russia's 'economic awakening'.[87] This was linked to – and, indeed, was part of – a more fundamental transformation which may be styled the achievement of Russia's political maturity, something acknowledged in western comments about St Petersburg's new sense of power and prestige. The process by which Catherine II's state became a great power involved nothing less than a transformation of Russian political culture. Full admission to Europe's political élite involved the adoption of a wide range of practices already established in the relations of the other leading states.[88] In the cases of Austria and Prussia the necessary political culture had been acquired over an extended period of time. For Russia, however, it was a much more compressed process which occupied the first half of the Empress' reign.

Various symptoms can be recognised. The first is the improbable but important topic of bribery. During the reigns of the Empresses Anna and Elizabeth, the Russian court had enjoyed the reputation of being one of the most venal in Europe. Since the great powers employed such corruption at minor courts and not in major states, this in itself revealed Russia's political inferiority. The widespread assumption was that the skilful application of money was essential for success in St Petersburg.[89] In the 1730s the British government had paid various Russian ministers the considerable sum of £32,000 to secure a commercial treaty.[90] Immediately before the Seven Years War, no less a figure than the Chancellor, Bestuzhev-Riumin, had been on the British payroll.[91] Whether the direction of Russian policy had actually been influenced by such payments must be doubted, though their existence and extent are clear.[92] In the mid-1740s Bestuzhev had been paid at least £10,000 by Britain, nominally in lieu of the conventional and much less valuable diplomatic

---

[86] Madariaga, *Russia*, 194; *SIRIO*, LVII. 183–6.
[87] P.H. Clendenning, 'The Economic Awakening of Russia in the Eighteenth Century', *Journal of European Economic History* 14 (1985), 443–72.
[88] These have recently been defined by Paul Schroeder (following Michael Oakeshott) as 'the understandings, assumptions, learned skills and responses, rules, norms, procedures, etc., which agents acquire and use in pursuing their divergent aims within the framework of a shared practice': *Transformation of European Politics*, p. xii.
[89] See the 'Mémoire sur la Russie', drawn up by the Austrian minister Ludwig Friedrich Julius Graf von Zinzendorf in July 1755 and printed in *Preussische und österreichische Acten*, ed. Volz and Küntzel, pp. 678–726, especially pp. 684, 694–7, 713 and 718; cf. Frederick the Great's view: 'Political Testament' of 1752, *Die politischen Testamente*, ed. Dietrich, pp. 334, 392.
[90] D.K. Reading, *The Anglo-Russian Commercial Treaty of 1734* (New Haven, CT, 1934), p. 146.
[91] Horn, *Hanbury-Williams*, pp. 184–7, 229; for details, *SIRIO*, CXLVIII. 405, 414, 415, 463–5.
[92] Mediger, *Moskaus Weg nach Europa*, p. 298.

presents, in the hope that this would bring about the signature of a subsidy convention; he had earlier been 'loaned' a similar sum which was never repaid and had never been intended to be repaid, and he probably received money from other governments as well.[93] When Elizabeth's death in January 1762 suggested a period of uncertainty and perhaps important changes at the Russian court, the extraordinary sum of £100,000 was immediately sent to the British minister, R.M. Keith, together with a list of those individuals who might be bribed to advance London's interests and, crucially, to bring about Russia's withdrawal from the anti-Prussian coalition.[94] To put this enormous figure into perspective: it was to be exactly the annual subsidy demanded by Panin and refused by London during unsuccessful Russo-British alliance negotiations in 1763–4. When Keith's successor, the Earl of Buckinghamshire, was appointed six months later, he was given £50,000 for bribery on the assumption that such payments would be essential if an alliance and a parallel commercial treaty were to be concluded.[95]

The change under Catherine II became starkly apparent when the new ambassador tried to bribe M.L. Vorontsov, who was now Chancellor. Buckinghamshire's approach was peculiarly inept: he was foolish enough to make an offer of £2,000 in writing. Vorontsov may have been willing and even anxious to take English bribes, and he had openly solicited such payments from a previous British diplomat.[96] Catherine was known to be firmly opposed, however, and so the offer was rejected by Vorontsov, who showed the letter to the Empress to protect his own position.[97] The matter did not end there. Buckinghamshire was discredited and soon recalled. This episode marked the disappearance of overt bribery of leading ministers: thereafter information could be purchased at the Russian court, but not influence.[98] St Petersburg had ceased to be a political market place, like Stockholm or Warsaw, capitals of second-rank states at which money was seen as an essential lubricant of political success. Instead, foreign diplomats in Russia henceforth used their funds in the same way they did in Paris or Vienna: to secure intelligence, usually from minor figures, not to corrupt leading ministers.[99] The Empress' determination to be politically independent, together with her generosity to her principal advisers, who

[93] A.I. Turgenev, ed., *La cour de la Russie il y a cent ans 1725–1783* (Berlin, 1858), pp. 110, 119–20, 128; Zinzendorf believed these payments to be simply a consequence of the poverty of Russian ministers, which contrasted sharply with the wealth of the favourite, Ivan Shuvalov: 'Mémoire sur la Russie', in *Preussische und österreichische Acten*, ed. Volz and Küntzel, p. 697.

[94] Newcastle to Bute, 6 Feb. 1762, BL Add. MSS 32934, fo. 205; the list is in BL Add. MSS 33024, fo. 124.

[95] See 'Most Secret Instructions', 13 Aug. 1762, PRO SP 91/70, fos. 79–80. This view was shared by Bernstorff, who assumed that such payments would be essential to advance the Holstein exchange: to Haxthausen, 8 Sept. 1762, *Bernstorff Corr.*, II. 93–4.

[96] Horn, *Hanbury-Williams*, p. 245. M.L. Vorontsov may also have taken French money in the past: Madariaga, *Russia*, p. 194.

[97] *The Fourth Earl of Sandwich*, ed. Spencer, p. 46; Roberts, pp., *Macartney in Russia*, pp. 12–13; Martens, *Recueil des traités*, IX (X). 222–3. See also M.L. Vorontsov to A.R. Vorontsov, 11 July 1763 OS, *AKV*, XXXI. 231. [98] Madariaga, *Russia*, p. 194.

[99] See Isabel de Madariaga 'The Use of British Secret Funds at St Petersburg, 1777–1782', *Slavonic and East European Review* 32 (1953–54), pp. 464–74.

received riches and titles, made it less likely that they would accept bribes, in sharp contrast to the situation under Elizabeth.[100] From the very beginning of her reign, Catherine II set her face very firmly against corruption throughout Russian government, repeated an edict passed in 1760 against graft, and sought to pay regular salaries to her ministers and advisers.[101] The wheel had gone full circle. Russia, previously an object of great power bribery, had joined the diplomatic élite.

A similar evolution was apparent over the imperial title. Russia's rulers had traditionally claimed that 'Tsar' was the equivalent of the European 'Emperor' and thus elevated them above mere kings in matters of diplomatic form and ceremonial.[102] In the eighteenth century it was important because such issues of precedence expressed a state's relative international standing. Russia's main opponents were France and the Habsburg Emperor. The French King believed himself to be Europe's second secular ruler, after the Emperor, and this status was clearly challenged, since an imperial title eclipsed a royal dignity. The Russian claim had caused friction from Peter I's reign onwards, when it had been revived and determinedly pursued, but an agreement between St Petersburg and Versailles had been patched up in 1744 when the issue was shelved. The question was reopened after 1762, during a decade when relations were in any case poor and when it both exacerbated relations and expressed their bad state. The bitter dispute with France led to diplomacy being reduced to the level of *chargé d'affaires* when a new French envoy's credentials omitted the word 'imperial'. A settlement was only reached in 1772, when Russian claims were largely accepted by France, now anxious to improve relations with St Petersburg.[103] Catherine II was insistent on the imperial dignity, believing it was an integral part of Russia's new status, enhancing her own prestige and that of her country.[104] At the beginning of her reign, Poland had been forced to recognise the Empress's title and the Ottoman empire did likewise when peace was made in 1774, while in 1767 Britain had to apologise formally when the Secretary of State's office accidentally bungled by omitting 'imperial majesty' from an official letter.[105]

Catherine II's sensitivity over Russia's new international standing was also evident over diplomatic ceremonial. In the eighteenth century these crucial formalities, which were part of every mission, displayed the relative standing of states and

---

[100] S.R. Vorontsov subsequently remarked that, after a lifetime of public service, M.P. Bestuzhev-Riumin (brother of the leading minister), 'was not rich, never having received a single gift from our rulers': *AKV*, v. 79.   [101] Soloviev, *History of Russia*, XLII. 111.

[102] The complex origins of the Russian imperial title have been re-examined in a major article by Isabel de Madariaga, 'Tsar into Emperor: The Title of Peter the Great', in Oresko *et al.*, eds., *Royal and Republican Sovereignty*, pp. 351–81.

[103] This dispute can be followed in the volumes of *SIRIO*: see, for example, LVII. 350–2; LXVII. 1–5, 437–43; for the settlement, see the 'Instructions' for Durand, 24 July 1772, in *Recueil: Russie*, ed. Rambaud, II. 286–8.

[104] See Panin to Choiseul, 23 Jan. 1768, *SIRIO*, CXLI. 388 (the definitive Russian reply over the imperial title).

[105] *SIRIO*, LI. 120, 398; Hammer, *Historire de l'empire Ottoman*, XVI. 393; H.S. Conway to Henry Shirley, 21 Aug. 1767, BL Add. MSS 37054, fo. 9.

were a direct expression of power and prestige.[106] Russia's position as a leading state was itself at stake in disputes over protocol. Unless the other European powers accepted her claims, whether to pre-eminence or simply to equality, her new-found political rank would not be confirmed beyond question. Panin clearly recognised this, declaring on one occasion that 'Etiquette strictly regulates forms of correspondence between states precisely because it serves as a measure of the mutual respect for each other's strength.'[107] Diplomatic ceremonial at the Russian court had previously been fluid and not elaborate or ornate, at least by the standards of the major western states.[108] This reflected its location on Europe's periphery and the fact that most countries were represented by diplomats of a lower rank, ministers or envoys: ambassadors were infrequent and usually appointed for a specific purpose.[109] During Elizabeth's reign there had been growing interest in diplomatic etiquette, and information on other courts had been collected, but there was no major change in Russia's practice.[110] The splendour which accompanied a French ambassador, the marquis de l'Hôpital, in 1757 and the considerable size of his retinue had been matters of amazed comment at the Russian court, still little used to such ornate display.[111] From the early 1760s, the situation changed very rapidly, as Russia adopted the formal diplomatic ceremonial practised by the other European states.[112] This new concern was institutionalised by the evolution of a Ceremonial Department within the College of Foreign Affairs during Catherine II's reign.

The Empress was insistent that the correct protocol should be followed.[113] The early months of her reign were marked by a sharp dispute with Vienna over her demand that foreign ambassadors should kiss her hand when they were formally presented, a practice which had been introduced by the Empress Anna and a point which Austria was finally forced to concede.[114] Catherine probably established the custom of receiving diplomats seated on a throne positioned on a raised dais, a practice associated above all with Louis XIV.[115] A similar evolution is evident over the

---

[106] Bielfeld, *Institutions politiques*, II. 235, and more generally Bielfeld, *Institutions politiques*, II. 234–62.

[107] Quoted in Sergei V. Bakhrushin and Sergei D. Skazkin, 'Diplomacy', translated in Marc Raeff, ed., *Catherine the Great: A Profile* (New York, 1972), pp. 181–96, at p. 194.

[108] See Macartney's comments in January 1765: *SIRIO*, XII. 196.

[109] This is apparent from the lists in *Repertorium*, II–III, *passim*.

[110] V.E. Grabar, *The History of International Law in Russia, 1647–1917: A Bio-Bibliographical Study*, transl. and ed. W.E. Butler (Oxford, 1990), p. 98.

[111] *AKV*, V. 30. This display had the obvious purpose of sealing a Franco-Russian alliance: Oliva, *Misalliance*, pp. 71–3.

[112] See, for example, the description of the formal audience by an Ottoman diplomat: Norman Itzkowitz and Max Mote, eds., *Mubadele: An Ottoman–Russian Exchange of Ambassadors* (Chicago, IL, 1970), pp. 93–6; Grabar, *History of International Law*, p. 159.

[113] See Solms' comments at the conclusion of his mission: Volz, ed., 'Katharina II.', pp. 213–16.

[114] Grabar, *History of International Law*, p. 164; see the Austrian diplomatic correspondence in *SIRIO*, XVIII and XLVI.

[115] This is suggested by the contemporary print of Catherine receiving an Ottoman ambassador, reproduced in Alexander Brückner, *Katharina die Zweite* (Berlin, 1883), p. 241; cf. Itzkowitz and Mote, eds., *Mubadele*, p. 94, for this practice. For the raised throne: *Un diplomate français à la cour de Catherine II 1775–1780: journal intime du Chevalier de Corberon*, ed. L.-H. Lalande (2 vols., Paris, 1901), I. 96–7.

language of the formal audience at which a diplomat presented his credentials or took his leave. Catherine insisted, apparently for the first time, that foreign representatives should speak French and she would reply in the same language. The use of diplomacy's universal language was intended to demonstrate Russia's full membership of the international system. When Buckinghamshire spoke in English, the Empress replied in Russian.[116] The point was that protocol demanded full reciprocity if St Petersburg's new status were to be established. Throughout Catherine's reign, Russian diplomats were particularly insistent on the correct ceremonial and on equal treatment, and tenacious over precedence. Prince Nikolai Repnin's extreme concern over protocol during his embassy to Constantinople in 1775–6 was to be a particularly interesting illustration of this. These years also saw the beginning of a prolonged diplomatic guerrilla war at Warsaw as Stackelberg unsuccessfully sought to undermine the precedence enjoyed by papal nuncios, who outranked the representatives of all secular rulers.[117]

This is part of a larger subject and one which historians of eighteenth-century Russia and her political emergence have not examined in sufficient detail. Viewed from the perspective of the other great powers, Catherine II's reign appears to be the point at which St Petersburg fully embraced the institutions, practices and techniques of modern diplomacy. The most famous manual of eighteenth-century diplomacy, *De la manière de négocier avec les souverains*, had been translated into English, German and Italian soon after its initial publication. Significantly, it was not to be translated into Russian until Catherine II's reign and only published in that language in 1772.[118] It is instructive that the Empress personally directed and encouraged such translations, which during her reign were on a wholly new scale.[119] The appearance in Russian of Callières and of other French and German works on diplomacy and international law facilitated a wider and enduring change in the prevailing political culture, which under the Empress came to resemble that of the other leading European states. Britain's representative, Macartney, plausibly claimed in the mid-1760s that 'It was not until this reign . . . that the common forms of business as practised in other courts have been introduced into this', and even declared that he had been told that 'during the Empress Elizabeth's time, Bestuzhev signed all his Treaties, Conventions, and Declarations without any full powers from his Sovereign'.[120]

---

[116] Bakhrushin and Skazkin, 'Diplomacy', p. 193. Macartney spoke in French and Catherine replied in that language: *SIRIO*, XII.195–6; cf. *SIRIO*, LVII.145; see also Grabar, *History of International Law*, p. 165.

[117] Itzkowitz and Mote, eds., *Mubadele*, pp. 10, 65, 71 n. 72, and *passim*; Lawrence Wolff, 'A Duel for Ceremonial Precedence: The Papal Nuncio versus the Russian Ambassador at Warsaw, 1775–1785', *International History Review* 7 (1985), 235–44, and the overlapping account in his *The Vatican and Poland in the Age of the Partitions: Diplomatic and Cultural Encounter at the Warsaw Nunciature* (Boulder, CO, 1988), pp. 97–114, though the author underestimates the wider Russian aim of securing equality. For Stackelberg, see below, pp. 235–6.

[118] Grabar, *History of International Law*, p. 133. An earlier diplomatic handbook, Abraham van Wicquefort's *L'ambassadeur et ses fonctions*, first published in 1681, had been translated into Russian under Peter I; but it had remained in manuscript: Grabar, *History of International Law*, pp. 40–1, 47, 86.   [119] Grabar, *History of International Law*, pp. 125 *et seq.*   [120] *SIRIO*, XII. 249.

Russia's entry into the international system had been delayed and piecemeal. Though St Petersburg had been incorporated in the diplomatic network during Peter I's reign,[121] there had been no immediate adoption of European-style diplomacy. During the first half of the eighteenth century a continuing shortage of trained personnel, to staff the new permanent embassies, had inhibited Russia's emergence.[122] Very few native Russians possessed the necessary knowledge of foreign languages, above all French, and of international law, which diplomats required by this period.[123] As late as the 1750s it had been difficult to find sufficient noblemen with some grounding in the relevant languages to serve abroad.[124] Since the close of the seventeenth century determined but sporadic efforts had been made to educate future diplomats, but these had not initially been successful. During Peter I's reign, there had been two proposals to establish a training school, clearly modelled on the celebrated *Académie politique* established by France's foreign minister Torcy in 1712, but neither succeeded. Under Elizabeth, the noted legal scholar F.G. Strube de Piermont revived these attempts, but his plan also foundered.[125] Instead, efforts were made to attach young nobles to Russia's own embassies, to enable them to learn foreign languages and to receive some relevant training, imitating other states.[126] In Russia this seems to have begun as early as 1699, when eight such students had been attached to A.A. Matveev's mission to the Dutch Republic, and it had been continued during the generation after Peter I's death. Once again it was only during Catherine II's reign that the education of potential diplomats was formalised and expanded. The 'nobles of the embassy' scheme was systematised and made permanent; the official table of appointments, issued in 1779, provided for two such students to be attached to each diplomatic mission and for these places to be funded, at least in theory. More important was a major expansion of teaching in international law and recent political history – subjects recognised as crucial for future diplomats – which Catherine personally encouraged, at the new University of Moscow, established as recently as 1755.[127]

The same objectives were apparent in the attempt to create a treaty collection. Such compilations were essential within an international system dominated by

---

[121] See above, p. 16.

[122] David J. Taylor, 'Russian Foreign Policy, 1725–1739' (PhD thesis, University of East Anglia, 1983), pp. 10–20, provides an illuminating discussion of Russia's difficulties in adjusting to the requirements of an active and western-style diplomacy. To some degree the employment of Germans, characteristic of Russian government at this period, was a consequence of this shortage.

[123] According to Bielfeld, the three key texts for any diplomat were Grotius, *De jure belli ac pacis*; Pufendorf, *Droit de la nature et des gens*; and Montesquieu, *De l'esprit des lois: Institutions politiques*, I. 14. [124] Anderson, *Rise of Modern Diplomacy*, p. 90.

[125] Grabar, *History of International Law*, pp. 52–3, 106–7; W.E. Butler, 'F.G. Strube de Piermont and the Origins of Russian Legal History', in R. Bartlett and J.M. Hartley, eds., *Russia in the Age of Enlightenment: Essays for Isabel de Madariaga* (London, 1990), pp. 125–41.

[126] When, e.g., M.P. Bestuzhev-Riumin represented Russia at the French court during the Seven Years War, four prominent young noblemen were attached to his mission: *AKV*, v. 75.

[127] Anderson, *Rise of Modern Diplomacy*, pp. 89–90; Grabar, *History of International Law*, pp. 90–1, 172–83.

precedent and regulated by previous treaties of peace and alliance, and they were employed both in training future diplomats and during actual negotiations. The most famous was the *Corps universel diplomatique du droit des gens* of the Dutchman, Jean Dumont de Carlscroon, which began publication in 1726 and eventually comprised twelve volumes. Most European states had begun to acquire such printed compendiums during or immediately after the age of Louis XIV. In Russia once again this did not commence until Catherine II's reign. The leading part was played by the noted historiographer and secretary of the Russian Academy of Sciences, G.-F. Müller.[128] In 1760, Müller had unsuccessfully proposed that he should compile and publish Russia's treaties and other international agreements, for the use of her diplomats. In 1763–4 he was consulted by the Empress on Russia's relations with China, on which he produced two memoranda. In late 1765 he renewed his proposal for a collection of diplomatic acts, but it was again rejected. In a related development Müller was appointed director of the Moscow archive of the College of Foreign Affairs in the following year. With the important support of Prince M.M. Shcherbatov, Müller finally secured Catherine II's approval in 1779 – significantly at exactly the point when Russia's European influence was considerably enhanced by her mediation at Teschen[129] – for a collection of all Russian treaties, modelled on Dumont's *Corps universel diplomatique*. The first volumes appeared during the next four years, until his death in 1783 brought the project to a halt.[130]

The growing sophistication of Russian diplomacy was also evident in the more formal instructions given to ministers and envoys at the outset of their missions.[131] These were more detailed and elaborate than previously and included matters such as ceremonial and the protection of Russian trade. On occasions they were even drawn up in French, the established language of diplomacy, which underlines the extent of the changes. The instructions which Russian diplomats received from relatively early in Catherine's reign bear comparison with those given to their French counterparts, which set the standard for the rest of Europe.[132] This certainly had not been the case before the 1760s, when they seem to have been cursory and lacking in political sophistication.

The forms of Russian diplomacy were thus becoming more sophisticated and

---

[128] For whom see J.L. Black, *G.-F. Müller and the Imperial Russian Academy* (Kingston and Montreal, 1986). [129] See below, p. 254.
[130] W.E. Butler, 'Treaty Collections in Eighteenth-Century Russia: Encounters with European Experience', in A.G. Cross, ed., *Russia and the West in the Eighteenth Century* (Newtonville, MA, 1983), pp. 249–58, but especially pp. 253–4; Grabar, *History of International Law*, pp. 108–9, 183–6.
[131] Particularly good examples are those given to von Asseburg, 11 Oct. 1774, *SIRIO*, cxxxv. 230–45, and to Stackelberg in August 1772, which has been printed and edited by Jerzy Lojek, 'La politique de la Russie envers la Pologne pendant le premier partage d'après un document secret de la cour Russe de 1772', *Canadian-American Slavic Studies* 8 (1974), pp. 116–35; see also the 'Additional Instructions' for S.R. Vorontsov (Mar. 1788), *AKV*, xviii. 82–8.
[132] These are assembled in the great series *Recueil des Instructions données aux ambassadeurs et ministres de France*.

complex, and corresponded more closely to the dominant European pattern.[133] A similar and more significant transformation can be seen in the content of Catherine II's diplomacy. Here Nikita Panin, *de facto* foreign minister from 1763 until 1781, was important in two ways. Panin was unusual among Russia's eighteenth-century ministers on account of his long service as a diplomat, having been Russian minister in Denmark and Sweden.[134] This had given him direct and prolonged experience of western-style diplomacy, and he was therefore able to conduct negotiations on an equal footing. The frequent complaints of foreign representatives that Panin was an obstinate and wily negotiator testified to his mastery of the diplomatic craft. His first-hand knowledge of Europe's politics also contributed to the unusually wide perspective which he brought to Russian policy. In partnership with the Empress, he pursued a more wide-ranging diplomacy than St Petersburg had hitherto attempted. The celebrated 'Northern System' was European-wide in its conception.[135] Though never fully realised in practice, it had three unusual aspects. It provided an integrated and sophisticated political system in which alliances were sought not for a single goal (usually to attack a mutual enemy, or to discourage aggression by a third party) but for broader and less immediate purposes, above all to protect Russia's security along the vulnerable western frontier and to permit internal reform and financial recovery. Panin's scheme was unusually comprehensive: it envisaged alliances with Prussia, Britain, Denmark, Poland and Sweden. Secondly, it assumed Russia's equality with the major European states and so underlined her new international status. Finally, it broke with St Petersburg's previous diplomacy by seeking treaties in order to preserve peace and not to prepare for war. In each respect, Panin's diplomacy was qualitatively different from that of his predecessors. Men such as G.I. Golovkin, who nominally controlled Russian policy from 1706 until his death in 1734, or A.I. Ostermann during the 1720s and 1730s, or Bestuzhev during the 1740s and 1750s, had been fully conscious of Russia's interests and had sought to advance them. But their political vision had been narrower, their policies less sophisticated, their conduct of negotiations less skilful than that displayed by the architect of the 'Northern System'. Significantly, Panin's experience as a Russian diplomat had been more extensive than most of his predecessors'. Golovkin had accompanied Peter I on his Great Embassy but had never been a permanent diplomat, while Ostermann had handled the negotiations with Constantinople after the disaster on the Pruth and also the extended discussions which produced the Peace of Nystad, but he had never been a resident ambassador.[136]

---

[133] In spring 1769, however, Frederick – clearly influenced by Russian policy in Poland – was dismissive of the political skill and knowledge of Europe possessed by the Empress and Panin, whom he declared lacked any finesse and knew only how to operate by force: *Pol. Corr.*, XXVIII. 260.

[134] For this, see Krummel, 'Nikita Ivanovic Panins aussenpolitische Tätigkeit 1747–1758'; Soloviev, *History of Russia*, XLII. 78; and Ransel, *Politics of Catherinian Russia*, pp. 15–27.

[135] See above, pp. 123–4.

[136] Taylor, 'Russian Foreign Policy', pp. 22 *et seq*, 102; cf. *Repertorium*, II. 314, 315, 320, for Bestuzhev's diplomatic career.

Only Bestuzhev could eclipse Panin's long diplomatic service, having spent two decades as a Russian representative in posts around the Baltic, and his ministry prepared the ground for developments after 1762.

Behind Panin stood the Empress whose individual contribution to Russian foreign policy was enormous, and who played a quite central role in its conduct. At the very first meeting which she attended of the College of Foreign Affairs, Catherine announced that she would receive full diplomatic reports, not the customary summaries, and this practice continued throughout her reign. In 1782 she boasted to Joseph II – with pardonable exaggeration – that she personally read all Russian diplomatic despatches.[137] Unlike the Prussian King, she did not actually draft letters herself. During the first decade and a half of her reign, that task was undertaken by Panin, as the senior member of the College of Foreign Affairs. Catherine II's personality and the new scale of her ambitions were the final link in the process by which Russia entered the ranks of the great powers. By thinking and acting like the ruler of a first-class state, the Empress ensured that her adopted homeland came to be accepted as one: an identical evolution to that which Frederick the Great had brought about after 1740.[138] She exploited the position created by Russian armies during the Seven Years War and confirmed Russia's political pre-eminence. By insisting, from the very beginning of her reign, on equality with all the major states, she forced the other great powers to recognise that Russia was now one of their number.[139] Catherine II's search for prestige for her state was equally a search for personal prestige. In the process she carved out a new and, as it proved, permanent role for Russia in the international system, which became fully evident during the later 1760s.

---

[137] Grabar, *History of International Law*, p. 138.   [138] See above, pp. 22–3, for this.
[139] Grabar, *History of International Law*, p. 139.

6

From peace to war, 1766–1768

I

In the summer of 1766 Prussia's representative in Vienna, Rohde, left on leave.[1] Shortly before his departure, Kaunitz went out of his way, in a rare extended conversation, to highlight the friendly relations between the former adversaries and to stress Austria's wish that these should continue, sentiments which were endorsed by Maria Theresa in the envoy's formal leave-taking audience.[2] There was more than diplomatic form to these reassurances, which were fully justified in view of the untroubled state of Prusso-Austrian relations and, in a wider sense, of continental politics three years after the Peace of Hubertusburg. Though the Bourbon powers periodically clashed with Britain, these confrontations were minor and confined to the colonial sphere, and they appeared unlikely to bring on a new war. Within Europe, there appeared no obvious threat to peace and stability in mid-1766, and everywhere governments continued the tasks of reconstruction and reform, resumed after the peaceful election of a new Polish King.

Rohde's departure was the latest episode in a prolonged squabble with the tight-fisted Prussian King over pay arrears and inadequate expenses.[3] In late January the envoy had submitted a semi-ultimatum: if he were not to be recalled outright, he demanded either an increase in pay and expenses – and for these actually to be paid – or five months' leave in order to return to East Prussia to attend to family affairs. The clear implication was that such an absence would enable him to improve his own financial situation, which was little short of desperate.[4] Frederick characteristically chose the cheaper option and granted the requested leave.[5] A *chargé d'affaires*, Edelsheim, assumed responsibility for diplomatic relations and, more importantly, for keeping the King informed about events in Austria. Yet the almost military discipline within the Prussian diplomatic service was such that the long-suffering

---

[1] He seems to have left in late June or early July, and he was to return on 19 Nov.: see the correspondence in GStAPK Rep. 96.46.H.

[2] See Rohde to Frederick II, 18 and 28 June 1766, GStAPK Rep. 96.46.H. Cf. *Pol. Corr.* xxv. 143, for the King's satisfaction at these assurances.

[3] See above, p. 101 n. 142, for earlier disagreements over money. The high cost of living in Vienna clearly exacerbated the fundamental problem of the Prussian King's parsimony.

[4] Rohde to Frederick II, 29 Jan. 1766, GStAPK Rep. 96.46.H. Prussia's ruler, it will be recalled, regarded diplomatic service as a form of covert taxation of the nobility: above, p. 100.   [5] *Pol. Corr.*, xxv. 32.

Rohde would have been kept at his post had there been any anxieties. The reverse was in fact true. Frederick's own confidence was real. In spring 1766, he had had two wide-ranging interviews with Panin's special envoy, the unpleasant Holsteiner Caspar von Saldern, who was in Berlin.[6] In the course of these, Prussia's ruler had made clear his conviction that Austria's weak situation guaranteed the continuation of peace.[7]

The early months of 1766 in fact had seen tentative Prussian approaches for a *rapprochement* with Vienna.[8] Whether the King believed that an alliance was possible at this point must be questioned: more likely the initiative was an attempt to put pressure on his Russian ally, and it had little immediate impact on Prusso-Austrian relations. These months also saw the failure of suggestions that Frederick and his youthful admirer, Joseph II, should meet. Both men were keen for such an interview, mainly out of a reciprocal sense of curiosity, but Kaunitz and especially Maria Theresa blocked the idea.[9] This rejection did not damage relations. Frederick's confidence was rooted in his assessment of Austria's continuing military and financial weakness, upon which he continued to collect information and from which he drew the reassuring conclusion that a new war was unthinkable for Vienna.[10] He appreciated that the general financial exhaustion of the leading states was the foundation of European peace, which he believed would continue.[11] The King persisted in his conviction that Anglo-Bourbon rivalry was the most probable source of renewed fighting, but judged that this lay some years in the future. Even the return of Britain's great war leader, William Pitt the Elder, to office in July 1766 did not initially appear the harbinger of a new war.[12] He was here more sanguine, and proved to be more realistic, than Austrian and French observers, who were inclined to view the British ministerial changes as likely to produce early hostilities, since the returning leader might seek to consolidate his position by attacking the Bourbons.[13]

Frederick's own security appeared to be guaranteed by his Russian alliance. Though he kept a careful watch on Austria's dealings with Russia, and never lost the opportunity to portray her actions to Panin in the worst possible light, principally as St Petersburg's opponent in Poland, he was still relatively confident in the strength of his own links with Catherine II.[14] He sought to bolster that alignment by a generalised support of Russian policy and, where necessary, by individual concessions. One example was the replacement of the Prussian representative in Constantinople, Rexin, in response to Panin's protests that he had been seeking to

---

[6] Saldern's reports are printed in *Pol. Corr.*, XXV. 350–64; cf. Brandt, *Caspar von Saldern*, pp. 134–40. Frederick's tart comments on Panin's envoy are in *Œuvres*, VI. 15.   [7] *Pol. Corr.*, XXV. 356–7.
[8] For these see A.H. Loebl, 'Österreich und Preussen 1766–1768', *AÖG* 92 (1903), pp. 392–406; Arneth, *GMT*, VIII. 103–7.
[9] The Emperor had in fact been angling for such a meeting in conversations with the Prussian envoy: see Rohde to Frederick II, 22 Mar., 23 Apr. and 7 June 1766, all in GStAPK Rep. 96.46.H.
[10] *Pol. Corr.*, XXV. 26, 88, 206, 261.   [11] *Pol. Corr.*, XXV. 268.   [12] E.g. *Pol. Corr.*, XXV. 204.
[13] E.g. Rohde to Frederick II, 15 Jan. 1766, GStAPK Rep. 96. 46. H; *Pol. Corr.*, XXV. 190.
[14] *Pol. Corr.*, XXV. 252–3.

persuade the Porte that Russia intended to carry out wide-ranging constitutional reforms in Poland.[15] Frederick, who was characteristically tenacious in trying to get to the bottom of this murky business, believed that Rexin was not culpable – except perhaps of an excess of zeal – and had been the victim of false accusations put about by Boscamp, Poland's agent in Constantinople. Whatever the truth or otherwise of the claims, Frederick was clear that the main priority was to protect the Russian alliance and so recalled Rexin. In May 1766 a new Prussian agent, Zegelin, arrived in the Ottoman capital. His public orders to co-operate with his Russian counterpart were blended with private instructions to seek, wherever possible, to undermine St Petersburg's position at the Porte.[16] This epitomised Frederick's ambivalence about his relations with Catherine II's empire: the alliance was essential to his own security, but he feared Russia's power and ambitions.[17]

At this point, as throughout the post-war period, Frederick took a particular interest in the Austro-French alliance.[18] Always alert for any hint of tension between Vienna and Versailles, he was reassured by its apparent stability. The King's concern was rooted in his established fear that a Russo-Austrian alliance was always a more natural alignment than his own treaty with Catherine II. He believed that a stable Austro-French alliance was an obstacle to the *rapprochement* between Vienna and St Petersburg which he dreaded.[19] Russo-French enmity was so deeply rooted that he believed the breakdown of Vienna's alliance with Versailles would have to precede any new links with St Petersburg.[20] The apparent stability of the Austro-French axis was at this period an additional source of the King's confidence.

Kaunitz's friendly and pacific assurances to Rohde were perfectly genuine. Austria's priorities were peace and domestic reconstruction. The Habsburgs were simply too weak to risk another war – exactly as Frederick believed – and hoped for an extended period of peace. These priorities were apparent in two separate initiatives at this time. The first was an unsuccessful proposal for a triangular neutrality agreement between Austria, France and Britain.[21] Against a background of rising Anglo-Bourbon tension, the Chancellor proposed that the two western powers should formally guarantee Austrian neutrality in any future war. Kaunitz hoped for declarations by France and Britain that they would not begin fighting in Germany: because of the Electorate of Hanover this would be the most likely location of any Anglo-French war in Europe. The initiative failed partly because of British suspicions, but principally because of Choiseul's thinly disguised opposi-

---

[15] *Pol. Corr.*, XXIV. 335, 336, 433; XXV. 10, 35, 56, 72, 247 and *passim*. [16] *Pol. Corr.*, XXV. 209.
[17] See his revealing letter to Solms, 25 Sept. 1766, *Pol. Corr.*, XXV. 235–6.
[18] This is especially emphasised by the most recent historian of the King's later foreign policy: Frank Althoff, *Untersuchungen zum Gleichgewicht der Mächte in der Aussenpolitik Friedrichs des Grossen nach dem Siebjährigen Krieg (1763–1786)* (Berlin, 1995).
[19] *Pol. Corr.*, XXV. 226, for an important acknowledgement of this.
[20] This remained the situation at the time of the first partition of Poland: see below, p. 113.
[21] There appears to be no specific study of these shadowy negotiations. Some correspondence concerning them can be found in HHStA England-Korrespondenz 112–13; see also AAE CP (Autriche) 305, fos. 237–40, 288.

tion. The French minister was determined to retain his freedom of action and also to control relations with Vienna.

The second initiative was a proposal for Austro-Prussian disarmament. In October 1766 Kaunitz canvassed Edelsheim about a mutual reduction in troop levels. The Chancellor's hope was that expenditure could be diverted from the army to domestic reconstruction, in contrast to the military build-up which Joseph II favoured.[22] This initiative was immediately rejected. Frederick was committed to a defence policy which kept his own forces in a state of immediate readiness and saw superiority in available troops numbers as a crucial foundation of Prussian security: it was, as far as the King was concerned, to be an armed peace.[23] That peace, however, was to be threatened and eventually overturned – with lasting implications for the post-war pattern of alliances – by two further developments during 1766: the launching of a more active French policy, and growing Russian intervention in Poland. Within three years these had brought on the new war which it was the common aim of the eastern powers to avoid. This conflict was to be launched by the Ottoman empire, which attacked Russia, in the process underlining that eastern Europe was not yet completely controlled by its three great powers.

II

The first threat was the sharp change in French policy brought about by Choiseul's return to the foreign office in spring 1766. Though he had retained overall control of France's diplomacy,[24] since 1761 the duc had focussed his ministerial attention and considerable energy upon the twin tasks of rebuilding the navy and reconstructing the army, both of which had been in very poor shape by the close of the Seven Years War. His cousin Praslin had handled day-to-day foreign policy. On 5 April Choiseul exchanged the naval portfolio with Praslin for that of foreign affairs. This was immediately followed by the implementation of an actively anti-Russian policy in Sweden and in the Ottoman empire. It aimed to involve Catherine II's empire in a war either on its vulnerable north-western frontier or across its exposed borderlands far to the south. Though it was clear within a few months that the duc's initiatives would not yield immediate results, France would continue to pursue measures directed against Russian power throughout the final four years of his ministry.

This campaign was one of these sudden and bold improvisations which characterised Choiseul's career.[25] Its precise motivation is unclear, though several

---

[22] See above, p. 76.

[23] *Pol. Corr.*, xxv. 225–6, for these exchanges; cf. above, pp. 98–9, for the doctrine of military deterrence after 1763.

[24] This was why Prussia's King was so unconcerned initially at his return to direct control of French foreign policy: see his correspondence for these months in *Pol. Corr.*, xxv *passim*.

[25] There is a particularly interesting portrait in *Souvenirs de Charles-Henri, Baron de Gleichen*, ed. Paul Grimblot (Paris, 1868), pp. 19–42. Gleichen was a German diplomat in Danish service and a friend of the duc. Frederick the Great styled Choiseul a 'madman who had abundant spirit', a hostile verdict which he questionably attributed to Pope Benedict XIV: *Pol. Corr.*, xxv. 175.

contributory factors can be suggested. The duc's return to day-to-day control of French diplomacy was linked to the slow progress of his plans for naval reconstruction, which were in any case over-ambitious. Since 1761 he had been personally directing the rebuilding of France's shattered navy and urging his Bourbon ally Spain to reconstruct her own fleet.[26] Naval parity – or near parity – in the all-important ships of the line was deemed essential before the planned *revanche* against Britain could be launched with any prospect of success. The British navy had reached new peaks of size and effectiveness during the Seven Years War, and its lead at sea further increased immediately after 1763.

During the early years of peace considerable success was achieved in rebuilding France's fighting navy. This progress was more impressive both because funds were not available on the scale required due to the financial problems of Louis XV's monarchy, and because of crucial shortages of manpower and *matériel*, above all timber. Less was at first accomplished south of the Pyrenees, though by the second half of the decade Spanish naval reconstruction was also moving ahead rapidly. In the longer perspective the Bourbon navies were to be rebuilt impressively and, during the next decade, would achieve superiority over their British rival.[27] In the short term, however, Choiseul's ambitious targets had not been met and this was decisive for France's wider international objectives. By the winter of 1765–6 the duc had concluded that it would still be several years before the Bourbon powers could fight their major adversary.[28] Rivalry with Britain and opposition to Russia were in no sense alternative policies for France. Preparations for a Bourbon war of revenge continued, though when Franco-Spanish discussions over a combined strategy took place in 1766–7 they were underpinned by the assumption that any conflict would be primarily defensive in nature.[29] There were, however, links between the postponement of the war against British power and the near-simultaneous adoption of an active anti-Russian strategy.

Choiseul always needed a course of action to follow. His impetuous temperament and willingness to embrace initiatives without thinking through their full implications flawed his whole career. By this point a growing challenge to his own dominance was evident. His position as leading minister was never to be so secure after the death in 1764 of his patron, Madame de Pompadour, as it had been when he enjoyed the important support of the King's official mistress. In the very next year there seems to have been some kind of crisis at the French court, and Choiseul

---

[26] See H.M. Scott, 'The Importance of Bourbon Naval Reconstruction to the Strategy of Choiseul after the Seven Years' War', *International History Review* 1 (1979), pp. 17–35, and the contrasting account in Glete, *Navies and Nations*, I. 271–94 *passim*.

[27] By 1770, the year of the confrontation over the Falkland Islands when an Anglo-Bourbon war almost broke out, France and Spain had a marginal advantage in terms of total naval tonnage: Glete, *Navies and Nations*, I. 271 (Table 23.13)

[28] See the comments on naval reconstruction in the 'Mémoire au roi' of December 1765: *Mémoires de Choiseul*, ed. Calmettes, pp. 404–9.

[29] R.E. Abarca, 'Bourbon "Revanche" against England: The Balance of Power, 1763–1770' (PhD thesis, University of Notre Dame, 1964), pp. 262–89, provides an account of these talks and prints (pp. 459–72) some of the relevant documents.

evidently believed that his continuation in office was threatened.[30] His anti-Russian initiatives were more to Louis XV's taste than an early war with Britain, which after the Peace of Paris was always anathema to the ageing and pacific King, whose dread of more fighting was well known. Choiseul's aim was that France would remain at peace while Russia became embroiled in a war, probably with the Ottoman empire or, possibly, with Sweden. Louis XV's animosity towards Catherine II and her empire was deeply rooted: futile opposition towards further Russian advances in eastern Europe was now the *secret*'s principal function. The duc's active opposition to Russia may have been intended to reconcile minister and King and so strengthen his own position. There was, in any case, an obvious link between France's two enemies. Britain and Russia were widely seen as natural allies, not least by Choiseul himself, and in the mid-1760s negotiations for a formal treaty were under way and were widely expected to succeed. The duc intended that the continent would be neutralised when the war against Britain broke out, but this aim was threatened by St Petersburg's growing might and links with London. In this sense, Choiseul's anti-Russian campaign was indirectly a blow against Britain as well.

These initiatives were primarily motivated by fear of Catherine II's power and influence, which were increasing in the early years of peace. Choiseul had always been fundamentally hostile towards Russia, though this opposition had been necessarily suspended during the Seven Years War and, for rather different reasons, not resumed after its conclusion: immediately after 1763 France had pursued a passive strategy in eastern Europe. This did not mean, however, that the duc was reconciled to Russia's enlarged role. On the contrary, his hostility was considerable, and it was strengthened by an awareness of France's own impotence. It found expression in the long-running dispute, which continued for a decade after Catherine II's accession, over the imperial title, which Choiseul resolutely refused to grant.[31] These clashes provided scope for some choice invective, and France's leading minister did not miss his opportunity. The fundamental antagonism was also apparent in France's prolonged refusal to recognise Poniatowski as King of Poland and in the parallel – and for a time successful – efforts to delay Ottoman recognition. In spring 1766, this hostility once more came to the forefront of French policy.

During the weeks after he returned to the foreign office, Choiseul announced this modified strategy in an important series of despatches. Relations with Prussia had been broken off in 1756 and not restored after the Seven Years War, while official diplomatic links with Poland had been severed in summer 1764 when first Paulmy and then Hennin were recalled as a futile protest against Russian control.[32] This breach was to continue until a French *chargé d'affaires* returned to Warsaw in 1775.[33]

---

[30] *Mémoires de Choiseul*, ed. Calmettes, pp. 381–2. The 'Mémoire justificatif présenté au Roi' of late 1765 was linked to this crisis; it is printed in *Mémoires de Choiseul*, ed. Calmettes, pp. 382–414.

[31] See above, p. 155.   [32] See the correspondence in AAE CP (Pologne) 282.

[33] Though France did receive news of events there from July 1766 onwards from an unofficial representative, Gérault, who was also an agent of the *secret*: AAE CP (Pologne) 289–90.

In the course of April 1766 France's remaining representatives in northern and eastern Europe all received new instructions. Choiseul's penetrating gaze fell first upon Scandinavia, where French policy had been drifting along established lines since the conclusion of the Seven Years War.[34] Traditionally, Versailles had aimed to preserve peace around the Baltic and to resist Russian encroachments by means of a French-dominated alignment of Denmark and Sweden, reinforced by subsidies to both states and by financial aid to the Hat party in Stockholm. The duc regarded such payments, especially to minor powers, as ineffective and wasteful,[35] and France was in any case determined to retrench. The two Scandinavian states, moreover, had now passed out of Versailles' control.[36]

Choiseul's verdict on Denmark was especially withering.[37] That state, he concluded, was no longer of any interest or utility to France.[38] He renewed a private correspondence with his old friend, the Danish foreign minister Bernstorff, simply in order to ram the message home in a brutal and thoroughly unattractive way.[39] Bewitched by the Holstein exchange, he concluded, Copenhagen was now a puppet of St Petersburg[40] and, rather more improbably, a client of Britain too. This latter verdict was clearly incorrect: Anglo-Danish relations at this point were poor, and London was certainly quite unwilling to pay the subsidies which Choiseul believed were already binding Copenhagen to Britain.[41] But the foreign minister was correct to view Denmark as dependent upon Russia. He therefore determined that only the remaining subsidy arrears, which had earlier been re-scheduled, would be paid, and even these were to be cut off in spring 1767 as a reprisal for Denmark's provisional settlement of the Holstein exchange in a treaty with Russia. France's changed policy was to be implemented by a new representative in Copenhagen. The capable though emollient Ogier, who had upheld French interests for a dozen years but was suspected of too much sympathy towards the Danish government, was replaced. His successor Blosset received instructions which spelled out very clearly Denmark's future unimportance.[42]

France's hopes in northern Europe would instead be concentrated upon Sweden, where a new policy was now launched.[43] The meeting of the *riksdag* then dragging

---

[34] Roberts, *British Diplomacy*, pp. 214–19, examines this reassessment within a Baltic context, though with a rather different emphasis.

[35] See, e.g., his comments in late 1765: *Mémoires de Choiseul*, ed. Calmettes, p. 390.

[36] *Mémoires de Choiseul*, ed. Calmettes, pp. 390–1, for some brutally realistic comments.

[37] To Ogier, 22 Apr. 1766, AAE CP (Danemark) 152, fo. 99.

[38] In a much more muted way, this had been France's response to the Dano-Russian treaty of the previous year: AAE CP (Danemark) 151, fos. 125, 258. Choiseul's view was both more extreme and more bluntly expressed.

[39] 15 Apr. 1766: *Correspondance entre le comte Johan Hartvig Ernst Bernstorff et le duc de Choiseul*, pp. 234–7; for Bernstorff's dignified reply of 24 May, pp. 238–48.

[40] AAE CP (Danemark) 152, fo. 124.

[41] See Roberts, 'Great Britain, Denmark and Russia', esp. pp. 242 *et seq.*

[42] These are dated 14 Oct. 1766 and printed in *Recueil: Danemark*, ed. A. Geffroy, pp. 180–90, *passim.*

[43] Choiseul to Breteuil, 23 Apr. 1766, AAE CP (Suède) 247, fos. 185–95. This dispatch amounted to new instructions, and it is substantially printed in *Recueil: Suède*, ed. A. Geffroy, pp. 407–13.

on in Stockholm had finally persuaded Choiseul that nothing was to be gained from continuing to support the Hats and trying to prolong the party dog-fight. The recent Swedo-British treaty of friendship, insignificant though it was, appeared to the duc as further evidence of the failure of traditional French policy in Stockholm. France, he believed, had secured very little either from continued support for the Hat party or from her subsidies during the Seven Years War, subsidies which had still not been paid in full. Instead French policy now became nothing less than the restoration of absolutism, which alone could make Sweden a worthwhile ally against Russia. The ambassador in Stockholm, Breteuil, was instructed to do everything he could to promote such a *coup*, which would strengthen the powers of the crown and simultaneously weaken both the *riksdag* and the Council. He was also provided with the necessary funds.

The scheme was breathtaking in its simplicity, and provides a good illustration of Choiseul's tendency to think in bold, imaginative, terms. It also faced severe practical problems, though its author ignored these. Swedish political life could not be re-shaped overnight to fit the new demands of French policy, while the present King, the timid and irresolute Adolf Frederik, could only with difficulty be cast in the role of heroic restorer of absolute monarchy. More might certainly be hoped for from Lovisa Ulrika, now the acknowledged leader of the Court faction, but her energetic intriguing had alienated almost as many as it had attracted. These and other objections were rehearsed by Breteuil in two massive and occasionally rambling despatches, devoted to the task of educating his superior in Swedish realities.[44] The ambassador's own membership of the *secret* was a further obstacle, as Choiseul may have realised. Louis XV's private diplomacy still aimed to support the Hats and so prolong the party strife, the traditional objectives of France's official policy which the duc had now overthrown. While the impact of this on Breteuil's actions cannot be precisely determined, it can only have strengthened his resistance to the foreign minister's bold initiative. By September 1766 Choiseul was prepared to admit that, for the present, nothing could be accomplished.[45] He therefore refused to pay the remaining subsidy arrears.[46] This provoked a series of bitter clashes, and reduced relations to a new low point. Yet Breteuil's pouring of cold water on an immediate restoration of absolutism had not destroyed this strategy, though it had imposed a realistic time-scale. While a royalist *coup* remained Choiseul's aim, he acknowledged that it would be several years before this could be attempted. Its agent was now to be the ambitious and able Crown Prince, Gustav, whom French diplomacy set out to cultivate.

---

[44] 27 May and 22 Aug. 1766: AAE CP (Suède) 247, fos. 236–73, and 248, fos. 103–26. In the interim, Choiseul had written on 10 July restating his position in its essentials, while admitting the practical problems: AAE CP (Suède) 248, fos. 8–13.

[45] To Breteuil, 20 Sept. 1766, AAE CP (Suède) 248, fos. 179–81.

[46] In March 1767 in pursuit of her new policy, France did pay off 1,200,000 *livres* of accumulated debts for Sweden's King and Queen: AAE CP (Suède) 249, fos. 206–7.

The lack of immediate success at Stockholm now led to a concentration upon Constantinople. Once again Choiseul's plan was characteristically striking: this time, an Ottoman declaration of war upon Russia was the goal. Once again this dream was to be shattered by inconvenient political reality. Two weeks after his return to the foreign office, Choiseul set out his thinking in a major despatch to the experienced French ambassador in Constantinople, the comte de Vergennes.[47] Since the Ottoman empire was the most promising source of a diversionary attack upon Russia, the Sultan must be made the pliable instrument of French designs. Vergennes was told that his mission's single purpose was to promote a declaration of war by the Porte. The outcome of this conflict was of no interest to Choiseul, who hoped only that an Ottoman attack would divert Russian resources to the Balkans and thereby weaken Catherine II's ascendancy in northern and eastern Europe. Above all it might reduce pressure on Poland where, in the duc's opinion, French influence might alone be resurrected. The Sultan and his empire were thus to be as much France's intended victims as the Empress herself.

Russo-Ottoman antagonism was a fixed point of international relations throughout the eighteenth century, yet Choiseul's hope reveals his desperation. Playing the Ottoman card was a familiar French stratagem, but by the 1760s it had lost much of its menace.[48] There is no doubt that France's alliance during the Seven Years War with the Porte's enemy Russia had weakened her standing at Constantinople. Both in 1763–4 and subsequently, the Ottoman government had resisted French suggestions that it might intervene over Poland. The Sultan and his ministers certainly disliked and feared Catherine II's growing influence at Warsaw and, partly as a sop to French pressure, they had delayed formal recognition of Poniatowski for ten months after his election: his new dignity was not acknowledged by the Porte until July 1765. Ottoman policy was far more independent of outside influence than Choiseul fondly believed, and in the mid-1760s Constantinople was preoccupied with internal problems and reluctant to adopt an active European role. This had indeed been the conclusion of the French foreign office, after the unsuccessful attempt to involve the Ottoman empire directly in the Polish election.[49] Yet in spring 1766 the ambassador in Constantinople was told that, once again, France's future interests in Europe depended on his own efforts and on the doubtful resolve of the Ottoman leadership.

The experienced Vergennes' response was cautious and – like that of his counterpart Breteuil – emphasised the real obstacles to success.[50] Once again Choiseul was obliged to work through a diplomat who was also a member of the *secret*, though this

---

[47] This was dated 21 Apr. 1766 and is printed in Bonneville de Marsangy, *Le Chevalier de Vergennes*, II. 304–8.

[48] Virginia Aksan, 'Ottoman–French Relations 1739–1768', in Sinan Kuneralp, ed., *Studies on Ottoman Diplomatic History* (Istanbul, 1987), pp. 41–58, provides helpful background.

[49] AAE CP (Turquie) 141, fos. 24–5, 227.

[50] Murphy, *Vergennes*, pp. 151 *et seq.*, provides a sketchy account of his reaction, which can be followed in detail in AAE CP (Turquie) 142, *passim.*

was to be less important in Constantinople, where the official and private diplomacies coincided almost exactly. When Vergennes tried to use the mechanism of the *secret* to deflect his superior's policies, he was sharply told by the King to try harder.[51] The ambassador was certainly less than whole-hearted in his diplomacy at the Porte, and before long this was fully apparent to Choiseul. Vergennes had been in Constantinople since 1755 and had himself previously favoured the exact strategy he was now ordered to pursue. But a decade of dealing with the Ottoman leaders had convinced him that they were now fearful of Russia and even of war itself, and that the limit of their undoubted resentment at Catherine II's gains would be empty threats and sabre-rattling. The ambassador believed Choiseul's plan was futile and immediately began to set out the barriers in its path.[52]

By mid-June Vergennes had convinced his superior that an immediate declaration of war was not to be expected and had modified the original strategy in an important respect.[53] The ambassador argued that the Ottoman empire might eventually attack Russia and that a sustained French diplomatic offensive at the Porte, stressing the extent of Catherine II's control over Poland, could best contribute to this.[54] This Vergennes pursued in the months that followed, though he was still less than whole-hearted in his efforts. The obstacles were, in any case, considerable. Since France dared not risk being implicated in any declaration of war, the ambassador was for long not permitted to submit any written memoirs, though these were the established method of conducting diplomacy in Constantinople. The Sultan and his advisers were pacific, and they proved much more independent of French pressure than anticipated. By August 1766 Choiseul was convinced that nothing was to be expected from the Ottoman empire and in the following month he admitted that the new strategy upon which he had so confidently embarked in the spring was unlikely to succeed.[55]

This was not the end of Choiseul's active policy in south-eastern Europe. In mid-1767 he once more tried to promote a war, this time by direct intervention in the Crimea. By the second half of the eighteenth century, the Muslim Khanate of the Crimea had lost much of its former prestige, though its location made it central to Russo-Ottoman relations.[56] The region, which had been an integral part of the Golden Horde, lay directly to the north of the Black Sea and consisted of a large, strategically-important quadrilateral of steppe. The Crimean Khanate had been one of the four constituent elements into which the Horde had dissolved in the mid-fifteenth century. After a brief period of independence, the Crimean Khanate had acknowledged Ottoman overlordship in the 1470s. The precise nature of the

---

[51] Murphy, *Vergennes*, p. 155.
[52] See Vergennes' lengthy initial reply: AAE CP (Turquie) 142, fos. 86–102.
[53] Choiseul to Vergennes, 19 June 1766, AAE CP (Turquie) 142, fo. 128.
[54] AAE CP (Turquie) 142, fos. 145–50.   [55] AAE CP (Turquie) 142, fos. 241, 267.
[56] Alan W. Fisher, *The Russian Annexation of the Crimea 1772–1783* (Cambridge, 1970), chs. 1 and 2, provides a scholarly introduction to the Khanate.

subsequent relationship was ambiguous and remains controversial. By the mid-eighteenth century, however, it was clear that the Tatar khans were substantially dependent upon Constantinople. The Sultan's original right to confirm each new khan in office, after he had been chosen by the Tatar chiefs, had become in practice the power to appoint and dismiss at will.

The Khanate remained important to the Ottoman empire. The southern Crimea, with its cluster of cities, was a significant zone for trade and enabled Constantinople to dominate Black Sea commerce. It was also an important source of troops for the Sultan's armies and especially of the light cavalry for which the region was famous. Above all, its strategic location made it crucial. Its historic role was that of a buffer state, protecting the Ottoman empire's northern flank. From the closing years of the seventeenth century, Russia's growing power and self-confidence had placed the Crimea in the front line against her southern expansion. It was a mantle which the Khanate was ill-equipped to assume, in view of its own weakness and internal divisions, and of the Sultan's diminishing ability to assist in defence. By the mid-1760s the Crimea appeared trapped between its powerful northern neighbour and its declining protector to the south.

In mid-1767 the Khanate suddenly assumed a central place in Choiseul's foreign policy, when in June the Baron François de Tott was sent there. Ostensibly he was to become France's consul in the Crimea and to develop French trade in the Black Sea region. His real mission was rather different.[57] Once again French policy sought to provoke a Russo-Ottoman War, this time through pressure exerted upon Constantinople by the anti-Russian Khan, though the prospects for success were never high and the initiative underlined the absence of alternative options available to French diplomacy. François de Tott was the son of a famous father who had fled Hungary after the Rakoczi rebellion and served his adopted French homeland, principally as a translator in its embassy in Constantinople.[58] The younger Tott, together with his father, had accompanied Vergennes when he began his mission to the Porte and had lived there until 1763. In the mid-1760s he was bombarding the French foreign office with a variety of improbable schemes for the expansion of France's commerce and political influence in the region, and this brought him to Choiseul's attention.

Though François de Tott's mission to the Crimea would last two years, it had been fatally undermined almost before it began. French hopes had been focussed upon Aslan Guerai Khan, but he died long before the consul reached the Crimea.

---

[57] His stridently anti-Russian Instructions are dated 6 July 1767 and can be found in AAE CP (Turquie–Supplément) 17, fos. 4–18.

[58] I am indebted to Dr Ferenc Tóth for sending me a copy of the parts of his thesis and of an article, which are informative on Tott: 'Ascension sociale et identité nationale: intégration de l'immigration hongroise dans la société française au cours du XVIIIe siècle (1692–1815)' (PhD thesis, Université de Paris-Sorbonne, 1995), pp. 106–110; and 'Voltaire et un diplomate français d'origine hongroise en Orient', *Cahiers d'études hongroises* 7 (1995), pp. 78–86.

His two successors were far more pacific and fearful of Russia. The personality of Tott himself was a further obstacle to success. A colourful individual, he craved publicity and diplomatic privilege, which made him a very poor secret agent. His objectives were soon widely known, and he accomplished next to nothing. He also committed the serious error of intervening directly in the Khanate's tumultuous politics, especially when he supported the wrong side. Two years later, in 1770, a further change of khans would force him to flee hurriedly from the Crimea. The intended political results were not achieved and Choiseul, who all along had been sceptical about the prospects of success, was soon forced to contemplate the wreckage of another anti-Russian initiative.[59] In the Crimea, as at Constantinople and in Stockholm, his policies had produced no immediate benefits for France.

The importance of these anti-Russian initiatives lay not in what they achieved but in their contribution to a gradual breakdown of diplomatic stability during the later 1760s. Though the duc's actions did not produce a war, they did confirm Catherine II and Panin in particular in their conviction that France was an enemy and also a real threat. In the later 1760s Russia appeared to be threatened by a revival of the *barrière de l'est*. Choiseul's new aims were quickly known in St Petersburg, where they fuelled established anxieties. Through Britain they knew as early as summer 1766 that French policy was now to work for the restoration of absolutism in Sweden, while the publicity surrounding de Tott's mission soon brought him to the attention of the Russian government. French intervention in the Crimea was clearly the more important and immediate danger, and this mission caused the Empress and her advisers some concern in 1767–8.[60]

The threat in Sweden, though equally serious, appeared a more long-term challenge to Russian interests. The *Ordinance* passed in the final stages of the *riksdag* secured Panin's immediate aims, while Adolf Frederik was not the man to lead a *coup*.[61] A more significant source of instability in Sweden was the acute problems soon faced by the new Cap government. The *riksdag*'s measures to stabilise the financial position were quickly revealed to be unsuccessful and by mid-1767 serious economic problems were undermining the Caps. Equally menacing was the political realignment after the *riksdag*.[62] The *Ordinance* did not, as Lovisa Ulrika had hoped, do anything to strengthen the crown's authority: on the contrary, it appeared to confirm the monarchy's impotence. This destroyed the fragile alliance between the Caps and the Court, who now began to realign with the Hats. By the second half of 1767 the Cap government was menaced by the emergence of a Court–Hat axis as well as by a deepening economic crisis. The situation at the end of the previous *riksdag*, which had appeared so favourable to Russian interests, was already breaking down.

[59] AAE CP (Turquie) 144, fos. 43, 105.   [60] Fisher, *Russian Annexation*, pp. 29–31.
[61] See above, p. 169.   [62] Roberts, *The Age of Liberty*, pp. 171–2.

III

The second and more significant source of international tension was the sharply deteriorating situation in Poland where, by 1768, a full-blown civil war was in progress.[63] Though the scale of the problems facing St Petersburg only became fully apparent during the second half of 1766, their origins went back to Poniatowski's election two years before. The peaceful accession of King Stanislas Augustus, as he became, had appeared a Russian triumph, but it soon became clear that the situation in the kingdom was both complex and unstable. This was due to the incompatibility of the main ingredients in the political equation. Catherine II had intended that the new King would be the pliable instrument of her policy, but in fact he harboured ambitions to be a reforming monarch and even to abolish the celebrated *liberum veto*, by which an individual nobleman could theoretically wreck an entire *Sejm* (Diet) and its whole legislative programme.[64] Stanislas Augustus aspired to create a stronger and hereditary monarchy, backed by a system of cabinet government and an effective administration, which was also to receive regular salaries. In addition he hoped to widen the *Sejm*'s membership to include not merely the nobility but other social groups, and to keep it permanently in session. Though these aspirations revealed his admiration for British constitutional practice, they were oddly at variance with the Russian military *coup* which had brought him to the throne: as his subjects were well aware.

Poland's ruler was well intentioned and extremely personable, but youthful and inexperienced. His origins in the middle ranks of the nobility meant that he lacked the kind of political experience, as head of a major lineage, together with the wealth and the support of a numerous clientage, which several of his aristocratic relatives possessed. Many Polish magnates viewed their new King as inferior socially and even politically. His own relations with the Family – the leading magnate lineage, the Czartoryski, of which he was a member – were not lacking in tension. The Czartoryski viewed him as an instrument of their policy, and they had their own programme of reforms, which they had forced through the Convocation *Sejm* (May–June 1764) and thereafter sought to defend. Their proposals were less root-and-branch than those of the new King, aiming only to make the existing constitutional arrangements work rather better, but they did envisage curbing and even abolishing the *veto*. Stanislas Augustus was determined to press on with his reforms, against the advice of his more cautious Czartoryski relations. He acknowledged his

---

[63] On Polish developments, see the well-written political biography by Adam Zamoyski, *The Last King of Poland* (London, 1992), chs. 8–11, and the important monograph by Lukowski, *The Szlachta and the Confederacy of Radom*. Lukowski has also written two informative articles: 'Towards Partition', and 'The Papacy, Poland, Russia and Religious Reform, 1764–8', *Journal of Ecclesiastical History* 39 (1988), pp. 66–94. The account which follows is largely based upon these studies.

[64] Richard Butterwick, *Poland's Last King and English Culture: Stanisław August Poniatowski, 1732–1798* (Oxford, 1998), pp. 146–71, discusses the King's reforming ideas and their indebtedness to English models.

obligations to the Family, but he was determined to be independent of its control, and also believed that his monarchical dignity exalted him above his own relatives. Personal tensions added a further ingredient to the complex political situation, as royal self-importance clashed with aristocratic *hauteur* and envy.

The King's position was soon revealed to be weaker than he recognised. The chaotic finances of the Polish monarchy at his accession made him dependent upon a pension from St Petersburg. His inexperience was apparent in the trust he at first placed in the good-will of Catherine II, upon whom he naïvely relied even when it became clear that his reforming ambitions were irreconcilable with the Empress' aims. The King was unaware of the secret clauses of the 1764 alliance, which laid down that Poland be maintained as a weak and divided country where Russian and, to a lesser extent, Prussian influence was to predominate, and he failed to recognise that St Petersburg now viewed and treated his realm as a dependency. He himself recognised Poland's need for international support, and put out feelers to Versailles and Vienna, both of which – along with Spain – had broken off relations at the time of his election, in protest at Russia's actions. One of his earliest reforms had been the creation of a Polish diplomatic service, intended to challenge the established role of individual magnates in Poland's foreign policy. But when, in late 1765, the King attempted to end the breach with France by despatching Sulkowski as ambassador, this was vetoed by St Petersburg. It left the Papacy as Stanislas Augustus' sole diplomatic conduit and one which extended only into Catholic Europe.

His own election, moreover, had marked the beginning of a new level of direct Russian involvement in Polish affairs. Its instrument came to be Panin's nephew, the ambassador in Warsaw Nikolai Repnin, who was youthful, arrogant and ambitious, and quickly began to go beyond his orders, though this was not at first apparent to St Petersburg: within a very few years he was effectively acting as Russia's viceroy and treating all opposition with increasing brutality. His power, at first exercised in co-operation with the Family, was buttressed by the Russian soldiers sent to Poland in growing numbers. The Seven Years War had established a military presence and this proved thereafter to be near-continuous, until Poland's destruction in 1795. By the late summer of 1764 as many as 14,000 Russian troops may have been present to supervise the royal election, and this number seems to have increased during the next few years.[65]

Poland had a distinct role in Catherine II's wider policies, as a passive member of the Northern System and, perhaps, a useful ally against the Ottoman empire in any future war.[66] The Empress and Panin were therefore willing to see an increase in the size of the Polish army (fixed at 24,000 in 1717, though by the 1760s its effective strength was barely half that figure), together with a strengthening of the monarchy and even the limitation or actual removal of the *veto*, which was proposed at this

---

[65] Zamoyski, *Last King*, p. 98.
[66] *SIRIO*, XXII. 364, for Panin's ideas and Frederick's sceptical response.

time. This was resolutely and successfully opposed by Frederick the Great, who had secured a say in the country's future in the 1764 treaty with Russia and intended that Poland be kept weak and divided, in order to facilitate his own ambitions. This was the second new element in the situation after Poniatowski's election.

Prussia's later role as the architect of the first partition of Poland, carried out in 1772, creates an obvious danger of teleology in writing about Frederick's ambitions towards his neighbour. His interest in acquiring Polish (or Royal) Prussia, which separated the Hohenzollern heartlands from the distant kingdom of East Prussia, was well established. It had been expressed as long ago as the early 1730s and confirmed in the first Political Testament of 1752. Yet the gap between territorial ambitions and actual annexations was wide and not easily crossed: especially for a ruler who feared a new war and also believed that future acquisitions would probably have to wait until a future reign.

At this period Frederick was more anxious to exploit the neighbouring Polish territories economically.[67] This was part of his wider aim after 1763 of increasing Prussia's wealth and thus safeguarding her position as a great power.[68] It was a continuation of his policies during the Seven Years War, when his forces had violated Polish territory, attacking Russian bases established there in 1759 and 1761, and raided at will into Greater Poland until 1765. During his occupation of Dresden at the very beginning of that conflict, Frederick had seized the dyes from which the Kingdom's currency was struck, and throughout the fighting he had issued debased Polish coins, whose circulation also had the effect of driving sound money out of Poland into the neighbouring Hohenzollern territories.[69] From this manipulation the King had made a profit which has been estimated to have been more than 25 million *taler*, and certainly contributed significantly to the costs of Prussia's Seven Years War. The resulting monetary problems for Poland were considerable and continued until the first half of 1765.

In that year a new stage was reached in this Prussian intervention in and exploitation of Poland. The General Tariff, introduced as part of the Family's reforms, was beginning to transform the parlous finances of the Polish monarchy.[70] Frederick the Great had no wish to see any strengthening of Poland, and in January 1765 he had protested against it on the quite specious grounds that its introduction without consultation ignored existing treaties between the two states. When these representations were rejected, Frederick resorted to direct action and established a customs'

---

[67] See the major study by Hans-Jürgen Bömelburg, *Zwischen Polnischer Ständegesellschaft und Preussischem Obrigkeitsstaat: vom Königlichen Preussen zu Westpreussen (1756–1806)* (Munich, 1995), esp. ch. 5. In exactly the same way the King sought to exploit economically his neighbour Saxony: Schulze, *Die Beziehungen zwischen Kursachsen*, p. 81. [68] Cf. above, p. 85.
[69] There is a detailed study of this complex subject by Jörg K. Hoensch, 'Friedrichs II. Währungsmanipulationen im Siebenjährigen Krieg und ihre Auswirkung auf die polnische Münzreform von 1765/66', *Jahrbuch für die Geschichte Mittel-und Ostdeutschlands* 22 (1973), pp. 110–75.
[70] See Jörg K. Hoensch, 'Der Streit um den polnischen Generalzoll 1764–1766', *JGO* NF 18 (1970), pp. 35–88.

post at Marienwerder.[71] This was the point at which his own territory of East Prussia bordered the river Vistula, the main artery of Poland's internal trade. He proceeded to collect customs' dues on traffic proceeding downstream to Danzig. These impositions started at 10 per cent and may have reached as high as 33 per cent for some goods, and they were backed by the unambiguous threat of military force: the fortified customs' post had ten cannon and was manned by 200 Prussian soldiers. Polish protests were brushed aside, and the matter was then raised with the Russian government. The prolonged and, at first, inconclusive diplomatic exchanges which followed revealed Frederick's great skill in balancing his overwhelming need for a Russian alliance with his desire to exploit Poland economically.[72] St Petersburg's ruling in March 1766, which determined the final settlement of this dispute, revealed Prussia's new importance in Poland's increasingly fractured politics. Russia was at this point unable to resist pressure from her ally, and so forced her satellite to abandon the General Tariff, with a consequent weakening of the Polish monarchy and its finances.

From the mid-1760s the principal source of Poland's internal strife came to be the vexed question of the rights of the dissidents, which quickly relegated all other issues to the margins of political life. It was a consequence of her size and diversity, and the religious pluralism which resulted. Her total population at this period was between 11 and 12 million. Around half of these were Roman Catholic, and a further 4 million were 'Uniate', that is to say members of the Greek Catholic Church, which since the sixteenth century had been in loose alliance with Catholicism in Poland. The dissidents, a term which covered both the Greek Orthodox and Protestant subjects of Stanislas Augustus, made up significantly less than 10 per cent of the total population. At the period of the first partition in 1772, it has been calculated that there were around half a million Orthodox and between 200,000 and 300,000 Lutherans and Calvinists.[73] Very few of the Orthodox were nobles, though significant numbers of Protestants were, particularly in Polish Prussia. In earlier times, these non-Catholics had enjoyed considerable religious and civic freedom, but these privileges had been squeezed out by the Catholicism which was the official religion. In the course of the eighteenth century the Protestants in particular had been politically marginalised. They could practise their faith and own property, but their civic rights were significantly reduced. While they could still vote in royal elections and serve in the army, they were otherwise barred from participation in public life, from membership of the *Sejm* and from state offices: restrictions which fell almost entirely upon the nobility. Yet, during the 1760s the dissidents came to have an importance out of all proportion to their numerical strength.

Their cause was taken up by the two powers which now controlled Poland's future. Frederick the Great cynically backed the cause of religious freedom because

---

[71] *SIRIO*, XXII. 364–5, sets out the King's basic position.   [72] These can be followed in *SIRIO*, XXII.
[73] These estimates are given by J.T. Lukowski, *The Partitions of Poland: 1772, 1793, 1795* (London, 1999), pp. 21–2. The Orthodox tended over time to be subsumed into the Uniate Church.

he recognised in the dissidents a means of keeping the country weak and divided, and also a vehicle for Prussia to intervene, which had been recognised in 1764.[74] Though Saxony had sought his protection for Poland's Protestants at the time of the interregnum, the King's subsequent support of this group was entirely opportunistic. He had no wish to see a tolerant Poland, which might deter the immigration into Prussia which his policies after 1763 sought to encourage, as one means of remedying the poverty of his own lands. By contrast both Catherine II and Panin were genuine supporters of religious toleration. In the spirit of the Enlightenment they were outraged by the discrimination which the non-Catholics faced and so determined to secure more equal treatment for them. The Empress was also a natural target for Orthodox appeals for assistance, and she was aware that her own position within Russia could be strengthened if she responded favourably. But both ruler and minister also appreciated the potential value of the dissidents to their future policy: protected by constitutionally guaranteed rights, they could serve as the 'Russian' party in Poland in years to come.

The first four years of Catherine II's reign had seen a notable and probably unprecedented enhancement of Russia's position in Europe.[75] Diplomatic and political successes had built upon the situation created by St Petersburg's armies during the Seven Years War. The Empress' candidate ruled in Poland, while her policy had succeeded in Stockholm. Alliances with Prussia and Denmark protected her position in northern Europe. Though these successes were real, the confidence which resulted encouraged the Empress and her leading minister to overplay their hand in Poland, where Russian policy quickly became dictatorial and also unrealistic.[76] The problems which Catherine II and Panin faced were complex, but their new-found confidence and even arrogance led them to mishandle these and especially their religious dimension. They never appreciated the strength and ubiquity of the Catholic fanaticism which opposed their policy.[77]

By 1766, Russian policy aimed to force an enlargement of the dissident rights through the *Sejm*. The resistance encountered merely made Catherine and Panin more determined to confront the firmly Catholic tone of Poland's official life. Roman Catholics might constitute only around half of the total population, but they dominated the public world: the country was still, as it had long been, the great north-eastern salient of Catholic orthodoxy, the scene of the Counter-Reformation's greatest triumph. Its monarchy and government were staunchly Catholic, its nobility – who monopolised political life – overwhelmingly opposed to

[74] See above, p. 116.

[75] Panin, indeed, declared that the Empress' accession was the point at which St Petersburg began to play such a leading international role: to Korff, 20 Oct. 1765 OS, *SIRIO*, LVII. 389; cf. Madariaga, *Russia*, p. 196.

[76] Cf. above, p. 129, for the wider development. In 1766 Britain's representative Macartney penned his famous verdict: see above, p. 131. This view was widely shared: see, e.g., the comments of Solms and, revealingly, of Frederick in a letter to Finckenstein and Hertzberg, where he speaks of Russia's 'despotic tone': *Pol. Corr.*, xx. 234, 201.   [77] Madariaga, *Russia*, pp. 199–200.

any extension of the rights of dissidents. This had been highlighted by the *sejmiki* elections of 1764 and 1766 when, in spite of considerable Russian and Prussian pressure, not a single instruction advocated any substantial improvement in their position.[78] The strength of the opposition was immediately apparent when Repnin and the Prussian representative Benoît took proposals to improve their status to the *Sejm* which met in November 1766.[79] These suggestions provoked an outcry and were thrown out. At the very end of November the *Sejm* largely confirmed the existing restrictions, though a handful of unimportant concessions were made for form's sake. These events made clear to St Petersburg, for the first time, that its demands would be resisted.

This initial effort to improve the dissidents' position through persuasion and consent had failed. It had run aground on the reef of Catholic intransigence and domination of public life. Frederick the Great, whose approach to Polish problems at this period was realistic and surprisingly moderate, was ready by the end of 1766 to abandon their cause, and ceaselessly urged caution upon his Russian ally.[80] He recognised that the *Sejm*'s simultaneous preservation of the *veto*, which both the Family and Stanislas Augustus had wanted to render obsolete by introducing majority voting, would prevent any extension of the rights of dissidents.[81] Prussia's King also feared that the growing strife in Poland would lead to the new war which he dreaded. During the winter of 1766–7 these fears were particularly acute, and seemed to have some basis in reality. In October Frederick had been puzzled by apparent Austrian mobilization in Bohemia and Moravia.[82] Prussia's extensive military intelligence network meant that, now and in the future, he had surprisingly detailed and apparently accurate knowledge of his rival's troop dispositions and movements. During the next few months these preparations (which were initially part of Joseph II's efforts to overhaul and build up the army, for which he was now directly responsible) continued and seem to have increased in scale,[83] causing Prussia's King considerable anxiety. The crisis certainly damaged relations,[84] though whether Frederick ever believed that war might break out is much less certain. He was convinced of Vienna's essential pacifism and believed, correctly, that sabre-rattling would be the limit of its response.[85]

Austria remained hostile to the growing control exercised by Russia over Poland. It had been considerable during the interregnum in 1763–4, and may have intensified thereafter. As a leading Catholic power, Austria was the target of appeals

[78] Lukowski, *The* Szlachta *and the Confederacy of Radom*, p. 107. The *sejmiki* were local assemblies of the nobility which preceded a meeting of the *Sejm* and guided the delegates sent to this.

[79] Britain and Denmark eventually provided limited diplomatic support for these demands: Madariaga, *Russia*, p. 198.

[80] *Pol. Corr.*, XXV. 59, 96, 173, 183, 185, 193–4, 211, 223, 260, 278, 282, 291, 312, 324, 336.

[81] *Pol. Corr.*, XXVI. 2.   [82] *Pol. Corr.*, XXV. 261–2.

[83] *Pol. Corr.*, XXV. 286, 291, 339–40; Loebl, 'Österreich und Preussen', pp. 417–18; Arneth, *GMT*, VIII. 128, and ch. 5 *passim*.   [84] See the King's comments in early March 1767: *Pol. Corr.*, XXVI. 85.

[85] *Pol. Corr.*, XXV. 321.

for support against the dissidents and their Russian and Prussian patrons both from within Poland and also from the Papacy and other Catholic states. Her ability to confront St Petersburg directly, however, was widely and correctly doubted. In mid-November 1766, Kaunitz frankly confessed to the French *chargé d'affaires* that the Habsburgs were powerless to resist Russia over Poland: letters would be useless and Vienna was in no position to fight.[86] Though his nerves occasionally got the better of him,[87] Frederick was confident for most of the time that a military demonstration would be the limit of the Austrian response.[88] This view was confirmed by the reports he received from Rohde, who was now back in Vienna. These emphasised that while there was considerable resentment at Russia's conduct and at the anticipated arrival of more troops, the Habsburgs had no stomach for a war.[89] Frederick put his own military preparations swiftly into effect, both to be quite certain and because this was his established response to any threat.[90] In particular the King set in motion the purchase of remounts for the cavalry, with the clear message that Prussia was ready to fight.[91] By spring 1767, however, it was apparent that Austria had no intention of intervening and that peace would prevail.

The heightened tension of these months possessed wider significance. It revealed Frederick's conviction that his own military and economic reconstruction was still incomplete and would not be finalised for 'some years' yet. His army was improving all the time, but more remained to be done. It would be another three years, the King admitted, before Prussia's forces could be restored to the level of effectiveness which they had attained before 1756.[92] Secondly, the episode heightened the King's established suspicion of Joseph II, whom he regarded as a youthful adventurer and a possible source of renewed fighting.[93] This made him more appreciative of Maria Theresa's pacific influence in Vienna. It was evident later in the same year, when she fell victim to smallpox and for a time appeared likely to die. Frederick was genuinely relieved when she recovered; as he wrote, her death would lead to 'many changes' and would threaten the peace which he so valued.[94]

The third and most important significance was the revelation of a subtle shift within the Russo-Prussian alliance. The leading position which Frederick had secured when it was signed in spring 1764 was being eroded by Russia's notable recovery. Increasingly, political initiative was coming from St Petersburg: as the King recognised.[95] He was particularly concerned that Russian actions could ignite

---

[86] AAE CP (Autriche) 306, fos. 278–82.   [87] *Pol. Corr.*, XXVI. 21, 42, 81–2.

[88] *Pol. Corr.*, XXVI. 4, 8, 12, 46, 54–5.

[89] His reports for the early months of 1767 are in GStAPK Rep. 96.46.J; see especially the long encyphered despatch of 4 Feb. 1767 and that of 25 Feb. 1767. (Some of the envoy's correspondence for early January is missing from this fascicle.)   [90] *Pol. Corr.*, XXVI. 86, 87, 97.

[91] *Pol. Corr.*, XXVI. 82–3.

[92] *Pol. Corr.*, XXVI. 77, 123. The fact that these admissions were both made in letters to his brother, Prince Henry, makes them particularly significant. Even this timetable proved optimistic: the King would later declare that Prussian military power had not reached a satisfactory state until 1774.

[93] E.g. *Pol. Corr.*, XXVI. 45.   [94] *Pol. Corr.*, XXVI. 181, 203–4, 216.

[95] See his revealing comment to Finckenstein, 11 Feb. 1767, *Pol. Corr.*, XXVI. 51.

a wider conflict over Poland, and at the very end of 1766 told Panin that if this happened he would regard the treaty as inoperative, since St Petersburg was clearly the aggressor.[96] It was why Prussia's King continually emphasised – and clearly exaggerated – the threat of direct Austrian intervention over Poland in his diplomacy at St Petersburg.[97] This might, he hoped, moderate Catherine II's policy and, at the same time, widen the gulf between Vienna and the Russian court and so make a *rapprochement* less likely.[98] Frederick's recognition of his gradual loss of the political initiative, and a parallel appreciation that events in Poland were running far beyond his control, were behind a further improvisation at this time. In spring 1767 he persuaded his Russian ally to sign a convention modifying the original treaty. This limited Prussian support over the dissidents to diplomatic backing. In the event of an Austrian attack on Russia, the provisions of the original defensive alliance would apply except that St Petersburg would indemnify him for the costs of intervention.[99]

Frederick's restless diplomatic activity was inventive, but it did nothing to restrain Russian actions in Poland, as he had clearly intended. Catherine and Panin, against the background of Russia's improving situation at home and abroad, would brook no opposition. Their aims had expanded during the past two years, and they now ordered Repnin to use force to secure their demands, which now went far beyond eighteenth-century notions of toleration and amounted to the full civic and religious rights of non-Catholics.[100] Their actions revealed that they viewed Poland as a satellite or even a province of Russia, rather than an independent country. For his part Repnin now appreciated the extent of opposition: proximity had made him more cautious, or merely realistic. During the winter of 1766–7 he had attempted to persuade his superiors to moderate their demands, but his pleas went unheeded in St Petersburg. His orders prescribed the use of force and this he duly did.[101] During the first half of 1767 Repnin sponsored the establishment of three confederations of Polish nobles, under the umbrella of Russian military power: one Protestant (at Thorn), one Orthodox (at Sluck), one general (that of Radom).[102] Each sought to impose religious freedom upon the unwilling Catholic establishment, and collectively they provided a more secure foundation for Russian control. The Radom Confederation, set up in late June, was much the most important and provided a competing source of authority to the King and his government, as well as a means of implementing St Petersburg's aims. Repnin's apparent success

---

[96] *Pol. Corr.*, XXV. 348–9; cf. *SIRIO*, XXII. 482–4.

[97] *Pol. Corr.*, XXV. 291, 340–1, 345–6; XXVI. 9, 24, 145.   [98] *Pol. Corr.*, XXVI. 130–1.

[99] *Pol. Corr.*, XXVI. 32–5 (a draft of the proposed convention), 122–3, 124–5; cf. Madariaga, *Russia*, pp. 202–3.

[100] See *Pol. Corr.*, XXV. 348–9, for Frederick's characteristically tart comments on Russia's demands by the end of 1766.   [101] Madariaga, *Russia*, pp. 200ff, summarises Russian policy at this point.

[102] A Confederation was an association of noblemen in pursuit of specific aims who proceeded not by unanimity but by majority vote. Confederations were an established and disruptive feature of pre-partition political life at periods of crisis, and were a constitutional means of pursuing opposition, almost invariably to the crown.

encouraged the Empress and Panin to press ahead with their demands and to ignore the resistance which was emerging. The extent of this opposition, encouraged by the Catholic leadership, was evident in the *sejmiki* which vigorously resisted St Petersburg's actions, except in Protestant Royal Prussia.

During the winter of 1767–8 Repnin, with the backing of considerable numbers of Russian troops, forced through significant improvements in the position of the dissidents. The *Sejm* which met in October was cowed first by the presence of 10,000 soldiers and, when this was insufficient, by the arrest of four noted opponents of concessions, who were taken to Russia and only released at the very beginning of 1773. In November 1767 it was converted into a Delegated *Sejm*, which was much easier to control since it contained far fewer noblemen, and it duly passed legislation increasing the rights of the dissidents. These changes, together with a statement of Poland's 'cardinal laws' (that is to say, the principal constitutional arrangements), were incorporated into a Perpetual Treaty between Russia and Poland, signed in mid-February 1768 and ratified the next month.[103] Panin had long been attracted by a Russian guarantee of the country's status and government, an idea which he had first put forward in 1764 and periodically pursued thereafter.[104] Its signature, and subsequent acceptance by the *Sejm*, indicated Poland's vassal status and underlined the almost unlimited power which St Petersburg now wielded over its neighbour. This dependent position was spelled out in Panin's notably blunt letter to King Stanislas Augustus, making clear that his Kingdom was now permanently a part of Russia's sphere of influence.[105]

Russia, however, had gone too far: as Repnin and Frederick the Great, in different ways, had feared. The rights now conferred upon dissidents and, even more, the way in which they had been imposed, produced a violent Polish reaction. This was deeply conservative, Catholic and patriotic in tone, and found expression in the establishment of the Confederation of Bar (in Podolia, in the extreme southeast of Poland) on 29 February 1768. During the months which followed the country rapidly descended into civil strife, as Russian troops were sent in even greater numbers to deal with the guerrilla war being waged against St Petersburg's protectorate. The residual private military power of Poland's magnates and of the nobility as a whole ensured that this confrontation would be armed, and that Russian interference, as it was viewed, would be resisted by force. Catherine II now faced a widening civil war, which would continue until the first partition four years later. These events, however, possessed a broader significance. They were crucial because of their international repercussions and especially the response of the Ottoman empire, with its long common frontier and traditional interest in Poland.

---

[103] The detailed terms are given by Lukowski, *The Szlachta and the Confederacy of Radom*, pp. 224–7.
[104] Lukowski, *The Szlachta and the Confederacy of Radom*, pp. 46, 59.
[105] 29 Nov. 1767 OS, *SIRIO*, LXVII. 524–7.

IV

These developments had been viewed with mounting hostility in Constantinople, and were the principal source of a new war declared in early October 1768.[106] The Russian empire's southward expansion had brought it into more direct contact with its Ottoman counterpart, and political rivalry had followed. From the middle of the eighteenth century, the Porte's resentment was focussed upon the influence which Russia had acquired and was consolidating in Poland and which posed a threat. It was feared in Constantinople that, in any future war, a Polish auxiliary army operating between the Dniester and Dnieper could be an important diversion. It might do something to replace Russia's lost ally, Austria, whose active role in south-eastern Europe had been ended by her preoccupation after 1740 with the struggle with Prussia. This was why the continuation of Poland's independence was viewed as an important Ottoman interest during the years when Mustafa III was Sultan (1757–74). Treaties signed with Russia in the early decades of the eighteenth century required her not to maintain troops in Poland, and Constantinople periodically sought and received assurances from St Petersburg over this.[107]

The Ottoman empire had not intervened directly in 1763–4, but its ill-will towards Russia had been apparent in the delayed recognition of Poland's new King.[108] St Petersburg's increasing interference in Polish affairs after 1764 was resented in Constantinople and the consequent hostility had been encouraged by both French and Austrian diplomacy.[109] The Sultan's attention was, in any case, drawn towards Poland by the frequent appeals for help which he received from the anti-Russian forces there. Relations were worsened by other sources of tension. In the mid-1760s the Ottoman empire had been racked by a series of revolts in its outlying provinces, and its government was well aware of the help Catherine II had furnished to the rebels in Montenegro. The Porte resented Russian penetration of its sphere of influence in Georgia, and St Petersburg's continuing intrigues among its Greek subjects.[110] There was also the running sore of the Crimea, a permanent point of friction which had been exacerbated by Russia's fortification of the southern frontier and direct intervention in the Khanate.

The main focus of Ottoman resentment, however, continued to be Poland and the Russian yoke over this. The resident in Constantinople, A.M. Obreskov, was

[106] Russo-Ottoman relations over Poland in the years before 1768 are covered by J.W. Zinkeisen, *Geschichte des Osmanischen Reiches in Europa* (7 vols., Gotha, 1840–63), v. 900–18; for the situation at the Porte, see Aksan, *An Ottoman Statesman*, pp. 100–23 *passim*.

[107] Lukowski, *The Szlachta and the Confederacy of Radom*, p. 205.

[108] See above, p. 170. Cf. Hammer, *Histoire de l'empire Ottoman*, XVI. 116–27.

[109] For Vergennes' activities, Bonneville de Marsangy, *Le Chevalier de Vergennes*, II. 308–75. See above, p. 171.

[110] Hammer, *Histoire de l'empire Ottoman*, XVI. 161–3, 172; Nikolas K. Gvosdev, *Imperial Policies and Perspectives towards Georgia, 1760–1819* (Basingstoke, 2000), esp. chs. 1–3; Ariadna Camariano-Cioran, 'La guerre russo-turque de 1768–1774 et les grecs', *Revue des études sud-est européennes* 3 (1965), pp. 516–20.

continually under pressure over Russia's military presence there. Early in 1768 he was sufficiently rattled to promise that the withdrawal of these troops would begin after the *Sejm* ended. Panin subsequently gave a measure of approval to his resident's assurances, announcing that this would begin in May.[111] Events in Poland made this impossible as the rising tide of resistance forced the sending of more Russian troops, rather than a reduction in their number. These forces, moreover, were operating increasingly in regions close to the Ottoman frontier. This had a serious impact at the Porte, where these months saw the growth of a war party, headed by the Sultan himself and encouraged by French diplomacy.[112] There was considerable popular sentiment in favour of fighting, and it was fostered by the military élite and by the theologians (*ulema*), who were very influential. The able Grand Vizier Muhsinzade Mehmed, in power since 1765, firmly resisted the pressure for war. He seemingly told Mustafa III during a private interview that military preparations should be completed and the frontiers made more defensible before any attack was launched, which displeased the Sultan who was determined upon hostilities.[113] This was the reason for the Grand Vizier's dismissal on 6 September. The next few weeks saw repeated councils which debated the question of war or peace.[114] By this point the Ottoman empire was resolved to fight: all that was needed was a suitable pretext. It was furnished by the violation of the Sultan's territory at Balta with the loss of Muslim lives and property, by Cossack irregulars in pursuit of Polish Confederates. More fundamental, in Ottoman eyes, may have been news of the surrender in August of the important Confederate stronghold of Cracow. News of this revealed more clearly than ever the scale of Russian successes in Poland and impelled Constantinople to act. Obreskov was arrested after a stormy interview with the Grand Vizier on 6 October 1768.[115] He was imprisoned in the Castle of the Seven Towers (Yedikule), an action which the Porte had always regarded as a formal declaration of war, believing that resident diplomats were simply hostages for the good behaviour of the rulers they represented.[116]

Over a century ago the celebrated diplomatic historian, Albert Sorel, penned a famous verdict, which has stood the test of time, on the Ottoman declaration of war. It had, he said, surprised and disconcerted everyone: the Ottomans who made it, the Russians whose actions had provoked it, the French who had prompted it, the Prussians who had advised against it and the Austrians who had dreaded it. No one, he continued, was prepared for this war, neither the belligerents nor the neutrals.[117]

---

[111] Lukowski, *The Szlachta and the Confederacy of Radom*, pp. 253–4; Madariaga, *Russia*, pp. 203–4.
[112] Hammer, *Histoire de l'empire Ottoman*, XVI. 172 *et seq.*
[113] Hammer, *Histoire de l'empire Ottoman*, XVI. 179–80.   [114] Aksan, *Ottoman Statesman*, 122.
[115] Accounts of this can be found in Bonneville de Marsangy, *Le Chevalier de Vergennes*, ii. 372–5, and Hammer, *Histoire de l'empire Ottoman*, xvi. 183–6 and 450–2. During this interview Obreskov made the damaging admission that there were now 27,000 Russian troops in Poland rather than the 7000 earlier claimed: Aksan, *An Ottoman Statesman*, p. 123.
[116] Aksan, 'Ottoman–French Relations 1739–1768', p. 44.
[117] Albert Sorel, *La question d'Orient au XVIIIe siècle* (2nd edn, Paris, 1889), p. 29.

Its unexpectedness, at least before the autumn of 1768, was one reason for the concerned reaction as news of Obreskov's seizure spread in the closing months of the year. More important, however, was the widespread fear that a general European war might be kindled by this spark, at a time when internal reconstruction was still the priority of all the leading powers.

This anxiety was itself a consequence of developments since the Seven Years War. There now existed two alliance systems which together covered much of the continent and which could easily become operative. The rival defensive alignments between Russia, Prussia and Denmark on the one hand (Panin's 'Northern System') and between France, Spain and Austria on the other (Choiseul's *Système du Midi*) were intended to insure against the outbreak of a new war. In practice they were also a guarantee that any conflict which involved more than one great power could very easily become generalised and involve several leading states. Only Britain, among Europe's political élite, was not tied by treaty to a potential belligerent. Paradoxically, London's failure to secure a major ally proved, in the later 1760s, to be a source of security.

Elsewhere rulers and their advisers looked anxiously at developments on Europe's south-east rim, and even more anxiously at the provisions of the 'defensive' alliances which they had so confidently contracted or confirmed only a few years before. The distinction between a 'defensive' and an 'offensive' alliance, so precise on paper, appeared less easy to define in the closing months of 1768. Everywhere, fear of a wider conflict increased sharply. In Vienna, Maria Theresa's despondency at the prospect of a new war was widely known, while Kaunitz, uncomfortably aware that Austria was France's ally and that Choiseul had prompted the Ottoman declaration of war, was driven to expressions of doom and despair.[118] In Potsdam, Frederick quickly conjured up the spectre of a general conflict being born out of the rupture between Russia and the Ottoman empire.[119] A year before the King had confidently predicted that there would be no war for several years to come, but he was now forced to confront the renewed conflict which he had long dreaded.[120]

In early October the King had enquired into his formal obligations to his Russian ally should an Ottoman war break out. The confirmation he received from Finckenstein, that his commitments under the 1764 treaty and the convention signed three years later, could be limited to a subsidy of 400,000 rubles, though in itself welcome, was tempered by a realisation that obligations which were on paper finite could easily be inflated by the march of events.[121] A month later, on 7 November – five days after word arrived of Obreskov's imprisonment – Frederick completed his second Political Testament.[122] In keeping with the King's changed

---

[118] Stormont to Rochford, Separate, 9 Nov. 1768, PRO SP 80/205; Rohde to Frederick II, 26 and 29 Oct. and 2 Nov. 1768, GStAPK Rep. 96.46.K.   [119] *Pol. Corr.*, XXVII. 397, 417–18.
[120] *Pol. Corr.*, XXVI. 216.   [121] *Pol. Corr.*, XXVII. 374–6.
[122] Definite news had reached Berlin on 2 Nov.: *Pol. Corr.*, XXVII. 417.

priorities after the Seven Years War, this massive survey of his statecraft gave most attention to the domestic foundations of Prussian power, military as well as administrative and economic, and the reconstruction and reform which had been commenced but not completed.[123] In the years to come these internal priorities would be overturned by the decisive twist given to European diplomacy by the Ottoman declaration of war.

---

[123] It is printed in *Die politischen Testamente*, ed. Dietrich, pp. 464–696; the sections on foreign policy begin at p. 614. Like its predecessor, it was not to be published until shortly after the First World War.

7

The partition of Europe, 1768–1772

I

The Ottoman declaration of war had, surprisingly enough, not been anticipated by the Russians, who were unprepared for the conflict they now faced. Until the very last moment Catherine II and Panin, preoccupied by Poland and the early stages of important internal reforms, had ignored the gathering storm clouds, believing that the usual resource of bribery in Constantinople could avert any threat.[1] Once Obreskov's imprisonment was known in St Petersburg, however, the Empress and her advisers demonstrated impressive vigour in preparing to fight. An informal Council – which was reminiscent of but did not replicate Elizabeth's Conference of the Seven Years War – was immediately set up. Its establishment was formally announced in mid-February 1769, by which point it had already been in existence for almost three months, and it was given overall responsibility for the conduct of the war and the peace negotiations.[2] This was a reverse for Panin. The new Council challenged not merely his policies, but his position as Catherine's principal adviser and his hopes of establishing himself as First Minister, with responsibility for all areas of government activity, and he opposed its creation. Since 1763 Panin had run Russian foreign policy with the Empress. His ascendancy, however, had been essentially personal in nature, and he had never possessed a secure institutional base, other than his role as senior member of the College of Foreign Affairs.[3] The Ottoman War was to weaken and, ultimately, undermine both his policies and his own position.

The Empress' priorities were turned upside down. Ambitious plans for political and administrative reform were shelved and their centrepiece, the Legislative Commission, was prorogued in December 1768. The new advisory Council instead prepared energetically for the coming campaign, making arrangements for troop dispositions and supply, appointing commanders, discussing strategy and, before long, war aims. The impressive vigour of these preparations, however, could not disguise the problems of defending Russia. At the inaugural meeting of the Council in mid-November, Panin had argued that no regiments were needed for defence against

---

[1] Hans Übersberger, *Russlands Orientpolitik in den letzten zwei Jahrhunderten*, vol. I (Stuttgart, 1913), pp. 282–3.   [2] Madariaga, *Russia*, p. 206.
[3] Griffiths, 'The Rise and Fall of the Northern System', p. 554.

Sweden's Finnish redoubt. The Northern System's creator was confident of its pro-phylactic qualities. He was opposed successfully by the military expert, Zachar Chernyshev – an established rival – who secured two regiments for the north.[4]

In the very next month a new crisis in Stockholm, driven on by Choiseul and the comte de Modène, the newly arrived French ambassador, temporarily increased Russia's security problems around the Baltic.[5] The Cap government had faced over-whelming political and financial problems.[6] Though now opposed by a Court–Hat alliance, the discredited and unpopular Caps could not be dislodged from government. In late 1768, in keeping with the embittered nature of political strife, officials in the Exchequer Court were threatened with prosecution. It opened the way for the King to act with unexpected resolve. In December, as part of the Court's continuing efforts to force the calling of a *riksdag*, Adolf Frederik went on strike. This, together with support from the government colleges, was sufficient to overcome the Cap-dominated Council's resistance, and on 20 December an extraordinary *riksdag* was summoned for the following spring, which defused the crisis at least temporarily. When this met, it restored the Hats to power.

These developments initially strengthened St Petersburg's links with Copenhagen, which was equally concerned that the Swedish monarch's powers should not be strengthened. Bernstorff realised the Ottoman War would place Denmark in the front line in the Baltic: it was evident to him that Russia would not fight on three fronts. In early 1769 Danish preparations for war began, to be immediately countered by French threats in defence of the Swedish crown, whose supporter Choiseul had become. Bernstorff turned to Russia for aid and, recognising St Petersburg's weakness – exactly as Prussia's King would do – argued that the alliance should be strengthened by the immediate implementation of the Holstein exchange. He feared that Catherine II or her son might die before this was resolved, since the ultimate heir to Holstein was Denmark's arch-enemy, the Swedish King. The Empress appreciated that the Duchy could be used as bait to retain Copenhagen's absolute loyalty and therefore blocked any final agreement.[7] In any case she wished to delay the exchange until much closer to Paul's own majority, in order to ensure that it had his full support and was therefore final. Catherine II was prepared, however, to conclude a new defensive alliance with Denmark, and this was signed in December 1769.[8] It included the provision that preparations should be made for a possible war against Sweden in the following spring and declared any constitutional change there an immediate *casus belli*.

[4] Soloviev, *History of Russia*, XLVI. 4–7. Three regiments, subsequently reduced to two, were simultaneously left to guard the Livonian frontier with Poland.
[5] Events can be followed in Modène's despatches for these weeks: AAE CP (Suède) 255. See more generally Amburger, *Russland und Schweden*, ch. 4 *passim*.
[6] For the political background, see Roberts, *The Age of Liberty*, ch. 4. See above, pp. 129–36, for the earlier party strife.   [7] *SIRIO*, LXXXVII. 411–12.
[8] It is printed in *Danske Tractater*, pp. 302–10. For these exchanges see Hübner, *Staatspolitik und Familieninteresse*, pp. 237–44; *Bernstorffsche Papiere*, III. 79–82, 88–9; *Bernstorff Corr.*, II. 369–78.

These events indicated Russia's vulnerability, with military operations far to the south and in Poland, where a guerrilla war was under way, and instability around the Baltic.[9] The Empress' recurring nightmare was of fighting at three points on the long and exposed western frontier, and during the Ottoman conflict this appeared possible on more than one occasion. This vulnerability was certainly evident to her ally, the Prussian King, who appreciated his opportunity and set out to take advantage of it.[10] During the year after the Ottoman declaration of war, he strengthened – or perhaps merely prolonged – his links with Russia. By the final weeks of 1768 Frederick was confident that he could limit his involvement in St Petersburg's military effort to a subsidy, albeit a hefty one for the miserly Prussian king.[11] He patiently awaited the moment when he could ruthlessly exploit Russian difficulties.[12] He continued his established campaign to persuade the Empress and her advisers that the situation in Poland was more serious than they appreciated. This was probably correct, and once again Frederick displayed a sharper understanding of Polish realities, but it was also an obvious way to increase his own influence.[13]

By early 1769 Frederick judged the moment opportune to launch a two-pronged diplomatic offensive cynically directed against his ally. The second strand in this was important as a harbinger of future developments, though it had little immediate impact. At the beginning of February the King sent a plan for a partition of Poland to his representative in St Petersburg, Solms. This project Frederick mendaciously declared to be the brainchild of a diplomat in Danish service, Graf Lynar, who had allegedly mentioned it to the King during a visit to Berlin for his daughter's marriage.[14] It was in fact Frederick's own scheme, and it anticipated very closely the contours of the first partition carried out three years later.[15] The Hohenzollerns were to annex Polish Prussia and Warmia and to secure a protectorate over Danzig, Austria would take Zips and part of Galicia, while Russia would secure such gains as she wished in eastern Poland. The three eastern powers would then unite against the Ottoman empire. The so-called Lynar project was forwarded to Solms, with orders – curiously understated and flexible for a ruler normally so decisive and autocratic as Frederick – that the envoy should show it to Panin if he deemed it appropriate. In the event Solms discussed the notion of a partition with the Russian minister, rather than letting him see the written scheme. Panin turned

---

[9] For Panin's recognition of the impact of the Ottoman War on Russia's position in Poland, see his letter to M.M. Filosofov, 27 Oct. 1768 OS, *SIRIO*, LXXXVII. 173–5.

[10] On Frederick's view of Russia at this period, see Stribrny, *Die Russlandpolitik*, pp. 22–8.

[11] See above, p. 185. The subsidy of 400,000 rubles may have been almost 3 per cent of the gross revenue of the Hohenzollern state: Stribrny, *Die Russlandpolitik*, p. 28; Lukowski, *The Partitions of Poland*, p. 48. When Russia asked for Prussian troops to be sent to Poland to bolster her own military effort there, Frederick refused outright and reiterated the view that his commitments under the alliance to Catherine's Ottoman War were limited to a subsidy: *Pol. Corr.*, XXVII. 472–3.

[12] *Pol. Corr.*, XXVII. 420, 432, 495, 512.

[13] *Pol. Corr.*, XXVII. 370–1; see especially his letter to Catherine II, 15 Dec. 1768, keeping up the pressure over Poland and announcing his wish to extend the alliance: *Pol. Corr.*, XXVII. 514–15.

[14] Rochus Friedrich, Graf von Lynar, though German by birth, had for long been in Copenhagen's service: for his diplomatic career, see *Repertorium*, II. 33, 42, 44.   [15] *Pol. Corr.*, XXVIII. 84.

it down, though a second conversation suggested that he was at least interested in the idea. For the moment, however, the Lynar project was no more than a testing of the waters. It revealed the King's established interest in acquiring Polish territory, if that were politically feasible, but it had little or no immediate impact on Russo-Prussian relations or on the wider diplomacy of the European powers.[16]

The first and more immediately important strand in the King's offensive was an attempt to prolong his Russian alliance.[17] A month earlier Frederick had launched his bid for a renewal and, more important, an extension of the treaty. First concluded in April 1764 for eight years, it would expire in 1772.[18] Immediately after he received definite news of the Sultan's declaration of war, the King had resolved to press for its prolongation.[19] The ostensible reason was that the Ottoman War, and the subsidy which the King was obliged to pay, had given Russia – and deprived Prussia of – the advantages of the alliance, and therefore Frederick argued that in equity he must be compensated by means of an extension of the chronological duration of the treaty.[20] The initiative, however, proceeded from the King's more fundamental anxieties about the stability and likely permanence of the alliance, seen as the foundation of his own security. He always professed to believe that a Russo-Austrian axis was more logical, since it could be directed either against himself in Germany or against the Ottomans in south-eastern Europe.[21] The Sultan's declaration of war seemed to make a Russo-Austrian *rapprochement* not merely possible but, in the future, more likely. Prussia's ruler also appreciated that the position of Panin, the alliance's architect, might come under pressure with the beginning of a new Ottoman war: as indeed it did. Frederick was anxious that his treaty should outlast Catherine II's most prominent adviser. This approach was strengthened by Panin's presentation of himself to Solms ever since spring 1764 as its principal defender.[22]

In mid-January 1769, the King opened negotiations for the alliance's renewal, together with an extension of its duration by another ten years, to run from 1772.[23] The discussions which followed were prolonged and proved to be difficult, extending over nine months. At first the King's believed that Russia's vulnerability and

---

[16] In the second Political Testament, completed in early November 1768, the King had declared that he believed that one day Poland's three neighbours would carry out a partition: *Die politischen Testamente*, ed. Dietrich, p. 670.

[17] Stribrny, *Die Russlandpolitik*, pp. 28–35, provides a brief and in some ways contrasting account of these exchanges.   [18] The modification in 1767 (above, p. 181) had not affected the treaty's duration.

[19] *Pol. Corr.*, XXVII. 432.   [20] e.g. *Pol. Corr.*, XXVII. 421, 472.

[21] See above, p. 164; see also his comments in the 1768 Political Testament: *Die politischen Testamente*, ed. Dietrich, p. 648.

[22] E.g. *SIRIO*, XXII. 141. See more generally the Prussian diplomatic correspondence printed in *SIRIO*, vols. XXII and XXXVII, *passim*. A French diplomat judged that the Empress and Panin were the only two important supporters of a Prussian connection (*SIRIO*, CXL. 472, 596) and it is certainly true that many influential advisers of Catherine II's first decade seem to have favoured an Austrian alliance, men such as A.P. Bestuzhev-Riumin, the Chernyshevs, the Orlovs and Kyrill Razumovsky: Griffiths, 'Russian Court Politics', p. 36.

[23] The negotiations can be followed in *Pol. Corr.*, XXVIII, and *SIRIO*, XXXVII, on which the account which follows is principally based. See also Soloviev, *History of Russia*, XLVI. 78–9.

need for his support would force the acceptance of his terms sooner or later. This optimism seemed well founded, given Russia's real need for assistance at this point, and it was reinforced by Panin's positive response. Before long, however, it was soon wearing thin. Frederick had recognised from the outset that the negotiations might be extended, because of St Petersburg's preoccupation with the war effort. In any case, any diplomacy involving Russia was likely to involve periodic and impenetrable delays as he was well aware.[24] By early April, however, the King was surprised and unhappy that no progress had been made, and by the end of that month his anxieties were acute.[25] Frederick had always recognised that the interval before the fighting began provided the best opportunity to extend the alliance. Once the Russian victories which he believed to be inevitable, given the clear military inferiority of the Ottoman armies, began to be secured, his own bargaining position would become appreciably weaker: this was why he wanted an early renewal of the treaty.[26]

There were two reasons for the delays. The first was the increased opposition to the Northern System itself and to its proponent which had been aroused in Russian governing circles by the Sultan's declaration of war.[27] The principal criticism of Panin's foreign policy had always been that it offered little protection against an Ottoman attack, and this charge was increasingly heard after the final weeks of 1768. Indeed, a majority of the new Council were unsympathetic to the diplomatic programme of the Northern System.[28] At the very end of that year, during one of its early meetings, Panin's system was openly challenged by Grigory Orlov, and others subsequently joined in this critique.[29] During the winter of 1768–9 the view that an Austrian alliance would be – as it had previously been – of greater utility against the Ottoman empire was heard more and more at the Russian court, particularly when it became clear that St Petersburg's Prussian ally intended to limit his assistance to the subsidy prescribed in the original treaty. Catherine II, who retained ultimate control over foreign policy, recognised that both Prussian and Austrian alliances had important supporters among her advisers, and was at first reluctant to sanction an extension of the 1764 treaty. This hesitation was possible because of Russia's simultaneous negotiations for a British alliance, which were the second reason for the hiatus in the Prusso-Russian discussions during the early months of 1769.

Frederick's anxieties would have been considerably greater had he fully appreciated that Panin was actually discussing a treaty with London. As in 1763–4, talks

---

[24] Cf. his experiences in 1763–4: above, pp. 109–15. [25] *Pol. Corr.*, XXVIII. 235, 286, 292.
[26] *Pol. Corr.*, XXVII. 481, 484.
[27] Both the British and French representatives in St Petersburg commented on this: *SIRIO*, XII. 411–12; CXL. 495. In autumn 1768 Frederick had feared that Panin's neglect of the Ottoman threat would weaken his position: *Pol. Corr.*, XXVII. 384.
[28] At least six (out of nine) advisers seem to have been: Kyrill Razumovsky, Zakhar Chernyshev, General A.M. Golitsyn, his namesake the Vice-Chancellor, Grigory Orlov and A.A. Vyazemsky: Ransel, *Politics of Catherinian Russia*, p. 197 and, more generally, ch. 7; Soloviev, *History of Russia*, xlvi. 53.
[29] Madariaga, *Russia*, pp. 205–6; cf. Soloviev, *History of Russia*, XLVI. 55.

with Britain went on side-by-side with the stalled negotiations for the renewal of the Prussian treaty.[30] The Ottoman declaration of war together with the near-simultaneous arrival of a new British ambassador in early autumn 1768 had produced a further initiative over the alliance.[31] The approaching hostilities modified Russia's terms. The demand for the 'Turkish clause', hitherto a *sine qua non*, was dropped. If it had not been, London could not have signed an alliance without simultaneously declaring war upon the Ottoman empire and that was unthinkable. In its place Panin sought a subsidy, together with additional financial support in Sweden, when negotiations began in October 1768. Russia, already short of money, faced the considerable expense of an Ottoman war, and her ministers were concerned at the extra expenditure necessitated by the likely summoning of the *riksdag*, the costs of which they hoped to transfer to London.[32]

Britain's new ambassador played a crucial part in the misunderstandings which followed. Baron Cathcart was a fatal mixture of enthusiasm, inexperience and gullibility. Determined to conclude the long-desired alliance, now seen in London as crucial to Britain's security in Europe, and to succeed where his predecessors had all failed, he seems to have been led by the nose by the crafty and experienced Panin. Fatally, the ambassador disregarded his explicit instructions and conveyed the impression that Britain was now willing to provide what she had always hitherto refused: a subsidy in peacetime.[33] When Russia's representative in London discovered that this was not on offer and that in fact Britain remained determined to refuse this, Panin was understandably irritated. In April and early May 1769 he first rejected Britain's stingy counter-offer of financial aid in Stockholm and then broke off the talks altogether.[34] This breakdown was immediately followed by the resumption of negotiations with Prussia. Progress towards a renewed treaty was now surprisingly swift, as Frederick quickly accepted a Russian demand that the extension should be for eight and not ten years, though in late summer 1769 a further, and much briefer, delay occurred.

It originated on the Prussian side and was a product of the second strand of the King's diplomacy at this period. This was a *rapprochement* with Vienna which would be quite crucial to the relations of the great powers in 1770–2. In Frederick's second Political Testament, finalised in the month after the Ottoman declaration of war, the value of links with Austria to curb Russia's growing power had been emphasised, and Prussia now sought such a *rapprochement*.[35] Its origins, apparent

---

[30] Cf. above, pp. 106, 109. To judge by the despatches printed in *Pol. Corr.*, XXVIII, and *SIRIO*, XXXVII, Frederick does not seem to have been fully aware of either the existence or the potential importance of Russo-British discussions at this point.

[31] For this latest round of alliance diplomacy, see Scott, *British Foreign Policy*, pp. 127–32.

[32] *SIRIO*, CXLI. 466. By April 1769, in preparation for the coming meeting, Russia's representative in Stockholm had spent over 900,000 livres: Amburger, *Russland und Schweden*, pp. 194 *et seq.*

[33] Panin certainly believed this was now on offer: Martens, *Recueil des traités*, IX(X). 270–1; cf. *SIRIO*, CXLI. 459, 469, 491, 502.   [34] *SIRIO*, XII. 432–3, 436–41.

[35] *Die politischen Testamente*, ed. Dietrich, p. 624.

before 1768, lay in the shared fear of a breakdown of the peace which was the main priority of both states, and a corresponding anxiety that the Russo-Ottoman conflict might widen into a more general continental war. Kaunitz was equally concerned at Russia's growing power and especially her dominance over Poland, and was anxious for a *rapprochement* with Prussia, which he believed was now the only way Catherine II's advance might be resisted.[36] Though both Joseph II and Maria Theresa were unconvinced that this was either feasible or desirable, Austrian diplomacy sought to persuade Frederick of Vienna's peaceful outlook and wish for friendly relations. In late 1768, shortly after news of Obreskov's imprisonment reached first Vienna and then Berlin, Austria's representative in the Prussian capital Nugent had canvassed a neutrality agreement between the two states, to prevent any extension of the fighting.[37] Though Frederick viewed this idea sympathetically, particularly since he believed – probably erroneously – that it had France's backing, he recognised that it could compromise the links with Russia he was currently seeking to extend, and so early in 1769 he politely turned down the suggestion while simultaneously welcoming the understanding which had been reached over neutrality. The Austrian initiative was correctly viewed by the King as further and welcome evidence that Vienna's outlook remained pacific.[38] The reports he was receiving from Rohde emphasised Austria's continuing financial weakness and resulting political passivity, and the King's conclusion was that the Habsburgs would not intervene either in Poland or in the Russo-Ottoman War, at least until the scale of Russian victories became clear.[39] He welcomed Vienna's attitude to the forthcoming fighting and the increasing convergence between the two states' foreign policies.

It was exemplified by a meeting between the Emperor Joseph II and his Prussian hero at Neisse in Silesia in late August 1769. Joseph remained keen on such an encounter, which had been blocked by Maria Theresa and, probably, Kaunitz three years earlier, and had continued to insinuate this to Prussia's resident in Vienna.[40] The Chancellor came to favour an interview, which could advance his projected *rapprochement* with Potsdam, and in November 1768 had once more broached the idea with Prussia. By 1769 its political advantages were much clearer, while the reciprocal curiosity between the two monarchs was at least as strong. By early in that year

---

[36] Arneth, *GMT*, VIII. 153ff, for his efforts. See also his memorandum of 3 Dec. 1768, printed in Beer, *Erste Theilung Polens*, III. 262–72. At the beginning of January of that year, the Chancellor had unsuccessfully pressed for agreement with the Prussian King to restrain Catherine II's conduct in Poland: Beer, *Erste Theilung Polens*, III. 1–5.

[37] See the account of his interview with the King, printed in *Pol. Corr.*, XXVII. 441–5. When Finckenstein, in an unusual and revealing intervention, expressed his scepticism over the idea, which he viewed in a traditional way, as an Austrian attempt to embroil Prussia with Russia, he received a shirty reply from Frederick: *Pol. Corr.*, XXVII. 452–4. See also Arneth, *GMT*, VIII. 157–60.

[38] *Pol. Corr.*, XXVII. 452: a particularly important and revealing statement since it was made in a letter to Prince Henry.

[39] See in particular Rohde to Frederick II, 4 Mar. 1769, GStAPK Rep. 96.47.A; *Pol. Corr.*, XXVII. 445, 446–7, 456.   [40] See above, p. 163.

a meeting had been agreed upon in principle; detailed arrangements were made, and in late August it took place.

The discussions, spread out over a week at Neisse, were very general in nature and seem to have confirmed each ruler's preconceptions where the other was concerned.[41] The fact that they met in Silesia was itself symbolically important: it appeared to confirm Vienna's renunciation of the lost province, which Habsburg diplomacy had emphasised since 1763. A renewed Austrian initiative proposing a neutrality convention for Germany was accepted by Frederick. It covered an Anglo-Bourbon War over the Falklands or any other new fighting in Europe, but still excluded any extension of the Balkan conflict through the intervention of one or more great powers. Nevertheless, it was an important stage in the emergence of political fault lines between eastern and western Europe. The Neisse agreement sought to prevent the two German powers being drawn into a renewed conflict between Britain and France. A second Austrian proposal, recalling an earlier initiative by Kaunitz,[42] for a reciprocal troop reduction was welcomed by the King as further evidence of Habsburg pacifism, but once again rejected as incompatible with Prussia's established strategy of military deterrence based upon her superior army. Yet the King had few anxieties about his relations with Austria. He believed that her burden of debt was such that Vienna would remain at peace for another fifteen years, and remained convinced that the Habsburgs would in any case not attack as long as the Russo-Prussian alliance existed.[43]

The King quite deliberately used the Neisse meeting, which had few immediate political results, to increase diplomatic pressure on Russia. The Prusso-Austrian *rapprochement* was a valuable weapon in his political armoury, as it would be during the next few years. By now Catherine II and her advisers were prepared to concede most of what Frederick had been demanding, since the initial campaign did not appear to be going well. In October 1769 the Russo-Prussian alliance was extended until 1780, that is to say, by a further eight years.[44] The King secured a Russian guarantee for his claim to Ansbach and Bayreuth, and in return promised in a secret article to invade Swedish Pomerania should there be any attempt to overturn the Constitution of 1720, as the Court now seemed to be attempting, or should Sweden attack Russia. The signature of the treaty came just in time for Frederick. By autumn 1769 the outcome of the first campaign against the Ottomans and the likely scale of Russian successes were becoming clear. The renewal of the alliance was accompanied by news of the major Russian gain of that year, the capture of Khotin.[45] The victories which Catherine II's armies were beginning to gain and

---

[41] The standard authority on the two interviews remains the long article (which includes a substantial documentary appendix) by Adolf Beer, 'Die Zusammenkünfte Josefs II. und Friedrichs II. zu Neisse und Neustadt', *AÖG* 47 (1871), pp. 383–527.   [42] Cf. above, p. 165, for this.

[43] See the extended and important analysis in his letter to Prince Henry, 26 Nov. 1769, *Pol. Corr.*, XXIX. 224–5. Frederick's only concern was that Joseph II might be more bellicose.

[44] The treaty can be found in Martens, *Recueil des traités*, VI. 48–51.   [45] *Pol. Corr.*, XXVIII. 124, 136–7.

which would continue throughout the first two campaigns of the war, was henceforth to be the major factor in the diplomacy of the eastern powers.

II

The fighting which began in earnest in spring 1769 would continue until peace was signed between the Ottoman empire and Russia in summer 1774.[46] During these years, political events were dependent upon the military struggle: this was why the first campaign saw little diplomatic activity of any significance, except for the Prussian King's successful attempt to extend his Russian alliance.[47] Throughout the war the ebb and flow of events in south-eastern Europe set the pace for diplomats all over the continent, particularly as the struggle's likely outcome became clear. Each successive Russian triumph was eagerly analysed and its significance discussed; every humiliating Ottoman reverse was gloomily received and its implications dissected. The distance from the major capitals at which these events were taking place, together with the renowned slowness and unreliability of communications with south-eastern Europe, ensured that at times the pace of diplomacy would be rather slow. The Russo-Ottoman conflict dominated international relations until 1771, when Poland became the leading issue. Its dual importance lay in the threat it posed to the continuation of peace between the great powers and in the specific French, Prussian and Austrian interests which were at stake, as the next few years would make clear.

Both Frederick the Great and Kaunitz, the two most perceptive observers of the diplomatic scene, declared that the Ottoman declaration of war changed Europe's political system.[48] Its decisive impact was due to the considerable military advantage which St Petersburg secured during the first two campaigns and, in spite of external and internal problems, retained throughout the conflict. In some ways this

---

[46] The most comprehensive introduction to the war is the old study by Richard Ungermann, *Der Russisch-türkische Krieg, 1768–1774* (Vienna, 1906). A well-informed Russian perspective is provided by Übersberger, *Russlands Orientpolitik*, I. 241–337, while the war's wider importance for the development of Russia as a military power is suggested by Bruce W. Menning, 'Russian Military Innovation in the Second Half of the Eighteenth Century', *War and Society* 2 (1984), pp. 23–41. Aksan, *An Ottoman Statesman*, pp. 100–69, and her overlapping articles, 'Feeding the Ottoman Troops on the Danube, 1768–1774', *War and Society* 13 (1995), pp. 1–14, and 'The One-Eyed Fighting the Blind: Mobilization, Supply, and Command in the Russo-Turkish War of 1768–1774', *International History Review* 15 (1993), pp. 221–38, are valuable for their perspectives from modern research on the Ottoman empire. The old narrative history of Hammer, *Histoire de l'empire Ottoman*, XVI. 209–400 *passim*, contains much military detail on the war. The Russian side of the campaigns of 1769–70 is set out in Soloviev, *History of Russia*, XLVI. 14–49 and 98–136, and with great penetration in Madariaga, *Russia*, pp. 205ff. Developments in the Crimea are the subject of Fisher, *Russian Annexation*, ch. 3. The best study of the complex diplomacy of these years is still Sorel, *La question d'Orient*.

[47] This emerges particularly clearly from the correspondence for that year in AAE CP (Autriche) 311–12 *passim* and from the despatches of Prussia's representative in Vienna, in GStAPK Rep. 96.47.C and D.

[48] *Œuvres*, VI. 6; Beer, *Erste Theilung Polens*, I. 293–6; and the Chancellor's *Vortrag* of 3 Dec. 1768, Beer, *Erste Theilung Polens*, III. 262–72.

was unexpected to Russian observers, since the Ottoman empire enjoyed three considerable strategic advantages in its eighteenth-century conflicts with Russia.[49] The first was that the fighting took place much closer to Ottoman bases and often in or close to Ottoman territory, which appeared to be protected by a network of fortresses around the Black Sea. The Sultan's armies could more readily draw supplies and reinforcements from lands at least nominally under Constantinople's control. By contrast, Russian armies operated far from their bases, with exposed and extended supply lines and no magazines to support their operations. The second advantage was a corollary of the first. Ottoman control of the Black Sea and its coastlines gave Constantinople the choice of the theatre of operations, together with the capacity to supply and reinforce its forces by sea. Finally, suzerainty over the Crimea provided a sally-port into Russian territory. The Khanate's importance was demonstrated during the early months of 1769, when in the first fighting of the war, Kirim Girai led a ramshackle and irregular force on a raid into southern Russia, causing considerable damage but securing no commensurate military advantage.

In the conflict of 1768–74, however, these advantages, together with the numerical superiority enjoyed by the Sultan's forces, were more than cancelled out by Russia's military organisation, which was relatively more efficient, and by the administrative and political shortcomings of the Ottoman empire. Though Catherine II's government also faced problems in Poland and, at times, around the Baltic, the military reforms since the Seven Years War and, more important, a willingness to improvise gave her the edge in the campaigns in the south. By contrast, the Sultan's army had enjoyed almost three decades of peace – the last fighting had been the conflict against Russia which ended in 1739 – and the regular Ottoman forces together with the army's supply services had effectively to be reconstructed from scratch in the winter of 1768–9. Russia's use of intelligence was far superior to her Ottoman adversary, which completely neglected its potential. Like its opponent, the Russian army faced significant problems of supply and logistics, but it overcame these more successfully. The fact that Catherine II's armies wintered in south-eastern Europe and conducted operations throughout the year was a further advantage against the Sultan's forces who usually campaigned only from spring to autumn. The Russian rank-and-file proved to be of higher quality, as did its leadership, especially the impressive Rumyantsev, who was experienced, dedicated, professional and flexible, and who supervised a series of significant victories. His skilful use of the superior Russian field artillery was to be particularly important, especially in the major victory at Falça in the second campaign of the war.[50] The discipline and firepower of the Russian armies proved decisive, particularly in set-piece engagements.

By contrast the Ottoman empire had acute recruitment, provisioning and financial problems, and suffered even more from the poor quality of its leadership. These

---

[49] Madariaga, *Russia*, p. 207.   [50] Fuller, *Strategy and Power*, p. 159.

problems were especially serious during the first half of the conflict; here, as in other respects, there was to be a noted improvement from 1771 onwards, as political leadership became much stronger. Field armies were often short of supplies, and at times of reinforcements as well. The Ottoman political and army leadership was also inferior, and its strategic thinking outdated and inflexible. It was compounded by divisions within the command structure, and by the lack of a clearly defined military hierarchy. The grand vizier, who commanded in person, and a supporting chancery accompanied the field army throughout the war, but a substitute grand vizier (*kaymakam*) with his own chancery remained in Constantinople. Contact between capital and battlefront was intermittent and characterised by tension and distrust. To these structural problems can be added the poor quality of grand viziers. By this period these men were the product of the administrative hierarchy rather than the army, but they were still expected to exercise military command, though they competed for authority with powerful provincial governors with their own contingents of troops. The shortcomings of the Grand Viziers during the crucial first two years of the war were decisive: none of them proved to be capable of fighting an extended campaign.[51] Silâdar Mehmed, who was in office from December 1770 until November 1771, was a noted improvement. His successor was the impressive though now veteran Muhsinzade Mehmed who alone of these men possessed previous military experience. He had been Grand Vizier in 1765–8, being dismissed on the eve of the Ottoman declaration of war.[52] He was in office throughout the second half of the struggle, dying shortly after the peace settlement in summer 1774, and provided firm and capable leadership.

The interval between the declaration of war and the start of serious fighting in late spring 1769 enabled Catherine II and her advisers to organise a significant military offensive. The target of the first campaign was Khotin, the most northerly outpost of the Ottoman empire. Despite supply problems, which affected both armies and at one point forced the Russians to retreat, Khotin was eventually and with considerable difficulty captured in the autumn, a success which enabled Catherine II's forces to occupy Bucharest and most of Moldavia and Wallachia by the end of 1769. St Petersburg's forces were concentrated against the Crimea during the war's second campaign. The fighting in 1770 saw a series of Russian triumphs, with Ottoman armies defeated first at Falça (July) and then Kartal (August), a considerable if hard-fought Russian victory in one of the very few large-scale engagement battles of the war. This success opened the entire region between the Danube and the Dniester to the Russian army. In the aftermath of Kartal, Catherine II's forces advanced along the Danube, capturing first Bender, the major Ottoman fort on the lower Dniester which menaced Russian supply lines, then Kili and finally Ismail; to the east, Russia's hold over the Crimea was consolidated.

---

[51] Aksan, *An Ottoman Statesman*, pp. 131–3, for these men and their considerable failings.
[52] Cf. above, p. 184.

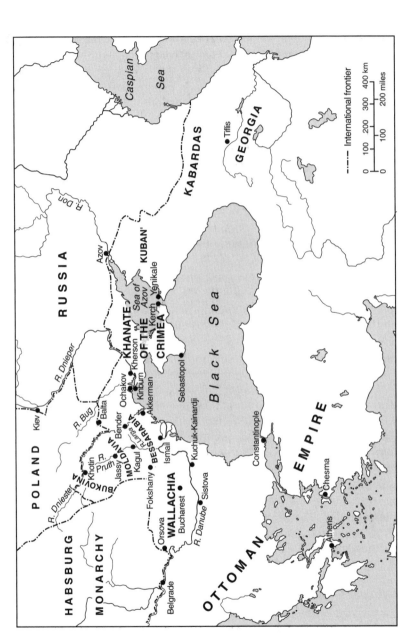

2. The campaigns of the Russo-Ottoman War

The major Ottoman defeats in 1770 were not confined to land. From the very beginning of the conflict, Russia had envisaged naval intervention in the Mediterranean.[53] The various squadrons in this force had made the long, slow and dangerous voyage from their bases in the eastern Baltic through the North Sea, into the Bay of Biscay and Atlantic, and then into the eastern Mediterranean. Ships and crews were often in poor condition, and only friendly ports – particularly in Britain[54] – in which to recuperate and undertake essential repairs enabled a Russian fleet to be assembled in the Aegean, where in July 1770 it won a dramatic victory over the Sultan's navy at Chesma (Chesmé), in the one decisive naval engagement of the entire conflict. The expedition had been led by Aleksey Orlov and initially proposed by his brother, Grigory, Catherine II's favourite. Success had been achieved against considerable odds: at Chesma the Russian squadrons were out-numbered and outgunned.[55] The significance of the Ottoman defeat was to be con-siderable. Though Russia's Mediterranean fleet accomplished very little during the rest of the war, the battle announced the appearance of Catherine II's empire as a major European naval power, a position which would be strengthened during the rest of her reign.[56]

The scale of Russian successes, at sea and on land, had surprised the Empress and her advisers, and they were celebrated with *Te Deums* and promotions: in particular Rumyantsev was elevated to Field-Marshal. Their impact was no less decisive on the vanquished Ottoman empire, which by mid-October 1770 was prepared to con-sider a negotiated settlement. But the striking Russian gains of 1769–70 were not built upon during the following campaigns, though the Crimea was declared inde-pendent and, more important, made subject to St Petersburg's control in the fol-lowing year. Russia, from an early stage in the war, had intervened in the Khanate's internal power struggle, taking the side of the nomadic and settled groups of Tatars, particularly the Nogays, against the Girai family (which had traditionally provided the Khans) and their supporters. The decisive point came in 1771 when, following a successful Russian invasion of the peninsula, Selim Girai fled, a puppet régime was established and Crimean independence proclaimed.[57]

Elsewhere a military stalemate was evident. The beginning of an extended search for a negotiated settlement in autumn 1770 was part of the explanation, as the Ottoman leadership sought by prolonged discussions to avoid further military defeats. The stalemate also reflected the strategic situation. By the end of the second campaign, Russia had been triumphant north of the Danube, in the tributary prin-cipalities of the Ottoman empire, and had occupied large swathes of former

---

[53] There is a detailed study by Andreas Bode, *Die Flottenpolitik Katharinas II. und die Konflikte mit Schweden und der Türkei (1768–92)* (Munich, 1979).
[54] See M.S. Anderson, 'Great Britain and the Russian Fleet, 1769–70', *Slavonic and East European Review* 31 (1952–3), pp. 148–63.   [55] See the figures in Madariaga, *Russia*, p. 21.
[56] See below, p. 252.
[57] Fisher, *Russian Annexation*, pp. 32–44, provides an account of these complex developments.

Ottoman territory. But south of the river the Sultan's forces were established in Muslim territory which remained firmly under Constantinople's control, and occupied a very strong defensive position, which they were careful not to abandon in the fighting which followed. After 1770, in contrast to the first two campaigns, the Ottoman high command would fight an overwhelmingly defensive war. Improvements in organisation and leadership, especially after Muhsinzade Mehmed became Grand Vizier, stiffened Ottoman resistance, and a military and – before long – diplomatic *impasse* came into existence which would only be broken in the final year of the struggle.

Russia's satisfaction at her victories over the Ottomans was tempered by renewed anxieties in autumn 1770 over relations with Copenhagen. Denmark had been ruled since 1766 by Christian VII.[58] The sixteen-year-old King, however, was weak, dissolute and mentally unstable, and unable to rule effectively; he was soon to be completely disabled by schizophrenia. In the same year he became King, he had married Caroline Mathilda, the youngest sister of Britain's George III. By the later 1760s the estranged royal couple were falling under the sway of Johann Friedrich Struensee, a German doctor, who first became court physician and then the lover of the isolated and neurotic Queen. By 1770 Struensee effectively controlled royal policy, with the complaisant King a prisoner in his own palace. During the second half of that year, with the support of his accomplice Enevold Brandt and a group of younger courtiers, he undermined and then removed Christian VII's old advisers.[59] In mid September a *coup* ousted J.H.E. von Bernstorff, the distinguished and by now veteran foreign minister. By the end of 1770 Struensee's power was total. During the following year he used this personal dictatorship to introduce wide-ranging enlightened reforms. Struensee's arrogance – he never seems to have learned Danish – together with his low birth and the scandalous nature of his power, aroused resentment and, eventually, opposition.

Bernstorff's fall alarmed Russian observers, who viewed him as the pillar upon which their Danish alliance rested.[60] Their anxiety was increased when it seemed likely that his successor would be Grev S.C. Rantzau-Ascheberg, who had risen in Struensee's entourage, and was viewed as a tool of France and therefore hostile towards Russia.[61] Catherine II protested vigorously at these developments and threatened that the Holstein exchange would not go ahead: once again this was

---

[58] H. Arnold Barton, *Scandinavia in the Revolutionary Era 1760–1815* (Minneapolis, MN, 1986), pp. 57–63, 67–76, provides the Danish background.

[59] The dangers for Copenhagen's foreign policy were set out by Bernstorff in a memoir to Christian VII, 18 July 1770, *Bernstorff Corr.*, II. 466–72.

[60] Panin to Filosofov, Draft, 15 July 1770 OS, *SIRIO*, XCVII. 104–8, for Russian anxieties almost two months before the minister's removal and testimony to his importance; Soloviev, *History of Russia*, XLVI. 190–6, for St Petersburg's subsequent reaction.

[61] Panin considered him to be the 'declared enemy' of any links with Russia: *SIRIO*, XCVII. 159; cf. *Bernstorffsche Papiere*, II. 371–2, 376, 385–6, 603–8, for the reactions of Christian VII's old advisers, who were of course concerned that this would imperil the Holstein exchange: exactly as St Petersburg threatened.

believed to provide diplomatic leverage at Copenhagen.[62] When these representations were ignored, the Empress recalled her envoy from the Danish court, where during the next two years Russia was represented by a *chargé d'affaires*.[63] The downgrading of diplomatic representation did not indicate a serious worsening of relations. Bernstorff's eventual successor, Grev A.S. von der Osten, was less anti-Russian than Rantzau and, as a former Danish diplomat in St Petersburg, was viewed favourably by the Empress and Panin.[64] Russia's Danish alliance, however, was to be less secure throughout Struensee's ascendancy (1770–2) than it had been when Copenhagen's policy was in Bernstorff's safe hands.

These anxieties had repercussions in Sweden, where Denmark's support had been especially welcome during the first two years of the Russo-Ottoman War.[65] Russia saw Choiseul's hand behind her wide-ranging problems at this period: to the Empress he was 'the cursed enemy of my state and my person'.[66] This was especially so in Sweden, where the *riksdag* which assembled in spring 1769 had been prolonged, necessitating considerable expenditure both by Ostermann and his French counterpart. Panin's anxieties were real and centred upon his fear that constitutional changes by the Hat–Court alliance might lead to a Swedish attack upon Russia.[67] The crisis passed, however, as the Hat *riksdag* ended early in 1770 without any major decisions being taken, save for the payment of the Swedish royal couple's debts. There was no strengthening of monarchical power, and thereafter Russian anxieties were somewhat reduced. Crown Prince Gustav's emergence as the leader of the Court party, together with the French backing he was receiving, were already viewed with concern in St Petersburg, though this was in some degree reduced by his departure in autumn 1770 on an extended visit to France. He was to be in Paris when he heard of his father's death in early 1771 and so became King as Gustav III.

The Ottoman War intensified Catherine II's difficulties not merely around the Baltic but also in Poland, where it encouraged her opponents and also weakened her own military effort.[68] Panin's Northern System had envisaged that Poland might provide military assistance in any Ottoman War, but by autumn 1768 this was unrealistic. Instead, St Petersburg faced a guerrilla war which consumed such troops as could be spared. Russia's opponents, unified under the umbrella of the Confederation of Bar and with some French support, effectively sustained resistance with an army which at its peak was 12,000 strong. Before 1772 St Petersburg never committed more than 26,000 troops to Poland, and usually around half that number. This was far too few to hold down a large, frequently hostile, country

[62] See Panin's very strong note to Scheel (Danish envoy in St Petersburg), 17 Oct. 1770 OS, *SIRIO*, XCVII. 158–61. For Russo-Danish relations at this period see Hübner, *Staatspolitik und Familieninteresse*, pp. 244–54.

[63] Filosofov left in Dec. 1770 and I.I. Mestmacher handled relations until the arrival of I.M. Simolin as envoy in late 1772: *Repertorium*, III. 350.   [64] E.g. *Bernstorffsche Papiere*, II. 139.

[65] Soloviev, *History of Russia*, XLVI. 91–5.   [66] Soloviev, *History of Russia*, XLVI. 156.

[67] *SIRIO*, XXXVII. 247–59.

[68] Soloviev, *History of Russia*, XLVI. 55–78, 172–86, for developments in 1768–70.

unreconciled to its Russian yoke.[69] One localised military threat could be defeated, but resistance immediately erupted in another region. In December 1768 Repnin resigned his post, recommending partition as the only solution. His successor, M.N. Volkonsky, had reached the same exasperated conclusion by March 1770. The frustrations of two successive viceroys would contribute to St Petersburg's acceptance of partition in 1771–2, as the failure of military repression encouraged a more radical approach to the problem of Poland.

III

Russia's striking victories during 1770 provided the first real opportunity for other powers to propose a negotiated settlement. Both belligerents were, in 1769–70, intent upon awaiting the outcome of the military struggle. This was why the half-hearted efforts at outside diplomatic intervention during the first two years of the war were doomed to failure.[70] Austria, Prussia and even Britain (still searching for a Russian alliance, now by way of Constantinople) were all, at different times, involved in efforts to secure Obreskov's release which was viewed as a breach of international law – a symptom of Russia's new found international maturity[71] – and was insisted upon by St Petersburg, as a precondition of any talks. The governments who pursued a negotiated agreement aimed initially to prevent the outbreak of fighting and then to produce a mediated peace.[72] Their efforts never had much prospect of success, as Frederick the Great always recognised. Neither Russia nor the Ottoman empire would consider any settlement until the war's likely outcome had become apparent.[73] In the late summer of 1770, however, in the aftermath of the defeats at Chesma and Kartal, the Sultan and his advisers accepted an Austrian offer of mediation first made in the previous year and renewed before the second campaign began: Vienna's concern at Russian successes was already apparent.[74] That same military struggle which had led Constantinople to favour negotiations, however, had simultaneously reduced the scope for any mediation not merely by inflating St Petersburg's terms, but by fostering the belief that peace should be negotiated directly with the defeated army by the Russian commander in the field.[75]

The winter of 1770–1 saw intensive but ultimately unsuccessful efforts to produce a mediated settlement, undertaken by Austria and Prussia. Britain, which earlier had been active but ineffective, was now wholly discredited in Ottoman eyes. The assistance provided in British shipyards to the Russian squadrons which made

---

[69] Lukowski, *Partitions of Poland*, pp. 45–6.
[70] E.g. Catherine II's comments on a possible British initiative: [Mar. 1769] *SIRIO*, LXXXVII. 349.
[71] Cf. above, p. 159.   [72] For Austria's efforts, see Arneth, *GMT*, VIII. 166–70, 201 ff.
[73] The documents printed in *Pol. Corr.*, XXX, for these months, convey very well the sense of waiting upon news of military events from the Russo-Ottoman front.
[74] Roider, *Thugut*, p. 28; Kaunitz to Thugut, 20 Feb. 1770, Arneth, *GMT*, VIII. 189–206.
[75] The Ottoman leadership initially interpreted this as a sign of Russian weakness!: Aksan, *An Ottoman Statesman*, p. 154.

the long voyage to the Mediterranean, and the way in which this was exploited by French diplomacy at the Porte, had ended any prospect of London's mediation being accepted by the Ottoman empire. By autumn 1770, however, the two German powers were moving in the same direction over the war in south-eastern Europe. They were united – as they had been since 1768 and, to some extent, since 1763 – by a common fear of a new European struggle, which the fighting in the Balkans appeared to be bringing closer, and increasingly by shared anxieties about the scale of Russian victories.

Frederick was publicly obliged to rejoice at his ally's military successes.[76] Privately he was increasingly concerned at Russia's likely territorial gains. No longer was it simply a matter of the King's dread of being dragged into a wider conflict: the implications of Catherine II's military successes threatened Prussia almost as much as Austria. Underlying his belief in the absolute necessity of a Russian alliance for Prussia's survival as a leading state had always been a more fundamental anxiety concerning Russian power and its implications in the longer term.[77] These fears gained ground as news arrived of the spectacular gains which the Russian empire was making at the expense of its Ottoman counterpart and which challenged ideas of a balance of power between the leading states. The consequent annexations, when peace was finally concluded, would not be matched by equivalent gains for the other two eastern powers, and would immeasurably strengthen Russia's position in south-eastern Europe and free the Empress to pursue a more vigorous policy in Poland and Sweden.

The implications of the Russian victories of summer 1770 were even more alarming for Austria.[78] They climaxed a growing concern at the direction of the Russo-Ottoman War and further undermined the policy of neutrality adopted in 1768.[79] Kaunitz's initial analysis had been rather different from that of the Prussian King. Whereas Frederick had, from the first, appreciated the potential of the Russian forces which he had faced on the battlefield, the Chancellor believed – or perhaps merely hoped – that two equally matched armies would weaken each other through an indecisive conflict and that this might benefit Austria.[80] During the first year of

---

[76] See in particular his letter to Catherine II, 12 Aug. 1770, *Pol. Corr.*, xxx. 72–3; cf. *Pol. Corr.*, xxx. 78–9, 206.

[77] This fundamental ambiguity was articulated in the second Political Testament, *Die politischen Testamente*, ed. Dietrich, 622–4, 646–8.

[78] A valuable guide to Austria's changing policy towards the Russo-Ottoman War at this point is provided by the 'Instructions' for Belgioioso, 22 Sept. 1770, HHStA, England-Korrespondenz 115.

[79] Roider, *Austria's Eastern Question*, pp. 110ff.

[80] Vienna's attitude to the Russo-Ottoman War can be examined in: Adolf Beer, *Die Orientalische Politik Österreichs seit 1774* (Prague and Leipzig, 1883), pp. 20–9; Roider, *Thugut*, pp. 23ff; Roider, *Austria's Eastern Question*, chs. 6–8. Much can also be gleaned from Arneth, *GMT*, viii, chs. vi–x, and Beer, *Erste Theilung Polens*, vols. i–ii. For the Chancellor's initial attitude, see his long and interesting, if rather speculative, memorandum of 3 Dec. 1768, printed in Beer, *Erste Theilung Polens*, iii. 262–72; cf. Kaunitz to Seilern, 18 Jan. 1769, HHStA, England-Korrespondenz 115, which provides an interesting and detailed statement of Vienna's initial attitude to the conflict, which was sent to the ambassador in London because of Britain's presumed role in any attempt to avert fighting.

the struggle, Vienna could – and did – do little more than observe developments in south-eastern Europe. By the end of 1769, however, the speed and scale of Russian successes were alarming Kaunitz.[81] During that winter a steady though not spectacular shift in Habsburg attitudes can be detected. In the previous September a new Austrian representative, the impressive and linguistically accomplished Thugut – one of the first graduates of the Vienna Oriental Academy – had reached Constantinople.[82] His notably pessimistic initial reports had increased the Chancellor's anxieties by confirming the wretched state of the Ottoman empire after only one campaign.[83] By the first half of 1770 Kaunitz's concern at the changing situation to the south was manifest and his despondency at the opening of the new campaigning season was public knowledge in Vienna.[84] He now recognised that Russia might before long dominate the Balkans. His earlier hope that a prolonged but indecisive struggle might weaken both combatants was replaced by a desire for an early end to the fighting, which he viewed as the one chance of restricting Russian territorial gains.[85]

Peace remained the principal Habsburg aim, but the extent of Ottoman defeats was making the accompanying policy of neutrality an ever more hazardous course of action.[86] The threat that St Petersburg might secure some kind of control over Moldavia and Wallachia when a settlement was concluded directly threatened traditional Austrian interests, economic as well as political, in this region.[87] It would bring Russian influence close to the Monarchy, and might even threaten Vienna's control over the Kingdom of Hungary. More generally, Russia's potential gains would dramatically alter the existing political balance. Kaunitz shared Frederick the Great's fear that, once peace had been concluded, Catherine II would be free to concentrate resources and energy on the subjugation of Poland: the extent of Russian control there remained a Habsburg anxiety, and now this seemed likely to increase. This in turn would give the Empress a dominant position throughout the eastern half of the continent.[88]

---

[81] E.g. the report of Rohde, 23 Dec. 1769, printed in *Pol. Corr.*, XXIX. 278 n. 1. The despatches of Prussia's representative in Vienna for the closing months of 1769 had charted this growing concern, created by news of Ottoman successes: GStAPK Rep. 96.47.B. For the role of Russian victories in 1769 on Kaunitz's attitude, see Roider, *Austria's Eastern Question*, pp. 112–13.

[82] Franz Maria, Freiherr von Thugut, was to serve in Constantinople until August 1776: *Repertorium*, III. 96.

[83] Roider, *Thugut*, pp. 24–5. The poor state of the Ottoman army caused especial concern: Rohde to Frederick II, 13 Dec. 1769, GStAPK, Rep. 96.47.B.

[84] See, e.g., Stormont to Rochford, 10 Feb. 1770 and 28 Apr. 1770, both in PRO SP 80/207, reporting two remarkably frank conversations with the Chancellor. Cf. Arneth, *GMT*, VIII. 203ff.

[85] Arneth, *GMT*, VIII. 203, for his view by late Feb. 1770.

[86] See the important analysis in Rohde to Frederick II, 10 Jan. 1770, GStAPK Rep. 96.47.C.

[87] According to Binder, one reason for Austrian involvement in the mediation attempted in 1770–1 was her hopes of developing Danube trade: HHStA Tagebuch Zinzendorf, vol. 15 (1770), fo. 130.

[88] By spring 1770 Russia was irritated by Vienna's refusal to allow her consul to take up his post at Trieste and by its willingness to allow Polish Confederates to take refuge on Habsburg territory, actions which Panin believed called in question Austria's professed neutrality and threatened the good relations which he wished to cultivate: *SIRIO*, XCVII. 39–40, 61–4.

By 1769–70, therefore, Austrian and Prussian concerns were similar, if not quite identical. It was the foundation of a significant *rapprochement*, which was the most important diplomatic development of these years.[89] It aroused real anxiety within the Empire, where it was feared that the two German great powers might use their hegemony to carry through the kind of partition which Poland would soon suffer.[90] The Neisse meeting had been an important stage in the emergence of this axis. It was less because any major decisions were taken, beyond the informal neutrality agreement, but because of the symbolic co-operation of the two established enemies, states whose rivalry had hitherto been viewed as a structural and probably permanent feature of the international system. Austro-Prussian antagonism had been established for a generation, though reduced in intensity after 1763. It was now overlaid by a period of important political co-operation, as Russia's threatening advance appeared more important than their own political rivalry.

The growing community of interest over the Russo-Ottoman War had been apparent throughout the year after the first interview. It was strengthened by a second meeting in autumn 1770. In the early days of September the two monarchs met at Neustadt in Moravia. Though once again this provided Frederick with additional diplomatic leverage against his Russian ally,[91] its main purpose was to permit discussions over the threatening situation to the south-east. Never one to miss a trick, Frederick and his officers dressed in the white of the Austrian army, rather than the familiar Prussian blue, to flatter his host.[92] This time Joseph II was relegated to the wings, being sent off to watch military manoeuvres in the pouring rain of the Moravian autumn, while Kaunitz (who accompanied the Emperor) talked to – or, more accurately, at – the Prussian King.[93] As at Neisse, no formal political agreement was signed, though the discussions did reveal the considerable identification of interests between the two states.[94] King and Chancellor did agree, however, that the time was now ripe for a joint attempt to mediate in the Russo-Ottoman War, and immediately after the meeting Frederick, who believed Austria's participation was essential to its success, set this in motion by an approach to his ally Catherine II.[95]

The considerable barriers to any outside diplomatic intervention now became clear. These had already been revealed during 1770 by the continuing efforts by

---

[89] It can be followed in Arneth, *GMT*, VIII, chs. VII–IX, and in *Pol. Corr.*, XXIX–XXX.

[90] This is emphasised, and probably exaggerated, by Cegielski, *Das Alte Reich*, esp. ch. 3. It provides ample evidence that such an onslaught was feared in the Empire, especially in 1769–72, but cannot establish that Austria and Prussia ever seriously intended to carry it out. See also Aretin, *Das Alte Reich*, III. 173–83. [91] Soloviev, *History of Russia*, XLVI. 150ff.

[92] Prince C.J.E. de Ligne, *Mémoire sur le roi de Prusse, Frédéric le Grand* (Berlin, 1789), p. 24.

[93] For the discussions, see the contrasting material in Arneth, *GMT*, VIII. 210–25; Beer, 'Die Zusammenkünfte Josefs II.', pp. 400–20, 446–71; and *Pol. Corr.*, XXX. 101–18 *passim*.

[94] Immediately after the Neustadt meeting, Frederick wrote that he and Kaunitz were 'assez d'accord dans nos principes et dans nos idées' on the crisis in the east: to Prince Henry, 9 Sept. 1770, *Œuvres*, XXVI. 324; while the Chancellor was said to be 'très content' with the King of Prussia: HHStA Tagebuch Zinzendorf, vol. 15 (1770), fo. 130.

[95] The King's considerable diplomatic efforts are apparent from *Pol. Corr.*, XXX. 125ff.

Austria, Prussia and Britain to promote a settlement, all of which had been firmly rejected by the two belligerents.[96] The most substantial obstacle was Russia's terms for peace, which were always considerable and had been inflated by her victories. In November 1768 the Council had laid down two principal war aims.[97] The first, in accordance with St Petersburg's policy since Peter I's reign, was freedom of navigation on the Black Sea, on which Russia was also to acquire a port and perhaps even annex the Crimea. Secondly, some extension of Russian territory was to be secured at Poland's expense. The tide of successes in 1769–70 crystallised additional war aims. By September 1770 Catherine II was also thinking in terms of the independence of the Crimea, whose Khan had hitherto ruled as an Ottoman vassal, rather than its outright annexation: at this point it was not deemed of sufficient value to be subjected to direct rule. St Petersburg was also seeking large areas of territory around the Sea of Azov, and as an indemnity for Russia's war costs, a twenty-five-year lease on Moldavia and Wallachia.[98]

These vast aims presented serious obstacles. The Crimea – unlike some of the other occupied lands – was Muslim territory. There was strong opposition in Constantinople to its cession, a stance which was reinforced by a numerous and vociferous group of Tatar exiles from the Khanate who were unwilling to see it given an independence which it did not wish and which would be a mask for Russian control.[99] Vienna remained particularly hostile to any Russian presence on the lower Danube, viewed as a traditional zone of Habsburg influence. In October 1770, moreover, Catherine II, aware that an attempt was about to be made to impose mediation upon Russia, instructed Field-Marshal Rumyantsev that he was to negotiate peace directly with the defeated Ottoman commander.[100] Obreskov's release was once more demanded and remained a precondition for any talks.[101] Together these two decisions revealed St Petersburg's determination not to submit to outside intervention in making a settlement with Constantinople.

Whether at this point the Empress and her advisers seriously believed that such an ambitious programme could be realised must be doubted. Yet Russia's spectacular successes in the first two campaigns forced the other states to take very seriously the threat of a considerable growth of her power on Europe's south-eastern rim. It was primarily the fear that St Petersburg might actually be able to impose its

---

[96] In late spring Panin had made clear to Solms that Russia would not consider peace until the outcome of the forthcoming campaign had become clear: *SIRIO*, XXXVII. 292.

[97] The development of Russia's war aims can be followed in Übersberger, *Russlands Orientpolitik*, I. 284 *et seq.*; cf. Soloviev, *History of Russia*, XLVI. 8, 27.

[98] Übersberger, *Russlands Orientpolitik*, I. 302. Catherine II seems rather to have favoured the independence of the two Principalities from Ottoman control: Madariaga, *Russia*, p. 223.

[99] Aksan, *An Ottoman Statesman*, p. 120.

[100] This intended way of making peace had first been communicated to Rumyantsev in August: Madariaga, *Russia*, pp. 219–20.

[101] This demand had been made at several earlier points (cf. above, p. 202), and had been renewed in the previous June: *SIRIO*, XXXVII. 291–2. It was now confirmed in an extended note given to Solms, 29 Sept. 1770 OS, *SIRIO*, XCVII. 150–7.

demands on a defeated and humiliated Ottoman empire, together with the established anxiety about a wider conflict, which drew the other powers ever more deeply into the war. It was also why this mediation was deliberately undertaken by two great powers acting together: the intention was to employ their combined political weight to prise the belligerents apart. One reason why earlier efforts had failed had been that they had mostly been unilateral initiatives, though the unwillingness of the combatants for any settlement was more important.

The Prusso-Austrian mediation was immediately revealed to be a diplomatic *cul-de-sac*.[102] The formal initiative was launched in mid-September 1770 immediately after the meeting in Moravia, and Frederick made a determined effort to convince his Russian ally that a negotiated settlement was the best way forward. His arguments and entreaties, however, encountered only blank opposition in St Petersburg. Its initial reply, to the effect that Rumyantsev had been ordered to negotiate peace directly, revealed to the King that mediation was extremely unlikely: as he frankly admitted to his brother Prince Henry and to his principal adviser Finckenstein in the final days of October 1770.[103] Though Frederick pressed ahead with his efforts, primarily to buttress his own growing political intimacy with Vienna, he was soon having to admit that the Russian Empress would not accept outside mediation, while the Ottoman leadership would only conclude peace in that way. Though less directly involved in this diplomacy, Kaunitz recognised that the orders to Rumyantsev effectively undermined St Petersburg's subsequent acceptance of the principle of mediation, and he was clearly irritated by Russia's deception.[104] In December Constantinople announced that it would never accept the Russian terms, would exclude any state which supported them, and would therefore only accept mediation by Austria and Prussia. By the final weeks of 1770 the shipwreck of Prusso-Austrian initiative was apparent.[105]

Out of deference to her ally, Catherine II responded to the Prussian request by formally announcing her terms for peace. These were declared to be the full realisation of her established war aims, with in addition a second Black Sea port and an amnesty for the Sultan's subjects who had fought on Russia's side.[106] Frederick immediately realised that St Petersburg's answer amounted to a final rejection of any outside involvement in its peace with the Ottoman empire.[107] When the King first received the Russian reply in early January 1771, he declared that the terms

---

[102] The exchanges can be followed in *SIRIO*, xxxvii, and *Pol. Corr.*, xxx, on which the account which follows is based.   [103] *Pol.Corr.*, xxx. 219, 221.

[104] See the report of a conversation with the Chancellor in Rohde to Frederick II, 17 Nov. 1770, GStAPK Rep. 96.47.D. By the end of Oct. Maria Theresa, who a month before had been hoping that Russia might still make peace on moderate terms, was bewailing the scale of St Petersburg's demands: *MT–MA*, I. 61,81.   [105] *Pol. Corr.*, xxx. 240, 246, 301, 302, 309, 321–2.

[106] For these see above, p. 206; Soloviev, *History of Russia*, xlvi. 155–6, gives the terms in full.

[107] This had earlier been suggested by the fact that Russia marginally increased the peace terms which she had set out as recently as September when the Ottoman empire accepted the Austro-Prussian mediation: Soloviev, *History of Russia*, xlvi. 166.

'made his hair stand on end', and he frankly described them to the Austrian representative in Berlin as 'exorbitant and intolerable'. He did not at first pass on the Empress' precise demands to Vienna and Constantinople, melodramatically declaring them to be equivalent to a declaration of war.[108] Characteristically inventive, Frederick sought to use this failure to strengthen his own links with Austria, while simultaneously making a final attempt to persuade Catherine II to moderate her terms.[109] When he did pass on Russia's demands to the Austrians, he accompanied the communication with some extremely negative prognostications about the prospects for a mediated settlement: which were only too realistic, as events soon proved. By early January 1771 – little more than three months after it had been launched – the failure of the mediation was public knowledge. Its principal author, the Prussian King, gloomily concluded that a wider war would quickly follow, probably as early as the coming spring, unless Russia moderated her demands, and this seemed improbable. Yet peace remained Frederick's greatest priority, convinced as he was that Prussia had still not recovered from the Seven Years War.[110]

Kaunitz had been equally alarmed when Catherine II's territorial aims were disclosed to him, and after an intense debate, Vienna's policy became more active and, potentially, belligerent in its opposition to Russia.[111] The winter of 1770–1 saw two significant developments in Habsburg foreign policy which were to be crucial for the emerging pattern of alliances. The first was France's collapse as a European power in the aftermath of Choiseul's dismissal on Christmas Eve 1770 and the consequent breakdown of her alliance with Vienna. Since the beginning of the Russo-Ottoman War Austria's political conduct had been circumscribed by her established French links, which were the basis of her foreign policy after 1763. The fundamental problem was that Vienna's ally was pursuing an actively anti-Russia strategy. This meant that, as since the Seven Years War, Austria's predicament was to be tied by treaty to France, whose foreign minister was the declared enemy of Russia. Yet Russia was also the power which had been Vienna's traditional ally and the attractions of whose alliance were apparent to observers in the Habsburg capital. The implications of this Russo-French antagonism were a central problem for Austrian policy-makers. Indeed, in the extensive instructions which he had drawn up to guide the Emperor during his interviews with Frederick at Neisse, the Chancellor

---

[108] *Pol. Corr.*, xxx. 357–8; 361–3.   [109] *Pol. Corr.*, xxx. 370–1.   [110] *Pol. Corr.*, xxx. 385, 404, 407.
[111] Beer, *Erste Theilung Polens*, II. 15–19, for his reaction and Joseph II's critique of his plans. The Emperor's views were set out in his 'Denkschrift' of 14 Jan. 1771, Beer, *Erste Theilung Polens*, III. 11–23. The Chancellor's reply of 23 Jan. is printed in Beer, *Erste Theilung Polens*, III. 23–6. For some interesting information on Vienna's military and financial preparations, which confirm that war was being seriously considered, see HHStA Tagebuch Zinzendorf, vol. 15 (1770), fos. 160, 161; vol. 16 (1771), fos. 1, 6, 7 (where Zinzendorf declared that Kaunitz 'coulait la guerre'). Shortly before 12 Jan. 1771, the Chancellor had treated Prussia's representative to an anti-Russian tirade which lasted for almost an hour, in the course of which he referred to Russia's 'inordinate ambition': Rohde to Frederick II, 12 and 16 Jan. 1771, GStAPK Rep. 96.47.E. See also: *MT–JII*, I. 321, 328–9, 330, and two highly revealing letters from Maria Theresa to Kaunitz, the first shortly before or on 19 Jan. 1771 and the second of that date, both in HHStA Nachlass Kaunitz (1765–92).

had frankly admitted the difficulties this created for Austria. Russia was her natural ally against both the Ottoman empire and Prussia, but she could not pursue a closer political relationship with St Petersburg as long as she maintained her links with Versailles.[112] Prussia's King made essentially the same point when he declared, shortly before Choiseul's fall, that the Austro-French alliance was an obstacle to his own diplomatic schemes.[113] As late as the autumn of 1770, however, Maria Theresa and Kaunitz had gone out of their way to inform France very fully of the discussions at Neustadt, conscious of the suspicion which the earlier interview had aroused.[114] At this point Vienna's French alliance was still the basis of her foreign policy.

In the closing months of 1770 Kaunitz had been obliged to consult Choiseul about Austria's involvement in the mediation. The French minister wanted to prolong the struggle, and therefore opposed any such diplomatic intervention, far less Habsburg participation. His blunt reply left Kaunitz with a stark choice: either he must abandon co-operation with Prussia to end the war, or he must abandon France.[115] The immediate collapse of the Austro-Prussian initiative saved him from this dilemma. Choiseul's fall, dismissed by the deeply pacific Louis XV who had become convinced that his minister was about to involve France in a war not in south-eastern Europe but with Britain over the distant Falkland Islands, removed the French monarchy as an active element in continental diplomacy.[116] A six-month interregnum followed, during which a courtier, the duc de la Vrillière, served as a locum at the foreign office. His incompetence was apparent on every despatch he wrote, and France simply ceased to have any foreign policy during an important period for continental alignments.[117] His eventual successor, the duc d'Aiguillon, was to pursue a rather different policy from the energetic Choiseul,[118] but it was almost a year before he could fully secure his position against court intrigue. France's temporary disappearance during the early 1770s, highlighting a more fundamental decline, was crucial for the diplomatic realignment of these years. The resulting breakdown of the Austro-French alliance was a precondition of Vienna's involvement in the first partition of Poland. It left Austria free to change her alignments, and so facilitated her growing political intimacy with Russia, which was to be so vital in the years to come.[119]

The second development was much more unexpected and was in fact the

---

[112] Arneth, *GMT*, VIII. 177.   [113] *Pol. Corr.*, XXX. 318.

[114] Maria Theresa to Kaunitz [undated but *c.* 10–12 Sept. 1770], and Kaunitz to Maria Theresa, 18 Sept. 1770, both in HHStA Nachlass Arneth 15; cf. Arneth, *GMT*, VIII. 578, and *MT–MA*, I. 60–1.

[115] Sorel, *La question d'Orient*, pp. 118–19; *MT–MA*, I. 90–100.

[116] Vienna was initially concerned at his fall, given the duc's strong support for the Austrian alliance, but was soon being reassured on this point: *MT–MA*, I. 115–16, 125.

[117] The despatches of the Prussian resident, Sandoz Rollin, for the first half of 1771 provide a strong picture of this collapse: GStAPK Rep. 96.27.C.   [118] Cf. below, pp. 222–4, for this.

[119] Albert Sorel's verdict was that Choiseul 'était le grand obstacle à une entente entre la Russie et l'Autriche': *La question d'Orient*, p. 132; cf. p. 137.

exact opposite of the first, though ultimately it was to prove another diplomatic *cul-de-sac*. During the first half of 1771, in response to a suggestion from the Porte, which was searching ceaselessly for foreign support against Russia, secret negotiations took place between the Ottoman and Austrian governments. In early July 1771 these produced an agreement, signed in the Ottoman capital, by which Austria – in return for a substantial subsidy and the promise of an eventual territorial rectification – undertook to provide mediation or, if that failed (as seemed probable), to enter the war against Russia.[120] The precise nature of this agreement – was it, or was it not, a formal treaty? – together with Vienna's purpose in concluding it, have been much debated. The Ottoman régime evidently believed that it had secured important support at the price of a substantial subsidy, the first instalment of which was actually paid.[121]

The moving spirit on the Austrian side was the Chancellor. The obstacles to any mediated settlement evident by late 1770, together with the scale of Russia's likely territorial gains when peace was concluded and determination to control Poland, had set in motion an intense debate in the Habsburg capital.[122] Maria Theresa, who retained final control over policy, was completely pacific, while the Chancellor was the most inventive, favouring co-operation with Prussia to keep Russia in check and military preparations along the Monarchy's southern border to support this diplomatic strategy, but also the least realistic. Joseph II's views were somewhere between these two extremes, though the Emperor was usually opposed to any war. The notion of securing an Ottoman paymaster was clearly Kaunitz's, aware as he was that Austria would be unable to fund any conflict, and the Chancellor may even have been prepared to fight a preventive war against Russia.[123] The eventual Austrian policy came to be a compromise between these contrasting attitudes. The Empress supported Kaunitz's wish to align the Monarchy on the side of the Ottoman empire, with whom alliance negotiations went ahead, but placed strict limits on the accompanying military preparations, which were intended to uphold peace. Maria Theresa also undermined this policy by reassuring St Petersburg that Vienna wanted to preserve peace: exactly as she would subsequently undermine Kaunitz's diplomacy over the Polish partition.[124] In the event, this stratagem was overtaken by

---

[120] It is printed in *Recueil des traités et conventions concernant la Pologne*, ed. J.L.C. d'Angeberge (Paris, 1862), pp. 92–5.

[121] Aksan, *An Ottoman Statesman*, pp. 118, 155. In July 1771, the same month that the treaty was signed, one fifth of the total subsidy, a sum of around two and a quarter million florins, was sent to Vienna by convoy.

[122] Beales, *Joseph II*, pp. 286ff, provides a notably incisive account of this and sets out an important challenge to the conventional view that these negotiations and especially the treaty were merely a diplomatic ploy which the Chancellor had no intention of upholding. The more traditional interpretation of these events can be found in the overlapping accounts in Roider, *Thugut*, pp. 30–3, and Roider, *Austria's Eastern Question*, pp. 117–26; it goes back to Arneth, *GMT*, VIII: e.g. pp. 264, 291, 442, 446.

[123] Beales, *Joseph II*, p. 293. His view is given important and probably decisive support by the two letters from Maria Theresa to Kaunitz of *c.* 19 Jan. 1771 cited above, n. 111.

[124] Beales, *Joseph II*, p. 290; see below, p. 217.

the progress of events. By summer 1771, when the Austro-Ottoman treaty was signed, Poland and not the Russo-Ottoman War had become the major diplomatic issue. During the autumn and winter of 1771–2 Austria's policy towards Constantinople was reversed and any thought of fighting to support the Sultan abandoned.[125] To Ottoman disappointment, Austria renounced the treaty in spring 1772, by which point its utility had long since disappeared.

IV

By early 1771 Frederick was close to despair.[126] The Austro-Prussian mediation had failed before it had begun, due to Russian and Ottoman intransigence. The consequent *impasse* in the Balkans threatened to produce the wider conflict which the King had feared throughout the past two years, while Austria's continuing military preparations exacerbated the situation and appeared likely to bring war closer: unlike Russia, Prussia had not been informed of Vienna's fundamental pacificism.[127] The eventual solution was both unexpected and dramatic: within eighteen months Poland's three powerful neighbours had carried out the first partition, implemented by treaties signed in August 1772. European diplomacy was dominated in 1771–2 by the fate of Stanislas Augustus' kingdom.[128] The partition signalled the full emergence of the eastern powers, and with it a new diplomatic pattern. Though Prussia's King would play the leading part, the responsibility for the scheme's launch belongs to his brother, Prince Henry. The Prince had found his own political role, after his military exploits during the Seven Years War, to be as restricted as it had been before the fighting began. His overbearing royal brother never permitted any of his siblings to play much part in government, and after 1763 Henry had returned to semi-private life. In the early months of 1771, however, he enjoyed a brief period at the very heart of Prussian policy-making. It provides the principal exception, in the period covered by this study, to the established generalisation that Frederick acted as his own foreign minister and did not allow either members of the royal family or the advisers in the *Kabinettsministerium* any significant share in the formulation of external policy.[129] His brother's importance at this period – which was to prove

---

[125] See in particular Kaunitz's letter to Thugut in Jan. 1771, setting out the manifold reasons against Austrian military intervention: Arneth, *GMT*, VIII. 442.

[126] His correspondence for this period is in *Pol. Corr.*, XXX. 351ff.

[127] See, in particular, Frederick to Prince Henry, 24 Jan. 1771, *Pol. Corr.*, XXX. 407.

[128] An up-to-date account of the first partition of Poland, based upon a full re-examination of the abundant manuscript material, is badly needed. The most recent study, H.H. Kaplan, *The First Partition of Poland* (New York, 1962), is both superficial and inaccurate and in no way meets this need; for some severe but perfectly justified criticisms by a noted Polish historian see J. Topolski, 'Reflections on the First Partition of Poland (1772)', *Acta Poloniae Historica* 27 (1973), pp. 89–104. Lacking a modern study, the most informative accounts remain Beer, *Erste Theilung Polens*, esp. vol. II, and Sorel, *La question d'Orient*. The recent studies by Michael G. Müller, *Die Teilungen Polens* (Munich, 1984), and Lukowski, *Partitions of Poland*, provide a valuable wider perspective.

[129] See above, p. 91.

ephemeral – lay not in establishing the idea of a partition but in persuading the King both that this was now feasible and, more significantly, that it presented a way out of the *impasse* created by the Russo-Ottoman War.

Frederick's interest in annexing Polish Prussia and thereby linking up the Hohenzollern heartlands with the Kingdom of East Prussia was long established.[130] He always believed that territorial gains, and the new subjects and resources which these brought, were essential and had been the basis of Prussia's emergence as a great power. This was an even greater imperative after 1763, since the principal conclusion the King drew from the Seven Years War was that his scattered possessions lacked the economic and demographic resources essential if the Hohenzollern monarchy were to establish its position as a leading European state. His most consistent target, among all the neighbouring lands upon which his acquisitive gaze fell, was Polish Prussia. The aim of annexing it had been set out in his first important political statement, the so-called Natzmer Letter composed in the early 1730s when he was Crown Prince. It had been confirmed in the first Political Testament, completed in 1752, and reaffirmed in its successor, finalised in November 1768. In both these documents, however, the acquisition of Polish Prussia was placed in the sections entitled 'Political Pipe-Dreams'.[131] This did not mean that it had ceased to be the King's objective, merely that he believed that favourable circumstances would have to arise and, for this reason, its annexation probably would have to be left until a future reign.

From the era of the Seven Years War onward, however, the economic exploitation of neighbouring Polish territories, rather than their outright annexation, had been the King's most immediate aim.[132] Frederick's sponsorship of the 'Lynar Project' in the initial months of the Russo-Ottoman War underlined his active and enduring interest in a partition, but also revealed the immense obstacles to any such scheme, particularly Russia's apparent opposition.[133] Panin's 'Northern System' incorporated Poland as a satellite, and this appeared to rule out any joint acquisitions at her expense. Yet the King remained avid for further territorial gains: as a remarkable and deliberately wide-ranging interview about possible territorial ambitions with the departing Austrian diplomat, Nugent, in early May 1770 had underlined.[134] This conversation, which eventually came round to Frederick's Polish ambitions, was the equivalent testing of the water in Vienna to the Lynar Plan, sent to St Petersburg fifteen months earlier.

Prince Henry's importance lay first in uncovering a new appetite in St Petersburg for Polish territory, and then in convincing his brother of the attractions and, more

---

[130] Zbigniew Kulak, 'The Plans and Aims of Frederick II's Policy towards Poland', *Polish Western Affairs* 22 (1981), pp. 70–101, provides a useful if rather nationalistic survey. See also the major recent study by Bömelburg, *Zwischen Polnischer Ständegesellshaft*, chs. 5–6 *passim*.

[131] *Die politischen Testamente*, ed. Dietrich, pp. 368, 372–4, 664.   [132] See above, pp. 176–7.

[133] See above, pp. 189–90.

[134] Arneth, *GMT*, VIII. 573; Madariaga, *Russia*, p. 221. The Austrian envoy's account of the interview is printed in *Pol. Corr.*, XXIX. 462–5.

important, the feasibility of a partition.[135] In summer 1770 the Prince had been sent to Stockholm to visit his elder sister, the Swedish Queen Lovisa Ulrika. This trip had a distinct political purpose. The renewal of Prussia's Russian alliance in October 1769 had committed Prussia to invade Swedish Pomerania in the event that any change were to be made to the 1720 Constitution, or that Sweden were to attack Russia.[136] One way in which Frederick had long sought to strengthen his links with Catherine II was by seeking to restrain his sister, and this had again been requested by Panin. The terms of the renewed alliance were thought to be too confidential, and also too inflammatory, to be committed to paper and so Henry was sent to inform the Queen privately, with the clear hope that this might frighten the court to moderate its aim of strengthening the Swedish monarchy.

While he was in Sweden, an invitation to extend his journey and visit Russia reached the Prince. The Prussian King, ever anxious to do anything and everything to fit in with the Empress' wishes and so (he hoped) strengthen the alliance and advance the mediation launched that autumn, enthusiastically urged his brother to accept. He seems to have been unaware that the invitation was not a spontaneous action on Catherine II's part, but resulted from an initiative by the Prince himself who had strongly hinted to her diplomatic representative in Prussia that he would like to visit Russia and renew his acquaintance with the Empress, whom he had known at Berlin when she was a young woman.[137] His extended sojourn at Catherine II's court during the winter of 1770–1 was, at the personal level, a great success, and established a lasting friendship, sustained by regular correspondence during the 1770s and deliberately fostered by Frederick in an attempt to strengthen the alliance.[138] Its immediate political importance was even greater, though this only became apparent at the very end of his visit and did not concern the Prusso-Austrian mediation, as might have been anticipated, but the fate of Poland.[139]

During the first week of January 1771 Prince Henry, whose own interest in annexing Polish Prussia was quite clear, had a series of conversations first with the Empress and then with some key advisers in which the possibility of a partition was floated.[140] Though Panin's Northern System appeared to preclude such annexations, elements at the Russian court had long been interested in such territorial gains.[141] During the middle decades of the eighteenth century these ideas had

[135] His role is the subject of two informative articles by G.B. Volz, 'Prinz Heinrich von Preussen und die preussische Politik vor der ersten Teilung Polens', *FBPG* 18 (1905), pp. 153–86, and 'Prinz Heinrich und die Vorgeschichte der ersten Teilung Polens', *FBPG* 35 (1923), pp. 193–211. The discussion in C.V. Easum, *Prince Henry of Prussia* (Madison, WI, 1942), pp. 254–71, is rather more penetrating, though it misrepresents the King's attitude. Frederick's correspondence with his brother for the period July 1770 until mid-February 1771 is both extensive and revealing; it can be found in *Pol. Corr.*, xxx. [136] See above, p. 194. [137] *Œuvres*, VI. 33. [138] e.g. *Pol. Corr.*, xxi. 384, 500
[139] E.g. *Pol. Corr.*, xxx. 123, 149, for the King's expectations.
[140] His account is in *Pol. Corr.*, xxx. 406; cf. Solms to Frederick II, 8 Jan. 1771, *SIRIO*, xxxvii. 339–40.
[141] See the helpful article by J.T. Lukowski, 'Guarantee or Annexation: A Note on Russian Plans to Acquire Polish Territory Prior to the First Partition of Poland', *Bulletin of the Institute of Historical Research* 106 (1983), pp. 60–5.

notably revived.[142] In 1744 the Empress Elizabeth and her ministers had drawn up a plan which envisaged seizing East Prussia and exchanging it with Poland, either for Courland or for lands in eastern Byelorussia. This aim had accompanied participation in the anti-Prussian coalition, though it had not been realised: Russia had occupied East Prussia in 1758, but had returned it to Hohenzollern rule in 1762. One legacy of Russian operations during the Seven Years War had been that military observers had come to appreciate the strategic attractions of annexations in eastern Poland. St Petersburg's eyes fell upon certain specific territories: Polish Livonia, the palatinates of Polotsk and Vitebsk, and part of that of Mstislav, which together would comprise around three-quarters of Russian annexations in 1772. These lands would, it was believed, complement territorial gains made from Poland in 1667 and from Sweden in 1721 and facilitate a more effective commercial exploitation of the region to the east and north-east of the rivers Dvina and Dnieper. They might also make possible the development of a profitable trading link between the Baltic and the Black Sea, which Russia would control. During the early years of Stanislas Augustus' reign, Russia had unsuccessfully sought to secure Polish Livonia by negotiation with Warsaw. The latent appetite for Polish territory was clear, and in summer 1767 Russian surveyors had conducted extensive and detailed surveys of possible gains in Poland's eastern regions north of the river Dvina. Immediately after the Seven Years War, at the time of the Polish interregnum, the vice-president of the College of War, Zachar Chernyshev, had advocated such annexations, but at this point had secured no effective support. In early 1771 during Prince Henry's visit he recommended a joint seizure of Polish lands to him.

In a more general sense, Russia's military role after 1763 and growing involvement in Poland's domestic affairs, together with the way in which she came to treat the kingdom as almost a Russian province, may have made partition more likely. The growing criticism of and even opposition to the Northern System in St Petersburg after the Ottoman declaration of war indirectly strengthened interest in such acquisitions, while the initial Russian statement of war aims included securing territory from Poland.[143] More immediately, Prince Henry's conversations took place shortly after Catherine II heard of Austria's continuing military preparations and also her decision to incorporate Zips, occupied two years previously, into her own territory.[144] In 1768, in an attempt to insulate its own lands both from the military activities of the Bar confederates and from the outbreak of plague, Vienna had established a military cordon along the Polish border, incorporating the small and rich enclave of Zips. This had been mortgaged to Poland in the early fifteenth century by Hungary's King. Its retention by Austria after 1768 was not a prelude to a Polish partition but a simple security measure. Its formal reincorporation into the Kingdom of Hungary on 20 November 1770 was the kind of border rectification

---

[142] LeDonne, *Russian Empire*, pp. 37–46.   [143] See above, p. 206.

[144] See Horst Glassl, 'Der Rechtsstreit um die Zips vor ihrer Rückgliederung an Ungarn', *Ungarn-Jahrbuch* 1 (1969), pp. 23–50.

familiar to all eighteenth-century governments, though its impact over the next two years was to be considerable. Since by now Frederick had himself run a *cordon sanitaire* across Polish Prussia, ostensibly to protect his own lands against the plague, and was beginning to turn it into a full military occupation, this meant that Russia alone among Poland's neighbours was not in possession of Polish territory, though her troops continued to occupy large areas of the country and to struggle to contain the guerrilla war still being waged there.

Prince Henry left St Petersburg convinced both that partition was now possible and that it could provide a way out of the *impasse* in the south-east. Immediately upon his return to Prussia, he had a series of crucial private discussions with the King, which took place at Potsdam during the week beginning 18 February 1771. Frederick had hitherto been cautious, even sceptical, about Henry's reports from the Russian court, but he was now won over by his brother's arguments in a remarkably short period of time. The cautious elder statesman, as Prussia's ruler had self-consciously become,[145] now emerged as the skilful architect of partition. Though the King was certainly interested in acquiring Polish Prussia, his rapid conversion to the view that this was not merely possible but also provided the best chance of averting a general European war was highly unusual. In the entire reign there is no other example of Frederick changing his mind so completely and so suddenly in the face of contrary arguments.[146] Henry then worked with Finckenstein on the crucial project which was sent to Catherine II, and also drafted the key despatch to Solms.[147] By the final days of February, Frederick had launched a diplomatic offensive on a broad front.[148] Russia would secure considerable gains at Poland's expense and therefore it was hoped be more moderate when her settlement with the Ottoman empire was made. In this way Austria's hostility to large-scale Russian annexations to the south-east and the danger that this might produce a wider conflict could be defused. Such, at least, were the King's original hopes, though in the event the Polish partition did nothing to restrict St Petersburg's gains from the Ottoman empire.[149] This was because these same Polish annexations were viewed by the Russian Empress and her advisers as a way of weakening Prussian and Austrian opposition to Russian annexations in south-eastern Europe.

The new priorities at Potsdam and, to a lesser extent, St Petersburg which became apparent in the early months of 1771 shaped European diplomacy until the late summer of the following year. The Russo-Ottoman War was eclipsed by the fate of Poland as the decisive issue for the eastern powers and especially Prussia's King.[150] The military stalemate in the south assisted this shift of emphasis. Indeed,

---

[145] E.g. Frederick's own characterisation of himself: *Pol. Corr.*, XXXI. 2.

[146] Easum, *Prince Henry of Prussia*, p. 270.

[147] The King's acknowledgement of his brother's vital role is in *Pol. Corr.*, XXXI. 29.

[148] On 26 Feb. 1771, Austria's new representative in Berlin, van Swieten, was reporting that Prusso-Russian talks to partition Poland were under way: Sorel, *La question d'Orient*, p. 149.

[149] See in this connection Panin to Saldern, Draft, 11 June 1771 OS, *SIRIO*, XCVII. 332–40. Cf. below, pp. 232–4, for more on this.   [150] E.g. *Pol. Corr.*, XXXI. 28.

Frederick's own attitude to the war was now reversed. His earlier desire for a prompt peace between Russia and the Ottoman empire gave way to a recognition that the continuation of the fighting could assist his plan to bring about a partition of Poland, principally by keeping up the pressure on Vienna. Austria remained unreconciled to Russian gains to the south and east of the Monarchy and this was played upon by Frederick, in a way which was now familiar, to put pressure on his ally Russia during the partition negotiations.[151]

These discussions were facilitated by a broader development which favoured Prussia and her King.[152] Hitherto, St Petersburg had held the political initiative between the two German states.[153] This situation had been reversed by the Russo-Ottoman War, which gave Frederick the diplomatic initiative between Russia and Austria.[154] It had been apparent since 1768–9, and would be particularly important during the extended negotiations which led to the seizures. Though he always rec-ognised that the participation of Poland's three neighbours was essential for success, the King's strategy from the outset was to arrange a partition with St Petersburg and then impose it upon Vienna.[155] In the confidential survey of foreign policy which formed part of the second Political Testament, the King had identified Russia as the greatest obstacle to success.[156] He now set about securing St Petersburg's support for his plans. Despite Russia's apparent interest in Polish gains uncovered by Prince Henry, the detailed discussions were extended and occasionally difficult. This was partly a question of attempting to equalise the value of the two states' respective shares, and partly the unique nature of what was being arranged. Though the eighteenth-century European states system enjoys a justified reputation for rapacity, it was the first occasion upon which major states acting together had seized large areas of territory from a country they had not earlier defeated in war or with whom they did not have an established dispute. Nor were these substantial annexa-tions justified by credible dynastic or legal claims. Though there was some presen-tation of 'rights', particularly by Austria, this was largely for form's sake. No partitioning power took such claims seriously: indeed, in a memoir to the King, Finckenstein and Hertzberg frankly admitted that Hohenzollern claims to Polish Prussia were 'neither important nor strong'.[157] The first partition was purely a matter of cynical power politics, and exemplified the new dominance of the great powers over other states.

Frederick's negotiations with St Petersburg were prolonged – exactly as the King anticipated[158] – by the usual delays of diplomacy involving Russia, particularly when St Petersburg was distracted by the Ottoman War and the onset of plague,

---

[151] E.g. *Pol. Corr.*, XXXI. 62.   [152] E.g. *Pol. Corr.*, XXXI. 32, 35, for the King's confidence.

[153] See above, p. 120.   [154] See above, p. 189.

[155] His diplomacy can be followed in detail in *Pol. Corr.*, XXXI–XXXII, *passim*, and in *SIRIO*, XXXVII; cf. his letter to Finckenstein, 14 May 1771, *Pol. Corr.*, XXXI. 148. Only a brief account is provided here.

[156] *Die politischen Testamente*, ed. Dietrich, p. 664.

[157] *Pol. Corr.*, XXX. 487. The memoir was undated but clearly belongs to February 1771.

[158] *Pol. Corr.*, XXXI. 38.

which had reached Moscow by late 1771. Though agreement in principle had been reached by July 1771, the details took some time to resolve.[159] The principal barrier was erected by Frederick himself. Against a threatening background, with Austria's intransigence over the future of Moldavia and Wallachia still threatening a wider conflict, and in keeping with his established view that no war should be undertaken without the prospect of territorial gain, Frederick demanded in the autumn that he should be allowed to include the thriving port of Danzig in his annexations.[160] This was rejected outright by Panin, and dropped by Prussia's King in order not to endanger either his alliance with Catherine II or the partition itself, though he would subsequently revive the claim. By the very end of the year final agreement was reached. In February 1772 a Russo-Prussian convention was signed,[161] setting out the two states' respective shares when the partition was implemented. Frederick then turned to the seemingly more difficult task of securing Austria's participation.

Attitudes in Vienna were complex and fluid. Each of the three leading figures viewed matters in a different way. The approach of the ageing Maria Theresa was the most clear-cut. She was always fundamentally opposed to any Polish partition, particularly if carried out jointly with the hated King of Prussia, and only gave her consent when persuaded by Kaunitz that there was no alternative. She was even more opposed to any further fighting. In autumn 1771 her indiscretion during a conversation with Rohde, to whom she admitted that Austria would never fight, revealing to Prussia's King that Kaunitz's firm stance was a bluff, weakened Habsburg efforts to resist partition.[162] She subsequently made a belated and unsuccessful attempt at the end of February 1772, after the signature of the Russo-Prussian convention, to interest Britain in Poland's fate, and never tired of bewailing the partition and its immorality.[163] Her son and Co-Regent, Joseph II, was also opposed in principle to any division of Poland. He wanted to maintain the Kingdom intact as a buffer zone between the Monarchy and Russia, and was in any case much more interested in possible gains from the defeated Ottoman empire. In a memorandum drawn up in autumn 1771 he described any Polish partition as the least favourable outcome for Austria.[164]

Kaunitz's attitude was much more complex and also far more ambiguous. The first partition demonstrated Austria's relative weakness as long as the Russo-Prussian alignment endured and made clear her inability to resist her two more

---

[159] *Pol. Corr.*, XXXI. 245.   [160] *Pol. Corr.*, XXXI. 359, 410, 425.

[161] It is printed in Martens, *Recueil des traités*, VI. 71–7.

[162] Joseph II's tart comments on his mother's revelation are in his letter to Leopold, 25 Sept. 1771, *MT–JII.*, I. 344–5. Kaunitz's reaction was only marginally less severe: see his letter to Maria Theresa, 23 Sept. 1771, printed in Beer, *Erste Theilung Polens*, III. 338–9.

[163] Stormont to Suffolk, 29 Feb. 1772, PRO, SP 80/211; same to same, Separate, 5 Dec. 1772, PRO, SP 80/212. The British ambassador who was the recipient of these lamentations was a friend and secret supporter of Poland and political confidant of her King, as she well knew. See *MT–JII*, I. 362, for the Empress' unhappiness at 'acting in the Prussian manner while trying to keep the appearance of honesty'.   [164] 26 Sept. 1771, printed in Beer, *Erste Theilung Polens*, III. 26.

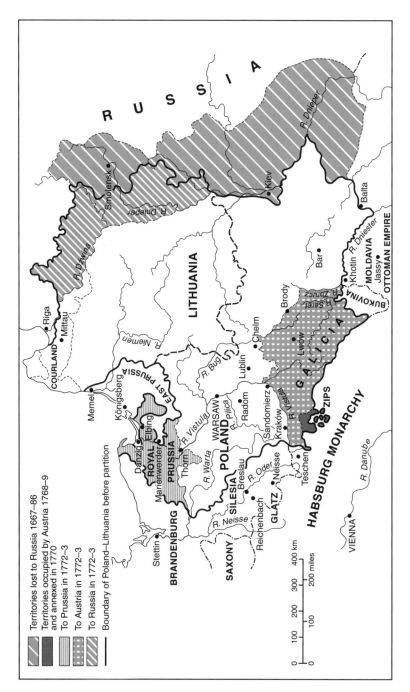

Territories lost to Russia 1667–86

Territories occupied by Austria 1768–9 and annexed in 1770

To Prussia in 1772–3

To Austria in 1772–3

To Russia in 1772–3

Boundary of Poland–Lithuania before partition

0   100   200   300   400 km
0   100   200 miles

3. The first partition of Poland

RUSSIA

Smolensk

R. Dnieper

R. Dnieper

Kiev

Balta

R. Dwina

Riga

Mittau

COURLAND

Memel

R. Niemen

LITHUANIA

Königsberg

EAST PRUSSIA

Bar

R. Dniester

Khotin

MOLDAVIA

Jassy

OTTOMAN EMPIRE

BUKOVINA

Brody

R. Seret

R. Zbrucz

Chelm

Lublin

R. Bug

Lwów

GALICIA

Elbing

ROYAL PRUSSIA

Danzig

Marienwerder

Thorn

PRUSSIA

R. Vistula

R. Warta

WARSAW

Radom

R. Pilica

Sandomierz

Kraków

R. Vistula

ZIPS

Teschen

HABSBURG MONARCHY

BRANDENBURG

Stettin

Breslau

SILESIA

R. Oder

Neisse

GLATZ

Reichenbach

R. Neisse

SAXONY

R. Danube

VIENNA

powerful eastern neighbours, evident since the Seven Years War. In 1771–2 Vienna's political options narrowed significantly, and eventually the Chancellor was persuaded that partition was inevitable and that Austria had no alternative to participation. He had long feared Prussian territorial ambitions at Poland's expense, but he was now forced to join in their realisation. This decision was only reached after sustained diplomatic efforts to avert partition, by seeking to divide the Russo-Prussian allies and even by threatening to fight alongside the Ottoman empire. All these initiatives were primarily Kaunitz's work.

During the Russo-Ottoman War the Chancellor produced a series of the flawlessly logical but politically improbable schemes which were his trademark. These envisaged various territorial gains for Austria: sometimes Silesia (which Frederick always refused to countenance handing back) or Ottoman territory, less often Polish lands, always seen as the least satisfactory outcome. Yet the Chancellor was always far more willing than either Maria Theresa or Joseph II to annex Polish territory.[165] Though usually opposed to such schemes, he ultimately played the decisive role during the crucial debates at the Habsburg court which began in mid-January 1772 and concluded a month later, when Maria Theresa agreed that partition and Vienna's involvement could go ahead.[166] The alternative was that Prussia and Russia would make substantial unilateral gains, which was unthinkable: exactly as the Prussian King had intended.

Thereafter, Kaunitz exploited the political initiative which Austria had been given to secure the largest share for the Habsburgs.[167] Since Prussia and Russia, having signed an agreement to partition Poland and setting out their own intended shares, now needed Austrian participation to implement it, Vienna had been handed an opportunity and this was not neglected: the Habsburgs, as Frederick the Great remarked on several occasions, had a 'good appetite' for Polish territory.[168] Six months' further negotiations were needed to determine Austria's share. Finally, in August 1772, a series of agreements between Austria, Prussia and Russia agreed upon partition and laid down the respective territorial gains of the three great powers from Poland. Austria's success in exploiting her favourable diplomatic position from February 1772 onwards was apparent in her substantial gains: Galicia and Lodomeria, an area of almost 32,000 square miles containing 2,650,000 new subjects. The new human and economic resources which Vienna acquired were impressive, though the strategic benefits were less than the other two eastern powers

---

[165] His willingness for such a division of Polish territory is, e.g., apparent from the Chancellor's memorandum of 3 Dec. 1768, on the situation created for Austria by the Ottoman declaration of war; this is printed in Beer, *Erste Theilung Polens*, III. 262–72.

[166] The debate can be followed in Arneth, *GMT*, VIII. 344 *et seq.*; the Empress' acceptance of partition is in her letter to Kaunitz, *c.* 12 Feb. 1772, *GMT*, VIII. 358–60, 595–6. Kaunitz's crucial memorandum of 20 Jan. 1772 is printed in Beer, *Erste Theilung Polens*, III. 42–8. Joseph II continued to argue for Austria to make her territorial gains from the Ottoman empire: see his 'Vorschläge' of 14 Feb. 1772, printed in Beer, *Erste Theilung Polens*, II. 343–4.

[167] For the Chancellor's diplomacy see Arneth, *GMT*, VIII, ch. 14.   [168] E.g. *Pol. Corr.*, XXXII. 139.

secured. Russia acquired the largest area, 36,000 square miles of new lands in eastern Poland which became the *gubernii* of Polotsk and Mogilev. Thinly populated, these contained only 1,300,000 inhabitants. Prussia gained least of all in terms of territory and population: a mere 14,000 square miles, with 580,000 new subjects. But control of the lower reaches of the Vistula brought important customs' revenues which paid for an increase in the size of Prussia's army and the possibility of guaranteed grain imports when famine threatened, while the strategic value of the new Prussian province of West Prussia eclipsed that of the Austrian and Russian gains. It linked the Hohenzollern heartlands with distant East Prussia, and created a solid wedge of territory which stretched across central and north-eastern Germany.[169]

These gains were only finalised after detailed discussions, both between the eastern powers and with commissioners from Poland, and these were not completed until 1777.[170] In these negotiations, as in the diplomacy which preceded the partition treaties in August 1772, the new doctrine of relative international power can be seen at work. It was accepted that each state would make approximately equal gains.[171] These were calculated not simply in terms of human and economic resources but of strategic value as well.[172] This was what contemporary statesmen meant when they spoke of the 'political worth' (*valeur politique*) of the respective gains by the partition.[173] They believed that the relative benefits could be precisely assessed, and in this way the shares of the partitioning states equalised.[174] This approach can be seen at work in the negotiations which arranged the partition in 1771–2 and in the detailed discussions which followed, to clarify the precise territories which each would seize. These exchanges demonstrated the way in which the theoretical approach to power, set out in the writings of Justi and Bielfeld during the later 1750s, had, by the early 1770s, become part of the practice of international relations.[175] The first partition of Poland, like its two successors, has been rightly condemned both at the time and since for its immorality. What has been insufficiently appreciated is that the seizures of Polish territory also accorded with the latest Enlightenment doctrines about the way relative political power could be assessed. The eastern powers had demonstrated a novel approach to international relations, though it was securely rooted in theoretical developments.

V

When Kaunitz came to inform France, still Austria's ostensible ally as well as Poland's traditional friend, of the partition – which had caused a 'sensation' at the

---

[169] These figures are given in the most recent study: Lukowski, *Partitions of Poland*, p. 100; see also LeDonne, *Russian Empire*, p. 46.   [170] See below, pp. 234–5.

[171] For this doctrine, see, e.g., Beer, *Erste Theilung Polens*, III. 127, 180.

[172] One of the best examples is Panin's memoir of May 1772, seeking to evaluate the 'valeur intrinsèque' of each state's share: this is printed in Beer, *Erste Theilung Polens*, III. 121–7.

[173] For this usage see, e.g., Kaunitz to van Swieten, 25 Jan. 1772, printed in Beer, *Erste Theilung Polens*, III. 175.   [174] Beer, *Erste Theilung Polens*, III. 184.   [175] See above, pp. 8–10.

French court[176] – and Habsburg participation in it, he sought to explain it away as a simple consequence of shifts within the international system. He claimed that the disappearance of France and Britain in the early 1770s had left Vienna with no choice but to join in the seizure of Polish lands.[177] Though nothing if not special pleading, it also touched on a fundamental issue. Frederick the Great, whether more cynical or simply more realistic, made essentially the same point. He penned a brutal political obituary of the two western powers, composed in the same month that the Russo-Prussian convention was signed.[178] The partition, the King declared, marked the end of the era of Anglo-French hegemony, during which the two states had dominated the international system. It was the culmination of a development which had become evident during the Seven Years War, as the rise of Prussia and Russia began to transform the relations of all the great powers. By the end of the 1760s it was evident that the eastern powers had their own very distinct political priorities, while their growing leadership of the international system was facilitated by the continuing rivalries and political eclipse of Britain and France. This was rooted in ignorance of what was being arranged in 1771–2. The partitioning powers were remarkably successful in disguising their intentions, something which was believed to be essential if their plans were to be realised.[179] Potsdam was the diplomatic nerve-centre, and here the habitual secrecy which surrounded Frederick's foreign policy worked to the advantage of the eastern states. It was early March 1772, two weeks after the key Russo-Prussian agreements had been signed, before Britain's representative in Berlin, the enterprising James Harris, secured the first definite news of the partition, and mid-April before French policy-makers fully appreciated what had been arranged, and then only because the Austrian ambassador informed d'Aiguillon.[180]

In Britain's case, ignorance was accompanied by an established disinterest in the continent in general and its eastern half in particular, and by a series of alternative domestic and colonial priorities, which together produced an official attitude which was close to isolationism.[181] Her European role, limited since 1763, was by the early 1770s becoming exiguous. Ministers were primarily concerned with relations with

---

[176] *MT–MA*, I. 315.

[177] This view was also articulated by Maria Theresa: see her letter of 2 July 1772, *MT–MA*, I. 320; cf. *MT–MA*, I. 420, for a subsequent expression of the same sentiment. France, it must be underlined, was unconvinced. For her strong and enduring resentment, see Mercy Argenteau to Lobkowitz (Austrian ambassador in Madrid), 26 Oct. and 18 Dec. 1772, HHStA Frankreich-Korrespondenz 35, fos. 79, 81–2; cf. *MT–MA*, I. 352.

[178] Frederick II to Sandoz Rollin, 7 Feb. 1772, *Pol. Corr.*, XXXI. 737. Prussia's agent in Paris had reported (26 Jan. 1772) on the growing Anglo-French *rapprochement*: *Pol. Corr.*, XXXI. 737. See above, p. 6.

[179] For Joseph II's appreciation of the need for secrecy, whatever policy were to be adopted, see his letters to Leopold, May 1771 and Apr. 1772, *MT–JII*, I. 342, 367–8; for Frederick's anxieties about the western powers, see *Pol. Corr.*, XXXII. 105, 206.

[180] See Harris to Suffolk, 1 Mar. 1772, *Diaries and Correspondence of James Harris*, ed. Earl of Malmesbury, I. 79–80; same to same, 7 Mar. 1772, PRO, SP 90/91, fols. 53–5, giving detailed confirmation of this; Lucien Laugier, *Un ministère réformateur sous Louis XV: le Triumvirat (1770–1774)* (Paris, 1975), p. 412.   [181] Scott, *British Foreign Policy*, pp. 177–81, and more generally ch. 7.

the Bourbons, much improved since the great confrontation over the Falkland Islands in 1770–1. A more immediate priority in 1772 was extricating the Queen of Denmark from the compromising and ultimately dangerous predicament in which she had been placed by her own reckless conduct.[182] In January Struensee had been overthrown by a military *coup*. Along with his principal accomplice, Brandt, he was tried and executed. Britain feared that George III's sister might be drawn into the judicial aftermath of Struensee's fall, and during the first half of 1772 became involved in a confrontation with Copenhagen, eventually securing the release of Caroline Mathilda, who went into exile in Hanover. This preoccupied ministers when the partition was being finalised, and ensured that Britain's immediate response to Poland's fate was that of indifference, tempered by *Schadenfreude*, at what was viewed as further evidence of the fall of the arch-enemy, France.

French political decline, evident since the Seven Years War, was by now complete, and in the early 1770s it was intensified by renewed and acute financial problems. The chaos which followed Choiseul's dismissal had lasted for six months, a period of 'anarchy' as Frederick the Great characterised it.[183] The eventual appointment of d'Aiguillon in June 1771 was followed by many months during which the new minister defended himself against court and governmental intrigues and sought to master the rudiments of his office.[184] Though the duc was hard-working and intelligent, when he became foreign minister he was ignorant both of the ways of diplomacy and of the European issues of the day.[185] At a crucial period, for Poland and for the wider international system, France ceased to have a policy beyond simple passivity.[186] This was accompanied by a breakdown in the Franco-Austrian alliance, which was a precondition of the first partition.[187] It was furthered by d'Aiguillon's inept and unsuccessful efforts during the second half of 1771 to bring about a *rapprochement* and even to conclude an alliance with Prussia.[188] Choiseul's energetic and adventurist policies had periodically alarmed and infuriated his Austrian counterpart, and this had been particularly true at the end of the 1760s.[189] Until December 1770 Kaunitz had almost always paid attention to French policies and interests: the alliance was secure until Choiseul's fall. Thereafter it was a different

---

[182] Scott, *British Foreign Policy*, pp. 171–7, for the confrontation with Copenhagen.

[183] *Pol. Corr.*, XXX. 477. In mid-Apr., Joseph II declared that France was in 'la plus grande fermentation': *MT–JII*, I. 336.   [184] *MA–JII*, II. 406, 407.

[185] See Sandoz Rollin to Frederick II, 20 June and 4 July 1771, GStAPK Rep. 96.27.C.

[186] As d'Aiguillon honestly admitted: to Rohan, 6 Feb. 1772, *Recueil: Autriche*, ed. Albert Sorel, p. 449. For Panin's testimony to the collapse of France and the impact of this upon Austria, see his letter to Saldern, 28 Aug. 1771 OS, *SIRIO*, XCVII. 416–17. Cf. *MT–MA*, I. 300, 305.

[187] A point emphasised by E. Rostworowski, 'Na drodze do pierwszego rozbioru: Fryderyk II wobec rozkladu przymierza francusko-austriackiego w latach 1769–1772', *Roczniki Historyczne* 18 (1949), pp. 181–204. I am indebted to Professor A. Kaminski, who was good enough to translate this article for me.

[188] For this initiative, see *Pol. Corr.*, XXXI. 278ff, and the correspondence for these months in GStAPK Rep. 96.27.C. Vienna's resentment is evident from *MT–MA*, I. 321.

[189] See the Chancellor's hostile political obituary: to Mercy, 5 Jan. 1771, *MA–JII*, II. 382–3.

story.[190] With France's effective collapse in the early 1770s, the Chancellor simply stopped taking account of Versailles in his policies: this was one dimension of the diplomacy of partition and of the emergence of the eastern powers.[191] This downward trajectory was appreciated by Frederick. He had hated and feared France's fallen minister, whom he had viewed as the principal threat to peace, and he welcomed his political demise. France's collapse after Choiseul's dismissal had, he believed, averted a wider conflict by denying Austria essential support and so weakened her politically.[192] The King, however, initially believed that the Franco-Austrian alliance would survive the French minister most closely associated with it.[193] In early August 1771 his view changed quite suddenly, when he received the secret French overtures for an alliance.[194] These were rejected out of hand, but they revealed the collapse of the Franco-Austrian axis: within a month Frederick was pronouncing it moribund.[195] This isolated Vienna, and was the final piece in the diplomatic jigsaw of partition. It was confirmed by the widespread failure of the harvest across much of the Habsburg Monarchy, which meant that Austria could not form magazines and so would not be able to fight.[196] The diplomatic changes of the early 1770s had in this way marginalised western Europe's two great powers. Britain's Southern Secretary, the Earl of Rochford, remarked on one occasion that the Polish partition 'had completely changed the political system of Europe', and his view was endorsed by the French foreign minister.[197]

D'Aiguillon was aware that France alone could do little against the partitioning powers. This led him, in 1772–3, to seek to create an Anglo-French *entente* and even an alliance to confront the eastern axis.[198] His efforts were unsuccessful, but they were an imaginative response to the new political world in which France now lived, and the one possible solution to the problems her foreign policy faced. Ever since he entered office in summer 1771 the duc had sought to improve relations with Britain. This in itself was unusual. The two states were traditional enemies and as recently as the final months of 1770 had come close to war over the Falkland Islands. In spring 1772, with his own position now more securely established and with the news of the Russo-Prussian agreement to partition Poland, d'Aiguillon sought to

---

[190] *MA–JII*, II. 400, 404.

[191] Though he professed to be anxious about possible diplomatic intervention by the western powers over partition: see Golitsyn's account of an interview with the Chancellor at the beginning of 1772, Soloviev, *History of Russia*, XLVIII. 20. [192] *Pol. Corr.*, XXXI. 66, 143, 202–3.

[193] *Pol. Corr.*, XXXI. 169–70, 184.

[194] *Pol. Corr.*, XXXI. 278ff. By mid-August 1772, Mercy was reporting that d'Aiguillon might not automatically support the Austrian alliance: *MA–JII*, II. 411.

[195] *Pol. Corr.*, XXXI. 284–5, 336, 339–40, 345. For Kaunitz's resentment, *MA–JII*, II. 402.

[196] *Pol. Corr.*, XXXI. 439, 461, 472. This view was shared by Joseph II, who had first-hand knowledge of the severity of the famine in Bohemia: *MT–JII*, I. 346. See also Arneth, *GMT*, VIII. 327.

[197] Quoted by Scott, *British Foreign Policy*, p. 181.

[198] The fundamental article is B. du Fraguier, 'Le duc d'Aiguillon et l'Angleterre', *Revue d'histoire diplomatique* 26 (1912), pp. 607–27; other accounts are provided by Michael Roberts, 'Great Britain and the Swedish Revolution, 1772–3', in Michael Roberts, *Essays in Swedish History* (London, 1967), pp. 301–8, 312–17, and Scott, *British Foreign Policy*, pp. 181–90.

turn the existing *détente* into full-blown political co-operation with London. His suggestion was that a *rapprochement* would be followed by a diplomatic offensive to restrain the eastern powers and even avert the proposed partition. These suggestions were taken up by several leading figures in the British government, headed by George III, and negotiations continued intermittently and largely in secret for a year, from spring 1772 until spring 1773. While the political logic of such a realignment was considerable, the practical difficulties were equally daunting and ultimately proved overwhelming. The francophobia of Britain's parliament and political nation was considerable, and this intimidated the various figures interested in co-operation with the national enemy. The most persistent supporter was Rochford, and even he eventually realised that political logic was not enough to overcome traditional and deeply ingrained prejudice, while Britain's changed position was not widely understood at this point.

In late January 1773, by which point the prospects for closer links with Britain were already poor, d'Aiguillon had a remarkably frank interview with the papal nuncio.[199] Freely confessing that France dare not risk war, he went on to admit that Poland was beyond help and might well be subjected to a further partition. The combined strength of the eastern powers was too great for any one state to challenge with any prospect of success.[200] Behind the three partitioning powers, in d'Aiguillon's estimation, could be glimpsed the hegemony of Russia, France's other traditional foe but a state whose advance she was now powerless to resist: as the duc admitted with a fury rooted in his appreciation of France's own impotence. This was the real significance of the failure of the Anglo-French negotiations. The established rivalry between the two leading western states, together with their divergent priorities and problems, contrasted sharply with the coherence and unity of the eastern powers, and contributed to their dominance.

The diminished importance of the western powers was linked to – and indeed formed part of – the growing division of Europe into two separate diplomatic systems. This had been apparent since the Seven Years War and had accelerated thereafter, though in the later 1760s it had been temporarily and partially disguised by Choiseul's anti-Russian initiatives in northern and eastern Europe. The informal neutrality agreement at Neisse was a significant stage in this political division and in the growing independence of the three great powers in the eastern half of Europe. In the second half of 1770, as an Anglo-Bourbon war over the Falkland Islands appeared likely, Prussia and Austria had both been robustly confident that it would not extend to Germany: unlike the fighting which had begun in 1756.[201] The political polarisation was most evident in the early 1770s, when the partition of Europe between the western states and the eastern powers accompanied and, to some extent, prepared the way for the partition of Poland.

---

[199] Giraud to Pallavicini, 25 Jan. 1773, AAE CP (Rome) 865, fos. 41–2; cf. fo. 4.
[200] See AAE CP (Prusse) 191, fo. 81, for a good example of d'Aiguillon's resentment at their dominance.
[201] *Pol. Corr.*, xxx. 197, 351; *MT–JII*, I. 310–18.

8

The advance of Russia, 1772–1775

I

Russia's involvement in partition had revealed not merely her territorial ambitions, but also her inability to resist Austrian and Prussian pressure. Sole control seemed to have been given up in exchange for shared domination over Poland exercised jointly with the two German powers. This was in keeping with Catherine II's considerable and mounting problems during the first half of the 1770s.[1] Though important victories had been won over the Ottoman empire, St Petersburg seemed unable to secure its peace terms, while it was recognised that imposing the territorial seizures upon Poland might prove difficult. The burdens of the fighting were considerable and ever increasing. On the eve of the war there had been a cash reserve of eight and a half million rubles, but this had quickly been consumed.[2] By 1771 annual military expenditure had soared to almost twenty-two million rubles: in 1768 it had been twelve and a half, while the small budgetary surplus which had existed in the last year of peace had, by 1772, become an annual deficit of over nine million rubles.[3] The fiscal effort required to support spending on this scale was beyond the capacity of Russia's protean state administration, while foreign credit was soon exhausted.[4] The solution was as predictable as it was to be disastrous: the government had recourse to the printing press, issuing *assignats* to cover the shortfall. By 1774, the final year of the war, the total amount of these paper notes in circulation was twenty million rubles: some two-thirds of annual expenditure.[5]

Human as well as financial resources were strained by the fighting. The extent of Russia's military commitments placed unprecedented pressure upon the recruitment system, with which it could only cope with difficulty. Though six levies between 1768 and 1773 had raised over 300,000 men, commanders at the front seldom received reinforcements on the scale required.[6] Military equipment was in short supply, while harvest failure in 1770–1 exacerbated the problems of feeding

---

[1] Brief and contrasting accounts are provided by John T. Alexander, *Autocratic Politics in a National Crisis: The Imperial Russian Government and Pugachev's Revolt, 1773–1775* (Bloomington, IN, 1969), pp. 11–23; Madariaga, *Russia*, esp. pp. 239–73; Ransel, *Politics of Catherinian Russia*, pp. 227–48.
[2] Simon Dixon, *The Modernisation of Russia 1676–1825* (Cambridge, 1999), p. 20.
[3] See the figures in Kahan, *The Plow*, p. 337, table 8.16, and p. 346, table 8.28.
[4] Riley, *International Government Finance*, p. 155.
[5] Alexander, *Autocratic Politics in a National Crisis*, 16.   [6] Madariaga, *Russia*, 233.

the troops and caused widespread suffering among the civilian population. One by-product of the fighting in south-east Europe was a severe typhus epidemic which reached Moscow in 1771, killing around 100,000 people in the city and its surrounding region, and causing serious social unrest in that autumn.[7] Even more serious were a series of direct challenges to the régime's stability. The early 1770s saw a severe court crisis, central to which was the position of Catherine's son, the Grand Duke Paul, who would shortly come of age and whom many believed had a better claim to the throne than the Empress herself.[8] In the summer of 1772 a conspiracy which aimed to make him ruler had been uncovered in a guards' regiment. In that autumn Catherine II's favourite for a decade, Grigory Orlov, was summarily removed when his infidelity became known to the Empress, an episode with wide-ranging political repercussions. Finally, the peasant-Cossack revolt led by Emelyan Pugachev, which assumed serious proportions by the autumn of 1773, posed a violent and large-scale challenge to social peace and even to the government itself. The details of these episodes are less important than their cumulative impact. The first half of the 1770s saw mounting problems culminating in the Pugachev rebellion, which forced the recall of troops from the Ottoman front to restore domestic peace. Yet these years also witnessed further Russian successes, due not least to the steadfastness demonstrated by the Empress herself, whose nerve held under severe pressure. The most important was the triumphant conclusion of the Ottoman War in summer 1774 and the vast territorial gains to the south which accrued, annexations which – together with the Polish acquisitions – decisively altered the territorial and political situation in eastern Europe and made Russia dominant there.

The successes achieved by the mid-1770s could not have been predicted, given the extent of the external challenges and domestic problems confronting Catherine II. In the same month that the eastern powers signed the treaties partitioning Poland – August 1772 – security around the Baltic was imperilled by the Swedish *coup* which had long been feared. On 19 August the young King, Gustav III, with the enthusiastic backing of France, summarily brought the Age of Liberty to an end and restored some – though far from all – of the powers of Sweden's monarchy. It was the most serious reverse in foreign policy which Catherine II had experienced to this point in her reign and caused real anxiety in St Petersburg.[9] France's presumed role aroused particular concern. Russia viewed the *coup* as the work of Louis XV's monarchy, which regarded Gustav III as its protégé, had favoured a strengthening of royal authority, had given the young king financial and diplomatic support, and

---

[7] See the lively study by John T. Alexander, *Bubonic Plague in Early Modern Russia: Public Health and Urban Disaster* (Baltimore, 1980).

[8] Paul's eighteenth birthday was in October 1772 and, while there was no formal law of succession in Russia and thus no established age of majority, it would be difficult to delay it much beyond this date. In the event, his majority was postponed until his marriage in October 1773: Madariaga, *Russia*, p. 257.

[9] Amburger, *Russland und Schweden*, p. 266; for the anxious reaction, Soloviev, *History of Russia*, XLVIII. 6off.

loudly acclaimed his success.[10] The revolution swept away the Constitution of 1720, which Russia aimed to uphold as a safeguard against Swedish revanchism: in the previous year the French diplomat Sabatier de Cabres had declared that not merely were memories of the battle of Narva alive in St Petersburg but the recollection of this shattering defeat at the hands of Charles XII in 1700 still influenced its policy.[11] The *coup* destroyed at a stroke two decades' work by Nikita Panin – as a diplomat in Stockholm in the 1750s and as foreign minister in St Petersburg in the 1760s – and in the longer perspective further weakened the Northern System.[12] More immediately, however, it threatened a Baltic war when Russia was already more than fully committed against the Ottoman empire and in Poland.

This was less because of the nature of Sweden's new régime than the exaggerated reactions it inspired. Gustav III did not restore anything approaching the absolutism which had prevailed before 1718. He rather strengthened the King's executive powers, while simultaneously obliging the monarch to consult his Council, which in certain circumstances could overrule him. His authority after 19 August 1772 blended older Swedish parliamentary traditions with newer ideas of enlightened rule: Gustav III, who was strongly influenced by Montesquieu, sought to create a balanced polity, rather than revive a full-blown absolutism. These refinements, however, have been more apparent to historians than they were to contemporaries, who were alert for any strengthening of the Swedish monarchy. As recently as the Russo-Danish treaty of 1769 any alteration in Sweden's constitutional arrangements had been declared a *casus belli*, and Copenhagen's reaction during the autumn and winter of 1772–3 was particularly bellicose.

The Swedish revolution came at a particularly difficult moment for Russia.[13] When rumours of a *coup* first reached St Petersburg, the military expert Zachar Chernyshev had carried out an immediate inspection of the empire's Finnish frontier. This revealed that the border fortresses were poorly manned and in a dilapidated condition, and underlined that Russia was extremely vulnerable to invasion from Swedish Finland. During the tense nine months which followed Gustav's *coup*, St Petersburg's policy was constrained by the fact that she lacked available military and naval muscle: her army was largely committed in Poland and in the south, while most of the Baltic fleet was operating in the Mediterranean and even the Black Sea.[14] Added to this was the lack of any negotiated settlement with the Ottoman empire. The early 1770s saw a stalemate on the Russo-Ottoman front, after the substantial Russian successes during the first two campaigns.[15] Constantinople drew the lesson from the initial defeats that major battles were to be avoided, and instead reinforced

---

[10] *SIRIO*, CXVIII. 211; Soloviev, *History of Russia*, XLVIII. 60; for France's policy, see Murphy, *Vergennes*, esp. pp. 184–206.   [11] *SIRIO*, CXLIII. 587.   [12] Hübner, *Staatspolitik und Familieninteresse*, p. 257.
[13] See Panin's testimony to this, written shortly after news arrived of the *coup*: to I.A. Ostermann, 27 Aug. 1772, *SIRIO*, CXVIII. 210–13. There is a careful and informative study by R.J. Misiunas, 'Russia and Sweden 1772–1778' (PhD thesis, Yale University, 1971), see esp. chs. 1–3; the same author's 'The Baltic Question after Nystad', *Baltic History* (1974), 71–90, puts these events into a broader context.
[14] *SIRIO*, CXVIII. 211, 395.   [15] See above, pp. 199–200.

the already strong defensive position which its forces occupied south of the Danube. The Russians, for their part, consolidated their position both on the river's northern bank and in the Crimea during 1771, but they were unable and also unwilling to attempt further decisive action. By March 1772 formal proposals for a truce had reached the Grand Vizier's camp, and this was signed and then successively extended to facilitate the peace conferences held at Fokshany (August–September 1772) and Bucharest (November 1772–March 1773).[16] The pause in the fighting, however, did not lead to the negotiated settlement which both sides genuinely wanted. This was because their respective terms for peace were incompatible. Central to the *impasse* was the Crimea, which by a treaty between its Khan and St Petersburg signed in November 1772 effectively became an independent state under a Russian protectorate. Constantinople was unwilling to concede this as part of a peace settlement, and the refusal led to a breakdown of the discussions at Fokshany. Negotiations were resumed in November at Bucharest, but the Khanate's independence remained the major stumbling block and by early April 1773, by which point the conference had broken up and the truce had expired, it was clear that a peace settlement would not be made without a decisive military victory.

With the benefit of hindsight it is clear that the failure of the talks prevented any Russian initiative against Gustav III.[17] Indeed, when news arrived of the Swedish revolution, instructions were sent to the Russian plenipotentiaries at Fokshany that the demand for Crimean independence should be dropped: in itself revealing confirmation of the seriousness with which the Baltic situation was viewed. But by the time these arrived the congress had been ruptured by an earlier Russian ultimatum over the Khanate.[18] Catherine II and Panin quickly accepted that aggressive action in the Baltic could only be undertaken once a settlement with the Porte had been secured. The frontier in Finland was reinforced, and in November 1772 when fighting appeared likely troops were actually recalled from the Ottoman front to strengthen Russia's northern ramparts. At the end of that month Stockholm was warned that any hostile move against Denmark would be viewed as aggression against Russia herself.[19] Though the Empress' forces mobilised with the aim of intimidating Gustav, an actual invasion of Swedish territory was never seriously contemplated. Yet in the prevailing mood of nervousness, defensive measures were interpreted as aggressive actions and so increased tension, and there was a real risk of war. These troops movements were viewed as provocative in Stockholm and as welcome in Copenhagen, and this increased international tension. Europe's two systems of defensive alliances threatened that any Baltic conflict might become more generalised: exactly as had been feared over the Russo-Ottoman War since 1768.[20]

---

[16] Aksan, *An Ottoman Statesman*, pp. 156–63, examines the Ottoman side of these negotiations and their failure. For a fuller account, see Hammer, *Histoire de l'empire Ottoman*, XVI. 333–47.
[17] Frederick, with his usual perception, had immediately pronounced that this would be the case: *Pol. Corr.*, XXXII. 466–7, 476.   [18] Madariaga, *Russia*, p. 227.   [19] *SIRIO*, CXVIII. 211, 395.
[20] See above, p. 185.

There were two periods during 1772–3 when hostilities appeared likely.[21] The first was in late October and November, when Copenhagen, which had mobilised and feared a Swedish invasion of Norway (ruled by Denmark), appeared on the point of launching a pre-emptive attack on Gustav III.[22] The Russo-Danish axis, so secure in the 1760s, had been much weaker since J.H.E. von Bernstorff's fall, and relations had become particularly strained during Struensee's ascendancy.[23] After his overthrow in January 1772, a strongly Danish régime headed by the Queen Mother Juliana Maria and Ove Høegh-Guldberg ruled for the schizophrenic Christian VII. The foreign minister, Grev A.S. von der Osten, had appeared to be less dependent upon Russia than Bernstorff had been. In fact, having earlier contemplated unilateral action against Gustav III, Osten now demonstrated considerable statesmanship in dealing with a Swedish ultimatum, and thereby averted war in the closing weeks of 1772. Prussia's King had also contributed to the preservation of peace. He was the brother of Sweden's Queen Mother and the uncle of the new king, and during these months he applied considerable pressure upon his relatives.[24] A series of admonitory and, increasingly, menacing letters cautioned against any Swedish invasion of Norway and warned of its dire consequences, while Frederick also tried to restrain Denmark. This peace diplomacy was in keeping with Panin's explicit request to his ally, but it also accorded with the King's fundamental wish to prevent any war unless he saw the possibility of gains for Prussia.[25]

The central role in the second crisis, in spring 1773, was played not by Denmark or even Russia (who was still prepared for military intimidation of Stockholm but not actual fighting)[26] but by France. In late February a new defensive alliance and a subsidy treaty were signed, by which the French monarchy undertook to provide Gustav III with an annual subsidy of 800,000 *livres* for three years, to be spent on building up his armed forces, and promised to send 10,000–12,000 troops to support him if he were to be attacked.[27] In the weeks which followed its signature a new Baltic crisis flared up, created by Russian troop movements which suggested – quite erroneously – that Catherine II's forces were about to seize Swedish Finland. In fact the failure of the Bucharest peace conference ensured that Russia would not go to war in the north, but in the tense atmosphere which prevailed her military manoeuvres were once again viewed as aggressive. They were answered by a French threat to send both the troops provided by treaty and a fleet into the Baltic to support her

---

[21] The best study of the international consequences of the Swedish *coup* is Michael Roberts, 'Great Britain and the Swedish Revolution', an article of much wider European significance than the title might suggest. (This paper was first published in *Historical Journal* 7 (1964).)

[22] For Frederick's real fears of war at this period, see *Pol. Corr.*, XXXIII. 38, 40–1, 82; for Kaunitz's, Edelsheim to Frederick II, 30 Sept., 24 Oct. and 21 Nov. 1772, all in GStAPK Rep. 96.47.K.

[23] See above, pp. 200–1.   [24] *Pol. Corr.*, XXXII. 442–3, 455, 456–8, 474–5, 518, 536, 574–5, 615–16.

[25] *Pol. Corr.*, XXXII. 508–9, for Russia's request for diplomatic support. The King had by this point begun his own campaign at Stockholm.   [26] Soloviev, *History of Russia*, XLVIII. 75–6, 152–6.

[27] Important material on Franco-Swedish relations at this point is contained in L. Bonneville de Marsangy, *Le comte de Vergennes: son ambassade en Suède 1771–1774* (Paris, 1898).

Swedish client.[28] Though preparations began at Toulon, these envisaged at most naval action in the Mediterranean, where Russian ships were still operating, and may have been simply a bluff, given the weakened condition of the French navy in the early 1770s. Versailles' mobilisation was predictably answered by its British rival which commissioned a fleet of its own and threatened France with superior naval force unless she backed down: which the French ministry duly did, thereby preserving peace in northern Europe.[29] This was consolidated by Catherine II's declaration in the spring that she viewed the new Swedish régime favourably, thereby reassuring Stockholm and further reducing tension.[30] The war scare of spring 1773 possessed one final importance. It ended any prospect – which had never in any case been particularly high – of an Anglo-French *rapprochement* and so removed the one possible threat to the leadership of the eastern states.[31]

In March 1773, shortly before the second crisis, Russia's position around the Baltic was strengthened by a political change in Copenhagen. Osten, whose reliability St Petersburg questioned – perhaps unfairly – and whose dismissal it had sought, left office.[32] He was succeeded by Andreas Peter von Bernstorff, who proved the political executor of his more famous uncle. The younger Bernstorff quickly restored the pro-Russian policies which had prevailed until 1770, and Copenhagen re-entered St Petersburg's political orbit. Russo-Danish harmony was considerably strengthened during 1773 by the final settlement of the Holstein problem.[33] Catherine II's son Paul, who would reach his majority in that autumn, gave his approval, and this agreement was finalised by a treaty signed on 1 June.[34] This provided for the exchange of ducal Holstein (which Russia's Grand Duke renounced) for Oldenburg-Delmenhorst, which passed to the junior line of the House of Oldenburg, a transfer which was formally carried out in the following month. This settlement finally removed Danish anxieties about the vulnerable southern frontier. It was followed on 12 August 1773 by a permanent defensive alliance between the two courts.[35] By attaching Copenhagen permanently to St Petersburg – the exchange was finalised on the basis of an unbreakable alliance – it consolidated Russia's position around the Baltic and made Denmark a Russian client for a generation to come. Copenhagen's efforts over half a century to resolve the problem of Holstein had eventually been crowned by success.[36] Though the ending of the

---

[28] For France's crucial role, see *Pol. Corr.*, XXXIII. 399, 406, 421. As in the earlier crisis, Prussia's King did what he could to preserve peace, though he clearly regarded the spring crisis as less acute.

[29] Though at the price of further damage to her political standing: *MT–MA*, I. 447.

[30] Ole Feldbaek, 'Denmark and the Baltic, 1720–1864', in Göran Rystad, Klaus-R. Böhme and Wilhelm M. Carlgren, eds., *In Quest of Trade and Security: The Baltic in Power Politics, 1500–1990*, vol. I: *1500–1890* (Stockholm, 1994), pp. 257–95, at p. 267.

[31] See above, pp. 223–4, for these shadowy negotiations. [32] Soloviev, *History of Russia*, XLVIII. 156–8.

[33] For the negotiations see Hübner, *Staatspolitik und Familieninteresse*, pp. 259–71, and the documents in *Bernstorffsche Papiere*, III. [34] It is printed in *Danske Tractater*, pp. 322–53.

[35] It is printed in *Danske Tractater*, pp. 365–72.

[36] For the settlement's importance to Denmark, see A.P. von Bernstorff to Ditlev Reventlou, 23 Oct. 1773, *Bernstorffsche Papiere*, III. 288.

Russo-Ottoman War did much to reassure her, by freeing Russia to play her traditional role as a powerful ally against Sweden, Denmark remained concerned by Gustav III's warlike posturings.[37] Fears persisted of a sudden Swedish attack on Zealand and Copenhagen, designed to force Denmark to yield Norway, and they were countered by a Danish strategy which aimed to retain naval supremacy in the Sound. As Russia's power grew during the next few years, Denmark's political independence was gradually lost, as an unequal alliance reduced her to a wholly subordinate status.[38]

St Petersburg's position around the Baltic was also strengthened, in the medium term at least, by Gustav III's *coup*.[39] This may seem paradoxical, given that Sweden's young king had been so aggressive and even bellicose in 1772–3. These months, however, had also revealed shortcomings in the Swedish military and naval establishments, and underlined the real disparity in power between the two Baltic neighbours. Russia, though overextended and vulnerable, had still proved far too strong for Sweden, whose weakness was evident.[40] A commission of enquiry was set up in 1774, to examine the Swedish armed forces in the light of the mobilisation two years earlier, and revealed that they were in a parlous condition. In 1776 a start was made on essential reforms, though it would be several years before real improvements in the army and the navy could be achieved.[41] These were accompanied by deliberate efforts by Gustav III to improve relations with Russia, seen as even more necessary after Louis XV's death in spring 1774 weakened the Franco-Swedish axis. They were facilitated by St Petersburg's recognition that Sweden was much less of a threat than hitherto believed.[42] Even with French subsidies and, potentially, armed support, and at a moment when Russia was extremely vulnerable, the new Swedish régime had offered only a limited threat in 1772–3 and had backed away from an open confrontation. This in turn weakened Russian assumptions about the need to guard against Swedish revanchism, thinking which had guided St Petersburg's policy for several decades.[43] Before long a *rapprochement* was under way, supported by each state. It was strengthened by Gustav III's visit to Russia in 1777 and a further meeting in Russian Finland in 1783, though it would break down during the next decade when ideas of revenge again moved up the political agenda in Stockholm.[44] In the 1770s, however, the growing friendship between the two adversaries strengthened Russia around the Baltic, and may even have contributed to her

---

[37] *Bernstorffsche Papiere*, III. 316, 317, 321.   [38] Feldbaek, 'Denmark and the Baltic', pp. 268, 289.

[39] The lavish exhibition catalogue *Catherine the Great and Gustav III* is informative on the relationship between the two rulers; see pp. 118–248 *passim* for the political dimension.

[40] This was apparent as early as spring 1773: see Panin's paper on the Baltic crisis and its resolution, 2 May 1773 OS, *SIRIO*, CXVIII. 394–7, esp. p. 396.

[41] Barton, *Scandinavia in the Revolutionary Era*, p. 112.

[42] Misiunas, 'Russia and Sweden, 1772–1778', p. 267.

[43] For this growing confidence, see the 'Instructions' for K.L.S. von Asseburg, 30 Sept. 1774, *SIRIO*, CXXXV. 233.

[44] *Catherine the Great and Gustav III*, pp. 153–69, for the King's first journey to St Petersburg.

increasing interest in further expansion to the south, at the Ottoman empire's expense.

By this point the *impasse* revealed by the Fokshany and Bucharest negotiations was Catherine II's sole problem in foreign policy. In spring 1773 a decisive military victory was once more sought. The rival armies were now reluctant to fight again: disease, desertion, supply problems and sheer exhaustion had all taken their toll. Russia's Council ordered a hesitant Rumyantsev to advance across the Danube and break through the strong Ottoman defensive position to the south of the river. The campaigns of 1773 and 1774, in which the legendary Russian commander A.V. Suvorov first achieved prominence, both began late after unusually heavy spring rains.[45] The first offensive was beaten back, though at the very end of the campaigning season Russian troops did secure a foothold on the Danube's southern bank. In the following year, after the failure of further peace talks, Rumyantsev led his forces across the river and attacked the Grand Vizier's camp. The battle which followed witnessed the rout of the Sultan's army and brought a rapid end to the war. Ottoman suggestions of a further truce were brushed aside by the Russian commander, who demanded an immediate peace. The Grand Vizier's army was surrounded and outnumbered, and lacked both supplies and reinforcements. Ottoman resistance simply could not be sustained, and there was no alternative to accepting Russia'speace terms which had earlier been put forward at the Fokshany and Bucharest conferences and were now renewed.

The peace of Kuchuk-Kainardji, negotiated by Nikolai Repnin and signed in Rumyantsev's headquarters on 21 July 1774, reflected Russia's ultimately overwhelming victory. In the longer perspective it can be seen to have established the Russian empire as the leading power in south-eastern Europe and, more widely, throughout the Middle East. The vague right which, it was subsequently and erroneously claimed by St Petersburg, had been secured to protect the Orthodox Christians would, in the next century, be a fertile source of ambiguity and conflict. Eighteenth-century contemporaries were more impressed by the scale of Catherine II's territorial gains and the resulting boost to Russia's international standing. The northern littoral of the Black Sea between the Bug and Dnieper was secured, together with the important ports of Kilburun, Yenikale and Kerch, while Azov and the region which surrounded it, gained in 1739, were confirmed as Russian possessions. St Petersburg also secured free navigation on the Black Sea and, for commercial ships, through the Straits and in the Mediterranean, a distinction which was in practice difficult to uphold. The independence of the Crimea which Constantinople had long opposed, was established. Though the Sultan retained the right to approve the new Khan, as the area's religious leader, and attached much importance to this, it was widely recognised that the Khanate's independence would be simply a

---

[45] Soloviev, *History of Russia*, XLVIII. 84–101, 162–70; Philip Longworth, *The Art of Victory: The Life and Achievements of Generalissimo Suvorov, 1729–1800* (London, 1965), pp. 73–98.

4. Territorial changes in eastern Europe, 1768–1775

prelude to Russian annexation. Finally, the Ottoman government was forced to pay a war indemnity of four and half million rubles. These terms were a severe set-back for the Porte, where Russia's power was seen as irresistible, and they brought radical domestic reform to the top of the agenda in Constantinople.

II

The dominance of the eastern powers and its corollary, the impotence of France and Britain, were evident to contemporaries.[46] The unity of this alignment, however, was more apparent than real, and principally impressed outside observers. Russia, Prussia and Austria were never formally allies. During and immediately after the Polish partition Panin sponsored the notion of a Triple Alliance.[47] This was immediately rejected by Kaunitz, ostensibly because it was incompatible with Vienna's French alliance which he wished to maintain:[48] though Austria's own involvement in the partition amounted to a repudiation of these links.[49] The Chancellor's real motive was his belief that, while the three powers could co-operate effectively over a single issue – such as Poland – shared hegemony over the eastern half of Europe would be intrinsically less stable and should be avoided.[50] It would also perpetuate that same Prussian ascendancy over Austria which he hoped eventually to undermine. Any three-power concert would relegate Vienna to permanent political subordination, which was unacceptable. Though Frederick necessarily responded more favourably to Panin's initiative, he too was fundamentally opposed to any Triple Alliance, which he believed could only advance the Russo-Austrian *rapprochement* which he himself feared.[51] Though such ideas would periodically re-emerge in the future,[52] the links between the eastern powers were always less solid than treaty obligations would have been. They were simply the 'trois cours' or the 'trois puissances', not a formal alignment.[53]

The principal cement was Poland and the need to impose partition, a task which took several years to complete. It had two dimensions: determining the precise extent of the individual annexations and so fixing boundaries, and imposing these and, perhaps, new constitutional arrangements upon the Poles themselves. Though the detailed negotiations in 1771–2 had sought to equalise the

---

[46] E.g. the views of A.P. von Bernstorff in March 1774: *Bernstorffsche Papiere*, III. 277; cf. *MT–MA*, II. 35, for French weakness and confusion in late summer 1773.

[47] E.g. *SIRIO*, LXXII. 58–60; *MT–JII*, I. 367.

[48] See Edelsheim to Frederick II, 5 Sept. 1772, GStAPK Rep. 96.47.K.

[49] Mercy-Argenteau's important analysis of the alliance's breakdown is in his letter of 17 Mar. 1773 to Maria Theresa: *MT–MA*, I. 435–6.

[50] See the 'Instruction Secrète' for van Swieten, 21 Jan. 1773, in Beer, *Erste Theilung Polens*, III. 186–90, for the Chancellor's coolness.

[51] *Pol. Corr.*, XXXII. 471–72, 482. See below, pp. 237–8, for more on this.

[52] E.g. *Pol. Corr.*, XXXIII. 246.   [53] E.g. Beer, *Erste Theilung Polens*, III. 157, for these usages.

234

three shares, much remained to be done. It was partly a question of the real limitations upon cartographical knowledge at this period. In the partition treaties Austria's gains were declared to extend eastwards as far as the river Podgórze, marked on a map published as recently as January 1772. In fact this was a phantom river, and when Austrian gains were finalised the Zbrucz, some twenty miles further east, was designated as the new Habsburg frontier.[54] Vienna's appetite for more lands and subjects was shared by the other two partitioning powers. Extended and detailed negotiations, both with Polish commissioners and between the three eastern courts, were required to settle the precise extent of the cessions, and these exchanges were ruthlessly exploited by the partitioning powers to extend their annexations: Frederick secured as many as 120,000 new subjects in this way.[55] It was July 1775 before Russian acquisitions could be prescribed in a treaty with Poland, the following February before Austria's convention could be signed, and as late as July 1777 before Prussia's share could be agreed with Warsaw.[56]

Poland and her king were powerless to resist these seizures, backed as they were by the overwhelming military might of Russia, Prussia and Austria. After 1772 a new Russian ambassador Otto Magnus von Stackelberg supervised the imposition of the territorial annexations and a new political settlement, and in so doing restored St Petersburg's control over the country.[57] Both Prussia and Austria recognised Russia's special interest in Poland, viewed by Catherine and her advisers as a satellite, and were happy to leave her to impose the partition. Stackelberg was pliable and adroit, in sharp contrast to his immediate predecessors, Volkonsky and Caspar von Saldern. He realigned Russian policy, which instead of using the dissidents to secure leverage at Warsaw, as had been attempted during the 1760s, now aimed to divide and rule by playing off Poland's political factions. This was evident in the more limited rights now accorded to the dissidents, which contrasted sharply with the demands earlier made on their behalf by St Petersburg. The King, Stanislas Augustus, could at most delay the political adjustments, rather than obstruct them fundamentally. Stackelberg supervised a series of constitutional changes, which further reduced the authority of the Polish monarch, who became little more than the 'honorary president' of the executive council which now governed.[58] The *veto*, at once symptom and

---

[54] Arneth, *GMT*, VIII. 423–5.

[55] *MT–JII*, II. 54, for the Emperor's view in Jan. 1775 that Prussia's King was manipulating these triangular discussions to his own advantage.

[56] For these discussions see Arneth, *GMT*, VIII. 492–533; *MT–JII*, II. 40; J. Topolski, 'La formation de la frontière polono-prussienne à l'époque du premier partage de la Pologne (1772–1777)', *La Pologne et les affaires occidentales* 5 (1969), pp. 96–127; Lukowksi, *Partitions of Poland*, pp. 90–2.

[57] Brief accounts are provided by Lukowski, *Partitions of Poland*, pp. 82–104, and the same author's *Liberty's Folly*, pp. 203–11; see also Soloviev, *History of Russia*, XLVIII. 109–36. Events in Poland after 1772 are viewed from the perspective of the papal nuncio Garampi in Wolff, *The Vatican and Poland*.

[58] Lukowski, *Liberty's Folly*, p. 207.

cause of the Kingdom's decline, was quite deliberately maintained. These and related changes were then incorporated into a new Russo-Polish treaty, signed in spring 1775. Russia's special interest in Poland and dominance there were apparent in the fact that – unlike the partition – there were no similar treaties with Prussia or Austria.

By the middle of the decade St Petersburg's recovery, in Poland as elsewhere, was to be impressive. Yet its problems in 1773–4 had been acute, with continuing upheavals at court, an unfinished war and the Pugachev rebellion.[59] These domestic priorities obscured the decisive impact of the early 1770s on Russia's foreign policy and wider international position. The Northern System, which had guided Catherine II's diplomacy since 1763, was now fatally weakened.[60] The Ottoman war, and St Petersburg's effective isolation during this, had been the first serious blow to Panin's policies and his own position. Events in 1772 dealt two further blows, and their impact was to prove fatal. The first partition was incompatible with the Northern System, which sought to incorporate the kingdom as a buffer state, while the Swedish revolution was exactly the event which Panin's diplomacy had aimed to prevent. Catherine II subsequently came to resent what she viewed as the way in which her ally Prussia had exploited her vulnerability to divide Poland. Though for the moment political exigency required the maintenance of the Prussian alignment, she subsequently came to view the partition as the point at which her links with Frederick ended.[61]

By this period, Panin's own position had also been seriously weakened.[62] Until 1768 he had enjoyed the Empress' full and unquestioned backing, and could rely upon her support against his critics. The creation of the Council at the beginning of the Ottoman War signalled the end of his privileged position; thereafter his policies came under increasing attack and his authority was less secure.[63] Though he remained Catherine II's leading minister throughout the 1770s, he was no longer as dominant as he had been in the previous decade. Panin's personal relations with the Empress were damaged by events in 1772–3. Catherine resented the minister's apparent efforts to cement and then exploit the fall of her favourite Grigory Orlov, while a second and more important source of tension was Paul's majority and the misunderstandings this aroused. One significant source of Panin's own power had been his position as *Oberhofmeister* (governor) to the Grand Duke, a post he had occupied since 1760. Paul's majority and marriage ended this role, and also caused tension with the Empress, due to the erroneous belief that her minister may have been attempting to place his protégé on the throne. Rumours that Panin would leave

---

[59] See, e.g., the comments of A.P. von Bernstorff, a friendly observer: *Bernstorffsche Papiere*, III. 274, 276. Cf. the view of Catherine II's leading historian that this was 'the most serious challenge to her domestic authority': Madariaga, *Russia*, p. 256.

[60] See Griffiths, 'The Rise and Fall of the Northern System', pp. 556ff, and in greater detail in the same author's, 'Russian Court Politics', esp. chs. 2–4.   [61] Soloviev, *History of Russia*, XLVIII. 78–80.

[62] Ransel, *Politics of Catherinian Russia*, pp. 194–201 and 227–61, provides an illuminating if perhaps overdrawn account of his personal and political fortunes.   [63] See above, pp. 187–8.

office were particularly widespread during 1773 and, while this did not happen, his position was less secure.[64]

In the short term the Northern System and its architect were saved by the victories of Russian armies. In the longer perspective, however, these same successes aroused ideas of further expansion to the south, at the expense of the enfeebled Ottoman empire and probably in partnership with Austria, and so undermined Panin and his policies. For the moment, more pressing problems hemmed in the Empress and her advisers, and there was no obvious alternative to the Prussian alliance. Panin in particular was dependent upon this alignment, and he went as far as to renew the treaty with Frederick for a further eight years in 1777, securing in return the final abandonment of determined Prussian efforts to incorporate Danzig in its gains by the first partition. Yet this did little to secure his own position. In exactly the same way it was a pyrrhic victory for Prussia's King. Formally the alliance was now due to expire in 1788, but this did nothing to prevent its final breakdown seven years earlier. By the second half of the 1770s the alignment existed more on paper than in spirit. In the summer of 1775 Solms, in a surprisingly outspoken and also realistic analysis, had underlined that the alliance was less secure, though he believed its breakdown was still some way off.[65] Four years later his successor Goertz found that the alignment was in tatters. By September 1779 when he first arrived in the Russian capital, it would be evident that the Empress no longer regarded herself as an active ally of Prussia and instead was preoccupied with ambitious plans for expansion at Ottoman expense, which demanded links with Austria.[66]

This shift was exactly mirrored in Russo-Austrian relations. By the mid-1770s a significant softening of St Petersburg's attitude towards Vienna, its erstwhile opponent over Poland and throughout the first half of the Ottoman War, was evident.[67] The fighting had revealed the possibility of further sweeping gains at the expense of the Sultan's declining empire. These were certainly the aim of Grigory A. Potemkin, who was the Empress' favourite in 1774–6, probably married her in secret, and remained a decisive influence – as viceroy of southern Russia – upon Catherine II's policies until his death in 1791.[68] Prussia might, for the moment,

---

[64] AAE CP (Russie) 91, fo. 221; 92, fos. 176–7, 204, 349–52. During the second half of July Panin made clear his fears of declining influence and even dismissal during a revealing conversation with Solms: *SIRIO*, LXXII. 372–9; cf. *SIRIO*, LXXII. 379–80. Prussia's envoy, it should be said, was more sanguine and proved to be more accurate: *SIRIO*, LXXII. 382–3. See also *Bernstorffsche Papiere*, III. 216; Ransel, *Politics of Catherinian Russia*, p. 238.

[65] See his despatch to Frederick II, 27 July 1775, GStAPK Rep. 96.58.G, fo. 29. This contrasted sharply with Panin's more roseate view, for which see, e.g., GStAPK, fos. 31–2.

[66] See Graf J.E. von Goertz, *Mémoire sur la Russie (1786)*, ed. Wolfgang Stribrny, in *Veröffentlichungen des Osteuropainstitut München* 34 (1969), pp. 9–75, at pp. 18–19. His predecessor Solms was marginally more optimistic in his memoir for Goertz, but still saw problems ahead: Volz, ed., 'Katharina II.', p. 208.

[67] See e.g. the Instructions for von Asseburg, 30 Sept. 1774 OS, *SIRIO*, CXXXV. 231–2, 235, 240.

[68] Madariaga, *Russia*, chs. 22 and 23. There is now a lively and informative biography by Simon Sebag Montefiore, *Prince of Princes: The Life of Potemkin* (London, 2000), which contains much new material on the 1770s.

remain Russia's formal diplomatic partner, but Austria more and more had the status of an ally in waiting.[69] Frederick was particularly concerned that Russo-Austrian co-operation to drive the Ottomans out of Europe would create the alliance which he dreaded.[70] Though there were moments when he believed a formal treaty less likely, he remained anxious at the *rapprochement* in progress.[71]

This change was quite fundamental, and its consequences were to be equally profound. It was also evident to the King at a surprisingly early stage. He recognised that the Polish partition might have averted a wider war and secured West Prussia, but it had also moved Austria decisively into Russia's political orbit. The alliance between the two eastern empires had been brought much closer by the Frederick's success in sponsoring partition, as well as by the wider developments which were simultaneously undermining the Northern System. This in turn threatened Prussia with international isolation and even the loss of her status as a great power. The same division of Europe into two separate diplomatic spheres, which the King recognised had facilitated the partition, also threatened to work to the disadvantage of Prussia and her international position in the longer term, if the other two eastern powers combined against him. It was not that Frederick feared the immediate loss of the alliance upon which Prussia's enhanced political status had depended since 1764. Though Solms' despatches from St Petersburg, based as they were upon uniquely favoured access to Panin[72] and incorporating his distinctive view of events, charted the foreign minister's decline and his own exaggerated sense of this, Frederick was more sanguine and proved to be more accurate. He seems to have believed that the minister would survive for several years, and instead was more concerned with Prussia's security in the medium and longer term, which he sought to protect through a series of initiatives.

The most obvious was an attempt to reinforce his own links with Russia while, simultaneously, seeking to disrupt the *rapprochement* between St Petersburg and Vienna and to place any obstacles he could in the way of this.[73] This was a continuation of the King's established approach, which was now pursued even more actively. While never neglecting his own interests and periodically asserting his political independence, Frederick demonstrated a remarkable willingness to support Russia by whatever means necessary: whether this involved the diplomatic intimidation of Sweden in 1772–3[74] or a more generalised adoption of many of Catherine II's objectives as his own. In time other stratagems were adopted in an attempt to prolong the alliance: in 1776 Prince Henry, with the King's enthusiastic backing, visited Russia for a second time and sought to exploit his undoubted

---

[69] E.g. *SIRIO*, LXXII. 479.   [70] *Pol. Corr.*, XXXII. 583.   [71] *Pol. Corr.*, XXXIII. 246–7, 528.

[72] It was plausibly claimed that the Prussian envoy saw everything, including Russian diplomatic despatches, in sharp contrast to the minister's marked reserve towards his Austrian counterpart: AAE CP (Russie) 91, fo. 46.

[73] The most recent study of relations during the 1770s is Stribrny, *Die Russlandpolitik*, pp. 49–127, though its emphases are rather different from the account which follows.   [74] See above, p. 229.

personal friendship with Catherine II to strengthen and extend Prussia's key alignment.[75] This was also the purpose of the splendid and ornate reception which the Grand Duke Paul received throughout the Hohenzollern territories and especially at the Prussian court later that same year when he travelled there in the company of the returning Prince Henry in order to inspect his new fiancée, the Princess Sophie Dorothea of Württemberg, who was Frederick the Great's niece.[76] The episode provides one of the more improbable sights of eighteenth-century Europe: that of the strongly misogynist King acting as a fairy godfather to the young couple. The purpose was clearly political: it was likely that Paul would, one day, become Russian ruler, and Frederick hoped to win him over to support the Prussian alliance.[77]

The second strand was an attempt to disrupt the conclusion of a Russo-Austrian alliance. The King's efforts were apparent as early as March 1772, the month after the Russo-Prussian convention to seize Polish territories, and were pursued intermittently thereafter.[78] The King's principal tactic came to be that of emphasising Austria's own considerable territorial ambitions and underlining that these made her a competitor to St Petersburg, particularly in the Balkans, and therefore a less satisfactory ally than Prussia – of course – had been. Vienna's efforts to extend its gains from Poland after 1772, and its annexation of the Bukovina in 1774–5, were valuable ammunition in this campaign, while Joseph II's restless ambition and supposed plans of territorial aggrandisement were repeatedly stressed.[79] The King also continued to emphasise Austria's military and financial weakness – in sharp contrast to Prussia's strength – in his diplomacy at St Petersburg. Whether these and similar stratagems did much to bolster his alliance or even to delay Russia's *rapprochement* with Vienna must be doubted. One fundamental problem was that Frederick was preaching to the converted, since Solms' principal point of contact was Panin: himself committed to maintaining and extending the alliance.[80] Here the Prussian diplomat's concentration upon the foreign minister, a feature of his entire mission, rebounded upon the envoy and his royal superior. Working through Panin had become a diplomatic *cul-de-sac*, in view of the political reconfiguration at the Russian court.

The importance of these initiatives lies rather in the revelation of the King's fundamental anxieties. From the moment of the first partition Frederick was working

[75] Easum, *Prince Henry of Prussia*, pp. 282–8; Robert Stupperich, 'Die zweite Reise des Prinzen Heinrich von Preussen nach Petersburg', *JGO* 3 (1938), pp. 580–600.
[76] See McGrew, *Paul I of Russia*, pp. 95–8. In 1773 Paul had married a Princess of Hesse-Darmstadt, but she had died in childbirth in April 1776. Sophia Dorothea had earlier been considered as a possible bride, but rejected on account of her youth. This marriage reinforced Russia's established links with Württemberg.
[77] These efforts evidently enjoyed some success: Goertz, *Mémoire sur la Russie*, ed. Stribrny, p. 20.
[78] *SIRIO*, LXXII. 53; cf. *SIRIO*, LXXII. 7–8.
[79] E.g. *Pol. Corr.*, XXXIX. 249. For the seizure of the Bukovina, see below, pp. 244–8.
[80] This is apparent from the Prussian despatches for this period: those for 1772–4 are in *SIRIO*, LXXII, while those for 1775 have not been printed and are in GStAPK Rep. 96.58 F and G.

to delay and, if he could not postpone indefinitely, to prepare for the diplomatic iso-lation which he dreaded and which he would face nine years later, with the conclu-sion of a Russo-Austrian alliance in spring 1781. One way in which he sought future security was by reopening links with London and Versailles, which he had disdained for a decade. From 1772 onwards a genuine attempt to rebuild relations with the two western powers was evident. Its purpose was to prepare the ground for a future alli-ance, preferably (as far as Frederick was concerned) with France, failing that with Britain, which would have to be attempted when the feared Austro-Russian treaty came to be signed. This strategy first became apparent in 1772–4, during a serious dispute with the British government over Danzig, which Prussia's King made a determined and prolonged effort to include in his territorial gains from the first par-tition.[81] Located at the mouth of the river Vistula, Danzig was the principal *entre-pôt* for Poland's external trade. Frederick believed that its annexation would enable him to levy tolls on its trade and also to divert some of the commerce to other Prussian ports, above all Stettin. This would enrich both the Hohenzollern state and its subjects, important objectives after the Seven Years War. The complicity of Russia and Austria in the partition and in the subsequent attempts to enlarge the shares of all three powers, together with St Petersburg's other problems at this point, enabled Frederick to pursue his aim through a mixture of diplomatic pres-sure and direct military force against the city. Britain emerged as an improbable champion of Danzig's cause. The town contained a sizeable British merchant com-munity which exerted pressure on the government in London. Danzig was also an important source of Baltic naval stores, upon which the Royal Navy was dependent. These considerations led to a series of bruising diplomatic exchanges. Prusso-British relations had been extremely poor since 1763 and these clashes caused a further deterioration.

This bad feeling, however, was largely on Britain's side. The dispute's wider importance was its demonstration of Frederick's new attitude. He certainly sneered in his familiar way at London's feeble representations, styling George III the 'Don Quixote of Danzig'.[82] Yet even more striking, at the end of a decade during which diplomacy had been poisoned primarily by the Prussian King's behaviour, was the surprising moderation which he now demonstrated in a dispute which could very easily have been inflamed.[83] At the height of the clashes he declared that he wished 'to live on good terms with that crown [Britain]'.[84] This rather surprising statement revealed his conviction that he must improve relations, and his anxiety that Prussia

---

[81] The only detailed study of this episode is still Wolfgang Michael, *Englands Stellung zur Ersten Teilung Polens* (Hamburg and Leipzig, 1890); a brief account from a British perspective is in Scott, *British Foreign Policy*, pp. 197–201.

[82] *Pol. Corr.*, XXXIII. 387; XXXIV. 16, 211, 226: the King never allowed a *bon mot* to go to waste!

[83] At this point the King also seems to have gone out of his way to favour Britain's new minister in Berlin, James Harris, by speaking to him frequently: AAE CP (Prusse) 192, fo. 22.

[84] *Pol. Corr.*, XXXIV. 7. This despatch to Solms, 3 July 1773, is illuminating on the King's more moder-ate attitude towards Britain by this point.

might one day be forced back into a British alliance, though for the moment any such re-alignment remained improbable. It was to remain his approach throughout the final decade of his reign, when diplomacy was rather more cordial than during the 1760s.[85] Indeed, in 1782 he went as far as to declare that Britain – rather than France, as he had hitherto believed – might represent Prussia's best route out of diplomatic isolation. Louis XVI's weak leadership had further reduced his monarchy's international reputation, while intervention in the American War had completely undermined the French financial system.[86]

In the 1770s, however, relations with London were less important. During this decade it was towards France that Frederick primarily looked for his insurance policy, convinced that her alliance with Austria had broken down over the Polish partition and that a *rapprochement* with Versailles was possible.[87] This was the object of the favourable treatment given from 1772–3 onwards to the new French representative in Berlin, the marquis du Pons.[88] For a King who treated the diplomatic corps with sovereign contempt, and notoriously devoted very little time to the formalities of diplomacy, his friendly behaviour towards France's minister was politically significant. Improved relations were also advanced by Vergennes' appointment in summer 1774. His predecessor d'Aiguillon had been generally hostile towards Frederick, after the failed *rapprochement* in 1771 and the King's leading role in the first partition. Vergennes by contrast wanted better relations, which he believed would be a way of putting pressure on Austria and regaining control over the established alliance with Vienna.[89] This objective coincided with Prussian intentions and made possible a marked improvement in diplomacy. It culminated in a series of informal approaches by Prussia for a French alliance in 1776–9.[90] These were rejected by Vergennes, who viewed them as disingenuous and a mere stratagem to weaken France's links with Austria.[91] In fact the overtures were a genuine attempt by Frederick to improve relations and so pave the way for an eventual alliance, though they were completely unsuccessful.

The King had contributed to Prussia's predicament and to the isolation which threatened. He himself had worsened relations with London by his propaganda

---

[85] The softening was noted by Horst Dippel, who was inclined to attribute it to Frederick's wish to develop commercial relations with Britain. This was undoubted, but it was less important than his political objectives at this period: 'Prussia's English Policy after the Seven Years War', *Central European History* 4 (1971), pp. 195–214, esp. pp. 204, 213–14.

[86] *Die politischen Testamente*, ed. Dietrich, pp. 716–18.

[87] These initiatives have not been the subject of a separate study. They are most apparent in the despatches of France's representatives in Berlin: AAE CP (Prusse) 190–8 *passim*. See especially 191, fo. 21; 192, fos. 214–15; 193, fos. 410–18.

[88] This did not, however, prevent the King denouncing France's representative as an Austrian stooge when the broader requirements of his policy required!: *Pol. Corr.*, XXXIX. 13. Pons arrived in Berlin in June 1772.   [89] Murphy, *Vergennes*, p. 214.

[90] A detailed study of Prusso-French relations at this period is badly needed. The overtures can be reconstructed from *Pol. Corr.*, XXXVIII–XLII, and AAE CP (Prusse) 195–8.

[91] See his despatch to Breteuil, 9 July 1777, AAE CP (Autriche) 332, fos. 92–3, for an important analysis of the Prussian approaches.

campaign against successive ministries during the 1760s and by the links which his representatives cultivated with the parliamentary opposition.[92] The poor state of diplomacy during the 1770s and early 1780s, in spite of Frederick's efforts, was due primarily to Britain's lingering and deep-rooted distrust of the King himself. This also existed at Versailles, where Frederick's behaviour during the 1740s and 1750s, when he appeared to have abandoned France on no fewer than four occasions, still inspired suspicion and resentment. Europe's chancelleries had long memories, and Prussia's King had an established reputation for duplicity, faithlessness, and opportunism. It was only partly deserved. The problem was that the clear-sighted and single-minded way in which he conducted his state's foreign policy took little account of the susceptibilities of actual or potential allies. The resulting suspicion of Prussia and her ruler was exacerbated by Frederick's malicious if often memorable *bon mots*.

There were more fundamental reasons why these initiatives failed. The political division of Europe into two separate spheres, advanced by the Seven Years War and completed by the early 1770s, was central to the King's problems. Frederick had been among the earliest to appreciate this structural change and its implications: his rejection of either western power as a potential ally after 1763 was based upon his recognition that neither could be guaranteed to support Prussia in central Europe, as well as his fear of being dragged into a new Anglo-French war. The problem was that this same change was now operating against Frederick's own foreign policy, by denying him the alliance with Britain or France which he believed one day would be essential but which the outbreak of the War of American Independence in 1775 made even less likely, since Vergennes – like Choiseul before him – intended to neutralise Europe while fighting Britain overseas. Even more important, however, was the simultaneously realignment of Austrian and Russian diplomacies, which was apparent to Prussia's King but which he was quite unable to influence, far less prevent.

III

The 1770s saw a reconfiguration of Habsburg policy towards Russia, supervised by Kaunitz whose control over Vienna's foreign policy was almost complete at this period. Frederick wrongly suspected that the Emperor was the principal advocate of a Russian alliance, when the Chancellor was becoming the key figure.[93] Though a formal agreement between the two powers was impossible as long as Maria Theresa lived and was not to be concluded until 1781, the ground was prepared by the *rapprochement* after the first partition.[94] It was rooted in the same concern at the growth of Russian power and influence to the south and south-east of the Monarchy

---

[92] Scott, *British Foreign Policy*, pp. 66, 200.   [93] *Pol. Corr.*, XXXII. 565.
[94] See Maria Theresa's revealing testimony to this: *MT–MA*, III. 334. For her firm opposition to any such treaty, see above, p. 119.

evident during the war of 1768–74.[95] Kaunitz – like Joseph II – had aimed hitherto to keep Russia at a distance from Habsburg territory, but by the mid-1770s this was becoming more and more difficult. The scale of St Petersburg's successes, and the considerable territorial gains to which these victories led at Kuchuk-Kainardji, alarmed the Chancellor and forced him to reconsider his diplomatic strategy.[96]

Kaunitz was especially concerned at the strategic implications of Russia's wide-ranging annexations along the northern littoral of the Black Sea. In particular control over the Crimea seemingly enabled Catherine II's state to attack Constantinople directly and, in the Chancellor's febrile imagination, to overthrow the Sultan's power at a stroke. After 1774 Kaunitz believed the Ottoman empire to be in terminal decline. It was why he rejected Thugut's suggestion that Austria should provide the Porte with a territorial guarantee as a way of resisting a further Russian advance, which the Chancellor viewed as inevitable. Hitherto the Khanate had served as an Ottoman sally-port into the Russian mainland.[97] It was now trans-formed into a potential launching pad for an amphibious Russian assault on the Sultan's capital. This in turn weakened one important foundation of Austro-Russian co-operation against the Ottomans during the first half of the eighteenth century. In any land war, Russia would have to campaign in the Danube basin. This would be facilitated by co-operation with Vienna, which in return secured diplo-matic leverage at St Petersburg. The conflict of 1768–74 demonstrated this was no longer the case, as Russia had been able to defeat the Ottoman empire without Habsburg support. Russian victories, moreover, had been gained without the active assistance of any ally and at a time of domestic upheaval, and they inevitably accel-erated a growing disparity in the relative power of the two states. By the 1770s the Chancellor, who had earlier viewed Catherine II's régime as weak and vulnerable, saw Russia as a dynamic power whose potential was unlimited.[98] Her favourable geo-strategic position made her all-but-invulnerable to attack and offered boundless possibilities of further demographic and economic growth: expansion which would only increase the relative weakness of Austria, who might decline to the status of a minor power or be reduced to a Russian client. Yet there was no obvious solution to Vienna's predicament.

Austria's fundamental problem, as throughout the eighteenth century, was that the scale of her commitments exceeded the resources which she could mobilise to support them. Kaunitz believed that the Monarchy needed the security provided by

---

[95] See above, pp. 203–4.

[96] His attitude is brought into sharp focus by Harvey L. Dyck, 'Pondering the Russian Fact: Kaunitz and the Catherinian Empire in the 1770s', *Canadian Slavonic Papers* 22 (1981), pp. 451–69, on which the following discussion largely depends. For his alarm at Russian gains, see Riedesel to Frederick II, 24 and 27 Nov. 1773 and 6 Aug. 1774 (reporting the Russo-Ottoman peace settlement) in GStAPK Rep. 96.47.L and Rep. 96.47.N. Johann Hermann Freiherr von Riedesel had replaced Edelsheim as envoy extraordinary in autumn 1773, arriving in Vienna in late September. He would remain there until 1785.   [97] See above, p. 196.

[98] See his view in 1776, quoted by Klueting, *Die Lehre von der Macht der Staaten*, p. 120.

its defensive alliance with France, which protected Habsburg interests in the southern Netherlands and the Italian Peninsula. Though this had collapsed in the early 1770s,[99] the appointment of Vergennes as French foreign minister in summer 1774 inaugurated a new era in relations. Though the Austro-French axis was never as secure as it had been under Choiseul, it revived during Vergennes' ministry (1774–87) when for a time it was to be one source of Vienna's security. The Chancellor also regarded rivalry with Prussia as ineradicable. The exigencies of the Russo-Ottoman War might have led him to work with Frederick, but such co-operation was transient or, at least, impermanent. Kaunitz believed Prussian power incompatible with Vienna's leadership in central Europe and was anxious to see it reduced, though he recognised this would have to wait until Frederick the Great died. This led him to reject any thought of permanent political co-operation with Potsdam, and instead to come to favour partnership and an eventual alliance with Russia.

The Chancellor had never abandoned his fundamental conviction that Austria and Russia were natural allies, against Prussia in Germany and against the Ottoman empire in the south-east: this had been the basis of an enduring alignment during the generation after 1726.[100] In the mid- and later 1770s, against a background of Russia's dynamic and seemingly irreversible advance, the idea of a future *rapprochement* with St Petersburg gained ground in Vienna.[101] Co-operation, not confrontation, would be the way in which Russian power would be curbed in the future. This implied active Austrian participation in future aggression against the declining Ottoman empire, a revival of Vienna's traditional policy in south-eastern Europe. The programme was implicit in the massive instructions drawn up in spring 1777 for the Chancellor's own son, Joseph Kaunitz, who was going as ambassador to Russia.[102] It had emerged over the preceding four or five years, and incorporated the lessons – as they were viewed in Vienna – of the Russo-Ottoman conflict. This realignment mirrored developments in the Russian capital, where attachment to the Northern System and to the Prussian alliance which stood at its heart was simultaneously being weakened.[103] By the mid-1770s a significant Austro-Russian *rapprochement* was under way, though for the moment it was doing no more than preparing the ground for future co-operation.

This is the context to the final territorial annexation of 1772–5, Austria's seizure

---

[99] See above, pp. 222–3.   [100] See above, p. 51.

[101] An early symptom was provided by Kaunitz's efforts to cultivate the Russian ambassador in Vienna, Prince D.M. Golitsyn: see Riedesel to Frederick II, 8 June and 13 July 1774, GStAPK Rep. 96.47.N. The ostensible reason was the question of the boundaries of Austria's Polish gains, but the Chancellor seems to have had longer-term aims.

[102] These instructions were glossed and partially printed by E. Winter, 'Grundlinien der österreichischen Russlandpolitik am Ende des 18. Jahrhunderts', *Zeitschrift für Slawistik* 4 (1959), pp. 94–110. Frederick, of course, saw the appointment of a Kaunitz to St Petersburg as especially alarming and was soon worrying about the new ambassador's efforts to undermine the Prusso-Russian alliance: *Pol. Corr.*, xxxix. 29, 134.   [103] See above, p. 237.

of the Bukovina.[104] During the second half of the Russo-Ottoman War there had been clear interest in Vienna in securing lands in any partition of the Sultan's territories. Maria Theresa was firmly opposed to such schemes, believing that Vienna had earlier abandoned the Ottoman empire when it was an ally and should not complete the betrayal by seizing territory when it was in no position to resist. The Empress' moral approach to foreign policy was as rare as it was to be irrelevant. Both the Emperor and Kaunitz were attracted by such gains. Various improbable projects were considered, though none was adopted. In 1773 Joseph II, who was an inveterate traveller, went on an extended tour of the Monarchy's eastern territories, including the provinces seized from Poland in the previous year.[105] In the course of this his acquisitive eye fell upon two areas of nominally Ottoman territory, Old Orsova in the north-west of Wallachia and the region in northern Moldavia which came to be known as the Bukovina. This was a quadrilateral of territory wedged between Transylvania and the new acquisition of Galicia. Its strategic value was considerable, since it would facilitate links between the Monarchy and its Polish gains, direct communications between which were all but impossible because of the intervening Carpathian Mountains.[106] The region would also be a valuable military base in any future war involving either the Ottoman empire or Russia. This was why Kaunitz in particular was keen to acquire the Bukovina.[107] Its economic value at the time was judged to be much less: in 1773 Joseph II pronounced it a 'real desert', though its agrarian development would later be notable.[108]

The Chancellor's own interest in securing Ottoman territory was considerable. In February 1773 he had put forward an abortive proposal to purchase 'little Wallachia' (the western region of the province which had been ruled by Austria between 1718 and 1739) from the Ottoman empire. He now transferred his attention to the potential gain identified by the Emperor. In July Austria's representative in Constantinople, Thugut, was instructed to secure the cession of the Bukovina. The secret Austro-Ottoman treaty signed two years before had provided that Vienna would be granted Ottoman territory as a reward for its assistance against Russia, and Kaunitz professed to believe that this was the Monarchy's right. Since Moldavia and Wallachia had been returned by the occupying Russians to the Porte, he claimed Austria was entitled to a territorial reward. But the treaty had never been ratified, and Vienna had given no effective support to the Sultan's war effort. When Thugut raised the question of ceding lands to the Habsburgs, Ottoman resentment

---

[104] There are accounts in Arneth, *GMT*, VIII. 469–89; Beer, *Erste Theilung Polens*, II. 261–75; and Roider, *Austria's Eastern Question*, pp. 131–50, on which the following discussion is principally based. There is also a volume entitled *Rapt de la Bukovine, d'après des documents authentiques* (Paris, 1875), which the British Library catalogue attributes to 'D.A. Sturdza'. An anniversary production, Romanian nationalist in tone and strongly anti-Austrian, its value lies in the substantial, though highly selective, extracts which it prints from the correspondence between Kaunitz and Thugut.

[105] For his journey, see the account in Beales, *Joseph II*, pp. 359–65.

[106] *MT–JII*, II. 47–8, for the Emperor's view of the advantages conferred by its acquisition.

[107] Dyck, 'Pondering the Russian Fact', p. 461.   [108] Beales, *Joseph II*, p. 301.

and opposition became very clear. At first Kaunitz ignored the advice provided by his shrewd and experienced representative in Constantinople, to the effect that the territory was only to be had by force and not by diplomacy, and continued to emphasise Austria's 'right' to a territorial gain. By the early summer of 1774, however, the Chancellor had come to recognise that Thugut was correct and that bullying backed by the threat of military intervention would have to be employed to secure the Bukovina. In keeping with this new approach Habsburg troops were sent to occupy parts of the Ottoman province of Moldavia, to support Vienna's claims and to put pressure on Constantinople, which was in no position to resist such demands, as Austria knew.[109]

Though the Bukovina was nominally under Ottoman suzerainty, it had been occupied by Russian troops for much of the war. In the immediate aftermath of the treaty of Kuchuk-Kainardji, Vienna secured the Russian commander Rumyantsev's agreement that, as his forces withdrew, Austria's soldiers would occupy the area. St Petersburg was not consulted but presented with a *fait accompli*.[110] On 20 August 1774 Habsburg regiments moved into the Bukovina. It remained to impose this annexation on a prostrate Ottoman empire. Austria's action was deeply resented in Constantinople, which sent reinforcements to Moldavia and Wallachia early in 1775. It was countered by Austrian military mobilisation in the early weeks of the year, and this intimidation proved more effective.[111] The Porte was unable to resist, and Thugut and Kaunitz rammed home the message that the defeated Ottoman empire had to accept this latest territorial encroachment, by a power which had appeared to be a friend and, briefly, even an ally.[112] The Chancellor rightly calculated that Russia would view favourably any Austro-Ottoman war, since it would assist St Petersburg in imposing the Kuchuk-Kainardji settlement on Constantinople.[113] Negotiations were quickly concluded. Austria agreed that Orsova might remain in Ottoman hands, but secured the Bukovina by an agreement finalised on the night of 2–3 April 1775. Its transfer was incorporated into a formal Austro-Ottoman treaty signed on 7 May 1775, by which Constantinople agreed to cede the province, which was then subjected to full-scale military government by Vienna.[114]

Austria had secured a significant territorial gain without having to fire a shot or

---

[109] For its weakness and vulnerability, see Thugut's extended report to Kaunitz, 3 Sept. 1774, printed in Hammer, *Histoire de l'empire Ottoman*, XV. 495–500; see also his later despatch of 4 Mar. 1775, *Rapt de la Bukovine*, p. 57.

[110] Arneth, *GMT*, VIII. 472; Madariaga, *Russia*, p. 617 n. 44; Kaunitz to Thugut, 20 Sept. 1774, in *Rapt de la Bukovine*, p. 29.   [111] See Riedesel's despatches for that period in GStAPK Rep. 96.48.A.

[112] See in particular Thugut to Kaunitz, 4 Jan. 1775, *Rapt de la Bukovine*, pp. 31–6, esp. p. 36.

[113] Arneth, *GMT*, VIII. 477.

[114] It is striking that Prussia's minister in Vienna was kept in the dark until the actual agreement had been signed. Riedesel was only able to report the formal annexation of the Bukovina in mid-June: see his despatches to Frederick II, 13 and 17 June 1775, GStAPK Rep. 96.48.A.

expend a substantial sum of money: in sharp contrast to Kaunitz's proposal two years earlier that upwards of 5 million *gulden* be offered for little Wallachia. In the context of the substantial territorial changes of 1772–4, the annexation of the Bukovina was a mere coda. But the episode possesses considerable wider significance. In the first place – and in contrast to Vienna's legalistic discourse which had accompanied the Polish partition – there was surprisingly little talk of enforcing Habsburg 'claims' to the area, though the usual search for a plausible pretext was made.[115] Nor could the annexation be portrayed as a trophy of war, a cession made to a victor by the defeated Ottoman empire. It was rather an act of pure *Realpolitik*: the brutal seizure, from a defeated state, of territory by a power which had claimed to be friendly. It was predictably bewailed by Maria Theresa, who admitted that there was no basis for it and then acquiesced in the annexation.[116] Yet it was more than simple political opportunism. The episode extended the principles which had underpinned the partition of Poland into south-eastern Europe. It also underlined the region's new importance and, as an essential corollary, of relations with St Petersburg for Habsburg policy-makers. Kaunitz, as he frankly admitted, would try to uphold the Ottoman empire's territorial position in Europe for as long as this could be done, but Austria would have to join in any partition of its lands which Russia might bring about.[117] Catherine II's assent to the Austrian military occupation and subsequent annexation amounted to passive support of Vienna's gain. While the final stages of the Pugachev revolt were a more immediate concern for the Empress, her attitude was also a portent of future developments.[118] So too was Panin's impotent and probably disingenuous opposition – directed towards Potsdam – and his resentment expressed to Solms at the whole transaction.[119] Significantly, Russia's foreign minister also told the Austrian ambassador that he personally favoured the annexation, but warned him Prussia might oppose it.[120] This revealed his conviction that alliance with Vienna would one day supersede the links he had upheld with Prussia, and his own political opportunism. In this perspective the seizure of the Bukovina revealed the new alignments in St Petersburg

---

[115] It was found in the claims to the Bukovina possessed by part of Austria's own gains by the first partition: *Rapt de la Bukovine*, p. 9.

[116] Beales, *Joseph II*, p. 301, for her view that 'We are completely in the wrong.' She subsequently expressed well-founded scepticism about Austria gaining more than Russia from a forward policy towards either the Ottoman empire or Bavaria: *MT–MA*, III. 99–100.

[117] To Thugut, 6 Jan. 1775, *Rapt de la Bukovine*, pp. 38–9.

[118] As Kaunitz noted: to Thugut, 7 Feb. 1775, *Rapt de la Bukovine*, p. 52.

[119] GStAPK Rep. 96.58.F, fos. 16, 21. When, between February and April 1775, Frederick sought to stir Russia into opposing the Austrian annexation, the minister told Solms that St Petersburg's greatest priority was now peace and added, with evident *Schadenfreude*, that in the previous year the King had rejected a similar *Russian* initiative!: GStAPK Rep. 96.58.F, fos. 54–5, 79–80, 93. When the King had first heard of the Austrian occupation of the Bukovina in autumn 1774, he had placed the preservation of peace above preventing Vienna's territorial gain: *Pol. Corr.*, XXXVI. 138–9.

[120] Arneth, *GMT*, VIII. 479–80.

which were transforming Russian foreign policy. In a broader sense it was the last in a series of wide-ranging territorial changes in 1772–5 which consummated the emergence of the eastern powers. Above all, it underlined Russia's dominant position within this axis and, more generally, within the eastern half of Europe.

Russia and the emergence of the eastern powers

Russia's territorial gains in 1772–5 were striking and, in the longer perspective, proved decisive.[1] They consolidated her leading position, created by her armies during the Seven Years War but not immediately exploited. It was further strengthened by a restoration of Russian control over Poland, where Stackelberg ruled as viceroy during the 1770s and 1780s. St Petersburg's Polish acquisitions and the annexations from the Ottoman empire were, however, rather different in nature. The first partition did not establish a new way for the great powers to expand their territories, with the exception of Austria's cynical annexation of the Bukovina and Frederick's simultaneous and ultimately unsuccessful efforts to seize Danzig. In keeping both with established ideas about the 'balance of power' and the political situation in 1771–2, Russian gains from Poland had been matched by approximately equal shares for the other eastern powers. This expressed the doctrine that no single state could be permitted to make unilateral acquisitions, since this would undermine the equilibrium which, in theory at least, existed between the great powers. This idea was to underpin the second and third partitions (1793; 1795) which were to excise Poland from the map of Europe, without a war being fought by the competing powers.[2] Together, the partitions were to move Russia's European frontier over 250 miles westwards, a process which began in 1772 and would enhance her ability to intervene in central Europe, while underlining her new political importance.

The annexations from the Ottoman empire were even more significant at the time. The gains secured in 1774 – like those later in Catherine II's reign – involved no equivalent acquisitions by any other state, with the single exception of Vienna's seizure of the Bukovina. Russia's decisive military victories, together with the new diplomatic pattern, made it impossible for either Constantinople or the other leading powers to limit her acquisitions, as prevailing ideas about the balance of power would have suggested. Efforts to do so during the 1768–74 war had all failed: exactly as every attempt to restrict St Petersburg's gains in this region during the 1780s and 1790s would do. This highlighted Russia's growing ascendancy throughout the eastern half of Europe. It also underlined warfare's decisive importance for

---

[1] Hochedlinger, *Krise und Wiederherstellung*, pp. 80–124, provides an incisive commentary on international relations between the mid-1750s and the late 1780s.

[2] Austria, of course, would not take part in the second partition, due principally to Vienna's preoccupation with the war against Revolutionary France.

the development of the eighteenth-century states system, though its impact is often ignored by civilian-minded international historians. The emergence of the eastern powers was driven primarily by the political consequences of two military struggles, those of 1756–63 and 1768–74. The settlement of Kuchuk-Kainardji, which concluded the second conflict, established Russia as a Black Sea power for the first time in a millennium, and was to be the origin of her nineteenth-century dominance of south-eastern Europe. There was, however, no immediate attempt to extend the position secured in 1774. With the return of peace, Catherine II's priority once again became internal reform, abandoned six years earlier. The urgent need for this had been made clear by the Ottoman War and especially the Pugachev revolt. The next few years were to see a significant overhaul of local government, together with other reforming initiatives.

The revelation of Ottoman weakness in the war of 1768–74, however, did encourage Russia's appetite for further acquisitions in the longer perspective. Potemkin, who became governor-general of the new territories and 'viceroy of the south', certainly harboured plans for further annexations from the Ottoman empire.[3] The Empress' favourite was to play a crucial role in the military conquest and colonisation of the southern lands, and also to exert remarkable influence over Catherine II's own political outlook. His ideas were one principal source of the ambitious if rather vague scheme known as the 'Greek Project', which by the late 1770s was influencing Russian policy. It envisaged the expulsion of the declining Ottoman empire from Europe and the re-establishment of an Orthodox Byzantine empire ruled by the Empress' own grandson, born in 1779 and significantly christened 'Constantine', with perhaps another principality for Potemkin himself. Recent scholarship has questioned how precise these aims ever were, and has added the important *caveat* that, at least in the later 1780s, Russia lacked the necessary military and financial resources to implement them.[4] It has also been emphasised that the 'Greek Project' was in origin and always remained a personal objective of Catherine and Potemkin:

---

[3] There is still much of interest in the article by Raeff, 'The Style of Russia's Imperial Policy', reprinted under the title 'In the Imperial Manner', in Raeff, ed., *Catherine the Great*, pp. 197–246. See also Madariaga, *Russia*, ch. 23, and the biography of Potemkin cited in the next footnote.

[4] The major contributions have been the major and sceptical article, surveying the secondary literature and printed sources, by Edgar Hösch, 'Das sogennante "griechische Projekt Katharinas II.": Ideologie und Wirklichkeit der russischen Orientpolitik in der zweiten Hälfte des 18. Jahrhunderts', *JGO* NF 12 (1964), pp. 168–206, and an overlapping series of articles by Hugh Ragsdale, incorporating the results of new research in Russian and European diplomatic archives: 'New Light on the Greek Project: A Preliminary Report', in R.P. Bartlett, A.G. Cross, and Karen Rasmussen, eds., *Russia and the World of the Eighteenth Century* (Columbus, OH, 1988), pp. 493–501; 'Montmorin and Catherine's Greek Project: Revolution in French Foreign Policy', *Cahiers du monde russe et soviétique* 27 (1986), pp. 27–44; 'Evaluating the Traditions of Russian Aggression: Catherine II and the Greek Project', *Slavonic and East European Review* 66 (1988), pp. 91–117; 'Russian Projects of Conquest in the Eighteenth Century', in Hugh Ragsdale, ed., *Imperial Russian Foreign Policy* (Cambridge, 1993), pp. 75–102, esp. pp. 82–100. The new biography by Montefiore, *Prince of Princes*, ch. 14, provides considerable evidence for Potemkin's decisive role in the genesis of the project: see esp. p. 220.

only four other individuals in St Petersburg (A.A. Bezborodko, who replaced Panin in 1781, and three officials) knew of these plans.[5]

The peace of Kuchuk-Kainardji marked an important stage in the genesis of the 'Greek Project'. From Peter I's reign onwards, stronger and closer ties had been forged between Russian Orthodoxy and Greek Orthodoxy. During the second half of the eighteenth century Greek hopes and expectations focussed increasingly upon Russia. As the Ottoman power waned, Catherine II came to be seen as the guardian of Orthodoxy and to appreciate the political potential of this role. In this respect the 1774 peace settlement and the position it supposedly gave to Russia as protector of Balkan Christianity were to prove a turning point. These developments were part of the intellectual background to the 'Greek Project', which aimed to restore the Christian Eastern Empire with Constantinople as its capital. Renewed expansion to the south-west, however, was at first to be driven as much by instability on the periphery as by a conscious imperialist policy imposed from the centre. After 1774 St Petersburg's treatment of the newly independent Crimea was to be strongly reminiscent of its policy in Poland a decade earlier.[6] Russian military power was used first to establish Sahin Girai as Khan and then to put down a revolt against his rule. Constantinople resented Catherine II's growing control, but was powerless to do anything effective to oppose it. Indeed, the Porte was obliged, by the Convention of Aynali Kavak signed early in 1779, to acknowledge the Empress' control of the Khanate, now more than ever a Russian satellite. Sahin Girai's refusal to accept his designated role of puppet ruler led to further military intervention and to the effective conquest of the Crimea by forces under Potemkin. The Khanate was then formally annexed in April 1783.

Its acquisition was to give new momentum to Russia's southern expansion and this, in turn, increased tension with Constantinople. The outcome was Catherine II's second Ottoman War of 1787–92. The Austrian alliance concluded in 1781, as the first important political act of Joseph II's personal rule, brought Habsburg military support, though this proved to be less important than had been anticipated.[7] This conflict was to be less successful than its predecessor, though the Empress' forces would eventually gain the upper hand. It was concluded by the Treaty of Jassy (1792) which strengthened Russia's position on the Black Sea through the acquisition of the fortress of Ochakov and the territory on its northern littoral between the Bug and the Dniester. These gains were less important than the annexations made during the Empress' first Ottoman War, which had established both a dominant Russian position there and brought the Crimea firmly into St

---

[5] Ragsdale, 'Evaluating the Traditions', p. 97.
[6] Fisher, *Russian Annexation*, chs. 4–7, covers events down to 1783.
[7] The standard authority on the conclusion of the alliance and the unusual form it took is Isabel de Madariaga, 'The Secret Austro-Russian Treaty of 1781', *Slavonic and East European Review* 38 (1959–60), pp. 114–45.

Petersburg's sphere of influence. The territories acquired from the Ottoman empire in 1774, 1783 and 1792 far eclipsed in scale and importance any unilateral acquisitions by other states in Europe during Catherine's lifetime. During the 1760s France had made two significant gains, Corsica and Lorraine, while a quarter century earlier Frederick the Great's seizure of Silesia had been the foundation of Prussia's own emergence as a leading state. But none of these gains approached in scale Russia's southern expansion, for which the war of 1768–74 had been decisive.

This dramatic expansion, together with the gains from Poland, marked out Catherine II's empire as the most successful and dynamic continental state during the second half of the eighteenth century. That impression was strengthened by the simultaneous and striking development of Russian power at sea.[8] Only during the Empress' reign did Russia become an international – as distinct from a merely regional – naval power. The first Ottoman War was to be the turning point. Russia's fleet had been confined to Baltic waters until the early years of that conflict, when squadrons accomplished a long and difficult voyage to the eastern Mediterranean, where they had won an important victory at Chesma. Though this success was not fully exploited, the impetus to naval expansion was undoubted. The second half of Catherine II's reign was to see a major programme of construction. The Baltic battle fleet which, around 1770, had been some 54,000 tons in total, doubled to reach 110,000 tons in 1785 and increased again to 145,000 tons by 1790.[9] The building of a Black Sea fleet, first in Kherson (on the Dnieper estuary) and then after 1783 in Sevastopol, was made possible by Russia's dramatic southern expansion. The acquisition of the Crimean fortresses of Kerch and Yenikale in 1774 had been crucial. They controlled the exit from the Sea of Azov, and so enabled Russian warships to sail into the Black Sea. The Khanate's subsequent annexation made Russia the major naval power there, though Catherine II at first pursued a defensive strategy which paralleled that adopted in the Baltic for much of the eighteenth century.[10] Though continuing Ottoman control of the Straits remained an important obstacle to further expansion into the Mediterranean and the Sultan's fleet at first outnumbered its new rival, the possibilities were apparent by the Empress' final decade. Within twenty years Russia had built the fourth largest fighting navy in the world: only the great Atlantic colonial powers, Britain, France and Spain, were now more formidable at sea.[11]

Russia's military potential within Europe was also enhanced at this time. Catherine II's success in finally removing the triple threat which Sweden, Poland and the Ottoman empire had posed since the mid-sixteenth century, together with

---

[8] There is a detailed study by Bode, *Die Flottenpolitik Katharinas II.*. A brief comparative account, with some interesting statistics, is provided by Glete, *Navies and Nations*, I. 235–8, 296–8 and 307.

[9] Glete, *Navies and Nations*, I. 297–8. These figures are in displacement tons.

[10] LeDonne, *Russian Empire*, pp. 38–9; see above, p. 19.

[11] Glete, *Navies and Nations*, I. 298; for the fleet's numerical strength on the eve of the second Ottoman War, see Madariaga, *Russia*, p. 396.

her impressive territorial gains in 1772–5, fundamentally altered the geo-political situation. It also facilitated the adoption of a new strategy of military defence during the later 1770s.[12] Hitherto, the ever present danger of attack from several different quarters had discouraged the establishment of a permanent defence perimeter. Troops had instead been based in Great Russia and sent out to the frontier when an invasion threatened or when a war was to be waged abroad. This had magnified the problem of distance faced by all Russian armies in their efforts to intervene decisively in Europe. Catherine II's success in removing the traditional threats and expanding her own empire enabled a new approach to territorial defence to be adopted. It was made possible by a notable expansion of the Russian army after 1774. By 1786 the infantry numbered almost 220,000, more than twice the total when peace was restored in 1763, and it rose again to 280,000 by the final year of the Empress' reign. In the 1790s Russia possessed the largest army among the eastern powers.[13] This enabled Russian garrisons to be established along the entire frontier from the Baltic to the Black Sea, with secure communications, a supply network and rudimentary administration. It not merely improved Russia's own security; it placed the majority of her troops closer to central Europe and so able to intervene more rapidly.

This concentration was facilitated by a *détente* with China.[14] Relations had been tense when Catherine II came to the throne, with the cessation of trade in 1764 and the threat of a full-scale war. They quickly improved, mainly because of the Manchu régime's indifference to relations with Russia and St Petersburg's acceptance of the *status quo* on the distant eastern frontier. This enabled troops to be withdrawn from the Chinese border during the second half of the Empress' reign, and for attention and resources to be concentrated on the western and south-western frontiers. Between the 1760s and the 1790s, Russia accepted that a forward policy on the Amur river was impossible. Instead, Catherine's government concentrated its energies on the creation of an administrative, military and economic infrastructure which would facilitate a future advance. The Russian push east from the Kazakh Steppe towards the Pacific had been becalmed since the Treaty of Kiakhta of 1727, and it was not to be resumed until the final years of the Empress' own life. Russia's enhanced European role under Catherine II was never seriously impaired by anxieties in the Far East.

During the later 1770s St Petersburg began to adopt a more ambitious diplomatic strategy in Europe, in keeping with its enhanced power and dominant position. Catherine II intervened first in the Austro-Prussian War of the Bavarian Succession (1778–9) and then in the War of American Independence (1775–83). Mediation –

---

[12] LeDonne, 'Outlines of Russian Military Administration', esp. pp. 328–33, on which the following discussion is based.

[13] LeDonne, 'Outlines of Russian Military Administration', pp. 322–4, 328, gives precise figures for the official establishment. During the same period the cavalry rose from around 44,600 (1765) to some 51,500 (1796). [14] LeDonne, *Russian Empire*, pp. 170, 175–6, 352; Madariaga, *Russia*, p. 474.

jointly with France – in the conflict over Bavaria pushed Russian influence much further into central Europe.[15] St Petersburg's role in this conflict was doubly decisive. Its threat to intervene militarily on the side of Prussia, still formally Russia's ally, forced Vienna to pull back from the advanced position it had adopted, while its diplomacy then mediated a settlement which raised its own prestige in Germany. The later 1770s saw St Petersburg's influence in Europe reach wholly new levels.[16] It was evident in the decision at this period to begin work on a Russian treaty collection.[17] Russia's role in securing the Peace of Teschen (1779), which concluded the Bavarian conflict, and the skill of her envoy, Prince Nikolai Repnin, during these negotiations were both highly unusual and exemplified the new sophistication of her diplomacy.[18]

The responsibility for the empire's constitution conferred by that treaty was also novel. The Peace of Westphalia (1648), which concluded the Thirty Years War, had made France and Sweden guarantors of the imperial constitution, and Russia was now given a similar role. It conferred prestige rather than precise juridical rights. After 1779 Catherine II could only act with the consent of the two original guarantors and possessed neither the special legal status of France and Sweden, nor their unlimited ability to intervene in imperial affairs.[19] Nevertheless, Russia's new position exemplified her increased prestige and enlarged role in central Europe by the later 1770s.[20] It had its counterpart a year or two later in the suggestions, encouraged by the Empress, that she should mediate in the War of American Independence. Though these efforts were unsuccessful, Catherine II's leadership of a league of Europe's commercial states, the famous Armed Neutrality of 1780, provided the first occasion upon which Russia was able to lay down principles of international maritime law and maintain them against the two western powers.[21] This was a further illustration of the new sophistication and self-confidence of Russian diplomacy and St Petersburg's enhanced position.

Russia's renewed political advance during the later 1770s and 1780s was to be highlighted in the state-sponsored propaganda of the period.[22] This employed a

---

[15] Hellmann, 'Die Friedensschlüsse von Nystad (1721) und Teschen (1779)'.

[16] Schroeder, *Transformation of European Politics*, p. 25.   [17] See above, p. 159.

[18] *SIRIO*, LXV, contains abundant material on this episode.

[19] Karl Härter, 'Möglichkeiten und Grenzen: der Reichspolitik Russlands als Garantiemacht des Teschener Friedens (1778–1803)', in Claus Scharf, ed., *Katharina II., Rußland und Europa: Beiträge zur internationalen Forschung* (Mainz, 2001), pp. 133–81, has here modified the established view of Russia's precise role in the empire after 1779, set out by K.O. Freiherr von Aretin, for example in his 'Russia as a Guarantor Power of the Imperial Constitution under Catherine II', *Journal of Modern History* 48 (1986): Supplement – *Politics and Society in the Holy Roman Empire 1500–1806*, S141–60.

[20] For the change in Russian policy at this period, see Scharf, *Katharina II.*, pp. 399–406.

[21] The standard authority is Isabel de Madariaga, *Britain, Russia and the Armed Neutrality of 1780: Sir James Harris's Mission to St Petersburg during the American Revolution* (London, 1962); see also the same author's comments in A.G. Cross, ed., *Great Britain and Russia in the Eighteenth Century: Contacts and Comparisons* (Newtonville, MA, 1979), p. 321.

[22] This subject has recently been renewed by Richard S. Wortman, *Scenarios of Power: Myth and Ceremony in Russian Monarchy*, vol. I: *From Peter the Great to the Death of Nicholas I* (Princeton, NJ, 1995), which should be read in the light of an admiringly critical review by Isabel de Madariaga, 'The Staging of Power', *Government and Opposition* 31 (1996), 228–40.

variety of ceremonies and imagery to emphasise the continuities from the Petrine era: as, for example, in the *Te Deum* and memorial service for Peter I held after the victory at Chesma. The southern expansion was glorified by official propaganda representing Russia's greatness as a nation and as a reborn Roman Empire, a metaphor which underlined the degree of integration which had taken place.[23] The transformation of Russia's international position was pinpointed by Bezborodko's remark in the mid-1780s, that Catherine II's empire could become the 'arbiter of Europe', a notion which would have been unthinkable a generation before.[24] This dominance, created between the 1750s and the 1770s, was fully apparent to European contemporaries. Vergennes remarked in 1785 that Catherine II believed that she gave the law to the entire continent.[25] Three years earlier Grand Duke Leopold of Tuscany had gone even further. The Empress' ambitions, he declared, extended to nothing less than overthrowing the Ottoman empire, establishing two empires in its place, and changing Europe's entire political system.[26] His fears were exaggerated, but these anxieties testified to Russia's new dominance.

It was particularly evident to observers in Vienna. After the Seven Years War, Austria's ability to pursue a truly independent foreign policy had been severely circumscribed by internal and external factors: continuing financial weakness and military inferiority, dependence upon an alliance with the weakened power of France, above all the existence of a secure Russo-Prussian axis. During the 1770s Kaunitz had realigned Habsburg foreign policy in the light of the simultaneous reconfiguration of Russian objectives at this time.[27] Vienna now looked towards an alliance, the need for which was underlined by the War of the Bavarian Succession. There was one essential difference, however. By this point the Chancellor had been eclipsed by the Emperor as Vienna's leading proponent of a Russian alliance. The sending of Russian troops to support Prussia over Bavaria had highlighted the crucial importance of such links. Only Maria Theresa remained hostile, declaring in the final year of her life that she regarded Catherine II 'with aversion and horror' and she would soon pass from the scene.[28] Joseph II began the negotiations for an alliance during his own visit to the Russian court in 1780, and concluded it in May and June of the following year, barely six months after his mother's death.[29] When that alliance was concluded in 1781, however, Austria quickly found that she had exchanged subordination to an overwhelming Russo-Prussian axis for dependence upon an overmighty ally. Throughout the 1780s Joseph II and Kaunitz were agreed that Vienna was the subordinate partner, and that its need for a Russian alliance was

---

[23] Wortman, *Scenarios of Power*, I. 128, 138, 169 and 110–69 *passim*.

[24] Cited by Frank Fox, 'Negotiating with the Russians: Ambassador Ségur's Mission to Saint-Petersburg, 1784–1789', *French Historical Studies* 7 (1971–2), pp. 47–71, at p. 55.

[25] *Recueil: Naples et Parme*, ed. Joseph Reinach, p. 126.

[26] To Joseph II, 16 Dec. 1782, in *Joseph II. und Leopold von Toscana: Ihr Briefwechsel von 1781 bis 1790*, ed. Alfred Ritter von Arneth (2 vols., Vienna, 1872), I. 141–6, at p. 142; cf. *Joseph II. und Leopold von Toscana*, ed. Arneth, I. 166–70, for more on Leopold's fear of Russian power.

[27] See above, pp. 242–4.　　[28] Quoted by Beales, *Joseph II*, p. 433.

[29] For this visit, see Beales, *Joseph II*, pp. 431–8.

considerably greater than Catherine II's reliance upon Austria.[30] The Monarchy could only pursue a forward policy against Prussia or against the Ottoman empire if she had a secure Russian alliance. This could not be assumed. During Joseph's personal rule (1780–90) – as throughout the period after the Seven Years War – St Petersburg always had the option of a renewed Prussian treaty and was more than ever dominant.

Russia's dominance was predicated upon France's continuing weakness, exacerbated by her intervention in the War of American Independence and its costs, which made the monarchy's very serious financial position quite critical. During the later 1770s and the early 1780s Austria had moved imperceptibly from a French-based to a Russian-based foreign policy. The War of the Bavarian Succession was crucial in this evolution.[31] Both Joseph II and Kaunitz had expected their French ally to provide military assistance in any war against Prussia, as prescribed by the treaty signed in 1756. France was about to intervene openly on the side of the American colonists, however, and had no intention of becoming embroiled in a parallel war within Europe: the fracturing of the international system into western and eastern halves and the long-term implications of French strategy after the Seven Years War were to be particularly clear during the first half of 1778. It was only Austria's lack of an alternative ally which led her to look towards France, at a period when the western states had come to inhabit a separate political world and had little impact upon their counterparts further east. Vergennes, however, did not merely refuse Vienna all aid under the defensive alliance, on the plausible pretext that Austria was herself the aggressor over Bavaria. He ensured that Prussia learned of this refusal, an action which encouraged Frederick to take up arms to resist the planned annexations from the Electorate. The Bavarian War thus revealed the continuing frailty of Franco-Austrian links,[32] as well as Russia's quite central role and therefore her attractions as an ally to Vienna, which was inclined to blame the political failure on France.

The Austro-Russian realignment had been facilitated by Vergennes' temporary abandonment, during the American struggle, of the confrontational policy pursued by Choiseul and d'Aiguillon towards St Petersburg. France's foreign minister instead unsuccessfully sought a *rapprochement* and tried to use co-operation to control Russian expansion: exactly as Kaunitz had earlier done. Vergennes subsequently resumed an anti-Russian stance and in 1783–4 even contemplated war to

---

[30] Arneth, ed., *Joseph II. und Leopold von Toscana*, ed. Arneth, I. 180–2; for Leopold's agreement, *Joseph II. und Leopold von Toscana*, ed. Arneth, I. 270–71 and 276–81; *Joseph II., Leopold II., und Kaunitz: ihr Briefwechsel*, ed. Adolf Beer (Vienna, 1873), pp. 246–50, esp. p. 247.

[31] For the war, see the notably discriminating account by Beales, *Joseph II*, pp. 386–427; Adolf Unzer, *Der Friede von Teschen* (Kiel, 1903), which, in spite of the title, is a full and very valuable study of the conflict and of the peace settlement; Paul Oursel, *La diplomatie de la France sous Louis XVI: succession de Bavière et paix de Teschen* (Paris, 1921); Buddruss, *Die französische Deutschlandpolitik 1756–1789*, ch. 6; and Aretin, *Das Alte Reich*, III. 183–212.

[32] As Maria Theresa did not fail to note: *MT–MA*, III. 150, 161, 262.

prevent the outright annexation of the Crimea.[33] The failure of his efforts high-lighted once again both the extent of French political decline and the irresistible power of Catherine II's empire, especially in Europe's eastern borderlands. The episode underlined the continuing importance of France's decline. The emergence of the eastern powers, and the rise of Russia in particular, had been facilitated by the French monarchy's disappearance from its dominant central role in great power politics.

Prussia was even more of a victim than Austria. One recurring theme of this study has been her flawed international position after the Seven Years War. To adapt Frederick's *bon mot* about the Hohenzollern monarchy at his own accession,[34] Prussia in 1763 was a great power in name but a leading second-class state in fact: exactly as Talleyrand would subsequently declare her to be. It is revealing that, in his survey of the international system which forms part of the second Political Testament, the King had not included his own state among the great powers.[35] This presumed inferiority was primarily a matter of resources, in Frederick's eyes at least, and it had been exacerbated by the annexations of 1772–5. Through the Polish par-tition, the King had acquired new human and economic resources, together with a land bridge to East Prussia, and these were important gains. The problem was that Austria and especially Russia had secured far more territory and subjects in these years. Even more significantly, events during the Russo-Ottoman War had also stimulated a *rapprochement* between Vienna and St Petersburg, and this gathered pace during the 1770s. The conclusion of a defensive alliance between Catherine II and Joseph II in 1781 consigned the ageing Frederick and his state to the isolation and insecurity which he had feared for a decade and which were to darken his final years.[36]

Prussia's great power position after 1763 was always more vulnerable than later historians have recognised. Aping the great powers was a necessity rather than a choice. The central problem for the King was that, after the Seven Years War, Russia usually held the balance of power between Potsdam and Vienna. The conclusion and subsequent renewal of an alliance with Catherine II provided much-needed security for over a decade, while Frederick's own towering reputation and that of the formidable Prussian army also helped to discourage an attack by Austria, in any case seriously weakened. The King defended Prussia's new-found position as a great power with more skill and finesse than is sometimes recognised: he was a ruth-less and single-minded foreign minister as well as a successful military commander. Yet while he might camouflage his own state's weakness, he could exert far less influ-ence upon shifts within the international system. By the early 1770s the political division of Europe, to which Prussia's own rise had contributed significantly, was

---

[33] See Robert Salomon, *La politique orientale de Vergennes (1780–1784)* (Paris, 1935).
[34] Above, p. 20.   [35] *Die politischen Testamente*, ed. Dietrich, p. 646.
[36] The latest account of the King's foreign policy in the 1780s is Althoff, *Untersuchungen zum Gleichgewicht*, chs. 8–9.

complete. It was a fundamental change, and one which worked against Prussian interests. In this sense Charles Jenkinson's analysis had been incomplete.[37] The eastern powers had emerged, but it soon became evident that Russia enjoyed a dominant international position which would be consolidated in the decades and generations to come.

[37] Above, p. 1.

Bibliography

MANUSCRIPT SOURCES

The extensive publication during the nineteenth and early twentieth centuries of sources and source-based narrative histories bearing upon international relations means that a significant proportion of the material upon which this book is based is already in print. This is particularly so for **Austria**. Alfred Ritter von Arneth, who first wrote the history of Maria Theresa's reign and did so almost entirely from manuscript sources, summarises and quotes extensively from diplomatic correspondence in his *Geschichte Maria Theresias*; he was also the principal editor of numerous additional volumes which published *in extenso* the correspondence of members of the Habsburg family and of the leading minister, Kaunitz. Arneth's contemporary Adolf Beer was scarcely less indefatigable as an editor and an author of source-based narratives. The *SIRIO* (vols. XVIII, XLVI, CIX, CXXV) contains the despatches of Austrian diplomats from St Petersburg for 1762–76, though only the reports and not the instructions are printed. Even more material is available for **Prussia**. The *Pol. Corr.*, which prints all the diplomatic correspondence of Frederick II, together with summaries and excerpts from the incoming despatches, is the single most important source for this study. The reports of the Prussian envoy in St Petersburg, Solms, for the period 1762–74, have been printed in full in the volumes of the *SIRIO* (vols. XXII, XXXVII, LXXII), which is also an incomparable source for all aspects of **Russia**'s foreign policy. By contrast, rather less material on **France** and her international position at this period is available in print, with the exception of the great *Recueil des instructions* and the volumes devoted to the *secret du roi*; the French despatches from St Petersburg for 1762–72 can be found in the *SIRIO* (vols. CXL, CXLI, CXLIII).

These considerations dictate the strategy adopted over manuscript research in writing this study. The printed sources have been extensively utilised, and have been complemented by manuscript material in the French foreign office archives and in Berlin, where the important correspondence from Austria 1763–75 and from Russia in 1775 (which was not printed in the *SIRIO*) was principally utilised. Some material from repositories in Vienna, London and Edinburgh has also been exploited.

Archives du Ministère des Affaires Etrangères, Paris

CP (Autriche) 294, 295, 303, 304, 305, 306, 308, 311, 312, 332
CP (Danemark) 151, 152
CP (Pologne) 282, 289
CP (Prusse) 71, 110, 179, 181, 190, 191, 192, 193, 194, 195, 196, 197,198, 204, 205
CP (Prusse – Supplément) 7
CP (Rome) 865

CP (Russie) 91, 92
CP (Suède) 247, 248, 249, 255
CP (Turquie) 141, 142, 144
CP (Turquie – Supplément) 17
MD (Autriche) 38
MD (Prusse) 2, 8

Geheimes Staatsarchiv Preussischer Kulturbesitz, Berlin-Dahlem

Rep. 96.27.C
Rep. 96.46.E
Rep. 96.46.F
Rep. 96.46.F1
Rep. 96.46.G1
Rep. 96.46.H
Rep. 96.46.J
Rep. 96.46.K
Rep. 96.47.A
Rep. 96.47.B
Rep. 96.47.C
Rep. 96.47.D
Rep. 96.47.E
Rep. 96.47.K
Rep. 96.47.L
Rep. 96.47.N
Rep. 96.48.A
Rep. 96.58.F
Rep. 96.58.G

Haus-, Hof- und Staatsarchiv, Vienna

England-Korrespondenz 109, 112, 113, 115
Familienarchiv Sammelbände 88
Frankreich-Korrespondenz 35, 125
Nachlass Arneth 15
Nachlass Kaunitz (1765–1792)
Tagebuch Zinzendorf

British Library, London

Egerton 1862
Add. MSS 6810, 32934, 33024, 37054

Public Record Office, London

SP 78/258, 272, 293, 294, 295
SP 80/204, 205, 207, 211, 212

Bibliography

SP 88/71
SP 90/47, 65, 66, 82, 85, 87, 90, 93, 101
SP 91/70
SP 95/109

National Library of Scotland, Edinburgh

NLS MS 5819, 12944

Service Historique de l'Armée de Terre, Vincennes

A¹ 3444, 3445, 3446, 3471, 3472, 3473, 3474, 3511, 3631

PRINTED SOURCES

Printed sources are generally listed under the author or subject rather than the editor.

Acta Borussica: Denkmäler der Preussischen Staatsverwaltung im 18. Jahrhundert – Die Behördenorganisation und die allgemeine Staatsverwaltung Preussens im 18. Jahrhundert, ed. G. Schmoller *et al.* (16 vols., Berlin, 1894–1982).

Aufzeichnungen des Grafen William Bentinck über Maria Theresias, ed. Adolf Beer (Vienna, 1871).

Correspondance ministérielle du comte J.H.E. Bernstorff 1751–1770, ed. P. Vedel (2 vols., Copenhagen, 1882)

Correspondance entre le comte Johan Hartvig Ernst Bernstorff et le duc de Choiseul (Copenhagen, 1871)

Bernstorffsche Papiere, ed. Aage Friis (3 vols., Copenhagen, 1904–13).

Bielfeld, J.F. von, *Institutions politiques* (2 vols., The Hague, 1760).

Bielfeld, J.F. von, *Institutions politiques* (3 vols., Leiden, 1767–72; described on the title page as 'N. Edition, revue, corrigée et augmentée' and incorporating the Political Gazetteer anticipated in the first edition of 1760).

Broglie, duc de, *Le secret du roi* (2 vols., Paris, 1879).

Correspondance secrète du comte de Broglie avec Louis XV (1756–1774), ed. D. Ozanam and M. Antoine (2 vols., Paris, 1956–61).

François de Callières: The Art of Diplomacy, ed. H. M. A. Keens-Soper and Karl W. Schweizer (Leicester and New York, 1983)

Un diplomate français à la cour de Catherine II 1775–1780: journal intime du Chevalier de Corberon, ed. L.-H. Lalande (2 vols., Paris, 1901).

Mémoires du duc de Choiseul 1719–1785, ed. F. Calmettes (Paris, 1904).

Doniol, Henri, *Histoire de la participation de la France à l'établissement des Etats-Unis d'Amérique* (5 vols., Paris, 1886–92).

Danske Tractater, 1751–1800 (Copenhagen, 1882).

Diderot, Denis, and d'Alembert, Jean Le Rond, *Encyclopédie, ou Dictionnaire raisonné* (17 vols., Paris, 1751–65).

A Memoir of the Right Honourable Hugh Elliot, ed. Countess of Minto (Edinburgh, 1868).

Œuvres de Frédéric le Grand, ed. J.D.E. Preuss (30 vols., Berlin, 1846–56).

Politische Correspondenz Friedrichs des Grossen, ed. J.G. Droysen *et al.* (46 vols., Berlin, 1879–1939).

Bibliography

Masson, F., ed., 'Berlin il y a cent ans', *Revue d'histoire diplomatique* 5 (1891), pp. 28–65.

Souvenirs de Charles-Henri, Baron de Gleichen, ed. Paul Grimblot (Paris, 1868).

Goertz, Graf J.E. von, *Mémoire sur la Russie (1786)*, ed. Wolfgang Stribrny, in *Veröffentlichungen des Osteuropasinstitut München* 34 (1969), pp. 9–75.

Hertzberg, Ewald Frédérique, comte de, *Huit dissertations . . . lues dans les assemblées publiques de l'Académie Royale des Sciences et Belle-Lettres de Berlin, tenues pour l'anniversaire du roi Frédéric II dans les années 1780–1787* (Berlin, 1787).

Sbornik imperatorskogo russkogo istorischeskogo obshchestva (148 vols., St Petersburg, 1867–1916).

Joseph II., Leopold II., und Kaunitz: ihr Briefwechsel, ed. Adolf Beer (Vienna, 1873).

Joseph II. und Leopold von Toscana: ihr Briefwechsel von 1781 bis 1790, ed. Alfred Ritter von Arneth (2 vols., Vienna, 1872).

Justi, J.H.G. von, *Die Chimäre des Gleichgewichts von Europa* (Altona, 1758).

'Denkschriften des Fürsten Wenzel Kaunitz-Rittberg', ed. Adolf Beer, *AÖG* 48 (1872), pp. 1–162.

Memoirs and Correspondence of Sir Robert Murray Keith, ed. Mrs Gillespie Smyth (2 vols., London, 1849).

Dreissig Jahr am Hofe Friedrichs des Grossen: Aus den Tagebüchern des Reichsgrafen Ernst Uhasverus Heinrich von Lehndorff, Kammerherrn der Königin Elisabeth Christine von Preussen, ed. Karl Eduard Schmidt-Lözen (1 vol., with 2 vols. of *Nachträge*, Gotha, 1907–13).

Ligne, Prince C.J.E. de, *Mémoire sur le roi de Prusse, Frédéric le Grand* (Berlin, 1789).

Diaries and Correspondence of James Harris, First Earl of Malmesbury, ed. Earl of Malmesbury (4 vols., London, 1844).

Briefe der Kaiserin Maria Theresia an ihre Kinder und Freunde, ed. Alfred Ritter von Arneth (4 vols., Vienna, 1881).

Maria Theresia und Joseph II: ihre Correspondenz, ed. Alfred Ritter von Arneth (3 vols., Vienna, 1867–8).

Marie-Antoinette: correspondance secrète entre Marie-Thérèse et le cte de Mercy-Argenteau, ed. Alfred Ritter von Arneth and M.A. Geffroy (3 vols., 2nd edn, Paris, 1874–5).

Martens, F. von, *Recueil des traités et conventions conclus par la Russie avec les puissances étrangères* (15 vols., St Petersburg, 1874–1909).

Correspondance Secrète du Comte de Mercy-Argenteau avec l'Empereur Joseph II et le Prince de Kaunitz, ed. Alfred von Ritter Arneth and Jules Flammermont (2 vols., Paris, 1889–91).

Memoirs and Papers of Sir Andrew Mitchell, K.B., ed. A. Bisset (2 vols., London, 1850).

The Parliamentary History of England from the earliest Period to the Year 1803 (36 vols., London, 1806–20).

Die politischen Testamente der Hohenzollern, ed. R. Dietrich (Cologne and Vienna, 1986).

Correspondence of William Pitt, Earl of Chatham, ed. W.S. Taylor and J.H. Pringle (4 vols., London, 1838–40).

Recueil des instructions données aux ambassadeurs et ministres de France, depuis les traités de Westphalie jusqu'à la Révolution Française (32 vols. to date, Paris, 1884–): *Autriche*, ed. Albert Sorel; *Danemark*, ed. A. Geffroy; *Naples et Parme*, ed. Joseph Reinach; *Pologne*, ed. Louis Farges; *Russie* I–II, ed. A. Rambaud; *Suède*, ed. A. Geffroy.

Recueil des traités et conventions concernant la Pologne, ed. J.L.C. d'Angeberge (Paris, 1862).

Bibliography

Repertorium der diplomatischen Vertreter aller Länder, ed. L. Bittner, L. Gross and L. Santifaller (3 vols., Berlin, Zurich and Graz, 1936–65).

The Fourth Earl of Sandwich: Diplomatic Correspondence 1763–1765, ed. F. Spencer (Manchester, 1961).

Ségur, L.P. de, *Politique de tous les cabinets de l'Europe pendant les règnes de Louis XV et de Louis XVI* (3 vols., Paris, 1802).

[Sturdza, D.A.?], *Rapt de la Bukovine, d'après des documents authentiques* (Paris, 1875).

Thiébault, Dieudonné, *Mes souvenirs de vingt ans de séjour à Berlin* (3rd edn, 4 vols., Paris, 1813).

Turgenev, A.I., ed., *La cour de la Russie il y a cent ans 1725–1783* (Berlin, 1858).

Preussische und österreichische Acten zur Vorgeschichte des Siebenjährigen Krieges, ed. G.B. Volz and Georg Küntzel (1899; reprinted Osnabrück, 1965).

Volz, G.B., ed., 'Katharina II. und ihr Hof 1779–80: Zwei preussische Denkschriften', *Zeitschrift für Osteuropäischen Geschichten* 7 (1933), pp. 193–229.

Arkiv kniazia Vorontsova, ed. P. Bartenev (40 vols., Moscow, 1870–95).

The Last Journals of Horace Walpole during the Reign of George III, from 1771 to 1783, ed. A. F. Steuart (2 vols., London, 1910).

Horace Walpole's Correspondence, ed. W. S. Lewis (48 vols., New Haven, CT, 1937–83).

Wraxall, N.W., *Memoirs of the Courts of Berlin, Dresden and Vienna in the Years 1777, 1778 and 1779* (2 vols., London, 1799).

Karl Graf von Zinzendorf – Aus den Jugendtagebüchern 1747, 1752–1763, eds. Maria Breunlich and Marieluise Mader (Vienna, 1997).

SECONDARY STUDIES

Abarca, R.E., 'Bourbon "Revanche" against England: The Balance of Power, 1763–1770' (PhD thesis, University of Notre Dame, 1964).

Acomb, F., *Anglophobia in France, 1763–1789* (Durham, NC, 1950).

Aksan, Virginia H., 'Feeding the Ottoman Troops on the Danube, 1768–1774', *War and Society* 13 (1995), pp. 1–14.

'The One-Eyed Fighting the Blind: Mobilization, Supply and Command in the Russo-Turkish War of 1768–1774', *International History Review* 15 (1993), pp. 221–38.

'Ottoman–French Relations 1739–1768', in Sinan Kuneralp, ed., *Studies on Ottoman Diplomatic History* (Istanbul, 1987), pp. 41–58.

An Ottoman Statesman in War and Peace: Ahmed Resmi Efendi 1700–1783 (Leiden, 1995).

Alexander, John T., *Autocratic Politics in a National Crisis: The Imperial Russian Government and Pugachev's Revolt, 1773–1775* (Bloomington, IN, 1969).

Bubonic Plague in Early Modern Russia: Public Health and Urban Disaster (Baltimore, 1980).

Altbauer, D., 'The Diplomats of Peter the Great', *JGO* NF 28 (1980), pp. 1–16.

Althoff, Frank, *Untersuchungen zum Gleichgewicht der Mächte in der Aussenpolitik Friedrichs des Grossen nach dem Siebenjährigen Krieg (1763–1786)* (Berlin, 1995).

Amburger, Erik, *Russland und Schweden 1762–1772: Katharina II., die schwedische Verfassung und die Ruhe des Nordens* (Berlin, 1934; repr. Vaduz, 1965).

Anderson, M.S., 'Great Britain and the Russian Fleet, 1769–70', *Slavonic and East European Review* 31 (1952–3), pp. 148–63.

Bibliography

The Rise of Modern Diplomacy 1450–1919 (London, 1993).

The War of the Austrian Succession 1740–1748 (London, 1995).

Anisimov, Evgeny V., *Empress Elizabeth: Her Reign and her Russia 1741–1761* (1986; Engl. trans. John T. Alexander, Gulf Breeze, FL., 1995).

Antoine, Michel, *Louis XV* (Paris, 1989).

Antoine, M. and D. Ozanam, 'Le secret du roi et la Russie jusqu'à la mort de la Czarine Elisabeth en 1762', *Annuaire-bulletin de la Société de l'histoire de France* (1954–5), 69–93.

Aretin, Karl Otmar Freiherr von, *Das Alte Reich 1648–1806* (3 vols., Stuttgart, 1993–7).

Heiliges Römisches Reich 1776–1806, vol. I (Wiesbaden, 1967).

'Russia as a Guarantor Power of the Imperial Constitution under Catherine II', *Journal of Modern History* 48 (1986): Supplement – *Politics and Society in the Holy Roman Empire 1500–1806*, S141–60.

Arneth, Alfred Ritter von, 'Biographie des Fürsten Kaunitz: Ein Fragment', *AÖG* 88 (1899), pp. 1–201.

Geschichte Maria Theresias (10 vols., Vienna, 1863–79).

Askenazy, Simon, *Die letzte polnische Königswahl* (Göttingen, 1894).

Baack, Lawrence J., 'State Service in the Eighteenth Century: The Bernstorffs in Hanover and Denmark', *International History Review* 1 (1979), pp. 323–48.

Bagger, Hans, 'The Role of the Baltic in Russian Foreign Policy, 1721–1773', in Hugh Ragsdale, ed., *Imperial Russian Foreign Policy* (Cambridge, 1993), pp. 36–72.

Bakhrushin, Sergei V. and Sergei D. Skazkin, 'Diplomacy', translated in Marc Raeff, ed., *Catherine the Great: A Profile* (New York, 1972), pp. 181–96.

Bangert, D.E., *Die russische-österreichische militärische Zusammenarbeit im Siebenjährigen Kriege in den Jahren 1758–59* (Boppard-am-Rhein, 1971).

Barrow, J., *Some Account of the Public Life of the Earl of Macartney* (2 vols., London, 1807).

Barthélemy, Eduard de, *Histoire des relations de la France et du Danemarck sous le ministère du comte de Bernstorff 1751–70* (Paris, 1887).

Barton, H. Arnold, *Scandinavia in the Revolutionary Era 1760–1815* (Minneapolis, MN, 1986).

Baugh, Daniel A., 'Withdrawing from Europe: Anglo-French Maritime Geopolitics, ca. 1750–1800', *International History Review* 20 (1998), pp. 1–32.

Beales, Derek, *Joseph II*, vol. I: *In the Shadow of Maria Theresa, 1741–1780* (Cambridge, 1987).

'Love and the Empire: Maria Theresa and her Co-Regents', in Robert Oresko, G.C. Gibbs and H.M. Scott, eds., *Royal and Republican Sovereignty in Early Modern Europe: Essays in Memory of Ragnhild Hatton* (Cambridge, 1997), pp. 479–99.

Beaulieu-Marconnay, Carl von, *Der Hubertusburger Friede* (Leipzig, 1871).

Béchu, Claire, 'Les ambassadeurs français au XVIIIe siècle: formation et carrière', in Lucien Bély, ed., *L'invention de la diplomatie: Moyen Age – temps modernes* (Paris, 1998), pp. 333–48.

Beer, Adolf, *Die Erste Theilung Polens* (3 vols., Vienna, 1873).

Die Orientalische Politik Österreichs seit 1774 (Prague and Leipzig, 1883).

'Die Zusammenkünfte Josefs II. und Friedrichs II. zu Neisse und Neustadt', *AÖG* 47 (1871), pp. 383–527.

Behrens, C.B.A., *Society, Government and the Enlightenment: The Experiences of Eighteenth-Century France and Prussia* (London, 1985).

Bibliography

Bély, Lucien, *Espions et ambassadeurs au temps de Louis XIV* (Paris, 1990).

Bély, Lucien, ed., *L'invention de la diplomatie: Moyen Age – temps modernes* (Paris, 1998).

Bérenger, Jean, *Finances et absolutisme autrichien dans la seconde moitié du XVIIᵉ siècle* (Paris, 1975).

Bernard, Paul P., *Joseph II and Bavaria* (The Hague, 1965).

Beutin, Ludwig, 'Die Wirkungen des Siebenjährigen Krieges auf die Volkswirtschaft in Preussen', *Vierteljahrschrift für Sozial- und Wirtschaftsgeschichte* 26 (1933), pp. 209–43.

Beyrau, D., *Militär und Gesellschaft im vorrevolutionären Russland* (Cologne, 1984).

Black, J.L., *G.-F. Müller and the Imperial Russian Academy* (Kingston and Montreal, 1986).

Black, Jeremy, 'Russia's Rise as a European Power, 1650–1750', *History Today* 36 (August 1986), pp. 21–8.

Blanning, T.C.W., *The French Revolutionary Wars, 1787–1802* (London, 1996).

Joseph II (London, 1994).

'Louis XV and the Decline of the French Monarchy', *History Review* 22 (1995), pp. 20–4.

Blart, Lionel, *Les rapports de la France et de l'Espagne après le pacte de famille, jusqu'à la fin du ministère du duc de Choiseul* (Paris, 1915).

Bode, Andreas, *Die Flottenpolitik Katharinas II. und die Konflikte mit Schweden und der Türkei (1768–92)* (Munich, 1979).

Bohlen, Avis, 'Changes in Russian Diplomacy under Peter the Great', *Cahiers du monde russe et soviétique* 7 (1966), pp. 341–58.

Böhme, Klaus-Richard, 'Schwedens Teilnahme am Siebenjährigen Krieg: Innen-und aussenpolitische Voraussetzungen und Rückwirkungen', in Berhard R. Kroener, ed., *Europa im Zeitalter Friedrichs der Gressen: Wirtschaft, Gesellschaft, Kriege* (Munich, 1989), pp. 193–212.

Bolkhovitinov, N.N., *The Beginnings of Russian–American Relations 1775–1815* (Engl. trans., Cambridge, MA, 1975).

Bömelburg, Hans-Jürgen, *Zwischen Polnischer Ständegesellschaft und Preussischem Obrigkeitsstaat: vom Königlichen Preussen zu Westpreussen (1756–1806)* (Munich, 1995).

Bonneville de Marsangy, L., *Le Chevalier de Vergennes: son ambassade à Constantinople* (2 vols., Paris, 1894).

Le comte de Vergennes: son ambassade en Suède 1771–1774 (Paris, 1898).

Boroviczény, Aladár von, *Graf von Brühl: der Medici, Richelieu und Rothschild seiner Zeit* (Zurich, Leipzig and Vienna, 1930).

Brandt, Otto, *Caspar von Saldern und die nordeuropäische Politik im Zeitalter Katharinas II.* (Erlangen and Kiel, 1932).

Braubach, Max, *Versailles und Wien von Ludwig XIV. bis Kaunitz: die Vorstadien der diplomatischen Revolution im 18. Jahrhundert* (Bonn, 1952).

Browning, Reed, *The War of the Austrian Succession* (Stroud, 1994).

Brückner, Alexander, *Katharina die Zweite* (Berlin, 1883).

Brunner, Otto, Werner Conze and Reinhart Koselleck, eds., *Geschichtliche Grundbegriffe: Historisches Lexikon zur politisch-sozialen Sprache in Deutschland* (8 vols., Stuttgart, 1972–97).

Buddruss, Eckhard, *Die französische Deutschlandpolitik 1756–1789* (Mainz, 1995).

Burkhardt, Johannes, *Abschied vom Religionskrieg: der Siebenjährigen Krieg und die päpstliche Diplomatie* (Tübingen, 1985).

Büsch, Otto, *Militärsystem und Sozialleben im alten Preussen 1713–1807* (Berlin, 1962).

Bibliography

Butler, Rohan, *Choiseul*, vol. 1: *Father and Son, 1719–1754* (Oxford, 1980).

'Paradiplomacy', in A.O. Sarkissian, ed., *Studies in Diplomatic History and Historiography in Honour of G.P. Gooch* (London, 1961), pp. 12–25.

Butler, W.E., 'F.G. Strube de Piermont and the Origins of Russian Legal History', in R. Bartlett and J.M. Hartley, eds., *Russia in the Age of Enlightenment: Essays for Isabel de Madariaga* (London, 1990), pp. 125–41.

'Treaty Collections in Eighteenth-Century Russia: Encounters with European Experience', in A.G. Cross, ed., *Russia and the West in the Eighteenth Century* (Newtonville, MA, 1983), pp. 249–58.

Butterwick, Richard, *Poland's Last King and English Culture: Stanisław August Poniatowski, 1732–1798* (Oxford, 1998).

Camariano-Cioran, Ariadna, 'La guerre russo-turque de 1768–1774 et les grecs', *Revue des études sud-est européennes* 3 (1965), pp. 516–20.

Carl, Horst, *Okkupation und Regionalismus: die preussischen Westprovinzen im Siebenjährigen Krieg* (Mainz, 1993).

Catherine the Great and Gustav III (Helsingborg, 1999).

Cegielski, Tadeusz, *Das Alte Reich und die erste Teilung Polens 1768–1774* (Stuttgart and Warsaw, 1988).

Christelow, Alan, 'Economic Background of the Anglo-Spanish War of 1762', *Journal of Modern History* 18 (1946), pp. 22–36.

Clendenning, P.H., 'The Economic Awakening of Russia in the Eighteenth Century', *Journal of European Economic History* 14 (1985), pp. 443–72.

Cross, A.G., ed., *Great Britain and Russia in the Eighteenth Century: Contacts and Comparisons* (Newtonville, MA, 1979).

Russia and the West in the Eighteenth Century (Newtonville, MA, 1983).

Crouzet, François, 'The Second Hundred Years War: Some Reflections', *French History* 10 (1997), pp. 432–50.

Delmas, Jean, ed., *Histoire militaire de la France, II: de 1715 à 1871* (Paris, 1992).

Dickson, P.G.M., *Finance and Government under Maria Theresia 1740–1780* (2 vols., Oxford, 1987).

Dippel, Horst, 'Prussia's English Policy after the Seven Years War', *Central European History* 4 (1971), pp. 195–214.

Dixon, Simon, *The Modernisation of Russia 1676–1825* (Cambridge, 1999).

Doran, P.F., *Andrew Mitchell and Anglo-Prussian Diplomatic Relations during the Seven Years War* (New York, 1986).

Dorn, W.L., *Competition for Empire 1740–1763* (New York, 1940).

Droysen, Hans, 'Tageskalender Friedrichs des Grossen, von 1. Juni 1740 bis 31. März 1763', *FBPG* 29 (1916), pp. 95–157.

Duchhardt, Heinz, *Balance of Power und Pentarchie: Internationale Beziehungen 1700–1785* (Paderborn, 1997).

Duffy, Christopher, *The Army of Frederick the Great* (Newton Abbot, 1974).

The Army of Frederick the Great (2nd edn, New York, 1996).

The Army of Maria Theresa (London, 1977).

Frederick the Great: A Military Life (London, 1985).

Russia's Military Way to the West: Origins and Nature of Russian Military Power 1700–1800 (London, 1981).

Bibliography

Dyck, Harvey L., 'Pondering the Russian Fact: Kaunitz and the Catherinian Empire in the 1770s', *Canadian Slavonic Papers* 22 (1981), pp. 451–69.

Dziembowski, Edmond, *Un nouveau patriotisme français, 1750–1770: la France face à la puissance anglaise à l'époque de la guerre de Sept Ans* (Oxford, 1998).

Easum, C.V., *Prince Henry of Prussia* (Madison, WI, 1942).

Elias, Karl, *Die preussisch-russischen Beziehungen von der Thronbesteigung Peters III. bis zum Abschluss des preussisch-russischen Bündnisses vom 11. April 1764* (Göttingen, 1900).

Evans, R.J.W., *The Making of the Habsburg Monarchy 1550–1700* (Oxford, 1979).

Feldbaek, Ole, 'Denmark and the Baltic, 1720–1864', in Göran Rystad, Klaus-R. Böhme and Wilhelm M. Carlgren, eds., *In Quest of Trade and Security: The Baltic in Power Politics, 1500–1990*, vol. I: *1500–1890* (Stockholm, 1994), pp. 257–95.

Fisher, Alan W., *The Russian Annexation of the Crimea 1772–1783* (Cambridge, 1970).

Fox, Frank, 'Negotiating with the Russians: Ambassador Ségur's Mission to Saint-Petersburg, 1784–1789', *French Historical Studies* 7 (1971–2), pp. 47–71.

Fraguier, B. du, 'Le duc d'Aiguillon et l'Angleterre', *Revue d'histoire diplomatique* 26 (1912), pp. 607–27.

Freudenberger, Herman, *The Industrialization of a Central European City: Brno and the Fine Woollen Industry in the 18th Century* (Edington, Wilts., 1977).

Fuller, William C., Jr, *Strategy and Power in Russia 1600–1914* (New York, 1992).

Gerhard, Dietrich, 'Kontinentalpolitik und Kolonialpolitik im Frankreich des ausgehenden ancien régime', *Historische Zeitschrift* 147 (1933), pp. 21–31.

Glassl, Horst, 'Der Rechtsstreit um die Zips vor ihrer Rückgliederung an Ungarn', *Ungarn-Jahrbuch* 1 (1969), pp. 23–50.

Glete, Jan, *Navies and Nations: Warships, Navies and State Building in Europe and America 1500–1860* (2 vols., Stockholm, 1993).

Grabar, V.E., *The History of International Law in Russia, 1647–1917: A Bio-Bibliographical Study*, transl. and ed. W.E. Butler (Oxford, 1990).

Griffiths, D. M., 'The Rise and Fall of the Northern System: Court Politics and Foreign Policy in the First Half of Catherine II's Reign', *Canadian-American Slavic Studies* 4 (1970), pp. 547–69.

'Russian Court Politics and the Question of an Expansionist Foreign Policy under Catherine II, 1762–1783' (PhD thesis, Cornell University, 1967).

Gruder, Vivian R., 'Whither Revisionism? Political Perspectives on the Ancien Régime', *French Historical Studies* 20 (1997), pp. 245–85.

Guglia, E., *Maria Theresia: ihr Leben und ihre Regierung* (2 vols., Munich and Berlin, 1917).

Gvosdev, Nikolas K., *Imperial Policies and Perspectives towards Georgia, 1760–1819* (Basingstoke, 2000).

Hahn, Peter-Michael, 'Aristokratisierung und Professionalisierung: der Aufstieg der Obristen zu einer militärischen und höfischen Elite in Brandenburg-Preussen von 1650–1725', *FBPG* NF 1 (1991), pp. 161–208.

Hall, Thadd E., *France and the Eighteenth-Century Corsican Question* (New York, 1971).

Hammer, J. de (Joseph von Hammer-Purgstall), *Histoire de l'empire Ottoman, depuis son origine jusqu'à nos jours* (18 vols., Paris, 1835–41).

Hammond, Robert, 'La France et la Prusse, 1763–1769', *Revue historique* 25 (1884), pp. 69–82.

'Mission du comte de Guines à Berlin (1769)', *Revue historique* 27 (1888), pp. 322–48.

Härter, Karl, 'Möglichkeiten und Grenzen: der Reichspolitik Russlands als Garantiemacht

Bibliography

des Teschener Friedens (1778–1803)', in Claus Scharf, ed., *Katharina II., Rußland und Europa; Beiträge zur internationalen Forschung* (Mainz, 2001), pp. 133–81.

Hartmann, Stefan, 'Die Rückgabe Ostpreußens durch die Russen an Preußen im Jahre 1762', *Zeitschrift für Ostforschung* 36 (1987), pp 405–33.

Hauser, O., ed., *Friedrich der Grosse in seiner Zeit* (Cologne and Vienna, 1987).

Hellmann, Manfred, 'Die Friedensschlüsse von Nystad (1721) und Teschen (1779) als Etappen des Vordringens Russlands nach Europa', *Historisches Jahrbuch* 97/8 (1978), pp. 270–88.

Hinsley, F.H., *Power and the Pursuit of Peace: Theory and Practice in the History of Relations between States* (Cambridge, 1963).

Hochedlinger, Michael, *Krise und Wiederherstellung: Österreichische Großmachtpolitik zwischen Türkenkrieg und 'Zweiter Diplomatischer Revolution' 1787–1791* (Berlin, 2000).

'Mars Ennobled: The Ascent of the Military and the Creation of a Military Nobility in Mid Eighteenth-Century Austria', *German History* 17 (1999), pp. 141–76.

Hoensch, Jörg K., 'Friedrichs II. Währungsmanipulationen im Siebenjährigen Krieg und ihre Auswirkung auf die polnische Münzreform von 1765/66', *Jahrbuch für die Geschichte Mittel- und Ostdeutschlands* 22 (1973), pp. 110–75.

Sozialverfassung und politische Reform: Polen im vorrevolutionären Zeitalter (Cologne, 1973).

'Der Streit um den polnischen Generalzoll 1764–1766', *JGO* NF 18 (1970), pp. 35–88.

Horn, D.B., *British Public Opinion and the First Partition of Poland* (Edinburgh, 1945).

Sir Charles Hanbury-Williams and European Diplomacy (1747–58) (London, 1930).

Hösch, Edgar, 'Das sogennante "Griechische Projekt Katharinas II.": Ideologie und Wirklichkeit der russischen Orientpolitik in der zweiten Hälfte des 18. Jahrhunderts', *JGO* NF 12 (1964), pp. 168–206.

Hubatsch, Walther, *Frederick the Great of Prussia: Absolutism and Administration* (Engl. trans., London, 1973).

Hübner, Eckhard, *Staatspolitik und Familieninteresse: die gottorfische Frage in der russischen Außenpolitik 1741–1773* (Neumünster, 1984).

Hüffer, Hermann, 'Die Beamten des älteren preussischen Kabinetts von 1713–1808', *FBPG* 5 (1892), pp. 157–90.

Itzkowitz, Norman and Max Mote, eds., *Mubadele: An Ottoman–Russian Exchange of Ambassadors* (Chicago, IL, 1970).

Jacobsohn, Ljubow, *Russland und Frankreich in den ersten Regierungsjahren der Kaiserin Katharina II. 1762–1772* (Berlin and Königsberg, 1929).

Jany, Curt, *Geschichte der Königliche Preussischen Armee bis zum Jahre 1807*, vols. II and III (Berlin, 1928–9).

Johnson, H.C., *Frederick the Great and his Officials* (New Haven, CT, 1975).

Kahan, Arcadius, *The Plow, the Hammer and the Knout: An Economic History of Eighteenth-Century Russia* (Chicago, IL, 1985).

Kaplan, Herbert H., *The First Partition of Poland* (New York, 1962).

Russia and the Outbreak of the Seven Years War (Berkeley and Los Angeles, 1968).

Keep, John L.H, 'Feeding the Troops: Russian Army Supply Policies during the Seven Years War', *Canadian Slavonic Papers* 29 (1987), pp. 24–44.

'Die russische Armee im Siebenjährigen Krieg', in Bernhard R. Kroener, ed., *Europa im Zeitalter Friedrichs des Grossen: Wirtschaft, Gesellschaft, Kriege* (Munich, 1989).

Soldiers of the Tsar: Army and Society in Russia 1462–1874 (Oxford, 1985).

Bibliography

Kennett, Lee, *The French Armies in the Seven Years' War: A Study in Military Organization and Administration* (Durham, NC, 1967).

Kieniewicz, S., ed., *History of Poland* (Warsaw, 1968).

Kley, Dale Van, *The Jansenists and the Expulsion of the Jesuits from France, 1757–1765* (New Haven, CT, 1975).

Klingenstein, Grete, *Der Aufstieg des Hauses Kaunitz: Studien zur Herkunft und Bildung des Staatskanzlers Wenzel Anton* (Göttingen, 1975).

'Between Mercantilism and Physiocracy: Stages, Modes and Functions of Economic Theory in the Habsburg Monarchy, 1748–63', in Charles W. Ingrao, ed., *State and Society in Early Modern Austria* (West Lafayette, IN, 1994), pp. 181–214.

'Institutionelle Aspekte der österreichischen Aussenpolitik im 18. Jahrhundert', in E. Zöllner, ed., *Diplomatie und Aussenpolitik Österreichs: Elf Beiträge zur ihrer Geschichte* (Vienna, 1977), pp. 74–93.

'"Jede macht ist relativ": Montesquieu und die Habsburger Monarchie', in Herwig Ebner et al., eds., *Festschrift Othmar Pickl* (Graz, 1987), pp. 307–24.

'Kaunitz kontra Bartenstein: zur Geschichte der Staatskanzlei, 1749–1753', in H. Fichtenau and E. Zöllner, eds., *Beiträge zur neueren Geschichte Österreichs* (Vienna, 1974), pp. 243–63.

'The meanings of "Austria" and "Austrian" in the Eighteenth Century', in Robert Oresko, G.C. Gibbs and H.M. Scott, eds., *Royal and Republican Sovereignty in Early Modern Europe: Essays in Memory of Ragnhild Hatton* (Cambridge, 1997), pp. 423–78.

Klingenstein, Grete and Franz A.J. Szabo, eds., *Staatskanzler Wenzel Anton von Kaunitz-Rietberg 1711–1794* (Graz, 1996).

Klueting, Harm, *Die Lehre von der Macht der Staaten: das aussenpolitische Machtproblem in der 'politischen Wissenschaft' und in der praktischen Politik im 18. Jahrhundert* (Berlin, 1986).

Kohnke, Meta, 'Das preussische Kabinettsministerium: ein Beitrag zur Geschichte des Staatsapparates im Spätfeudalismus' (PhD thesis, Humboldt University, Berlin, 1968).

Konopczynski, W., 'Later Saxon Period, 1733–1763', in W.F. Reddaway, J.H. Penson, O. Halecki and R. Dyboski, eds., *The Cambridge History of Poland 1697–1935* (Cambridge, 1941), pp. 25–48.

Koser, Reinhold, *Geschichte Friedrichs des Grossen* (3 vols., 6th-7th edns, Berlin, 1925).

'Die preussischen Finanzen im Siebenjährigen Kriege', *FBPG* 13 (1900), pp. 153–217 and 329–75.

'Die preussischen Finanzen von 1763 bis 1786', *FBPG* 16 (1903), pp. 101–32.

Kretschmayr, H., *Maria Theresia* (Gotha, 1925).

Kroener, Bernhard R., ed., *Europa im Zeitalter Friedrichs des Grossen: Wirtschaft, Gesellschaft, Kriege* (Munich, 1989).

'Die materiellen Grundlagen österreichischer und preussischer Kriegsanstrengungen 1756–1763', in Bernhard R. Kroener, ed., *Europa im Zeitalter Friedrichs des Grossen: Wirtschaft, Gesellschaft, Kriege* (Munich, 1989), pp. 47–78.

'Militärischer Professionalismus und soziale Karriere: der französische Adel in den europäischen Kriegen 1740–1763', in Bernhard R. Kroener, ed., *Friedrichs des Grossen: Wirtschaft, Gesellschaft, Kriege* (Munich, 1989), pp. 99–132.

Krummel, Werner, 'Nikita Ivanovic Panins aussenpolitische Tätigkeit 1747–1758', *JGO* 5 (1940), pp. 76–141.

Bibliography

Kulak, Zbigniew, 'The Plans and Aims of Frederick II's Policy towards Poland', *Polish Western Affairs* 22 (1981), pp. 70–101.

Kunisch, Johannes, 'Der Aufstieg neuer Großmächte im 18. Jahrhundert und die Aufteilung der Machtsphären Ostmitteleuropa', in Grete Klingenstein and Franz A.J. Szabo, eds., *Staatskanzler Wenzel Anton von Kaunitz-Rietberg 1711–1794* (Graz, 1996), pp. 70–89.

'Der Ausgang des Siebenjährigen Krieges: ein Beitrag zum Verhältnis von Kabinettspolitik und Kriegsführung im Zeitalter des Absolutismus', *Zeitschrift für Historische Forschung* 2 (1975), pp. 173–222.

'Die Grosse Allianz der Gegner Preussens im Siebenjährigen Krieg', in Bernhard R. Kroener, ed., *Europa im Zeitalter Friedrichs des Grossen: Wirtschaft, Gesellschaft, Kriege* (Munich, 1989), pp. 79–97.

Das Mirakel des Hauses Brandenburg: Studien zum Verhältnis von Kabinettspolitik und Kriegsführung im Zeitalter des Siebenjährigen Krieges (Munich and Vienna, 1978).

Kunisch, Johannes, ed., *Expansion und Gleichgewicht: Studien zur europäischen Mächtepolitik des ancien régime* (Berlin, 1986).

Küntzel, Georg, 'Friedrich der Grosse am Ausgang des siebenjährigen Krieges und sein Bündnis mit Russlands', *FBPG* 13 (1900), pp. 75–122.

Fürst Kaunitz-Rittberg als Staatsmann (Frankfurt, 1923).

Laue, T.H. von, *Leopold Ranke: The Formative Years* (Princeton, NJ, 1950).

Laugier, Lucien, *Un ministère réformateur sous Louis XV: le Triumvirat (1770–1774)* (Paris, 1975).

Lebeau, Christine, *Aristocrates et grands commis à la cour de Vienne (1748–1791)* (Paris, 1996).

LeDonne, John P. 'Outlines of Russian Military Administration 1762–1796. Part I: Troop Strength and Deployment', *JGO* NF 31 (1983), pp. 321–47.

Ruling Russia: Politics and Administration in the Age of Absolutism 1762–1796 (Princeton, NJ, 1984).

The Russian Empire and the World, 1700–1917: The Geopolitics of Expansion and Containment (New York, 1997).

Leonard, Carol S., *Reform and Regicide: The Reign of Peter III of Russia* (Bloomington and Indianapolis, 1993).

'The Reputation of Peter III', *The Russian Review* 47 (1988), pp. 263–92.

'A Study of the Reign of Peter III of Russia' (PhD thesis, Indiana University, 1976).

Liechtenhan, Francine-Dominique, *La Russie entre en Europe: Elisabeth Ire et la Succession d'Autriche (1740–1750)* (Paris, 1997).

Loebl, A.H., 'Österreich und Preussen 1766–1768', *AÖG* 92 (1903), pp. 363–482.

Lojek, Jerzy, 'La politique de la Russie envers la Pologne pendant le premier partage d'après un document secret de la cour Russe de 1772', *Canadian-American Slavic Studies* 8 (1974), pp. 116–35.

Longworth, Philip, *The Art of Victory: The Life and Achievements of Generalissimo Suvorov, 1729–1800* (London, 1965).

Lossky, Andrew, 'France in the System of Europe in the Seventeenth Century', *Proceedings of the Western Society for French Historical Studies* (1974), pp. 32–48.

Louis XIV and the French Monarchy (New Brunswick, NJ, 1994).

Lukowski, J.T., 'Guarantee or Annexation: A Note on Russian Plans to Acquire Polish Territory Prior to the First Partition of Poland', *Bulletin of the Institute of Historical Research* 106 (1983), pp. 60–5.

Liberty's Folly: The Polish-Lithuanian Commonwealth in the Eighteenth Century 1697–1795 (London, 1991).

'The Papacy, Poland, Russia and Religious Reform, 1764–8', *Journal of Ecclesiastical History* 39 (1988), pp. 66–94.

The Partitions of Poland: 1772, 1793, 1795 (London, 1999).

The Szlachta and the Confederacy of Radom, 1764–1767/68: A Study of the Polish Nobility (Antemurale, XXI; Rome, 1977).

'Towards Partition: Polish Magnates and Russian Intervention in Poland during the Early Reign of Stanislaw August Poniatowski', *Historical Journal* 28 (1985), pp. 557–74.

McGrew, Roderick E., *Paul I of Russia 1754–1801* (Oxford, 1992).

McKay, Derek and H.M. Scott, *The Rise of the Great Powers 1648–1815* (London, 1983).

Madariaga, Isabel de, *Britain, Russia and the Armed Neutrality of 1780: Sir James Harris's Mission to St Petersburg during the American Revolution* (London, 1962).

Catherine the Great: A Short History (New Haven, CT, 1990).

Russia in the Age of Catherine the Great (London, 1981).

'The Secret Austro-Russian Treaty of 1781', *Slavonic and East European Review* 38 (1959–60), pp. 114–45.

'The Staging of Power', *Government and Opposition* 31 (1996), pp. 228–40.

'Tsar into Emperor: The Title of Peter the Great', in R. Oresko, G.C. Gibbs and H.M. Scott, eds., *Royal and Republican Sovereignty in Early Modern Europe: Essays in Memory of Ragnhild Hatton* (Cambridge, 1997), pp. 351–81.

'The Use of British Secret Funds at St Petersburg, 1777–1782', *Slavonic and East European Review* 32 (1953–4), pp. 464–74.

Malia, Martin, *Russia under Western Eyes: From the Bronze Horseman to the Lenin Mausoleum* (Cambridge, MA, 1999).

Marx, Karl, *Secret Diplomatic History of the Eighteenth Century* (London, 1899 edn).

Mathy, Helmut, *Franz Georg von Metternich: der Vater des Staatskanzlers* (Meisenheim-am-Glan, 1969).

Mediger, Walther, 'Friedrich der Grosse und Russland', in O. Hauser, ed., *Friedrich der Grosse in seiner Zeit* (Cologne and Vienna, 1987), pp. 109–36.

Moskaus Weg nach Europa: der Aufstieg Russlands zum europäischen Machtstaat im Zeitalter Friedrichs des Grossen (Brunswick, 1952).

Melton, Edgar, 'The Prussian Junkers, 1600–1786', in H.M. Scott, ed., *The European Nobilities in the Seventeenth and Eighteenth Centuries* (2 vols., London, 1995), II. 71–109.

Melton, James Van Horn, 'The Nobility in the Bohemian and Austrian Lands, 1620–1780', in H.M. Scott, ed., *The European Nobilities in the Seventeenth and Eighteenth Centuries* (2 vols., London, 1995), II. 110–43.

Menning, Bruce W., 'Russian Military Innovation in the Second Half of the Eighteenth Century', *War and Society* 2 (1984), pp. 23–41.

Metcalf, Michael F., *Russia, England and Swedish Party Politics 1762–1766: The Interplay between Great Power Diplomacy and Domestic Politics during Sweden's Age of Liberty* (Stockholm and Totowa, NJ, 1977).

Michael, Wolfgang, *Englands Stellung zur Ersten Teilung Polens* (Hamburg and Leipzig, 1890).

Middleton, R., *The Bells of Victory: The Pitt-Newcastle Ministry and the Conduct of the Seven Years War (1757–1762)* (Cambridge, 1985).

Bibliography

Misiunas, R.J., 'The Baltic Question after Nystad', *Baltic History* (1974), pp. 71–90.

'Russia and Sweden 1772–1778' (PhD thesis, Yale University, 1971).

Mittenzwei, Ingrid, *Preussen nach dem Siebenjährigen Krieg: Auseinandersetzungen zwischen Bürgertum und Staat um die Wirtschaftspolitik* ((East) Berlin, 1979).

Montefiore, Simon Sebag, *Prince of Princes: The Life of Potemkin* (London, 2000).

Muhlack, Ulrich, 'Das europäische Staatensystem in der deutschen Geschichtsschreibung des 19. Jahrhunderts', *Annali dell' Istituto Storico Germanico in Trento* 16 (1990), pp. 43–92.

Müller, Klaus, *Das kaiserliche Gesandtschaftswesen im Jahrhundert nach dem Westfälischen Frieden (1648–1740)* (Bonn, 1976).

Müller, Micheal G., 'Nordisches System-Teilungen Polens-Griechisches Projekt: Russische Aussenpolitik 1762–1796', in Klaus Zernack, ed., *Handbuch der Geschichte Russlands*, vol. II:ii, *1613–1856* (Stuttgart, 1988), pp. 567–623.

'Das "petrinische Erbe": Russische Grossmachtpolitik bis 1762', in Klaus Zernack, ed., *Handbuch der Geschichte Russlands*, vol. II:i, *1613–1856* (Stuttgart, 1986), pp. 402–44.

'Russland und der Siebenjährige Krieg', *JGO* NF 28 (1980), pp. 198–219.

Die Teilungen Polens (Munich, 1984).

Muret, Pierre, *La prépondérance anglaise 1715–1763* (2nd edn, Paris, 1942).

Murphy, Orville T., *Charles Gravier, Comte de Vergennes: French Diplomacy in the Age of Revolution 1719–1787* (Albany, NY, 1982).

The Diplomatic Retreat of France and Public Opinion on the Eve of the French Revolution, 1783–1789 (Washington, DC, 1998).

Naujoks, Eberhard, 'Die Persönlichkeit Friedrichs des Grossen und die Struktur des preussischen Staates', *Historische Mitteilungen* 2 (1989), pp. 17–37.

Nordmann, Claude, *Grandeur et liberté de la Suède (1660–1792)* (Paris, 1971).

Novotny, Alexander, *Staatskanzler Kaunitz als Geistige Persönlichkeit* (Vienna, 1947).

Oliva, L. Jay, *Misalliance: A Study of French Policy in Russia during the Seven Years War* (New York, 1964).

Opitz-Belakhal, Claudia, *Militärreformen zwischen Bürokratisierung und Adelsreaktion: das französische Kriegsministerium und seine Reformen im Offizierskorps von 1760–1790* (Sigmaringen, 1994).

Oresko, Robert, G.C. Gibbs and H.M. Scott, eds., *Royal and Republican Sovereignty in Early Modern Europe: Essays in Memory of Ragnhild Hatton* (Cambridge, 1997).

Otruba, Gustav, 'Die Bedeutung englischer Subsidien und Antizipationen für die Finanzen Österreichs 1701 bis 1748', *Vierteljahrschrift für Sozial- und Wirtschaftsgeschichte* 51 (1964), pp. 192–234.

Oursel, Paul, *La diplomatie de la France sous Louis XVI: succession de Bavière et paix de Teschen* (Paris, 1921)

Pintner, Walter M., 'The Burden of Defense in Imperial Russia, 1725–1914', *Russian Review* 43 (1984), pp. 231–59.

Russia as a Great Power, 1709–1856 ('Kennan Institute Occasional Papers', 33, Washington, DC, 1976).

'Russia's Military Style, Russian Society and Russian Power in the Eighteenth Century', in A.G. Cross, ed., *Russia and the West in the Eighteenth Century* (Newtonville, MA, 1983), pp. 262–70.

Pommerin, Reiner, 'Bündnispolitik und Mächtesystem: Österreich und der Aufstieg

Bibliography

Russlands im 18. Jahrhundert', in Johannes Kunisch, ed., *Expansion und Gleichgewicht: Studien zur europäischen Mächtepolitik des ancien régime* (Berlin, 1986), pp. 113–64.

Raeff, Marc, 'In the Imperial Manner', in Marc Raeff, ed., *Catherine the Great: A Profile* (New York and London, 1972), pp. 197–246.

'The Style of Russia's Imperial Policy and Prince G.A. Potemkin', in G.N. Grob, ed., *Statesmen and Statecraft of the Modern West: Essays in Honor of Dwight E. Lee and H. Donaldson Jordan* (Barre, MA, 1967), pp. 1–51.

Raeff, Marc, ed., *Catherine the Great: A Profile* (New York and London, 1972).

Ragsdale, Hugh, 'Evaluating the Traditions of Russian Aggression: Catherine II and the Greek Project', *Slavonic and East European Review* 66 (1988), pp. 91–117.

'Montmorin and Catherine's Greek Project: Revolution in French Foreign Policy', *Cahiers du monde russe et soviétique* 27 (1986), pp. 27–44.

'New Light on the Greek Project: A Preliminary Report', in R.P. Bartlett, A.G. Cross and Karen Rasmussen, eds., *Russia and the World of the Eighteenth Century* (Columbus, OH, 1988), pp. 493–501.

'Russian Projects of Conquest in the Eighteenth Century', in Hugh Ragsdale, ed., *Imperial Russian Foreign Policy* (Cambridge, 1993), pp. 75–102.

Ragsdale, Hugh, ed., *Imperial Russian Foreign Policy* (Cambridge, 1993).

Rain, Pierre, *La diplomatie française d'Henri IV à Vergennes* (Paris, 1945).

Ransel, David L., *The Politics of Catherinian Russia: The Panin Party* (New Haven, CT, 1975).

Rashed, Z.E., *The Peace of Paris 1763* (Liverpool, 1951).

Reading, D.K., *The Anglo-Russian Commercial Treaty of 1734* (New Haven, CT, 1934).

Reddaway, W.F., *et al.*, eds., *The Cambridge History of Poland 1697–1935* (Cambridge, 1941).

Riley, James C., 'French Finances, 1727–1768', *Journal of Modern History* 59 (1987), pp. 209–43.

International Government Finance and the Amsterdam Capital Market, 1740–1815 (New York and Cambridge, 1980).

The Seven Years War and the Old Regime in France: The Economic and Financial Toll (Princeton, 1986).

Ritter, Gerhard, *Frederick the Great* (Engl. trans., London, 1968).

Roberts, Michael, *The Age of Liberty: Sweden 1719–1772* (Cambridge, 1986).

British Diplomacy and Swedish Politics, 1758–1773 (London, 1980).

'Great Britain and the Swedish Revolution, 1772–3', in Michael Roberts, *Essays in Swedish History* (London, 1967), pp. 286–347.

'Great Britain, Denmark and Russia, 1763–70', in Ragnhild Hatton and M.S. Anderson, eds., *Studies in Diplomatic History: Essays in Memory of David Bayne Horn* (London, 1970), pp. 236–67.

Macartney in Russia (*English Historical Review*, Supplement 7; London, 1974), p. 38.

Rödenbeck, K.H.S., *Tagebuch oder Geschichtskalender aus Friedrichs des Grossen Regentleben (1740–1786)* (3 vols., Berlin, 1840–2).

Roider, Karl A., Jr, *Austria's Eastern Question 1700–1790* (Princeton, 1982).

Baron Thugut and Austria's Response to the French Revolution (Princeton, 1987).

'The Oriental Academy in the *Theresienzeit*', *Topic* 34 (1980), pp. 19–28.

Rostworowski, E., 'Na drodze do pierwszego rozbioru: Fryderyk II wobec rozkladu przymierza francusko-austriackiego w latach 1769–1772', *Roczniki Historyczne* 18 (1949), pp. 181–204.

Bibliography

'The Saxon period, 1697–1763/4', in S. Kieniewicz, ed., *History of Poland* (Warsaw, 1968), pp. 272–312.

Ruata, Ada, *Luigi Malabaila di Canale: Riflessi della cultura illuministica in un diplomatico piemontese* (Deputazione subalpina di Storia Patria, Turin, 1968).

Salomon, Robert, *La politique orientale de Vergennes (1780–1784)* (Paris, 1935).

Sandgruber, Roman, *Ökonomie und Politik: Österreichische Wirtschaftsgeschichte vom Mittelalter bis zur Gegenwart* (Vienna, 1996).

Savage, Gary, 'Favier's Heirs: The French Revolution and the Secret du Roi', *Historical Journal* 41 (1998), pp. 225–58.

Savory, Sir Reginald, *His Britannic Majesty's Army in Germany during the Seven Years War* (Oxford, 1966).

Schaefer, A., *Geschichte des Siebenjährigen Krieges* (2 vols., Berlin, 1867).

'Urkundliche Beiträge zur Geschichte des siebenjährigen Krieges', *Forschungen zur Deutschen Geschichte* 17 (1877), pp. 1–106.

Scharf, Claus, *Katharina II., Deutschland und die Deutschen* (Mainz, 1995).

Schieder, Theodor, *Friedrich der Grosse: ein Königtum der Widersprüche* (Frankfurt-am-Main, 1983).

Schilling, Lothar, *Kaunitz und das Renversement des Alliances: Studien zur aussenpolitischen Konzeption Wenzel Antons von Kaunitz* (Berlin, 1994).

Schmidt, K. Rahbek, 'Wie ist Panins Plan zu einem Nordischen System entstanden?', *Zeitschrift für Slawistik* 2 (1957), pp. 406–22.

Schroeder, Paul W., *The Transformation of European Politics 1763–1848* (Oxford, 1994).

Schulze, O., *Die Beziehungen zwischen Kursachsen und Friedrich dem Grossen nach dem Siebenjährigen Krieg bis zum Bayrischen Erbfolgekriege* (Jena, 1933).

Schweizer, Karl W., *Frederick the Great, William Pitt and Lord Bute: The Anglo-Prussian Alliance, 1756–1763* (New York, 1991).

Schweizer, Karl W. and Carol S. Leonard, 'Britain, Prussia, Russia and the Galitzin Letter: A Reassessment', *Historical Journal* 26 (1983), pp. 531–56.

Scott, H.M., *British Foreign Policy in the Age of the American Revolution* (Oxford, 1990).

'France and the Polish Throne, 1763–1764', *Slavonic and East European Review* 53 (1975), pp. 370–88.

'Frederick II, the Ottoman Empire and the Origins of the Russo-Prussian Alliance of April 1764', *European Studies Review* 7 (1977), pp. 153–75.

'Great Britain, Poland and the Russian Alliance, 1763–1767', *Historical Journal* 19 (1976), pp. 53–74.

'The Importance of Bourbon Naval Reconstruction to the Strategy of Choiseul after the Seven Years' War', *International History Review* 1 (1979), pp. 17–35.

'Prussia's Royal Foreign Minister', in R. Oresko, G.C. Gibbs and H.M. Scott, eds., *Royal and Republican Sovereignty in Early Modern Europe: Essays in Memory of Ragnhild Hatton* (Cambridge, 1997), pp. 500–26.

Scott, H.M., ed., *The European Nobilities in the Seventeenth and Eighteenth Centuries* (2 vols., London, 1995).

Seraphim, E., *Geschichte Liv-, Est- und Kurlands* (2 vols., Reval, 1895–6).

Showalter, Dennis, 'Hubertusburg to Auerstädt: the Prussian Army in Decline', *German History* 12 (1994), pp. 286–307.

The Wars of Frederick the Great (London, 1995).

Bibliography

Simsch, Adelheid, 'Armee, Wirtschaft und Gesellschaft: Preussens Kampf auf der "inneren Linie"', in Bernhard R. Kroener, ed., *Europa im Zeitalter Friedrichs des Grossen: Wirtschaft, Gesellschaft, Kriege* (Munich, 1989), pp. 35–46.

Soloviev, Sergei M., *History of Russia from the Earliest Times*, vol. XLI: *Empress Elizabeth – Domestic Affairs in the Seven Years War 1757–1761*, trans. by Peter C. Stupples (Gulf Breeze, FL, 1997).

History of Russia from the Earliest Times, vol. XLII: *A New Empress: Peter III and Catharine II, 1761–1762*, ed. Nicholas Lupinin (Gulf Breeze, FL, 1990).

History of Russia from the Earliest Times, vol. XLIII: *Catherine the Great in Power – Domestic and Foreign Affairs 1763–1764*, trans. by Daniel L. Schlafly, Jr (Gulf Breeze, FL, 1998).

History of Russia from the Earliest Times, vol. XLV: *The Rule of Catherine the Great: The Legislative Commission (1767–1768) and Foreign Affairs (1766–1768)*, ed. William H. Hill (Gulf Breeze, FL, 1986).

History of Russia from the Earliest Times, vol. XLVI: *The Rule of Catherine the Great: Turkey and Poland 1768–1770*, ed. Daniel L. Schlafly, Jr (Gulf Breeze, FL, 1994).

History of Russia from the Earliest Times, vol. XLVIII: *The Rule of Catherine the Great: War, Diplomacy and Domestic Affairs, 1772–1774*, ed. George E. Munro (Gulf Breeze, FL, 1991).

Sorel, Albert, *La question d'Orient au XVIIIe siècle* (2nd edn, Paris, 1889).

Stribrny, Wolfgang, *Die Russlandpolitik Friedrichs des Grossen (1764–1786)* (Würzburg, 1966).

Strohmeyer, Arno, *Theorie der Interaktion: das europäische Gleichgewicht der Kräfte in der frühen Neuzeit* (Vienna, Cologne and Weimar, 1994).

Stupperich, Robert, 'Die zweite Reise des Prinzen Heinrich von Preussen nach Petersburg', *JGO* 3 (1938), pp. 580–600.

Swann, Julian, *Politics and the Parlement of Paris under Louis XV, 1754–1774* (Cambridge, 1995).

Szabo, Franz A.J., *Kaunitz and Enlightened Absolutism 1753–1780* (Cambridge, 1994).

Tarkiainen, Kari, 'The Finland of Gustav III and of Catherine II', in *Catherine the Great and Gustav III* (Helsingborg, 1999), pp. 128–31.

Taylor, David J., 'Russian Foreign Policy, 1725–1739' (unpublished Ph.D. thesis, University of East Anglia, 1983).

Topolski, J., 'La formation de la frontière polono-prussienne à l'époque du premier partage de la Pologne (1772–1777)', *La Pologne et les affaires occidentales* 5 (1969), pp. 96–127.

'Reflections on the First Partition of Poland (1772)', *Acta Poloniae Historica* 27 (1973), pp. 89–104.

Tóth, Ferenc, 'Ascension sociale et identité nationale: intégration de l'immigration hongroise dans la société française au cours du XVIIIe siècle (1692–1815)' (PhD thesis, Université de Paris-Sorbonne, 1995).

'Voltaire et un diplomate français d'origine hongroise en Orient', *Cahiers d'études hongroises* 7 (1995), pp. 78–86.

Tribe, Keith, *Governing Economy: The Reformation of German Economic Discourse 1750–1840* (Cambridge, 1988).

Übersberger, Hans, *Russlands Orientpolitik in den letzten zwei Jahrhunderten*, vol. I (Stuttgart, 1913). [Only one volume was ever to be published.]

Ungermann, Richard, *Der Russisch-türkische Krieg, 1768–1774* (Vienna, 1906).

Bibliography

Unzer, Adolf, *Der Friede von Teschen* (Kiel, 1903).

Venturi, Franco, *The End of the Old Regime in Europe, 1768–1776: The First Crisis*, trans. R. Burr Litchfield (Princeton, NJ, 1989).

The End of the Old Regime in Europe, 1776–1789 (trans. by R. Burr Litchfield, 2 vols., Princeton, NJ, 1991).

Venturi, Franco, *Settecento riformatore, v: l'Italia dei lumi (1764–90)*, part 1 (Turin, 1987).

Volz, G.B., 'Prinz Heinrich von Preussen und die preussische Politik vor der ersten Teilung Polens', *FBPG* 18 (1905), pp. 153–86.

'Prinz Heinrich und die Vorgeschichte der ersten Teilung Polens', *FBPG* 35 (1923), pp. 193–211.

Waddington, Richard, *La guerre de Sept Ans: histoire diplomatique et militaire* (5 vols., Paris, 1899–1915).

Louis XV et le renversement des alliances: préliminaires de la guerre de sept ans, 1754–1756 (Paris, 1896).

Walter, Friedrich, *Die Geschichte der Österreichischen Zentralverwaltung in der Zeit Maria Theresias (1740–1780)* (Vienna, 1938).

'Kaunitz' Eintritt in die innere Politik: ein Beitrag zur Geschichte der österreichischen Innenpolitik in den Jahren 1760–61', *Mitteilungen des Instituts für österreichische Geschichtsforschung* 46 (1932), pp. 37–79.

Männer um Maria Theresia (Vienna, 1951).

Walter, Friedrich, ed., *Vom Sturz des Directoriums in Publicis et Cameralibus (1760/61) bis zum Ausgang der Regierung Maria Theresias: Aktenstücke (II. Abteilung, vol. 3 in the series Die österreichische Zentralverwaltung)* (Vienna, 1934).

Wangermann, Ernst, *The Austrian Achievement, 1700–1800* (London, 1973).

Wilson, Peter H., *German Armies: War and German Politics, 1648–1806* (London, 1998).

'Social Militarization in Eighteenth-Century Germany', *German History* 18 (2000), pp. 1–39.

Winter, E., 'Grundlinien der österreichischen Russlandpolitik am Ende des 18. Jahrhunderts', *Zeitschrift für Slawistik* 4 (1959), pp. 94–110.

Wolff, Lawrence, 'A Duel for Ceremonial Precedence: The Papal Nuncio versus the Russian Ambassador at Warsaw, 1775–1785', *International History Review* 7 (1985), pp. 235–44.

Inventing Eastern Europe: The Map of Civilization on the Mind of the Enlightenment (Stanford, CA, 1994).

The Vatican and Poland in the Age of the Partitions: Diplomatic and Cultural Encounters at the Warsaw Nunciature (Boulder, CO, 1988).

Wortman, Richard S., *Scenarios of Power: Myth and Ceremony in Russian Monarchy*, vol. 1: *From Peter the Great to the Death of Nicholas I* (Princeton, NJ, 1995).

Zamoyski, Adam, *The Last King of Poland* (London, 1992).

Zimmermann, J., *Militärverwaltung und Heeresaufbringung in Österreich bis 1806* (Munich, 1983).

Zinkeisen, J.W., *Geschichte des Osmanischen Reiches in Europa* (7 vols., Gotha, 1840–63).

Zöllner, E., ed., *Diplomatie und Aussenpolitik Österreichs: Elf Beiträge zur ihrer Geschichte* (Vienna, 1977).

Index

Single entries and passing mentions of places or persons are not generally indexed. For rulers, regnal years are given; for other individuals, dates of birth and death are provided where these can be established. For foreign ministers and diplomats, dates and places of service for the period covered by this study are also included.

Index

Louis XVI, King of France (1774–93) 5, 70, 241
Lovisa Ulrika (1720–82), Queen of Sweden (1751–71) and sister of Frederick the Great 131, 133, 134, 169, 173, 212, 229
'Lynar Project' 189, 190, 212

Macartney, Sir George, British diplomat in Russia 1764–7
  cited 151, 152, 157
  quoted 50
Magdeburg, Hohenzollern province of 20, 84
Maria Theresa, ruler of the Habsburg Monarchy (1740–80) and Empress (1745–80)
  hostility towards Prussia 78, 193
  hostility towards Russia 46, 119, 242, 255
  opposes first partition of Poland 217, 219
  opposes further territorial annexations in 1770s 245, 247
  outlook after 1763 76, 77–8, 79
  pacifism of 185, 210
  political role of 83
  mentioned 7, 23, 27, 28, 45, 53, 54, 73, 75, 84, 111, 162, 163, 180, 209
  see also Austria; Francis Stephen
Marienwerder, Prussian customs' post at 177
Mecklenburg-Schwerin, 15, 18
Mediterranean Sea 199, 203, 227, 230, 252
Mitchell, Sir Andrew, British diplomat in Prussia (1708–71) 114, 148–9, 150
Moldavia 197, 204, 206, 217, 245, 246
Moravia, Habsburg province of 25, 28, 74, 179, 205
Moscow
  epidemic in, 226
  University of 158
  mentioned 48, 159, 217
  see also Russia
Muhsinzade, Mehmed (c. 1700–74), Ottoman general and statesmen 184, 197, 200
Müller, Gerhard Friederich (1705–83), Russian official and historian 159
Mustafa III, Ottoman Sultan (1757–74) 183, 184

Neisse, meeting at (1769) 193–4, 205, 208, 224
Neustadt, meeting at (1770) 93, 205, 209
Nivernais, Louis-Jules Barbon-Mazarini-Mancini (1716–98), duc de, French diplomat to Prussia Jan.–June 1756 147, 149
North America 28, 33, 138
Norway, territory ruled by Denmark 128, 134, 229, 231

Obreskov, A.M. (1720–87), Russian resident in Constantinople 1751–68 183–4, 185, 187, 193, 202, 206
Oder, river 20, 25, 48

Oriental Academy, in Vienna 142, 204
Orlov, Aleksey G., Count (1737–1808), Russian military and naval commander 199
Orlov, Grigory, Prince (1734–83), Russian general and favourite of Catherine II 191, 199, 226, 230
Orsova 246
  Old Orsova 245
Osten, A.S. von der, Danish diplomat, and foreign minister 1700–73 201, 229
Ostermann, I.A., count (1725–1811), Russian diplomat in Sweden 1760–74 130, 135, 138, 160, 201
Ottoman empire
  disadvantaged in 1768–74 war with Russia 196
  French diplomacy in 170–3
  and negotiations with Austria (1771) 210–11; treaty with Austria (1771) 210, 245
  and search for peace in 1768–74 war with Russia 202–11 passim
  and situation in Poland after 1763–4 182, 183–6
  vulnerability of by mid-eighteenth century 3
  and war with Russia (1768–74) chapters 7–8 passim
  mentioned 2, 3, 4, 5, 12, 13, 36, 51, 64–5, 66–7, 76, 106, 110, 112, 113–14, 115, 122, 123, 124, 133, 142, 153, 155, 164, 165, 175, 249, 250, 252
  see also Mustafa III

Panin, Nikita I., Count (1718–83), Russian statesman in charge of foreign policy 1763–81
  advocates Triple Alliance in 1770s 234
  Baltic policy undermined 227
  foreign policy of 106, 107, 115, 116, 160, 173, 247
  'Northern System' of 120–36 passim, 160, 191, 213, 214, 217, 236–7, 238, 239, 244
  on Poland's value 104–5, 175; policy in 175, 178–82 passim
  policy in Russo-Ottoman war 191–5, 200–2, 217, 228
  position weakened by Ottoman war 187–8, 190, 191, 214, 236
  response to proposed Polish partition (1769) 189–90
  mentioned 6, 17, 19, 45, 47, 137, 152, 156, 161, 163, 181, 184, 185, 251
  see also Catherine II; Russia
Paul I (1754–1801), Russian Emperor (1796–1801), son of Catherine the Great, as Grand Duke, 47, 73, 127, 128, 188, 226, 230, 236, 239

282

CAMBRIDGE STUDIES IN EARLY MODERN HISTORY